studies in jazz

Institute of Jazz Studies, Rutgers University
General Editors: *Dan Morgenstern & Edward Berger*

PEE WEE SPEAKS

A Discography of Pee Wee Russell

by
Robert Hilbert
in collaboration with
David Niven

Studies in Jazz, No. 13

The Scarecrow Press, Inc.

Metuchen, N.J., & London

1992

Also by Robert Hilbert from Scarecrow Press:

Scott Brown and Robert Hilbert, A Case of Mistaken Identity: The
Life and Music of James P. Johnson (1986)

Frontispiece: Pee Wee Russell

British Library Cataloguing-in-Publication data available

Library of Congress Cataloging-in-Publication Data

Hilbert, Robert, 1939-
    Pee Wee speaks : a discography of Pee Wee Russell / by Robert
Hilbert in collaboration with David Niven.
        p.   cm. -- (Studies in jazz ; no. 13)
    Includes index.
    ISBN 0-8108-2634-8 (acid-free paper)
    1. Russell, Pee Wee--Discography. 2. Jazz--Discography.
I. Niven, David, 1942- . II. Title. III. Series.
ML156.7.R88H5 1992
788.7'165'092--dc20
[B]   92-37522

CONTENTS

EDITOR'S PREFACE

Most people think of discographies as useful reference and research tools (which they are). To me, however, a good discography is a great read; ever since I first became seriously interested in jazz and acquired Charles Delauney's *Hot Discography* I have been a passionate peruser of this arcane branch of literature.

The volume at hand is state-of-the-art, as behooves its subject: Charles Ellsworth Russell deserves nothing less than the best. Fortunately, he was recorded frequently throughout his long career; the trip Bob Hilbert takes us on here stretches from the early 1920s to the late 1960s. Great changes occurred in jazz during those four decades, but Pee Wee was always ahead of the pack -- from that break on "Ida" (both takes, each very different) that put him on the map to those magical late ballad performances.

The landmark sessions -- "One Hour" and "Hello Lola" with McKenzie et al., the Rhythmakers stuff, etc. -- are here in all their incarnations, from 78s to CDs, but it is instructive to see just how many different settings our man recorded in until it became possible to make a living playing just jazz, period. Pee Wee was an expert reed doubler in his younger days, and it would have been interesting to hear his tenor sax later on. But there was no need for him to touch any saxophone by then, nor to sit in a big-band section. It is a real kick, though, to hear him burst out of the ensemble on Louis Prima's "Cross Patch," or add his wry comments to Bobby Hackett's "Sunrise Serenade" -- both on clarinet, of course.

Speaking of Prima: Pee Wee did lots of work with him, and it should be better known. The man himself always spoke warmly of his years with the New Orleans trumpeter and showman. There are some gems on those records. The amount of music Pee Wee made with Eddie Condon-associated groups, live and in the studios, is staggering, and Hilbert has sorted it all out neatly here. Experienced collectors will also appreciate Bob's diligence in tracking down all the permutations of the notorious "Dixieland All Stars" sessions of June, 1959 -- truly a Herculean task!

Some newly discovered material was added at the last minute, and there is bound to be more. Pee Wee lived well into the tape era, thankfully, so who knows what remains to be discovered. As it stands between these covers, however, the recorded work of Pee Wee Russell is an imposing monument to a musician who never blew a meretricious note, who had the guts always to be his own man, and whose spirit was jazz incarnate. May these many indices lead the reader to Russellian statements yet unheard, for this was a man who did not repeat himself. And if you want to know about his life, pick up Bob Hilbert's biography.

Dan Morgenstern
Director
Institute of Jazz Studies
Rutgers University

INTRODUCTION

Pee Wee Russell was one of the most interesting and controversial musicians in jazz history. He was born Charles Ellsworth Russell, Jr., in St. Louis, Missouri, on March 27, 1906, but much of his childhood was spent in Muskogee, Oklahoma. A rebellious youth, he was sent to Western Military Academy in Alton, Illinois, where he lasted a year before being dismissed. By age 16, Russell was on the road playing alto and tenor saxophones and clarinet with a variety of dance bands, including the Herbert Berger Orchestra of St. Louis, with whom he made his first recordings and from whom, before he was fully grown, he acquired his nickname. While still a youngster, he joined the legendary band led by Peck Kelley in Houston, a band which included New Orleans clarinetist Leon Roppolo and Texas' own trombonist, Jack Teagarden. Other early jobs included an association with Wingy Manone in San Antonio, Texas, and a long, close friendship with Bix Beiderbecke who greatly influenced Russell's early style.

In 1927, Russell hit the big time when he played and recorded with cornetist Red Nichols in New York. Following a 1929 cross-country tour with Nichols and the Cass Hagan band, Russell returned to St. Louis for several months, during which time he changed his clarinet style, utilizing a variety of vocalizations in his playing; including the frequent use of a "dirty" tone, guttural grunts, and bent notes. When he returned to New York and resumed playing with Nichols groups, his new style was praised by some as brilliantly inventive and scorned by others who maintained he simply did not know how to play his instrument. Such diverse opinions persist among listeners and musicians to this day.

New Orleans trumpeter and showman Louis Prima hired Russell to join his successful group at The Famous Door, first in New York and then in Hollywood, where they also appeared in motion pictures. In 1937, Russell began a ten-year stint at Nick's in Greenwich Village, where he was featured almost continuously, in the company of Eddie Condon, Bobby Hackett, Miff Mole and Muggsy Spanier, and others. He recorded frequently for Milt Gabler's Commodore label and appeared in almost all of the Condon-associated jazz concerts and radio broadcasts produced by Ernest Anderson during that time.

But by the late 1940's, Russell's playing had deteriorated, as had his physical and psychological condition. His life-long addiction to alcohol had taken its toll and on New Year's eve, 1950, he collapsed on a bandstand in San Francisco. Little hope was held for his recovery, but he astounded his doctors, friends and fans by surviving a major operation. Within a year he had begun the most productive and, some believe, most fruitful part of his career. Shrugging off his long association with "Nicksieland" jazz, he began playing frequently with mainstream musicians such as Buck Clayton and Ruby Braff. Eventually, he recorded with such modernists as Thelonious Monk, and Jimmy Giuffre, and co-led a quartet with trombonist Marshall Brown which explored the then-modern repertoire.

With the encouragement of his wife, Mary, he took up oil painting and became quite proficient at it. His musical creativity flourished as well and he became a mainstay at jazz festivals throughout the United States. He toured Europe both as a single and as a member of George Wein's Newport All Stars, and played in Australia, New Zealand and Japan as a member of Eddie Condon's all-star ensemble.

When Mary died suddenly in 1967, however, Russell began drinking heavily again, all but abandoning his music and painting. On February 15, 1969, he died in Alexandria, Virginia.

This discography includes all known recorded performances by Russell, including films, radio and television broadcasts, concerts and private recordings, although no claim of completeness can be made for these types of non-commercial recordings. Undoubtedly, many more undocumented tapes exist; but it was considered important to include those that are known to help fill out Russell's recording career.

Although a discography attempts a chronological listing of an artist's recordings, it is not always possible to know in which order takes of a particular tune were recorded. It was assumed that "take" numbers provided such information about a recording session -- take 1 presumably having been recorded before take 2. But usually "take" numbers were assigned after the session to indicate the producer's order of choices for issue rather than the actual sequence of recording. Thus it is not possible to know the true sequence of takes in many instances, though the experienced listener will know that variations in tempo and length are often valid clues. Releases shown for each title are listed in alphabetical order for easy reference, with the original issue or issues indicated by a marker. Band names and song titles are listed as they appear on original issues.

Many collectors throughout the world were helpful in contributing their knowledge and time to this project. Special thanks must be given to my collaborator on this decade-long project, David Niven, the British researcher, who pulled together all the existing sources of discography relating to Russell, from the works of Rust, Jepsen, Bruyninckx, and many specialized discographies. Jack Litchfield and John Miner were especially helpful in reviewing a draft of the discography as well as providing a continuing stream of information. Dan Morgenstern and the staff of the Institute of Jazz Studies provided access to their vast holdings. A special thanks to my wife, Betsy, and daughter, Miriam, for their patience while I muttered about record numbers for the last ten years.

I most gratefully acknowledge the invaluable assistance of Stephen Adamson; Tony Agostinelli; Henry Alberro; Ernest Anderson; Jay Anderson; Jeff Atterton; Doug Armstrong (Canada); George Avakian; Ray Avery; Bill Bacin; Dick M. Bakker (Holland); Whitney Balliett; Henry Behnke; John Bitter; Joe Boughton; Jack Bradley; Ruby Braff; Hank Bredenberg; Ace Brigode; Les Buchman; Paul Burgess; Mark Cantor; Hayden Carruth; Lou Carter; Dick Cary; David Chertok; John Chilton (England); Mac Clark; Gerhard Conrad (Germany); Ken Crawford; Michael Cuscuna; Kenny Davern; Bob DeFlores; John Dengler; Frances A. Donelson; Frank Driggs; William Dunham, Wendell Echols; Don Ellis; Philip Evans; Tom Faber (Netherlands); John Featherstone (England); John Fell; Bud Freeman; Milt Gabler; Jim Galloway (Canada); Russell George; Joe Giorando; Vince Giordano; David Goldenberg; Don Goldie; Lee and Estelle Goodman; Sol and Vera Goodman; Robin Goodman; Jim Gordon; Bob Graf; Kenneth Gross; Ed Grossmann; Tommy Gwaltney; Richard Hadlock; James R. Hamilton; Ray Hatfield; Stanley Hester; Warren Hicks; Dick Hill; Art Hodes; Paul J. Hoeffler (Canada); Franz Hoffman (Germany); Steven Holzer; Peanuts Hucko; Dennis Huggard (New Zealand); Tom Hustad; Robert Inman; Ed Jablonski; Sid Jacobs; Max Kaminsky; Harold Kaye; Jack Keller; Peter Kennedy (England); Deane Kincade; Larry Kiner; Shirley Klett; Wolfram Knauer (Germany); Gene Kramer; Paul A. Larson; Steven Lasker; Ed Lawless; Floyd Levin; Giorgio Lombardi (Italy); Jim Lowe (England); Earl Lyon; Tor Magnusson (Sweden); Irving Manning; Tina McCarthy; John McDonough; Jim McHarg (Canada); Ann McKee; Jimmy McPartland; Johnson McRee; Eugene Miller (Canada); Keith Miller (Canada); Bill Miner; Jack Mitchell (Australia); Jamie Muller (Brazil); Joe Muranyi; John Nelson (Canada); M. Nishiguchi (Japan); Hank O'Neal; Ted Ono; Pat Patterson; Forrest "Fuzz" Pearson; Eugene Perkins; Don Peterson; Nat Pierce; Ed Polic; Jon Pollack; Barrett Potter; Frank Powers; Jim

Prohaska; Al Pyle; Larry R. Quilligan; Dick Raichelson; Charles Rehkopf; Dolf Rerink (Netherlands); Ed Reynolds; Evelyn Rich; Brian A. L. Rust (England); Jack Sadler (Canada); Tom Saunders; Duncan Schiedt; Dick Schindling; Rolf Schmidt (Germany); Yasuo Segami (Japan); Manfred Selchow (Germany); Hans J. Schmidt; Paul Sheatsley; Dick Shindeling; Joe Showler (Canada); Lola Shropshire; Herbert L. Shultz; Dan Simms; Jerry and Wanda Simpson; Chuck Slate III; Jack Sohmer; Jess Stacy; Alice Stevens; Jack Stine; Klaus Stratemann (Germany); Dick Sudhalter; Mike Sutcliffe (Australia); Ralph Sutton; Bill Thompson; Bob Thompson; Elmer Truch; Neville Twist (New Zealand); Warren Vache, Sr.; Jerry Valburn; Ute Vladmir, George Wein; Bob Weir (England); Bozy White; Bert Whyatt (England); Hal Willard; Satoshi Yuze (Japan).

Those who provided considerable and valuable assistance to David Niven included Trevor Huyton, Derek Coller and Roy Bower in the United Kingdom and Shirley Klett, Rolph Fairchild, Tom Lord and Bozy White in the USA.

Robert Hilbert
Coral Gables, Florida 1992

A detailed biography, *Jazzman: The Jazz Life of Pee Wee Russell,* by Robert Hilbert, is published by Oxford University Press.

ABBREVIATIONS

8T	Eight-track audio tape
33	33 1/3 rpm audio disc
45	45 rpm audio disc
78	78 rpm audio disc
AFRS	Armed Forces Radio Service
AFRTS	Armed Forces Radio and Television Service
Arg	Argentina
Au	Australia
C	Canada
CD	Compact disc
CT	Cassette tape
Cz	Czechoslovakia
D	Denmark
E	England (Great Britian)
Eu	Europe
F	France
FDC	For Discriminate Collectors
G	Germany
H	Holland
HRS	Hot Record Society
I	Italy
In	India
Ir	Ireland
J	Japan
NZ	New Zealand
RT	Open-reel audio tape
Sc	Scandinavia
Sd	Sweden
Sp	Spain
Sw	Switzerland
TX	Transcription disc
UHCA	United Hot Clubs of America
VD	Video disc
VOA	Voice of America
VT	Video tape (VHS format)
Yugo	Yugoslavia

> indicates original issue.

DISCOGRAPHY

Herbert Berger's St. Louis Club Orchestra
NYC, c. December 4, 1922

Probable personnel: Andy McKinney, Gene McCollum, trumpets; Sonny Lee, trombone; Pee Wee Russell, alto, clarinet, Carl Hohengarten, alto, arranger; Francis Nicolay, tenor; Joe Johnson, violin; Herbert Berger, piano; Bob Quain, banjo; Perry Bailey, tuba; Dee Orr, drums.

S-71-075-C   Lady Of The Evening
   78:   >Okeh 4745, Parlophone (E) E-5228

S-71-076-C   Trot Along
   78:   >Okeh 4753

S-71-077-B   The Fuzzy Wuzzy Bird
   78:   >Okeh 4753

S-71-078-C   Eleanor
   78:   >Okeh 4755, Parlophone (E) E-5114

NOTE: Pee Wee Russell remembered his first recording was "The Fuzzy Wuzzy Bird," which has a two note clarinet break at the end, conceivably played by him. A photograph exists of the band, taken circa 1924-25, which shows the personnel listed above.

Herbert Berger's St. Louis Club Orchestra
NYC, c. December 6, 1922

Probable personnel: Andy McKinney, Gene McCollum, trumpets; Sonny Lee, trombone; Pee Wee Russell, alto, clarinet; Carl Hohengarten, alto, arranger; Francis Nicolay, tenor; Joe Johnson, violin; Herbert Berger, piano; Bob Quain, banjo, guitar; Perry Bailey, tuba; Dee Orr, drums.

S-71-083-C   Who Did You Fool After All?
   78:   >Okeh 4758

S-71-084-   November Rose (waltz)
   78:   >Okeh 4765, Parlophone (E) E-5036

1

Herbert Berger's Coronado Hotel Orchestra
                                    St. Louis, Missouri, November 3, 1924

Probable personnel: Andy McKinney, Gene McCollum, trumpets;
Sonny Lee, trombone; Pee Wee Russell, alto, clarinet; Carl
Hohengarten, alto, arranger; Francis Nicolay, tenor; Joe Johnson,
violin; Herbert Berger, piano; Bob Quain, banjo, guitar; Perry Bailey,
tuba; Dee Orr, drums.

B-31144-3 Gee Flat
    Unissued

B-31145-2 Shanghai Shuffle
    Unissued

NOTE: This session was recorded for Victor. Russell's presence is not
confirmed, but since he was still associated with the Berger orchestra
around this time it is a strong possibility. Herbert Berger and his
Coronado orchestra recorded three more sessions for Victor during
December, 1925, but at that time Russell was playing with Frank
Trumbauer's band at the Arcadia ballroom in St. Louis so his presence
is unlikely.

*Previous discographies have shown Russell present on the April 2,
1927, session by Carl Fenton's Orchestra for Brunswick (E-22223 Doll
Dance; E-22226 Delirium). However, Pee Wee recalled arriving in
New York the day before the following session by Red Nichols and His
Five Pennies, so his involvement with the Fenton recordings five
months earlier is most unlikely.*

Red Nichols And His Five Pennies
                            NYC, August 15, 1927 (morning session)

Red Nichols, cornet; Leo McConville, Mannie Klein, trumpet; Miff
Mole, trombone; Pee Wee Russell, clarinet; Lennie Hayton, piano;
Dick McDonough, guitar; Adrian Rollini, bass sax; Vic Berton, drums,
harpophone.

E-24224 Riverboat Shuffle (Algarabia del Bote)
    78: >Brunswick 3627
    33: Classic Jazz Masters (Sd) CJM-25, Swaggie (Au) 837

2

E-24225   Riverboat Shuffle (Algarabia del Bote)
   78:   >Brunswick 3627, Brunswick 3698, Brunswick 6820,
           Brunswick (Au) 3627, Brunswick (C) 3627, Brunswick (E)
           2134, Brunswick (E) 01806, Brunswick (F) A-500400,
           Brunswick (G) A-7601
   45:   Brunswick 97021 (9-80166)
   33:   ABC (Au) L-38704, Affinity (E) AFS 1038, ASV Living Era
           (E) AJA 5025, BBC (E) REB-664, Brunswick BL 54047,
           Brunswick BL 58027, Classic Jazz Masters (Sd) CJM-25,
           Coral (G) COPS 6795, Coral (G) LPCM 97016, Swaggie
           (Au) 837, Time-Life STL-J17 (P 15733), Time-Life (Au)
           STL-J17, Time/Life (C) STL-J17
   TX: AFRS DB 309
   CD: ABC 36185, ASV Living Era (J) CD AJA 5025R, BBC (E)
           CD 664, Emarcy (J) 25JD-10150
   CT: ASV Living Era (E) ZC AJA 5025, BBC (E) ZCF 664,
           Neovox (E) 721, Time-Life 4TL-J17
   8T: Time-Life 8TL-J17

E-24228   Eccentric (Excentrico)
   78:   >Brunswick 3627, Brunswick 3698, Brunswick 6820,
           Brunswick (Au) 3627, Brunswick (C) 3627, Brunswick (E)
           01806, Brunswick (E) 02000, Brunswick (F) A-500400,
           Brunswick (G) A-7601, Columbia (Au) DO-1354
   45:   Brunswick 97021 (9-80166)
   33:   Affinity (E) AFS 1038, ASV Living Era (E) AJA 5025,
           Brunswick BL 54008, Brunswick BL 54047, Brunswick BL
           58027, Brunswick (C) BL 54008, Brunswick (C) BL 54047,
           Brunswick (E) LAT 8307, Classic Jazz Masters (Sd) CJM-25,
           Coral (G) COPS 6795, Coral (G) LPCM 97016, Coral (J)
           LPCM 2010, Festival (Au) B12 1488, Swaggie (Au) 837,
           Swaggie (Au) JCS 33745
   CD: ASV Living Era (J) CD AJA 5025R
   CT: ASV Living Era (E) ZC AJA 5025, Neovox (E) 721

(Same date, afternoon session) Omit McConville and Klein. Rollini
also plays goofus on mx. E-24235.

E-24230   Ida! Sweet As Apple Cider (Dulce, como la miel)
   78:   >Brunswick (Au) 3626
   33:   Classic Jazz Masters (Sd) CJM-25, Swaggie (Au) 837

E-24232   Ida! Sweet As Apple Cider (Dulce, como la miel)
   78:   Banner 32517, >Brunswick 3626, Brunswick 6819, Brunswick 80069, Brunswick (Au) 3626, Brunswick (C) 3626, Brunswick (E) 3626, Brunswick (E) 0l536, Brunswick (F) A-50040l, Brunswick (G) A-7559, Coral (G) 91015, Melotone M-12443, Perfect 15648, Vocalion 4654, >Vocalion l5622
   33:   Affinity (E) AFS 1038, Brunswick BL 54008, Brunswick BL 54047, Brunswick BL 58009, Brunswick (Au) B12 1488, Brunswick (C) BL 54008, Brunswick (C) BL 54008, Brunswick (E) LAT 8307, Brunswick (J) SDL 10299B, Classic Jazz Masters (Sd) CJM-25, Coral (G) COPS 6795, Coral (G) LPCM 97016, Coral (J) LPCM 2010, MCA (J) MCA 3012, Swaggie (Au) 837, Swaggie (Au) JCS 33745, Time-Life STL-J17 (P 15733), Time-Life (Au) STL-J17, Time-Life (C) STL-J17, Universal Record Club (Au) VJ-462
   CT: Neovox (E) 721, Time-Life 4TL-J17
   8T: Time-Life 8TL-J17

E-24235   Feelin' No Pain (No me Importe)
   78:   Banner 32517, >Brunswick 3626, Brunswick 6819, Brunswick 80069, Brunswick (C) 3626, Brunswick (E) 3626, Brunswick (E) 0l536, Brunswick (F) A-500401, Brunswick (G) A-7559, Coral (G) 91015721, Melotone M-12443, Perfect 15648, Vocalion 4654, >Vocalion 15622
   33:   Ace of Hearts (E) AH 63, Affinity (E) AFS 1038, ASV Living Era (E) AJA 5025, Brunswick BL 54008, Brunswick BL 54047, Brunswick BL 58009, Brunswick (Au) B12 1488, Brunswick (C) BL 54008, Brunswick (C) BL 54047, Brunswick (E) LAT 8307, Brunswick (J) SDL 10299B, Classic Jazz Masters (Sd) CJM 25, Coral (G) COPS 6795, Coral (G) LPCM 97016, Coral (J) LPCM 2010, MCA (J) MCA 3012, Swaggie (Au) 837, Swaggie (Au) JCS 33745, Time-Life STL-J17 (P 15733), Time-Life (Au) STL-J17, Universal Record Club (AU) VJ-462
   CD: ASV Living Era (J) CD AJA 5025R
   CT: ASV Living Era (E) ZC AJA 5025, Neovox (E) 721, Time-Life 4TL-J17
   8T: Time-Life 8TL-J17

NOTE: Melotone and Perfect issues as by The Red Heads. Brunswick (Au) 3627 as by Red Nicholls (sic) and His Five Pennies. The last title is rumored to exist on Romeo as by the Alabama Red Peppers. Fud Livingston is the arranger of "Riverboat Shuffle," "Eccentric," and "Feelin' No Pain." Lennie Hayton is the arranger of "Ida! Sweet As Apple Cider" Brunswick (E) 02000 contains only an excerpt of E-24228 and is entitled "A Short Survey of Modern Rhythm." Brunswick 80069 is part of Brunswick album B-1019. Emarcy (J) 25JD-10150 is part of a 4-CD set.

Miff Mole And His Little Molers

NYC, August 30, 1927

Red Nichols, cornet; Miff Mole, trombone; Pee Wee Russell, clarinet, tenor; Arthur Schutt, piano; Dick McDonough, banjo (on matrix 81297-B only); Eddie Lang, guitar; Adrian Rollini, bass sax; Vic Berton, drums.

W-81296-B   Imagination
    78: Columbia 35687, Odeon (Arg) 193092, Odeon (F) 165192, Odeon (H) A-189145, >Okeh 40890, Parlophone (Au) A-7618, Parlophone (E) R-2286, Parlophone (E) R-3420
    33: ABC (Au) L 38266, BBC (E) REB 590, EmArcy (J) 30JD-10099, Parlophone (E) PMC 7120, Swaggie (Au) S 1295, World (E) SH 503
    CD: ABC 36182, BBC (G) CD 590, EmArcy (J) 30JD-10099
    CT: ABC (Au) C 38266, BBC (E) ZCF 590, Neovox (E) 721

W-81297-B   Feelin' No Pain
    78: Columbia 35687, Odeon (Arg) 193092, Odeon (F) 165192, Odeon (G) 028536, Odeon (H) A-189145, >Okeh 40890, Parlophone (Au) A-7600, Parlophone (E) R-2269, Parlophone (E) R-3420, Parlophone (Sw) PZ 11290, Vocalion 3074,
    33: ABC (Au) L-38704, BBC (E) REB 664, Columbia CL 1521, Columbia (C) CL 1521, Franklin Mint 65, Parlophone (E) PMC 7120, Philips (E) BBL 7431, Philips (H) B47071L, Swaggie (Au) S 1295, World (E) SH 503
    CD: ABC 36185, BBC (E) CD 664
    CT: BBC (E) ZCF 664, Neovox (E) 721

W-81298-B Original Dixieland One Step
- 78: Brunswick 8243, Columbia 36010, Odeon (F) 165276, Odeon (H) A-189106, >Okeh 40932, Parlophone (E) R-3530
- 33: ABC (Au) L-38704, ASV Living Era (E) AJA 5025, BBC (E) REB 664, Columbia CL 1521, Folkways Vol. 7, Folkways FP 67, Folkways FJ 2807, Parlophone (E) PMC 7120, Philips (H) B47071L, Philips (E) BBL 7431, Swaggie (Au) S 1295, World (E) SH 503
- TX: AFRS H62-127
- CD: ABC 36185, ASV Living Era (J) CD AJA 5025R, BBC (E) CD 664, Emarcy (J) 25JD-10150
- CT: ASV Living Era (E) ZC AJA 5025, BBC (E) ZCF 664, Neovox (E) 721

NOTE: Columbia 36010, part of Columbia Album C-46, lists Fud Livingston, clarinet, on the label. Columbia CL 1521 is part of Columbia album C4L 18. Emarcy (J) 25JD-10099 and 25JD-10150 are both parts of 4-CD sets.

Miff Mole And His Little Molers
                                                    NYC, September 1, 1927

Red Nichols, cornet; Miff Mole, trombone; Pee Wee Russell, clarinet, tenor; Arthur Schutt, piano; Eddie Lang, guitar; Dick McDonough, banjo; Adrian Rollini, bass sax; Joe Tarto, tuba; Vic Berton, drums.

W-81413-B My Gal Sal
- 78: Odeon (F) 165276, Odeon (H) A-189106, >Okeh 40932, Parlophone (E) R-3530,
- 33: Columbia CL 1522, Columbia (C) CL 1522, Parlophone (E) PMC 7120, Philips (E) BBL 7432, Swaggie (Au) S 1295, World (E) SH 503
- CT: Neovox (E) 721

6

W-81414-B   Honolulu Blues
  78:   Brunswick 8243, Odeon (Arg) 193171, Odeon (F) 165328,
          Odeon (H) A-189122, Odeon (Sp) 182.280, >Okeh 40984,
          Parlophone (E) R-3441
  45:   Fontana (E) TFE 17266, Fontana (H) 367 092 TE
  33:   ABC (Au) L-38704, ASV Living Era (E) AJA 5025, BBC (E)
          REB 664, Columbia CL 1522, Columbia (C) CL 1522,
          Franklin Mint 47, Parlophone (E) PMC 7120, Philips (H)
          B4708L, Philips (E) BBL 7432, Swaggie (Au) S 1295, World
          (E) SH 503
  CD: ABC 36185, ASV Living Era (J) CD AJA 5025R, BBC (E)
          CD 664, Emarcy (J) 25JD-10150
  CT: ASV Living Era (E) ZC AJA 5025, BBC (E) ZCF 664,
          Neovox (E) 721

W-81415-C   The New Twister
  78:   Odeon (Arg) 193171, Odeon (F) 165328, Odeon (H) A-
          189122, Odeon (Sp) 182.280, >Okeh 40984, Parlophone (E)
          R-3441, Vocalion 3074
  45:   Fontana (E) TFE 17266, Fontana (H) 367 092 TE
  33:   Columbia CL 1522, Columbia (C) CL 1522, Parlophone (E)
          PMC 7120, Philips (E) BBL 7432, Swaggie (Au) S 1295,
          World (E) SH 503
  CT: Neovox (E) 721

NOTE: Columbia CL 1522 is part of Columbia album C4L-18.
Emarcy (J) 25JD-10150 is part of a 4-CD set.

The Charleston Chasers (under the direction of "Red" Nichols)
                                     NYC, September 6, 1927

Red Nichols, cornet, Leo McConville, trumpet; Miff Mole, trombone;
Pee Wee Russell, clarinet, tenor;   Lennie Hayton, piano; Dick
McDonough, banjo, guitar; Jack Hansen, tuba; Vic Berton, drums;
Craig Leach, vocal.

W-144625-3 Five Pennies (Cinco Centavos)
  78:   >Columbia 1229-D, Columbia (E) 4797
  45:   Fontana (E) TFE 17267, Fontana (H) 467093TE
  33:   Columbia CL 1523, Columbia (C) CL 1523, Philips (E) BBL
          7433, VJM (E) VLP 26
  CT: Neovox (E) 733

W-144626-3 Sugar Foot Strut (Paso Dulce) (CL vocal)
   78:   >Columbia 1260-D, Columbia (E) 4877, Columbia (J) 441
   45:   Fontana (E) TFE 17267, Fontana (H) 467093TE
   33:   Columbia CL 1523, Columbia (C) CL 1523, IAJRC 28,
         Philips (E) BBL 7433, VJM (E) VLP 26
   CT: Neovox (E) 733

NOTE: Arrangements of both tunes are by Fud Livingston. The
vocal on matrix 144626 has been removed on Columbia CL 1523 and
Philips BBL 7433. Columbia CL 1523 is part of Columbia album C4L-
18. Russell plays tenor on mx. 144625 only. Royal blue wax pressings
exist of Columbia 1229-D.

The Charleston Chasers (under the direction of "Red" Nichols)
NYC, September 8, 1927

Red Nichols, cornet; Leo McConville, trumpet; Miff Mole, trombone;
Bill Trone, mellophone; Pee Wee Russell, clarinet; Fud Livingston,
clarinet, tenor; Lennie Hayton, piano; Dick McDonough, guitar, banjo;
Jack Hansen, tuba; Vic Berton, drums.

W-144649-2 Imagination (Imaginacion)
   78:   >Columbia 1260-D, Columbia (E) 4877, Columbia (J) 441
   33:   Columbia CL 1523, Columbia (C) CL 1523, Philips (E) BBL
         7433, VJM (E) VLP 26
   CT: Neovox (E) 733

Add Wingy Manone, cornet; Carl Kress, guitar. Hayton plays celeste.

W-144650-2 Feelin' No Pain (No Siento Dolor)
   78:   >Columbia 1229-D, Columbia (E) 4797
   45:   Fontana (E) TFE 17267, Fontana (H) 467093TE
   33:   Columbia CL 1523, Columbia (C) CL 1523, Philips (E) BBL
         7433, VJM (E) VLP 26
   CT: Neovox (E) 733

NOTE: Both arrangements are by Fud Livingston. Clarinet and tenor
solos on W-144649 are by Livingston. On W-1446950, Pee Wee plays
the clarinet solo and Livingston plays the tenor solo. Columbia CL
1523 is part of Columbia album C4L-18. Columbia 1229-D exists on
blue wax pressings. Four takes of 144649 and three of 144650 were
cut.

Pee Wee Russell is usually listed as having participated in the Arksansas Travellers session of September 14, 1927. However, the clarinetist, the only reed player on the session, is Fud Livingston.

The Red Heads

NYC, c. September 16, 1927

Red Nichols, cornet; Miff Mole or Bill Rank, trombone; Pee Wee Russell, clarinet, alto, tenor (on 107783); Arthur Schutt, piano; Vic Berton, drums, harpophone.

107782-1   A Good Man Is Hard To Find
    78:   Mouldy Fygge 101, >Pathe Actuelle 36701, Pathe Actuelle (F) X. 6225, >Perfect 14882, Salabert (F) 765
    33:   Columbia CL 1524, Columbia (C) CL 1524, Fountain (E) DFJ-110SDL, Historical HLP-25, Philips (E) BBL 7434, Ristic (E) 50
    CT: Neovox (E) 817

107782-2   A Good Man Is Hard To Find (Es duro encontrar un humbre Cueno)
    78:   >Cameo 1260, >Lincoln 2725, >Romeo 494
    33:   Ristic (E) 50

107783-1   Nothin' Does Does Like It Used To Do Do Do
    78:   >Pathe 36707, Pathe Actuelle (E) 11515, Perfect 14888
    33:   Fountain (E) DFJ-110, Ristic (E) 50
    CT: Neovox (E) 817

107783-2   Nothin' Does Does Like It Used To Do Do Do
    78:   >Perfect 14888
    33:   Ristic (E) 50

Add Wingy Manone, cornet.

107784-1   Baltimore
    78:   Pathe Actuelle (E) 11515, Pathe Actuelle (F) 6213-X, >Perfect 14882, Salabert (F) 764
    33:   Fountain (E) DFJ-110, Ristic (E) 50
    CT: Neovox (E) 817

107784-2   Baltimore
  78:   >Pathe Actuelle 36701, >Perfect 14882
  33:   Columbia CL 1524, Columbia (C) CL 1524, Philips (E) BBL
        7434, Ristic (E) 50

NOTE: Cameo, Lincoln and Romeo issued as Alabama Red Peppers.
Columbia CL 1524 is part of Columbia album C4L-18.

Cass Hagan And His Park Central Hotel Orchestra
NYC, September 30, 1927

Ray Lodwig, Bob Ashford, Bo Ashford, trumpet; Al Philburn,
trombone; Jack Towne, clarinet, alto, baritone; Pee Wee Russell,
clarinet, tenor; Roy Thrall, alto; Frank Crum, tenor; Cass Hagan, violin;
Fred Frank, piano; Jim Mahoney, banjo; Al Weber, tuba; Chick
Condon, drums. Lewis James, Frank Luther, Elliott Shaw, vocals.

W-144618-5   Broadway (LJ vocal)
  78:   >Columbia 1138-D

W-144815-2   Manhattan Mary (Maria De Manhattan) (LJ, FL, ES
vocal)
  78:   >Columbia 1138-D

Red And Miff's Stompers
NYC, October 12, 1927

Red Nichols, cornet; Miff Mole, trombone; Pee Wee Russell, clarinet,
alto; Fud Livingston, clarinet, tenor; Lennie Hayton, piano; Carl
Kress, guitar; Jack Hansen, brass bass; Vic Berton, drums, harpophone.

BVE-40168-1   Slippin' Around (Deslizandose)
  78:   >Vic 21397
  33:   Franklin Mint 91, Jazz Studies (C) 2, New World NWR 274,
        OFC (Arg) 36, RCA (F) PM 43179, RCA (F) NL 89606,
        Saville (E) SVL 146
  CD: Bluebird 3136-2-RB
  CT: Bluebird 3136-4-RB, Emporium (E) 019, Neovox (E) 733

BVE-40169-2   Feelin' No Pain
    78:    >Vic 21183
    33:    OFC (Arg) 36, RCA (F) PM 43179, RCA (F) NL 89606,
           Saville (E) SVL 146
    CD: Bluebird 3136-2-RB
    CT: Bluebird 3136-4-RB, Neovox (E) 733

NOTE: Nat Shilkret was the recording director. Two takes of 40168
and three of 40169 were cut. Arrangements were by Fud Livingston.

Frankie Trumbauer And His Orchestra
                                                    NYC, October 25, 1927

Bix Beiderbecke, cornet; Bill Rank, trombone; Pee Wee Russell,
clarinet, alto; Frank Trumbauer, C-melody sax; Don Murray, baritone
sax, clarinet; Joe Venuti, violin; Frank Signorelli, piano; Eddie Lang,
guitar; Adrian Rollini, bass sax; Chauncey Morehouse, drums.

W-81570-C   Crying All Day
    78:    Columbia 35956, HJCA 601, Odeon (Arg) 193217, Odeon
           (F) 165291, Odeon (F) 279713, Odeon (H) A-189125, >Okeh
           40966, Parlophone (Au) A-6449, Parlophone (E) R-2176,
    45:    Columbia G-4-10, Columbia 7-1644, Fontana (E) TFE-
           17252, Fontana (H) 467 037 TE
    33:    Bix Volume 6, CBS (E/G) CBS 22179, CBS (E) 54271, CBS
           (Eu) 66367, CBS (F) 62374, CBS (F) 88030, CBS (J) SOPB
           55018, CBS (J) PMS 116C 193171, Columbia GL 508,
           Columbia CL 845, Columbia ML 4812, Columbia (Arg)
           8037, Columbia (C) GL 508, Electrola (G) 1 C 134-52
           768/69, Jazz Time JZTL 1003, Joker (I) SM 3562, Music for
           Pleasure (E) GX 2513, Music for Pleasure (E) MFP 5828,
           Odeon (G) MOEQ 27008, Parlophone (E) PMC 7064,
           Supraphon (Cz) 1015 3108, Swaggie (Au) S-1242, Time-Life
           STL-J04 (P 14780), Time-Life (Au) STL-J04, Time-Life (C)
           STL-J04, World (E) SH 414
    CD: CBS (E) 466967, Columbia CK 46175, Flapper (E) 9765,
           IRD (I) BIX 4, Music for Pleasure EMI (E) CD MFP 6046
    CT: CBS (E) 40-22179, Columbia CT 46175, Electrola (G) 1 C
           434-06 706 M, Neovox (E) 723, Time-Life 4TL-J04, World
           (E) TCSH 414
    8T: Time-Life 8TL-J04

11

W-81571-B   A Good Man Is Hard To Find
  78:   Columbia 35956, HJCA 601, Odeon (Arg) l93217, Odeon (F)
        l65291, Odeon (H) A-189125, >Okeh 40966, Parlophone (E)
        R-3489
  45:   Columbia G-4-9, Columbia 7-1644, Fontana (E) TFE-17060,
        Fontana (H) 462032TE
  33:   Bix Volume 6, CBS (E/G) CBS 22179, CBS (E) 54271, CBS
        (Eu) 66367, CBS (F) 62374, CBS (F) 88030, CBS (J) PMS
        116 CBS (J) SOPB 55018, Columbia GL 508, Columbia CL
        845, Columbia ML 4812, Columbia (Arg) 8037, Columbia
        (C) GL 508, Electrola (G) 1 C 134-527 68/69, Jazz Time
        JZTL 1003, Joker (I) SM 3562, Parlophone (E) PMC 7064,
        Supraphon (Cz) 1015 3108, Swaggie (Au) S-1242, World (E)
        SH 414
  CD: CBS (E) 466967, Columbia CK 46175, Electrola (G) 1 C
        434-06 706 M, IRD (I) BIX 4, Pro Arte Fanfare CDD 490,
        World (E) TCSH 414
  CT: Columbia CT 46175, Neovox (E) 723

NOTE: Some red label copies of Okeh 40966 are pressed from dubbed
masters 17066 and 17067 respectively. HJCA 601 is a 12-inch disc
with two titles on each side. Columbia 7-1644 is part of Columbia
album A-1079. Bix Volume 6 is part of a 20-LP boxed set produced by
Sunbeam Records. IRD (I) BIX 4 was issued singly and as part of a 9-
CD set which was designated BIX BOX. Pee Wee Russell solos on
mx. 81570 and Don Murray solos on mx. 81571.

Red Nichols' Stompers
                         NYC, October 26, 1927 (Morning session)

Red Nichols, cornet; Leo McConville, Bob Ashford, trumpet; Miff
Mole, Bill Rank, trombone; Max Farley, alto; Frank Trumbauer, C-
melody sax; Pee Wee Russell, clarinet, tenor; Arthur Schutt, piano;
Carl Kress, guitar; Adrian Rollini, bass sax; Jack Hansen, brass bass;
Chauncey Morehouse, drums. Jim Miller, Charlie Farrell, vocals

BVE-40512-1 Sugar (Azucar) (JM, CF vocal)
  78:   HMV (Cz) AM-1211, HMV (E) B-5433, >Victor 2l056
  33:   RCA (F) PM 43179, RCA (F) PM 43267, RCA (F) NL
        89606, Saville (E) SVL 146

12

BVE-40513-1   Make My Cot Where The Cot-Cot-Cotton Grows
(Quiero un Saco Hechoenla Tierra del Algodon) (JM, CF vocal)
   78:   HMV (Cz) AM-1211, HVM (E) B-5433, >Victor 21056,
   33:   RCA (F) PM 43179, RCA (F) NL 89606, Saville (E) SVL
      146

NOTE: Arthur Schutt arranged 40512 and Glenn Miller arranged
40513. Three takes were recorded of each title.

*The label of Br (E) 01856, "Chinatown, My Chinatown," by Red
Nichols, recorded on February 5, 1929, lists Pee Wee Russell. The
clarinet on this session is played by Benny Goodman.*

The Whoopee Makers
NYC, June 6, 1929

Jimmy McPartland, Tommy Gott (?), trumpet; Jack Teagarden,
trombone; Jimmy Dorsey, Gil Rodin, clarinet, alto; Bud Freeman, Pee
Wee Russell, clarinet, tenor; Vic Breidis, piano; Dick Morgan, banjo,
vocal; Harry Goodman, tuba; Ray Bauduc, drums; Jack Kaufman,
vocal.

8761-5   After You've Gone (JK vocal)
   78:   >Banner 6441, >Conqueror 7389, >Domino 4381, >Jewel
      5648, >Oriole 1624 >Regal 8826

8761-6   After You've Gone (JK vocal)
   78:   reported on >Oriole 1624

8762-6   Twelfth Street Rag (DM vocal)
(108931-6)
   78:   >Banner 6441, >Conqueror 7382, >Domino 4369, >Jewel
      5648, >Oriole 1624, >Pathe Actuelle 37036, >Perfect 15217,
      >Regal 8813
   33:   Ariston (I) AR LP 12057, Connoisseur (Sd) CR 523

Jack Teagarden, trumpet, trombone and vocal.

8763-5   It's So Good (JT and band vocal)
(108930-5)
>   78: >Banner 6483, >Conqueror 7382, >Domino 4369, >Jewel
5685, >Oriole 1668, >Pathe Actuelle 37036, >Perfect 15217,
>Regal 8813, UHCA 39
>   33: CSP JLN 6044, CBS Sony (J) SOPB 55014, Columbia (E)
33SX1545, Epic SN 6044 (LN 24045), Harrison LP-D,
Time-Life STL-J08 (P 15007), Time-Life (Au) STL-J08,
Time-Life (C) STL-J08
>   CD: Jazz Archives (F) 157022
>   CT: Time-Life 4TL-J08
>   8T: Time-Life 8TL-J08

NOTE: Produced by Ed Kirkeby. Jewel and Oriole issued as Dixie
Jazz Band. UHCA issued as Jack Teagarden and His Whoopee
Makers. Banner 6483, Conqueror 7382, Regal 8813 issued as Gil
Rodin's Boys. Pathe Actual 37036, Perfect 15217 issued as Whoopee
Makers. Mx. 8763-5 on Domino 4369 issued as Gil Roden (sic) and
His Boys. Other 78 rpm records were issued as Jimmy Bracken's Toe-
Ticklers. CSP JLN 6044 has Epic printed on the box, but shows CSP
Collectors Series on the labels. The clarinet solo on 8763-5, although it
sounds very much like Pee Wee, is by Bud Freeman.

Louisiana Rhythm Kings

NYC, June 11, 1929

Red Nichols, cornet; Jack Teagarden, trombone, vocal; Pee Wee
Russell, clarinet; Bud Freeman, tenor; Joe Sullivan, piano; Dave
Tough, drums.

E-30029 That Da Da Strain
>   78: Brunswick (E) 02731, Decca (H) M-30216, HJCA 612, HRS
7, >Vocalion 15828
>   33: Affinity (E) AFS 1036, Family (I) SFR-DP 649, Franklin
Mint 65, Swaggie (Au) 840
>   CD: Tax (Sd) S-5-2
>   CT: Neovox (E) 801

E-30030-A   Basin Street Blues (JT vocal)
   78: Brunswick (E) 02506, HJCA 612, Decca (E) BM O2506,
        Decca (F) 74.540, >Vocalion 15815
   33: Ace of Hearts (E) AH 168, Affinity (E) AFS 1015, Coral (G)
        COPS 3442, Coral (G) 6.21851, Decca DL 4540, Decca DL
        74540, Folkways Vol. 7, Folkways FP 67, Folkways FJ 2807,
        Gaps (I) 180, MCA 227, MCA (Arg) MCAB 5062, Swaggie
        (Au) 840, Time-Life STL-J08 (P 15007), Time-Life (Au)
        STL-J08, Time-Life (C) STL-J08
   CD: Jazz Archives (F) 157022, Tax (Sd) S-5-2
   CT: Neovox (E) 801, Time-Life 4TL-J08
   8T: Time-Life 8TL-J08

E-30031   Last Cent
   78: Brunswick (E) 02506, Decca (E) BM 02506, HJCA 612,
        >Vocalion 15815
   45: Coral (G) 94269
   33: Family (I) SFR-DP 649, Swaggie (Au) 840
   CD: Tax (Sd) S-5-2
   CT: Neovox (E) 801

NOTE: HJCA 612 is a 12-inch disc, with two titles on each side. At least some, if not all, copies of HRS 7 have no issue number. Matrix E-30029 is entitled "Da Da Strain."

Red Nichols And His Five Pennies
NYC, June 12, 1929

Red Nichols, cornet; Mannie Klein, Tommy Thunen, trumpet; Jack Teagarden, Glenn Miller, trombone; Bill Trone or Charles Butterfield, mellophone; Pee Wee Russell, clarinet; Bud Freeman, tenor; Joe Sullivan, piano; Eddie Condon, banjo; Art Miller, bass; Dave Tough, drums; Red McKenzie, vocal.

E-30056-A Who Cares? (A quien importe?) (RMcK vocal)
   78: >Brunswick 4778, Brunswick 6831, Brunswick (Au) 4778,
        Brunswick (C) 4778
   33: Family (I) SFR-DP 693

E-30056-G Who Cares?
   Unissued

E-30057-A Rose Of Washington Square (Rosa de in Plaza Washington)
    78:    >Brunswick 4778, Brunswick 6831, Brunswick (Au) 4778,
           Brunswick (C) 4778, Brunswick (E) 1204, Brunswick (E)
           01204, Brunswick (F) A-500200, Brunswick (I) 4730
    45:    Brunswick 9-7021 (9-80169)
    33:    Ace of Hearts (E) AH 63, Brunswick BL 54008, Brunswick
           BL 58027, Brunswick (Au) B-12-1488, Brunswick (C) BL
           54008, Brunswick (E) LAT 8307, Coral (G) LPCM 97016,
           Coral (G) 96016LPC, Coral (J) LPCM 2010, Festival (Au)
           B12-1488, Franklin Mint 47, Gaps (I) 180, Swaggie (Au) JCS
           33763, Universal Record Club (Au) UJ 462
    CD: Tax (Sd) S-5-2
    CT: Neovox (E) 745

NOTE: Arrangements on both titles by Glenn Miller. Brunswick 4778
was released May 29, 1930. E-30056-G was an instrumental version.

Red Nichols And His Five Pennies

                                                   NYC, c. July, 1929

Red Nichols, cornet; Herb Taylor, trombone;   Pee Wee Russell,
clarinet; Irving Brodsky, piano, Eddie Condon, banjo, Vega lute, vocal;
George Beebe, drums.

Ida! Sweet As Apple Cider
    TX: Vitaphone 870 1-2

Nobody's Sweetheart (EC vocal)
    TX: Vitaphone 870 1-2

Who Cares (EC vocal)
    TX: Vitaphone 870 1-2

Add one or two trumpets, possibly Tommy Thunen and/or John Egan

China Boy
    TX: Vitaphone 870 1-2

NOTE: The 16-inch, 33 1/3 rpm disc, pressed by Victor, was issued to
be used by movie theatres for synchronous use with Vitaphone film
870. The short subject was released by Vitaphone Corporation in 1929.
One additional selection, "Whispering," does not include Russell.

Red Nichols And His Five Pennies

NYC, August 20, 1929

Red Nichols, cornet; Tommy Thunen, John Egan, trumpet; Jack
Teagarden, Glenn Miller, Herb Taylor, trombone; Pee Wee Russell,
clarinet; Jimmy Dorsey, alto, clarinet; Fud Livingston, tenor; Henry
Whiteman, Maurice Goffin, violin; Irving Brodsky, piano; Tommy
Felline, banjo; Jack Hansen, tuba; George Beebe, drums; Scrappy
Lambert, Red McKenzie, vocal.

E-30502-A I May Be Wrong (But, I Think You're Wonderful) (Puede
Que Este Equi Vocado) (SL vocal)
78: >Brunswick 4500, Brunswick 6753, Brunswick (Arg) 4500,
Brunswick (Au) 4500, Brunswick (C) 4500, Brunswick (F)
A-8493, Brunswick (G) A 8493, Brunswick (G) A 9520,
Brunswick (I) 4891
33: Sunbeam MFC-12
CD: Tax (Sd) S-5-2

E-30503-B I May Be Wrong (But, I Think You're Wonderful)
78: ? Brunswick (F) A-8493, ? Brunswick (G) A-8493

E-30503-G I May Be Wrong (But, I Think You're Wonderful)
78: ? Brunswick (G) A-9520

E-30504-A The New Yorkers (Los Newyorkinos) (RMcK vocal)
78: >Brunswick 4500, Brunswick (Arg) 4500, Brunswick (Au)
4500, Brunswick (C) 4500, Brunswick (F) A-8493,
Brunswick (G) A-8493, Brunswick (G) A-9520
33: MCA 1518, Sunbeam MFC-12
CD: Tax (Sd) S-5-2
CT: MCA 1518

E-30505-G The New Yorkers
78: ? Brunswick (G) A-9520

NOTE: MCA 1518 issue of E-30504 is take A, despite liner notes.
Brunswick 6753 issued as Red Nichols and His Orchestra. Fud
Livingston arranged the first title and F. Sullivan the second. The
alternate takes listed above have not been confirmed.

Red Nichols And His Five Pennies

NYC, August 27, 1929

Red Nichols, cornet; Tommy Thunen, John Egan, trumpet; Jack Teagarden, Glenn Miller, Herb Taylor, trombones; Pee Wee Russell, clarinet, possibly tenor; Jimmy Dorsey, alto, clarinet; Fud Livingston, tenor; Irving Brodsky, piano, celeste; Tommy Felline, banjo; Jack Hansen, brass bass; George Beebe, drums. Scrappy Lambert, vocal; unknown announcer on all XE matrices.

E-30712-A   They Didn't Believe Me (Ellos no me creyeron) (SL vocal)
    78:   >Brunswick 4651, Brunswick 6827, Brunswick (C) 4651,
            Brunswick (F) A-8655, Brunswick (G) A-8655
    33:   Gaps (I) 180
    CD: Tax (Sd) S-5-2

E-30713-G   They Didn't Believe Me
    Unissued

XE-30714-A   Say It With Music/They Didn't Believe Me (SL vocal)
    78:   >Red Nichols Broadcast No. 29, Program E, part 3
    33:   Fanfare 20-120, Jazz Archives JA-43, Sandy Hook SH 2105

XE-30715-A   Say It With Music/I May Be Wrong (But, I Think You're Wonderful) (SL vocal)
    78:   >Red Nichols Broadcast No. 30, Program E, part 5
    33:   Fanfare 20-120, Jazz Archives JA-43, Sandy Hook SH 2105

XE-30716-A/B The New Yorkers
    78:   >Red Nichols Broadcast No. 31

XE-30717-A   Say It With Music/On The Alamo (SL vocal)
    78:   >Red Nichols Broadcast No. 32, Program E, part 4
    33:   Fanfare 20-120, Jazz Archives JA-43, Sandy Hook SH 2105

XE-30718-A   Say It With Music/That's A Plenty
    78:   >Red Nichols Broadcast No. 33, Program E, part 6
    33:   Fanfare 20-120, Jazz Archives JA-43, Sandy Hook SH 2105

NOTE: Fanfare 20-120 includes "On the Alamo" although it is omitted on the label and cover. Teagarden researcher Joe Showler doubts Teagarden's presence on this session. Glenn Miller wrote the arrangement for the first title; Fud Livingston for "I May Be Wrong," F. Sullivan for "The New Yorkers," and Bobby Van Eps for "On the Alamo." The German Brunswick issue of E-30712 is subtitled "Man Glaubt Mir Nicht/Incredula." No copy of matrix XE-30716-A/B is known to exist and therefore the program and part numbers are unknown.

Red Nichols And His Five Pennies

NYC, September 6, 1929

Red Nichols, cornet; Tommy Thunen, John Egan, trumpet; possibly Jack Teagarden, Glenn Miller, Herb Taylor, trombone; Jimmy Dorsey, Pee Wee Russell, clarinet, alto; Fud Livingston, tenor; Henry Whiteman, Maurice Goffin, violin; Irving Brodsky, piano; Tommy Felline, banjo; Jack Hansen or Joe Tarto, bass; George Beebe, drums. Scrappy Lambert, Dick Robertson, vocals.

E-30531-A/B Wait For The Happy Ending (Espera el final dichoso) (SL vocal)
  78: >Brunswick 4510, Brunswick (C) 4510, Brunswick (F) 1043
  33: Emanon ESL-1, Gaps (I) 180
  CD: Tax (Sd) S-5-2

E-30532-G Wait For The Happy Ending
  Unissued

E-30533-A/B Can't We Be Friends? (No podramos ser amigos?) (DR vocal)
  78: >Brunswick 4510, Brunswick 6827, Brunswick (C) 4510, Brunswick (F) 1043
  33: Gaps (I) 180
  CD: Tax (Sd) S-5-2

E-30534-G Can't We Be Friends?
  Unissued

NOTE: Fud Livingston wrote both arrangments.

The Midnight Airdales

NYC, September 13, 1929

Red Nichols, cornet; Tommy Thunen, John Egan, trumpet; Glenn Miller, trombone; two unknown alto and clarinet; Pee Wee Russell, tenor; Henry Whiteman, Maurice Goffin, violins; Rube Bloom, piano; Joe Tarto, bass; Gene Krupa, drums; Red McKenzie, vocal.

149002-3 Swanee Shuffle (Meneito Suave) (RMcK vo)
    78:   >Columbia 1981-D, Columbia (Arg) A-8332
    33:   Emanon ERM-2

149003-2 I Gotta Have You (Quiero Tenerte A Mi Lado) (RMcK vo)
    78:   >Columbia 1981-D, Columbia (Arg) A-8347, Columbia (E) CB-14
    33:   Emanon ERM-2

NOTE: Red Nichols was the leader of this session. Fud Livingston, who has been listed as playing the tenor solos on these titles, may be present as one of the other reed players. The clarinet work heard on these titles is probably not by Russell, but I believe the tenor sax solos are.

Irving Mills And His Hotsy-Totsy Gang

NYC, September 20, 1929

Mannie Klein, Leo McConville, trumpet; Miff Mole, trombone; Jimmy Dorsey, Arnold Brilhart, clarinet, alto; Pee Wee Russell, clarinet, tenor; Hoagy Carmichael, piano, celeste, vocal; Joe Tarto, brass bass; Chauncey Morehouse, drums.

E-30958 Harvey (HC vocal)
    78:   >Brunswick 4559
    33:   MCA Coral (G) 0052.056 (COPS 8868), Retrieval (E) FJ 123, TOM TOM-12
    CT: Neovox (E) 773

E-30959 Harvey
    Unissued

E-30960   March Of The Hoodlums
   78:   >Brunswick 4559
   33:   Retrieval (E) FJ 123, TOM TOM-12
   CT: Neovox (E) 773

E-30961   Stardust
   78:   >Brunswick 4587
   33:   Retrieval (E) FJ 123, TOM TOM-12
   CT: Neovox (E) 773

NOTE: Produced by Irving Mills. MCA Coral (G) 0052.056 shows E-30959, but it is identical to E-30958. Dorsey plays the clarinet solo on E-30958, Russell on E-30960, and Brilhart on E-30961.

Irving Brodsky And His Orchestra
NYC, October 1, 1929

Red Nichols, cornet; Tommy Thunen or John Egan, trumpet; Glenn Miller, trombone; Jimmy Dorsey, clarinet, alto; Pee Wee Russell, Fud Livingston, clarinet, tenor; Henry Whiteman, Maurice Goffin, violin; Irving Brodsky, piano; Tommy Felline, banjo; Joe Tarto, brass bass; George Beebe, drums; Irving Kaufman (as Robert Wood), vocal.

149076-1   If You Believed In Me (IK vocal)
   78:   >Diva 3021-G, >Harmony 1021-H, >Publix 1053-P, >Sunrise
        1053-P, >Velvet Tone 2021-V
   33:   Collectors Must..! (I) M-8004

149077-2   The End Of the Lonesome Trail (IK vocal)
   78:   >Diva 3041-G, >Harmony 1041-H, >Velvet Tone 2041-V
   33:   Collectors Must..! (I) M-8004

149078-2   I May Be Wrong But I Think You're Wonderful (IK vocal)
   78:   >Diva 3021-G, >Harmony 1021-H, >Publix l063-P, >Sunrise
        1063-P, >Velvet Tone 2021-V
   33:   Collectors Must..! (I) M-8004

NOTE: Although 149076-2 has been reported to have been issued, its existence is doubtful. Both Publix and Sunrise issued as The Paramounteers. Russell is not audible on this session and all clarinet solos are by Jimmy Dorsey.

Mound City Blue Blowers

NYC, November 14, 1929

Red McKenzie, comb; Glenn Miller, trombone; Pee Wee Russell, clarinet; Coleman Hawkins, tenor; Eddie Condon, banjo; Jack Bland, guitar; Al Morgan, bass; Gene Krupa, drums.

BVE-57145-3   Hello, Lola (Que Hay, Lola?)
- 78: Bluebird B-6270, Bluebird B-10037, Electrola (G) EG 7729, HMV (Au) EA-2963, HMV (E) JO-149, HMV (E) B-6168, HMV (E) B-8952, HMV (F) K-6501, HMV (F) K-8525, HMV (In) B-8952, HMV (Sw) JK 2260, HMV (Turkey) AX 4108, >Vic V-38100, Vic (Arg) 62-0058
- 45: HMV (E) 7EG 8096, RCA WEJ-10, RCA (F) 75.697, "X" EVAA-3005, "X" (C) EVAA 3005
- 33: BBC (E) REB 698, Bluebird 9683-1-RB, Bluebird (E) NL 90405, Book of the Month Club 41-7552, Camden CAL 339, Camden (Arg) CAL 339, Camden (Au) 95, Camden (C) CAL 339, Camden (E) CDN 139, Camden (I) LCP-51, Franklin Mint Jazz-013A, Gardenia (H) 4008, Giants of Jazz (E) LPJT 51, Jazztone J 1249, Jolly Roger 5030, Neiman Marcus Fourth Series (RCA Special Products DDM4-0456), Pickwick (E) CDM-1059, RCA LEJ 10, RCA (F) FXM1 7325, RCA (F) PM 43267, RCA (F) NL 89277, RCA (F) 741.103, RCA (F) 800.211, RCA (I) LCP 51, RCA (J) RA-87, RCA (J) RA 5801-20 (AX-50), Shinseido (J) RCA 8227, Time-Life STL-J06 (P 14683), Time-Life (Au) STL-J06, Time-Life (C) STL-J06, Victor (J) RA 5334, Victor RCA (J) RA 5359, "X" LX 3005, "X" (Can) LX 3005
- TX: AFRS APM 144, AFRS APM 198, AFRS APM 274, AFRS APM 602, AFRS SY 61, VOA WOJ 19, VOA WOJ 48
- CD: BBC (E) CD 698, Bluebird 9683-2-RB, Bluebird (E) ND 90405, Classics (F) 587, Jazz Archives (F) 758
- CT: BBC (E) ZCF 698, Bluebird 9683-4-RB, Bluebird (E) NK 90405, Book of the Month Club 51-7553, Camden (I) KLCP-51, Franklin Mint Jazz Tape 13, Neovox (E) 733, Time-Life 4TL-J06
- 8T: Time-Life 8TL-J06

BVE-57146-3   One Hour (Una Hora)
- 78: Bluebird B-6456, Bluebird B-10037, Electrola (G) EG 7729, HMV (Au) EA 2963, HMV (E) JO-149, HMV (E) B-6150, HMV (E) B-8952, HMV (F) K-6501, HMV (F) K-8525, HMV (In) B-8952, HMV (Sw) JK-2260, >Vic V-38100, Vic (Arg) 62-0058
- 45: HMV (E) 7EG 8096, RCA WEJ-5, RCA (F) 75.697, "X" EVAA-3005, "X" (C) EVAA 3005
- 33: BBC (E) REB 698, Bluebird 9683-1-RB, Bluebird (E) NL 90405, Camden CAL 339, Camden (Arg) CAL 339, Camden (Au) 95, Camden (C) CAL 339, Camden (E) CDN 139, Camden (I) LCP 51, Camden (J) CL 5030, Gardenia (H) 4008, Giants of Jazz (E) LPJT 51, Jolly Roger 5030, Musica Jazz (I) 2MJP-1008, Neiman Marcus First Series (RCA Special Products DDM 4-0261), Pickwick (E) CDM-1059, RCA LEJ 5, RCA (F) FXM1 7325, RCA (F) NL 89.277, RCA (F) 730.566, RCA (F) 741.103, RCA (F) 800.211, RCA (I) LPC 51, RCA (J) RA-87, RCA (J) RA 5801-20 (AX 50), Time-Life STL-J06 (P 14783), Time-Life (Au) STL-J06, Time-Life (C) STL-J06, Victor LPV 501, Victor (G) LPV 501, Victor (J) VRA 5012, Victor (J) RA 5334, Victor (J) RA-5380, "X" LX 3005, "X" (C) LX 3005
- TX: AFRS DB 310, AFRS APM 196, AFRS APM 193, AFRS QCS 375
- CD: BBC (E) CD 698, Bluebird 9683-2-RB, Bluebird (E) ND 90405, Classics (F) 587, Jazz Archives (F) 758
- CT: BBC (E) ZCF 698, Bluebird 9683-4-RB, Bluebird (E) NK 90405, Neovox (E) 733, Time-Life 4TL-J06
- 8T: Time-Life 8TL-J06

NOTE: Vic (Arg) 62-0058 is included in album A-20. Bluebird B-10037, HMV B-8952, HMV JO-149, HMV AX 4108 issued as by Red McKenzie and the Mound City Blue Blowers. HMV AX 4108 is labeled "His Master's Voice Series of Jazz Classics, No. 8" and is coupled with a Benny Goodman recording.

The Ben Selvin recording session of November 27, 1929, has been suggested as including Pee Wee Russell. Titles recorded were "When I Am Housekeeping For You" (149645-2), "I Have to Have You" (149646-1) and "Ain'tcha?" (149647-3). However, none of the identifiable reed work on any of the titles sounds like Russell.

HIT OF THE WEEK RECORDINGS

Pee Wee Russell may have appeared on some Hit of the Week records, but as a section man, not a soloist. In an interview by Dom Cerulli (Down Beat, May 15, 1958), Russell recalled some paper records he made with Don Voorhees. Voorhees recorded for Hit-of-the-Week in December, 1929; February and July, 1930; June 20 and August, 1931.

There are two clarinet solos on Voorhees' recording of "Roll On, Mississippi, Roll On," but neither sounds like Russell. There is no identifiable reed work on any of the other titles Voorhees recorded for Hit of the Week. "Mysterious Mose," by Bobby Dixon's Broadcasters on Hit of the Week 1061, the rarest of the paper records, has been suggested as a possibility but the clarinet solo on it does not sound like Russell.

Bix Beiderbecke And His Orchestra
NYC, September 8, 1930

Bix Beiderbecke, cornet; Ray Lodwig, trumpet; Boyce Cullen, trombone; Jimmy Dorsey, Benny Goodman, Pee Wee Russell, clarinet, alto; Bud Freeman, tenor; Joe Venuti, violin; Irving Brodsky, piano; Eddie Lang, guitar; Min Leibrook, brass bass; Gene Krupa, drums. Weston Vaughan, vocal.

BVE 63630-1 Deep Down South (WV vocal)
- 45: >Natchez (Arg) WEP 804
- 33: Bix Volume 18, Everest FS-317, Historical HLP 28, Jazz Line (G) 33-125, Joker (I) SM 3122, Joker (I) SM 3570, RCA (F) PM 43267, RCA (F) 731.131, RCA (J) RA 20
- CD: IRD (I) BIX 9

BVE 63630-2 Deep Down South (Muy el Sur) (WV vocal)
- 78: HMV (E) B-8419, HMV (F) K-6238, >Victor 23018, Victor 25370
- 33: ASV Living Era (E) AJA 5080, Bix Volume 18, Bluebird 6845-1-RB, Bluebird (E) NL 86485, Jazz Line (G) 33-125, Joker (I) SM 3570, OFC (Arg) 34, RCA (F) CL 70.125, RCA (F) 731.037, RCA (J) RA 20
- CD: ASV Living Era (E) CD AJA 5080, Bluebird 6845-2-RB, Bluebird (E) ND 86485, Flapper (E) 9765, IRD (I) BIX 9
- CT: ASV Living Era (E) ZC AJA 5080, Bluebird 6845-4-RB, Bluebird (E) NK 86485, Neovox (E) 785

BVE 63631-1 I Don't Mind Walkin' In The Rain (When I'm Walking
In the Rain with You) (No Me Importa caminar en la Lluvia) (WV
vocal)
- 78: HMV (E) B-4889, >Vic 23008
- 33: Bix Volume 18, Jazz Line (G) 33-125, Joker (I) SM 3570,
  OFC (Arg) 34, RCA (F) CL 70.125, RCA (F) 731.037, RCA
  (J) RA 20
- CD: IRD (I) BIX 9
- CT: Neovox (E) 785

Omit Venuti and Lang. Leibrook switches to string bass.

BVE 63632-2 I'll Be A Friend With Pleasure (Camigo de Parrandas)
(WV vocal)
- 78: >Vic 23008
- 33: Bix Volume 18, Jazz Line (G) 33-125, Joker (I) SM 3570,
  RCA (E) RD 27225, RCA (F) CL 70.125, RCA (F) 731.037,
  RCA (I) LJ-50004, RCA (I) LPM 50004, RCA (J) RA 20,
  RCA (J) RA 5298, Victor LPM 2323, Victor (C) LPM 2323
- CD: IRD (I) BIX 9
- CT: Neovox (E) 785

BVE 63632-3 I'll Be A Friend With Pleasure (Camigo de Parrandas)
(WV vocal)
- 78: HMV (E) B-4889, HMV (E) B-8419, >Vic 23008, Victor
  26415
- 33: Bix Volume 18, Bluebird 6845-1-RB, Bluebird (E) NL
  86485, Jazz Line (G) 33-125, Joker (I) SM 3570, OFC (Arg)
  34, RCA (F) 731.037, RCA (J) RA 20
- CD: Bluebird 6845-2-RB, Bluebird (E) ND 86485, Flapper (E)
  9765, IRD (I) BIX 9
- CT: Bluebird 6845-4-RB, Bluebird (E) NK 86485, Neovox (E)
  785

NOTE: Matrix 63631 labeled "Joe Venuti, directing" on Victor 23008.
Mx. 63632 labeled "Ray Lodwig, directing" on Victor 23008. Victor
25370 is part of Victor album P-4. Bix Volume 18 is part of a 20-LP
boxed set, produced by Sunbeam records. IRD (I) BIX 9 was issued as
a single CD and as part of a 9 CD boxed set, as BIX BOX. Russell
solos on 63631, Goodman on 63630 and Dorsey on 63632. Recorded
at Victor studio #2, 24th Street, the first two titles from 10 a.m. to 1:30
p.m., and the third title after lunch between 2:30 and 4 p.m. A test
pressing of matrix BVE 63632-1 is rumored to exist.

Hoagy Carmichael And His Orchestra

NYC, September 15, 1930

Bix Beiderbecke, cornet; Ray Lodwig, trumpet; Jack Teagarden, Boyce Cullen, trombone; Jimmy Dorsey, clarinet, alto; possibly Pee Wee Russell or Arnold Brilhart, alto; Bud Freeman, tenor; Joe Venuti, violin; Irving Brodsky, piano; Eddie Lang, guitar; Min Leibrook, bass sax; Chauncey Morehouse, drums; Hoagy Carmichael, vocal.

BVE-63653-1 Georgia (On My Mind) (HC vocal, arranger)
- 78: HJCA HC-100, HMV (Au) EA-1200, HMV (Au) EA 8549, HMV (E) B-4885, HMV (E) B-6133, HMV (E) B-8549, HMV (F) K-6525, HMV (G) K-6525, >Victor 23013, Victor 25494, Victor (Arg) 25494
- 45: HMV (E) 7EG 8037, Victor EPBT 3072 (947-0228)
- 33: Bix Volume 19, Bluebird 8333-1-RB, Bluebird (E) NL 88333, Divergent (H) D-302, HMV (E) DLP 1106, Jazz Line (G) 33-125, Joker (I) SM 3570, RCA CPL 1-3370(e), RCA (E) LSA 3180, RCA (E) INTS 5181, RCA (F) CL 70.125, RCA (F) NL 89.096, RCA (F) 731.037, RCA (I) LPC-31007, RCA (J) RA 20, Victor LPT 3072, Victor (C) LPT 3072
- TX: AFRS APM 708, AFRS TBC 501
- CD: Bluebird 2192-2-RB, Bluebird 8333-2-RB, Bluebird (E) ND 88333, IRD (I) BIX 9
- CT: Bluebird 2192-4-RB, Bluebird 8333-4-RB, Bluebird (E) NK 88333

Omit Beiderbecke.

BVE-63654-1 One Night In Havana (Una Noche en la Habana) (HC vocal)
- 78: HMV (E) B-4885, >Victor 23013
- 33: Bix Volume 19, Jazz Line (G) 33-125, Joker (I) SM 3570, RCA (F) 731.037, RCA (J) RA 20
- CD: Bluebird 8333-2-RB, Bluebird (E) ND 88333, IRD (I) BIX 9
- CT: Bluebird 8333-4-RB, Bluebird (E) NK 88333

Beiderbecke returns.

BVE 63655-1 Bessie Couldn't Help It (No Culpen a Isabel) (HC vocal)
  78: >Vic 22864
  45: HMV (E) 7EG 8037, Victor EPBT 3072 (947-0228)
  33: Bix Volume 19,HMV (E) DLP 1106, Jazz Line (G) 33-125,
       Joker (I) SM 3570, RCA (F) CL 70.125, RCA (F) 731.037,
       RCA (I) LPC-31007, RCA (J) RA 20, Victor LPT 3072,
       Victor (C) LPT 3072
  CD: IRD (I) BIX 9

BVE 63655-2 Bessie Couldn't Help It (HC vocal)
  78: Jazz Classic 532, >Vic 25371
  33: Bix Volume 19, Divergent (H) D-302, Jazz Line (G) 33-125,
       Joker (I) SM 3570, RCA (E) LSA 3180, RCA (E) INTS 5181,
       RCA (F) NL 89.096, RCA (F) 731.037, RCA (J) RA 20,
       Time-Life STL J04 (P 14781), Time-Life (Au) STL-J04,
       Time-Life STL-J04
  TX: AFRS APM 213
  CD: Bluebird 8333-2-RB, Bluebird (E) ND 88333, IRD (I) BIX 9
  CT: Bluebird 8333-4-RB, Bluebird (E) NK 88333, Time-Life
       4TL-J04
  8T: Time-Life 8TL-J04

NOTE: Russell does not solo on this session and may not be present;
the clarinet solo on matrix 63655 is by Jimmy Dorsey. Victor 25371 is
part of Victor album P-4. HJCA and Jazz Classic issued as Bix
Beiderbecke with Hoagy Carmichael and His Orchestra. Bix Volume
19 is part of a 20-LP boxed set, produced by Sunbeam records. IRD (I)
BIX 9 was issued as a single CD and as part of a 9 CD boxed set, as
BIX BOX. Recorded in Victor studio 2, 24th Street, from 1:15 p.m. to
5:10 p.m. The last twelve seconds of 63654-1 are omitted on Bluebird
8333-2 (and -4)-RB.

Jack Teagarden And His Orchestra
                                              NYC, October 14, 1931

Charlie Teagarden, Sterling Bose, trumpet; Jack Teagarden, trombone,
vocal; Pee Wee Russell, clarinet; Joe Catalyne, clarinet, tenor; Max
Farley, clarinet, alto, tenor, arranger, Fats Waller, piano, vocal; Hilton
"Nappy" Lamare, guitar; Adrian Rollini, bass sax; Artie Bernstein,
bass; Stan King, drums.

W-151839-1 You Rascal You (Picaro) (JT, FW vocal)
- 78: >Columbia 2558-D, Columbia (Au) DO-667, Columbia (E) CB 424, Columbia (G) DW-4075, HJCA 611
- 33: ASV Living Era (E) AJA 5040, ASV (E) AJA 5059, CBS (Eu) 63366, CBS Sony (J) SOPB 55014, Columbia CJ 40847, Columbia (E) 33SX1545, CSP JLN 6044, CSP P2-15027, Conifer (E) CHD 153, Epic SN 6044 (LN 24045), Epic (C) SN 6044 (LN 24045), Jazz Panorama 1807, Time-Life STL-J15 (STLJ-5015-B), Time-Life (Au) STL-J15, Time-Life (C) STL-J15
- CD: ASV Living Era (G) CD AJA 5040 R, ASV (E) 5059, Columbia CK 40847, Jazzmen (G) 625.50.008
- CT: ASV Living Era (E) ZC AJA 5040, ASV (E) CDAJA 5059, Columbia CJT 40847, Time-Life 4TL-J15
- 8T: Time-Life 8TL-J15

W-151840-1 That's What I Like About You (Eso Es Lo Que Me Gusta De Ti) (JT, FW vocal)
- 78: >Columbia 2558-D, Columbia (Au) DO-667, Columbia (Eu) DC 144, HJCA 611
- 33: ASV Living Era (E) AJA 5040, CBS (Eu) 63366, Columbia (E) 33SX1545, CSP JLN 6044, Conifer (E) CHD 153, Epic SN 6044 (LN 24045), Epic (C) SN 6044 (LN 24045), Jazz Panorama 1807, Time-Life STL-J08 (P 15008), Time-Life (Au) STL-J08, Time-Life (C) STL-J08
- CD: ASV Living Era (G) CD AJA 5040 R, Jazz Archives (F) 157022
- CT: ASV Living Era (E) ZC AJA 5040, CBS Sony (J) SOPB 55014, Time-Life 4TL-J08
- 8T: Time-Life 8TL-J08

W-151841-2 Chances Are (JT vocal)
- 78: >Clarion 5442-C, >Harmony 1403-H, >Okeh 41551, >Velvet Tone 2502-V
- 33: CBS (Eu) 63366, CBS Sony (J) SOPB 55015, Columbia (E) 33SX1553, CSP JLN 6044, Conifer (E) CHD 153, Epic SN 6044 (LN 24046), Epic (C) SN 6044 (LN 24046), Time-Life STL-J08 (P 15008), Time-Life (Au) STL-J08, Time-Life (C) STL-J08
- CT: Time-Life 4TL-J08
- 8T: Time-Life 8TL-J08

W-151842-1 I Got The Ritz From The One I Love (JT vocal)
   33: Conifer (E) CHD 153, >Rarest Fats Waller RFW-4, Time-
          Life STL-J08 (P 15008), Time-Life (Au) STL-J08, Time-Life
          (C) STL-J08, TOM TOM-61
   CT: Time-Life 4TL-J08
   8T: Time-Life 8TL-J08

NOTE: Harmony, Clarion, Velvet Tone issued as Roy Carroll and His
Sands Point Orchestra; Okeh as Cloverdale Country Club Orchestra
(reverse is by a different band, although the same artist credit is used).
HJCA 611, a 12-inch disc with two titles per side, was issued as Jack
Teagarden and Fats Waller. Despite some listings, no alternate takes
are known of any titles from this session. Although the Harmony,
Clarion and Velvet Tone issues of matrix 151841 show 100589-1 as the
matrix and take number, and the Okeh has it as 405143-A, these are
control numbers. A test pressing of this title clearly shows the actual
matrix and take as W-151841-2. Royal blue wax pressings exist of
Columbia 2558-D. The Time/Life issues of 151842-1 have superior
sound to the other releases.

Gene Austin
NYC, November 10, 1931

Charlie Teagarden, Sterling Bose, trumpet; Jack Teagarden, trombone;
Matty Matlock or Gil Rodin, clarinet, alto; Pee Wee Russell, Eddie
Miller, clarinet, tenor; Fats Waller or Gil Bowers, piano (as indicated);
Nappy Lamare, guitar; Adrian Rollini, bass sax; Harry Goodman, bass;
Ray Bauduc, drums, Gene Austin, vocal.

10976-1 China Boy (FW piano)
   33: >Meritt #6

10977-1 Lies (GB piano, GA vocal)
   78: Ace (C) 51024, >Banner 32325, Domino (C) 51024, >Oriole
         2380, >Perfect 15542, >Romeo 1752, Royal (C) 91235,
         Sterling (C) 91235

10978-3 I'm Sorry, Dear (GB piano, GA vocal)
   78: Ace (C) 51024, >Banner 32325, Domino (C) 51024, >Oriole
         2380, >Perfect 15542, >Romeo 1752, Royal (C) 91235,
         Sterling (C) 91235

10979-1 Tiger Rag (FW piano)
   33: >Meritt #6

NOTE: All issues of mx. 10977 and 10978 as by Gene Austin. Ace (C) 51024 and Domino (C) 51024, are "double length" 10-inch records with both "I'm Sorry Dear" and "Lies" on the A side of the disc. Both introductions have been "clipped" to shorten them enough to fit on one side. During the dubbing process, two turntables were used with the title started a fraction of a second apart to create an "echo" effect. Matrix 10977 is labeled "Life" on Romeo 1752.

Billy Banks And His Orchestra
NYC, April 18, 1932

Henry "Red" Allen, trumpet, vocal; Pee Wee Russell, clarinet, tenor; Joe Sullivan, piano; Eddie Condon, banjo; Jack Bland, guitar; Al Morgan, bass; Zutty Singleton, drums; Billy Banks, vocal.

11716-1 Bugle Call Rag
- 78: >Banner 32459, Brunswick (E) 01590, Brunswick (F) A-500198, Columbia (Sd) DS 1509, Commodore 109, HMV (Ir) IP-385, Kristal (H) 211 81, Kristall (G) 211 81, Kristall (G) 25052, >Oriole 2483, Parlophone (E) R-2893, Parlophone (I) B-71080, Parlophone (Sw) PZ-11063, >Perfect 15615, >Romeo 1856, UHCA 109
- 33: CBS Realm (E) 52732, Collector's Classics (D) CC-14, IAJRC IAJRC-4, Jolly Roger 5025, OFC (Arg) 9, Time-Life STL-J16 (P 15519), Time-Life (Au) STL-J16, Time-Life (C) STL-J16, VJM (E) VLP 53
- CD: BBC (E) BBC CD 685
- CT: Time-Life 4TL-J16
- 8T: Time-Life 8TL-J16

11716-2 Bugle Call Rag
- 33: >Meritt 26

11717-1 Oh! Peter (You're So Nice) (HA vocal)
- 78: >Columbia 35841
- 33: CBS Realm (E) 52732, Collector's Classics (D) CC-14, IAJRC IAJRC-4, Jazz Archives JA-1, Jolly Roger 5025, OFC (Arg) 9, Time-Life STL-J16 (P 15519), Time-Life (Au) STL-J16, Time-Life (C) STL-J16, VJM (E) VLP 53
- CT: Time-Life 4TL-J16
- 8T: Time-Life 8TL-J16

11717-2 Oh, Peter (HA vocal)
  33: Collector's Classics (D) CC-55, >Jazz Archives JA-1, Time-Life STL-J27 (P 15966), Time-Life (Au) STL-J27, Time-Life (C) STL-J27
  CT: Time-Life 4TL-J27
  8T: Time-Life 8TL-J27

11718-1 Margie (BB vocal)
  78: >Banner 32462, Brunswick (E) 01561, Brunswick (F) A-500199, Commodore 110, >Oriole 2487, Parlophone (E) R-2929, Parlophone (In) DPE 104, Parlophone (Sw) PZ-11064, >Perfect 15620, Polydor (F) 580007, Polydor (G) 580007, >Romeo 1861, UHCA 110
  33: CBS Realm (E) 52732, Collector's Classics (D) CC-14, IAJRC IAJRC-4, Jolly Roger 5025, OFC (Arg) 9, Time-Life STL-J16 (P 15519), Time-Life (Au) STL-J16, Time-Life (C) STL-J16, VJM (E) VLP-53
  CT: Time-Life 4TL-J16
  8T: Time-Life 8TL-J16

11719-2 Spider Crawl (BB vocal)
Unissued

NOTE: Supervised by Herman Rose. Columbia 35841 as The Rhythmakers; Brunswick A-500198, Brunswick A-500199 as Eddie Condon's Chicago Rhythm Kings; Polydor as Chicago Rhythm Kings, Romeo 1856 as Billy Banks and Blue Rhythm Boys. Liner of Collector's Classics CC-55 lists 11717-1, but it is take 2. Conversely, the liner notes of CBS Realm 52732 lists 11717-2, but it is take 1. Pee Wee Russell plays tenor and clarinet on 11718.

Billy Banks And His Orchestra

NYC, May 23, 1932

Henry "Red" Allen, trumpet, vocal; Pee Wee Russell, clarinet, tenor; Joe Sullivan, piano; Eddie Condon, banjo; Jack Bland, guitar; Al Morgan, bass; Zutty Singleton, drums; Billy Banks, vocal.

11717-3 Oh Peter! (You're So Nice) (BB vocal)
    78: >Banner 32462, Brunswick (E) 01561, Brunswick (F) A-500199, Columbia 35841, Commodore 110, >Oriole 2487, Parlophone (E) R-2929, Parlophone (In) DPE 104, Parlophone (Sw) PZ-11064, >Perfect 15620, >Romeo 1861, UHCA 110
    33: CBS Realm (E) 52732, Collector's Classic (D) CC-14, IAJRC IAJRC-4, Jazz Archives JA-1, OFC (Arg) 9, Time-Life STL-J17 (P 15733), Time-Life (Au) STL-J17, Time-Life (C) STL-J17, VJM VLP 53
    CT: Time-Life 4TL-J17
    8T: Time-Life 8TL-J17

11717-4 Oh, Peter (BB vocal)
    33: Collector's Classics (D) CC-55, >Jazz Archives JA-1, Musica Jazz (I) 2MJP-1010

11719-4 Spider Crawl (BB vocal)
    78: >Banner 32459, Brunswick (E) 01590, Brunswick (F) A-500198, Columbia (Sd) DS 1509, Commodore 109, HMV (Ir) IP-385, Kristal (H) 21 181, Kristall (G) 21 181, Kristall (G) 25052, >Oriole 2583, Parlophone (E) R-2893, Parlophone (I) B-71080, Parlophone (Sw) PZ-11063, >Perfect 15615, >Romeo 1856, UHCA 109
    33: CBS Realm (E) 52732, Collector's Classics (D) CC-14, IAJRC IAJRC-4, Jolly Roger 5025, OFC (Arg) 9, Time-Life STL-J27 (P 15966), Time-Life (Au) STL-J27, (C) STL-J27, VJM (E) VLP 53
    CT: Charly (E) ST 784, Time-Life 4TL-J27
    8T: Time-Life 8TL-J27

11881-1   Who's Sorry Now? (BB vocal)
- 78:   Commodore 112, >Domino 123, Imperial (Cz) 6006, Imperial (G) 18003, >Oriole 2521, >Perfect 15642, >Regal 346, >Romeo 1895, UHCA 112, Vocalion (E) S-9
- 33:   CBS Realm (E) 52732, Collector's Classics (D) CC-14, Columbia CJ 40833, Franklin Mint 47, IAJRC IAJRC-4, Jazz Panorama 1808, OFC (Arg) 9, VJM (E) VLP 53
- CD: Columbia CK 40833
- CT: Columbia CJT 40833

11882-1   Take It Slow And Easy (BB vocal)
- 78:   >HRS 17
- 33:   CBS Realm (E) 52732, Collector's Classics (D) CC-14, IAJRC IAJRC-4, Jolly Roger 5025, OFC (Arg) 9, VJM (E) VLP 53

11883-1   Bald Headed Mama (BB vocal)
- 78:   Commodore 112, >Domino 123, Imperial (Cz) 6041, Imperial (G) 18003, >Oriole 2521, >Perfect 15642, >Regal 346, >Romeo 1895, UHCA 112, Vocalion (E) S-9
- 33:   CBS Realm (E) 52732, Collector's Classics (D) CC-14, IAJRC IAJRC-4, Jazz Panorama 1808, OFC (Arg) 9, Time-Life STL-J17 (P 15733), Time-Life (Au) STL-J17, Time-Life (C) STL-J17, VJM (E) VLP 53
- CT: Time-Life 4TL-J17
- 8T: Time-Life 8TL-J17

NOTE: Supervised by Herman Rose. Domino 123 as Harlem Hot Shots; Brunswick A-500198 and Brunswick A-500199 as Eddie Condon's Chicago Rhythm Kings; Vocalion 9 and all Imperial issues as Billy Banks' Chicago Rhythm Kings, Romeo 1856 as Billy Banks and Blue Rhythm Boys. Some copies of matrix 11719-4 on Kristall 211 81 as "Stider Crawl." Pee Wee Russell plays tenor and clarinet on matrix 11881.

The Rhythmakers

Henry "Red" Allen, trumpet; Jimmy Lord, clarinet; Pee Wee Russell, tenor; Fats Waller, piano; Eddie Condon, banjo; Jack Bland, guitar; Pops Foster, bass; Zutty Singleton, drums; Billy Banks, vocal.

12119-1   I'd Do Anything For You (Hare cualquier cosa por ti) (BB vocal)
- 78:   Brunswick (F) A-500316, >Melotone M-12457, >Perfect 15651,
- 33:   CBS (F) 63366, CBS Realm (E) 52732, Collector's Classics (D) CC 55, IAJRC IAJRC-4, VJM (E) VLP 53

12119-2   I'd Do Anything For You (BB vocal)
- 78:   Brunswick (E) 02508, >Banner 32530, Commodore 105, >Oriole 2534, UHCA 105
- 33:   CBS Realm (E) 52732, Collector's Classics (D) CC-14, IAJRC IAJRC-4, Jazz Panorama 1808, Jolly Roger 5025, OFC (Arg) 14, Swaggie (Au) JCS 33764, Time-Life STL-J17 (P 15733), Time-Life (Au) STL-J17, Time-Life (C) STL-J17, VJM (E) VLP 53
- CT: Time-Life 4TL-J17
- 8T: Time-Life 8TL-J17

12120-1   Mean Old Bed Bug Blues (BB vocal)
- 78:   >Banner 32502, Brunswick (F) A-500315, Commodore 105, Imperial (Cz) 6003, Imperial (G) 18012, >Melotone M-12457, >Oriole 2554, >Perfect 15669, UHCA 105, Vocalion (E) S-20, Vocalion (E) V-1021
- 33:   CBS (F) 63366, CBS Realm (E) 52732, Collector's Classics (D) CC-14, IAJRC IAJRC-4, Jazz Panorama 1808, Jolly Roger 5025, Swaggie (Au) JCS 33764, Time-Life STL-J15 (STLJ-5015-B), Time-Life (Au) STL-J15, Time-Life (C) STL-J15, VJM (E) VLP 53
- CT: Time-Life 4TL-J15
- 8T: Time-Life 8TL-J15

12120-2   Mean Old Bed Bug Blues (BB vocal)
- 78:   >Columbia 35882
- 33:   CBS Realm (E) 52732, Collector's Classics (D) CC 55, IAJRC IAJRC-4, OFC (Arg) 14, Swaggie (Au) JCS 33764, VJM (E) VLP 53

12121-2 Yellow Dog Blues (BB vocal)
  78: >Columbia 35882
  33: CBS Realm (E) 52732, IAJRC IAJRC-4, OFC (Arg) 14, Swaggie (Au) JCS 33764, Time-Life STL-J15 (STLJ-5015-C), Time-Life (Au) STL-J15, Time-Life (C) STL-J15, VJM (E) VLP-53
  CT: Time-Life 4TL-J15
  8T: Time-Life 8TL-J15

12121-3 Yellow Dog Blues (BB vocal)
  78: >Banner 32502, Brunswick (F) A-500315, Commodore 107, Imperial (Cz) 6003, Imperial (G) 18012, >Melotone M-12481, >Oriole 2554, Parlophone (Au) A-7399, Parlophone (E) R-2810, Parlophone (In) DPE 9, Parlophone (Sw) PZ 11148, >Perfect 15669, UHCA 107, Vocalion (E) S-20, Vocalion (E) V-1021
  33: ABC (Au) L38415, BBC (E) REB 598, CBS (Eu) 67273, CBS (F) 63366, CBS (H) 67273-2, CBS Realm (E) 52732, Collector's Classics (D) CC-14, Columbia KG 31564, IAJRC IAJRC-4, Jazz Panorama 1808, OFC (Arg) 14, Swaggie (Au) JCS 33764, VJM (E) VLP 53
  CD: BBC (G) CD 598
  CT: ABC (Au) C 38415, BBC (E) ZCF 598

12122-1 Yes, Suh! (BB and band vocal)
  33: Collector's Classics (D) CC 55, >Jazz Archives JA-1

12122-2 Yes, Suh! (BB and band vocal)
  78: >Banner 32530, Brunswick (E) 02078, Brunswick (F) A-9940, Commodore 107, >Melotone M-12481, >Oriole 2534, Parlophone (Au) A-7399, Parlophone (E) R-2810, Parlophone (In) DPE-9, Parlophone (Sw) PZ 11148, >Perfect 15651, UHCA 107
  33: CBS (F) 63366, CBS Realm (E) 52732, Collector's Classics (D) CC-14, IAJRC IAJRC-4, Jazz Panorama 1808, OFC (Arg) 14, Swaggie (Au) JCS 33764, VJM (E) VLP 53

NOTE: Supervised by Herman Rose. Perfects as Jack Bland and His Rhythmakers; Brunswick A-500315, 500316 and Vocalion S-20 as Chicago Rhythm Kings; Brunswick 02078 and A-9940 as Eddie Condon and His Rhythmakers; Imperials as Billy Banks' Chicago Rhythm Kings; UHCA 105, 107 and Vocalion V-1021 as Billy Banks' Rhythmakers; all other issues as The Rhythmakers. Label of UHCA 107 lists Al Morgan, bass. Brunswick (E) 02078 is included in the British Federation of Rhythm Clubs album.

Jack Bland And His Rhythmakers

NYC, October 8, 1932

Henry "Red" Allen, trumpet, vocal; Tommy Dorsey, trombone; Pee Wee Russell; clarinet; Happy Caldwell, tenor; Frank Froeba, piano; Eddie Condon, banjo; Jack Bland, guitar; Pops Foster, bass; Zutty Singleton, drums; Chick Bullock, vocal.

12452-1   Who Stole The Lock (HA vocal)
78:   >Col 35841
33:   CBS Realm (E) 52732, Collector's Classics (D) CC 55, ESC 101, IAJRC IAJRC-4, Jolly Roger 5025, OFC (Arg) 14, VJM (E) VLP 53

12452-2   Who Stole The Lock (Quien se Ilevo el Candado?) (HA vocal)
78:   >Banner 32605, Brunswick (E) 01737, Brunswick (F) A-500317, Commodore 104, Kristal (H) 21182, Kristall (G) 21182, >Melotone M-12513, >Oriole 2593, Parlophone (E) R-2812, Parlophone (I) B-71147, Parlophone (Sw) PZ 11142, >Perfect 15694, >Romeo 1966
33:   Collector's Classics (D) CC 14, Franklin Mint 47, Jazz Panorama 1808, VJM (E) VLP 53

12453-1   A Shine On Your Shoes (Lustre en tus Zapatos) (CB vocal)
78:   Commodore 111, >Melotone M-12510, >Oriole 2588, >Perfect 15689
33:   CBS (E) 67273, CBS (F) S67273-1, Collector's Classics (D) CC-14, Columbia KG 31564, OFC (Arg) 14, VJM (E) VLP-53

12453-2   A Shine On Your Shoes (CB vocal)
33:   Collector's Classics (D) CC 55, >Jazz Archives JA-1

12453-3   A Shine On Your Shoes (CB vocal)
33:   Collector's Classics (D) CC 55, >Jazz Archives JA-1

12454-2   It's Gonna Be You (Tendra que sur tu) (CB vocal)
78:   Brunswick (F) A-500316, Commodore 111, >Melotone M-12510, >Perfect 15689
33:   Collector's Classics (D) CC-14, OFC (Arg) 14, VJM (E) VLP 53

36

Omit Dorsey, trombone.

12455-1 Someone Stole Gabriel's Horn (Alguiense Ilevo la Corneta de Gabriel) (HA vocal)
    78:   >Banner 32605, Brunswick (E) 01737, Brunswick (F) A-500317, Commodore 104, Kristal (D) 211 82, Kristall (G) 211 82, >Melotone M-12513, >Oriole 2593, Parlophone (E) R-2812, Parlophone (I) B-71147, Parlophone (Sw) PZ 11142, >Perfect 15694, Polydor (F) 580007, Romeo 1966
    33:   Collector's Classics (D) CC-14, Jazz Panorama 1808, Jolly Roger 5025, OFC (Arg) 14, VJM (E) VLP 53

12455-2 Someone Stole Gabriel's Horn (HA vocal)
    33:   Collector's Classics (D) CC 55, >Jazz Archives JA-1

NOTE: Supervised by Herman Rose. Columbia 35841 as The Rhythmakers. Brunswick, Parlophone and Polydor as Chicago Rhythm Kings. Com 104 and 111 are master pressings. Matrix 12452-2 is titled "Who Stole De [sic] Lock?" on Kristal 21182.
The reissue on Harrison Y of "In the Dim, Dim Dawning" (matrix 12629-1) by Cliff Martin has a clarinet solo that sounds "convincingly like Pee Wee Russell," according to the liner notes. My opinion, however, is that the clarinetist is not Russell.

Adrian Rollini And His Orchestra
NYC, July 29, 1933

Possibly Bunny Berigan, trumpet; probably Al Philburn, trombone; Pee Wee Russell, clarinet; Arthur Rollini, tenor; Fulton McGrath, piano; Dick McDonough, guitar; Adrian Rollini, bass sax; celeste (on mx. 13663 and 13676), vibraphone (on Mx. 13675), possibly Merrill Klein or Artie Miller, bass; unknown drums; Red McKenzie, Howard Philips, vocal.

13663-1 Ah, But Is It Love (HP vocal)
    78:   >Banner 32826, Crown (C) 91594, Decca (E) F-3702, >Melotone M-12756, >Oriole 2736, >Perfect 15799, Rex (E) 8052, >Romeo 2109, Royal (C) 91594
13664-1 I've Gotta Get Up And Go To Work (RMcK vocal)
    78:   >Banner 32826, Crown (C) 91594, Decca (E) F-3702, >Melotone M-12756, >Oriole 2736, >Perfect 15799, Royal (C) 91594
13675-1 If I Had Somebody To Love (HP vocal)
    78:   >Banner 32837, Crown (C) 91608, >Melotone M-12766, >Oriole 2743, >Perfect 15805, Rex 8035, >Romeo 2116

13676-1   Dream On (RMcK vocal)
   78:   >Banner 32837, Crown (C) 91608, >Melotone M-12766, >Oriole 2743, >Perfect 15805, >Romeo 2116

NOTE: Rex 8035 as Bob Causer and His Cornellians; Rex 8052 as Ed Lloyd and His Orchestra. Some issues of mx. 13664 on Perfect 15799 show take 2 in the wax, but the performance is identical to the more common take 1. Although Herb Weil is usually listed as the drummer on this session, he denied ever recording with Red McKenzie.

Adrian Rollini And His Orchestra
NYC, September 14, 1933

Bunny Berigan, trumpet; Al Philburn, trombone; Pee Wee Russell, clarinet; Arthur Rollini, tenor; Fulton McGrath, piano; Dick McDonough, guitar; Adrian Rollini, bass sax, celeste, vibraphone; Artie Miller, bass; Herb Weil, drums and vocal.

13999-1   By A Waterfall (HW vocal)
   78:   >Banner 32867, >Conqueror 8220, >Domino 139, >Melotone M-12788, Melotone 91619, >Oriole 2757, >Perfect 15817, >Romeo 2130

14000-1   Sittin' On A Back Yard Fence (HW vocal)
   78:   >Banner 32867, Decca (E) F-3827, >Domino 139, >Melotone M-12788, Melotone 91619, >Oriole 2757, >Perfect 15817, >Romeo 2130

14001-1   I'll Be Faithful (HW vocal)
   78:   >Banner 32863, >Conqueror 8279, >Domino 141, >Melotone M-12790, Melotone (C) 91621, >Oriole 2759, >Perfect 15819, >Romeo 2132

14002-1   Beloved (HW vocal)
   78:   >Banner 32863, >Conqueror 8279, Decca (E) F-3848, >Domino 141, >Melotone M-12790, Melotone (C) 91621, >Oriole 2759, >Perfect 15819, >Romeo 2132

NOTE: Copies of all four titles exist with takes 1 and 3, which are aurally identical. The "remake sessions" for take 3, usually listed as October 23 and November 17, 1933, are probably mastering or dubbing dates. Matrices 14001-2 and 14002-2, both listed in Rust, are not known to exist.

Eddie Condon And His Orchestra

NYC, October 21, 1933

Max Kaminsky, trumpet; Floyd O'Brien, trombone; Pee Wee Russell, clarinet; Bud Freeman, tenor; Alex Hill, piano; Eddie Condon, Vega lute; Artie Bernstein, bass; Sid Catlett, drums.

B-14193-A   The Eel
- 78:   >Columbia 35680, Decca (E) M-30368, Lucky (J) 5074
- 45:   Philips (E) bbe 12497, Philips (E) 436.008AJE
- 33:   CBS Sony (J) SOPL 186, Family (I) SFR 697, Franklin Mint 66, Jazz Panorama 1805, Musica Jazz (I) 2MJP-1010, Swaggie (Au) 1358, Tax (Sd) m-8019
- TX: VOA WOJ 19?
- CD: Dejavu (Austrian) 5119-2
- CT: Neovox (E) 819

B-14193-B   The Eel
- 33:   CBS (E) 67273, CBS (H) 67273-1, >Columbia KG 31564, Musica Jazz (I) 2MJP 1042, Swaggie (Au) 809

B-14194-A   Tennessee Twilight
- 78:   >Brunswick (E) 01690, Brunswick (F) A-500406, Columbia 36009, Columbia (Sd) DS-1574, Decca (E) M-30366, Parlophone (Au) A-7554, Parlophone (E) R-2938, Parlophone (In) DPE-108, UHCA 64
- 45:   Philips (E) bbe 12497
- 33:   CBS Sony (J) SOPL 186, Columbia (E) 33SX1499, Epic SN 6042 (LN 24027), Epic (C) SN 6042, (LN 24027), Family (I) SFR 697, Folkways FP 65, Folkways FJ 2806, Jolly Roger 5018, Tax (Sd) m-8019, Swaggie (Au) 1358, VJM (E) VLP 55,
- CT: Neovox (E) 819

B-14194-B   Tennessee Twilight
- 78:   >Columbia 36009, Columbia (J) M-673
- 45:   Philips (E) 436.008AJE
- 33:   CBS Sony (J) SOPL 186, Columbia (J) ZL 1091, Family (I) SFR 697, Franklin Mint 65, Swaggie (Au) 1358, Tax (Sd) m-8019, Time-Life STL-J17 (P 15733), Time-Life (Au) STL-J17, Time-Life (C) STL-J17
- CT: Time-Life 4TL-J17
- 8T: Time-Life 8TL-J17

B-14195-A   Madame Dynamite
   78:   >Brunswick (E) 0l690, Brunswick (F) A-500406, Columbia
         (Sd) DS 1574, Decca (E) M-30366, Parlophone (E) R-2938,
         Parlophone (Au) A-7554, Parlophone (In) DPE-108, UHCA
         63
   45:   Philips (E) bbe 12497, Philips (E) 436.008AJE
   33:   CBS Sony (J) SOPL 186, Columbia (E) 33SX1499, Family
         (I) SFR 697, Jolly Roger 50l8, Swaggie (Au) 1358, Tax (Sd)
         m-8019, Time-Life STL-J17 (P 15733), Time-Life (Au) STL-
         J17, Time-Life (C) STL-J17, VJM (E) VLP 55
   CT: Neovox (E) 819, Time-Life 4TL-J17
   8T: Time-Life 8TL-J17

B-14195-B   Madame Dynamite
   33:   CBS Sony (J) SOPL 186, Columbia (E) 33SX1499, >Epic
         SN 6042 (LN 24027), Epic (C) SN 6042 (LN 24027), Family
         (I) SFR 697, Swaggie (Au) 1358, Tax (Sd) m-8019
   CT: Neovox (E) 819

B-14196-A   Home Cooking
   78:   >Columbia 35680, Lucky (J) 5074
   45:   Philips (E) bbe 12497, Philips (E) 436008AJE
   33:   CBS Sony (J) SOPL 186, Columbia JZ-1, Columbia (E)
         33SX1499, Columbia (J) SL-3022, Epic SN 6042 (LN
         24027), Epic (C) SN 6042 (LN 24027), Family (I) SFR 697,
         Jazz Panorama 1805, Philips (H) B 07100 L, RTB (Yugo)
         LPV 4301, Swaggie (Au) 1358, Tax (Sd) m-8019, Time-Life
         STL-J17 (P 15733), Time-Life (Au) STL-J17, Time-Life (C)
         STL-J17
   TX: AFRS BS 274?
   CT: Time-Life 4TL-J17, Neovox (E) 819
   8T: Time-Life 8TL-J17

NOTE: Columbia 36009 is part of Columbia album C-46. The earlier
pressings of this issue used take A. Despite Epic SN 6042 notes, the
take used of 14196 is A, not B. UHCA 63/64 issued as by Chicago
Rhythm Kings. It has not yet been established if AFRS BS (Bill
Stewart series) 274 is 14196-A or take B from the Nov. 17 session, nor
if VOA WOJ 19 is 14193-A or take C from the Nov. 17 session. Alex
Hill arranged "Tennessee Twilight" and "Madame Dynamite."

Eddie Condon And His Orchestra

NYC, November 17, 1933

Max Kaminsky, trumpet; Floyd O'Brien, trombone; Pee Wee Russell, clarinet; Bud Freeman, tenor; Joe Sullivan, piano; Eddie Condon, banjo; Artie Bernstein, bass; Sid Catlett, drums.

B-14193-C   The Eel
- 78:   >Brunswick 6743, Brunswick (E) 02006, Brunswick (F) A-81914, Brunswick (F) A-500328, Brunswick (G) A-9738, Columbia (Sd) DS 1398, Decca (E) BM 30368, Parlophone (Au) A-7483, Parlophone (E) R-2807,
- 45:   Jass (H) 607
- 33:   CBS Sony (J) SOPL 186, Columbia (E) 33SX1499, Epic SN 6042 (LN 24027), Epic (C) SN 6042 (LN 24027), Family (I) SFR 697, Jazz Panorama 1805, Jolly Roger 5018, Swaggie (Au) 1358, Tax (Sd) m-8019, VJM (E) VLP 55
- TX: VOA WOJ 19?
- CT: Neovox (E) 819

B-14196-B   Home Cooking
- 78:   >Brunswick 6743, Brunswick (E) 02005, Brunswick (F) A-81914, Brunswick (F) A-500328, Brunswick (G) A-9737, Columbia (Sd) DS 1398, Decca (E) BM 30368, Parlophone (Au) A-7459, Parlophone (E) R-2807
- 45:   Jass (H) 607
- 33:   CBS Sony (J) SOPL 186, Columbia JZ-1, Family (I) SFR 697, Folkways FJ 2811, Jazz Panorama 1805, Jolly Roger 5018, Swaggie (Au) 1358, Tax (Sd) m-8019, Time-Life STL-J27 (P 15966), Time-Life (Au) STL-J27, Time-Life (C) STL-J27, VJM (E) VLP 55,
- TX: AFRS BS 274?
- CT: Neovox (E) 819, Time-Life 4TL-J27
- 8T: Time-Life 8TL-J27

NOTE: 14196-B was used on a few copies of Columbia JZ-1 in error. Brunswick A-500328 as Chicago Rhythm Kings. See note on previous session regarding the transcription issues.

Red McKenzie And His Orchestra

NYC, December 28, 1933

Jack Teagarden, Tommy Dorsey, trombone; Pee Wee Russell, clarinet; Bud Freeman, tenor; Casper Reardon, harp; Red Norvo, xylophone; Fulton McGrath, piano; Eddie Condon, guitar; Art Miller, bass; Stan King, drums, Red McKenzie, vocal.

B-14497-A   Whispering
      Unissued

B-14498-B   Delta Bound
      Unissued

B-14499-A   Mean To Me (RMcK vocal)
      33: >IAJRC IAJRC-28

NOTE: TO 1160 (indicating a special "test only" pressing) is embossed on the reverse side of the test pressing of B-14499-A. The session was recorded by ARC.

Vic Berton And His Orchestra

NYC, March 25, 1935

Sterling Bose, Henry Levine, Louis Garcia, trumpet; Art Foster, trombone; Matty Matlock, clarinet; Jimmy Granato, clarinet, alto; Pee Wee Russell, clarinet, tenor; unknown baritone; Irving Brodsky, piano; Darrell Calker, guitar, arranger; Merrill Klein, bass; Vic Berton, drums; Chick Bullock, vocal.

16785-3   Taboo (CB vocal)
    78:   Brunswick (F) A-500558, >Vocalion 2974
    33:   Harrison LP-O

17175-1   Mary Lou (CB vocal)
    78:   Brunswick (F) A-500559 Brunswick (G) A-81075,
          >Vocalion 2944
    33:   Harrison LP-O

17176-1   In Blinky, Winky, Chinky Chinatown (CB vocal)
    78:   Brunswick (F) A-500559, >Vocalion 2964
    33:   Harrison LP-O, Stash ST-116

17177-1 Blue
    78: Brunswick (F) A-500560, >Vocalion 2974
    33: Harrison LP-O

17178-1 Lonesome And Sorry
    78: Brunswick (F) A-500560, >Vocalion 2944
    33: Harrison LP-O

NOTE: Matrix 17175 on Brunswick A-500559 as "Hary Lou." Matrix 17178 on Brunswick A-500560 as "Lonesome and Blue." Brunswick A-81075 as Vic Burton (sic) and his Orchestra; Brunswick A-500560 as Vic Berton and His Rhythm. Spencer Clark, who is usually listed as playing bass sax on this session, denied his presence and pointed out that the instrument used is a baritone sax. (Other saxophonists insist that the instrument is a bass sax.) He thought it sounded something like Charlie Bubeck, who played in the Ozzie Nelson band of the period. George Tooley has also been suggested. Russell plays the clarinet solos after the vocal on 17176, the first clarinet solo on 17177 and the solo following the tympany break on 17178. All other clarinet work is by Matty Matlock.

A Chick Bullock session of May 10, 1935, is usually listed as including Pee Wee Russell. There is a clarinet solo on "Chasing Shadows" that resembles Russell's style but, in my opinion it is not Pee Wee.

Louis Prima And His New Orleans Gang

NYC, May 17, 1935

Louis Prima, trumpet, vocal; Pee Wee Russell, clarinet; Frank Pinero, piano; Garry McAdams, guitar; Jack Ryan, bass; Sam Weiss, drums.

B-17612-1 The Lady In Red (LP vocal)
    78: >Brunswick 7448, Brunswick (F) A-500575, Lucky (J) 60144
    33: CBS (E) 67273, Columbia KG 31564, Jazz Panorama 1819, Reader's Digest RD4-206 (RD4-206-5), Time-Life STL-J17 (P 15733), Time-Life (Au) STL-J17, Time-Life (C) STL-J17, TOM-38
    CT: Time-Life 4TL-J17
    8T: Time-Life 8TL-J17

B-17613-1 Chinatown, My Chinatown (LP vocal)
- 78: >Brunswick 7456, Brunswick (F) A-500561, Decca (E) F-5626, Lucky (J) 60144
- 33: Decca (E) RAL 511, Historia (G) H-651, Jazz Panorama 1819, TOM-38

B-17614-1 Chasing Shadows (LP vocal)
- 78: >Brunswick 7448, Brunswick (F) A-500575, Decca (E) F-5621
- 33: Bellaphon (G) 625 50 017, Columbia CJ 40847, Decca (E) RAL 511, Jazz Panorama 1819, Time-Life STL-J17 (P 15733), Time-Life (Au) STL-J17, Time-Life (C) STL-J17, TOM-38
- CD: Columbia CK 40847
- CT: Time-Life 4TL-J17, Columbia CJT 40847
- 8T: Time-Life 8TL-J17

B-17615-1 Basin Street Blues (LP vocal)
- 78: >Brunswick 7456, Brunswick (F) A-500561, Decca (E) F-5626, Polydor (F) 580009, Polydor (G) 580009
- 33: Columbia CL 1036, Columbia (J) YL-146, Jazz Panorama 1819, Franklin Mint 47, TOM-38

NOTE: Although Lucky 60144 has matrix 17613-2 in the wax, it is a dub of take 1.

Louis Prima And His New Orleans Gang

NYC, June 27, 1935

Louis Prima, trumpet, vocal; Pee Wee Russell, clarinet; Frank Pinero, piano; Garry McAdams, guitar; Jack Ryan, bass; Sam Weiss, drums.

B-17739-1 In A Little Gypsy Tea Room (LP vocal)
- 78: >Brunswick 7479, Lucky (J) S-26, Lucky (J) 60510
- 33: New World NW 250, TOM-38

B-17740-1 Let's Swing It (LP vocal)
- 78: >Brunswick 7479

B-17740-2 Let's Swing It (LP vocal)
- 78: >Brunswick 7479
- 33: TOM-38

Louis Prima And His New Orleans Gang

NYC, July 2, 1935

Louis Prima, trumpet, vocal; Pee Wee Russell, clarinet; Frank Pinero, piano; Garry McAdams, guitar; Jack Ryan, bass; Sam Weiss, drums.

B-17762-1   Plain Old Me (LP vocal)
   78:   >Brunswick 7499
   33:   TOM-38

B-17763-1   How'm I Doin'? (LP vocal)
   78:   >Brunswick 7531, Brunswick (F) A-9869

B-17763-2   How'm I Doin'? (LP vocal)
   78:   >Brunswick 7531, Brunswick (F) A-9869, Decca (E) F-5692
   33:   Decca (E) RAL 511, Historia (G) H-651, Swingfan (G) 1015, TOM-38

B-17764-1   Weather Man (LP vocal)
   78:   >Brunswick 7499, Decca (E) F-5777
   33:   Decca (E) RAL 511, Historia (G) H-651, Special Editions (Au) No. 1, TOM-38

B-17765-1   Solitude (LP vocal)
   78:   >Brunswick 7531, Brunswick (F) A-9869, Decca (E) F-5692
   33:   Decca (E) RAL 511, Swingfan (G) 1015, TOM-38,

NOTE: B-17763-1 titled "How'm I Doin', Hey! Hey!" on Decca (E) F 5692. B-17762-3 has been listed as being made at a remake session, September 14, 1935, in New York, but this is a dubbing of take 1. (The band was in Los Angeles at the time.)

Shortly after arriving in Los Angeles in August, 1935, Louis Prima and his band appeared in a short subject, "Star Reporter in Hollywood," number 2, also known as "Talent Discovery." Prima is listed as having played "Chinatown" in the film. It was released in November, 1935.

Another film which included Prima -- and possibly his band -- is "The Champ's A Chump," shot in Hollywood in 1936 by Columbia. Neither film has been available for audition.

Louis Prima And His New Orleans Gang
Los Angeles, November 30, 1935

Louis Prima, trumpet and vocal; Pee Wee Russell, clarinet; Frank Pinero, piano; Garry McAdams; guitar; Jack Ryan, bass.

LA-1078-B Sweet Sue - Just You (LP vocal)
    78:   >Brunswick 7596, Brunswick (F) A-9975, Decca (E) F-5911
    33:   Historia (G) H-651, TOM-38

LA-1079-B I'm Shooting High (LP vocal)
    78:   >Brunswick 7586, Regal Zonophone (Au) G-22696
    33:   TOM-38

LA-1080-B I Love You Truly (LP vocal)
    78:   >Brunswick 7596, Brunswick (F) A-9975, Decca (E) F-5911
    33:   Decca (E) RAL 511, TOM-38

LA-1081-A I've Got My Fingers Crossed (LP vocal)
    78:   >Brunswick 7586

LA-1081-B I've Got My Fingers Crossed (LP vocal)
    78:   >Brunswick 7586, Regal Zonophone (Au) G-22696
    33:   TOM-38

Louis Prima And His New Orleans Gang
Los Angeles, February 28, 1936

Louis Prima, trumpet, vocal; Pee Wee Russell, clarinet; Joe Catalyne, tenor; Frank Pinero, piano; Garry McAdams, guitar; Jack Ryan, bass; George Pemberty, drums.

LA-1101-A It's Been So Long (LP vocal)
    78:   >Brunswick 7628, Columbia (J) M 104, Lucky (J) 60132
    33:   TOM-39

LA-1102-A At the Darktown Strutters' Ball (LP vocal)
    78:   >Brunswick 7657, Decca (E) F-6001, Lucky (J) 60155
    33:   TOM-39

LA-1103-A Dinah (LP vocal)
    78: >Brunswick 7666, Brunswick (F) A-81011, Brunswick (G)
         A-81011, Columbia (E) 5065, Columbia (I) CQ 1432, Decca
         (E) F-6001
    33: Franklin Mint 47, Historia (G) H-651, Swingfan (G) 1015,
         TOM-39

LA-1104-A Lazy River (LP vocal)
    78: >Brunswick 7666, Brunswick (F) A-81011, Brunswick (G)
         A-81011
    33: TOM-39

LA-1105-A Alice Blue Gown (LP Vocal)
    78: >Brunswick 7657, Lucky (J) 60155
    33: TOM-39

LA-1106-A Sing, Sing, Sing (LP and band, vocal)
    78: >Brunswick 7628, Columbia (E) 5030, Columbia (J) M 104,
         Lucky (J) 60132
    33: TOM-39

Louis Prima and his "Famous Door Orchestra" appeared in a 10-minute film short, "Vitaphone Varieties," (Vitaphone 3623, release number 1603), filmed around this time in Los Angeles. The film was directed by Roy Mack and copyrighted in March, 1936. The band apparently appeared in only one number, probably "Chinatown." A copy of the film and the soundtrack exist at the Library of Congress.

Louis Prima And His Orchestra
                                        Los Angeles, c. April, 1936

Louis Prima, trumpet, vocal; Pee Wee Russell, clarinet; Frank Pinero, piano; Garry McAdams, guitar; Jack Ryan, bass.

'Way Down Yonder in New Orleans
    Unissued

Isle of Capri
    Unissued

Basin Street Blues
    Unissued

Up A Lazy River
    33:   >Extreme Rarities 1008

Dinah
    Unissued

NOTE: These performances are included in the short subject, "Swing It," released by RKO and copyrighted July 3, 1936. Some of the interior scenes were shot in the Famous Door. Russell has several lines of dialog. Directed by Leslie Goodwin. The film is also notable for including one of the first screen appearances of Lucille Ball.

Louis Prima And His New Orleans Gang

Los Angeles, May 17, 1936

Louis Prima, trumpet and vocal; Gene Lafreniere, Denny Donaldson, trumpet; Bill Atkinson, trombone; Pee Wee Russell, clarinet, tenor; George Moore, Peyton Legare, alto; Joe Catalyne, tenor; Frank Pinero, piano; Garry McAdams, guitar; Jack Ryan, bass; George Pemberty, drums.

LA-1111-A Let's Get Together and Swing (LP, The Three Stafford Sisters vocal)
    78:   >Brunswick 7740, Columbia (E) 5065, Columbia (I) CQ
          1432, Lucky (J) S-23
    33:   TOM-39

LA-1112-A Cross Patch (LP vocal)
    78:   >Brunswick 7680, Lucky (J) 60165
    33:   Time-Life STL-J17 (P 15733), Time-Life (Au) STL-J17,
          Time-Life (C) STL-J17, TOM-39
    CT: Time-Life 4TL-J17
    8T: Time-Life 8TL-J17

LA-1113-A Swing Me A Lullaby (LP vocal)
    78:   >Brunswick 7680, Lucky (J) 60165
    33:   TOM-39

LA-1114-A The Stars Know (I'm In Love With You) (LP vocal)
    78:   >Brunswick 7740, Lucky (J) 60202
    33:   TOM-39

LA-1114-B The Stars Know (I'm In Love With You) (LP vocal)
    78:   >Brunswick 7740

LA-1115-A Confessin' (LP vocal)
    78:   >Brunswick 7709
    33:   TOM-39

LA-1116-A Let's Have Fun (LP vocal)
    78:   >Brunswick 7709, Lucky (J) 60202
    33:   TOM-39

NOTE: Pee Wee Russell solos on LA 1114-A; a solo by Prima replaces his on the alternate take.

Louis Prima And His Orchestra
                                      Los Angeles (?), May 23, 1936

Louis Prima, trumpet, vocal; Pee Wee Russell, clarinet; Frank Pinero, piano; Garry McAdams, guitar; Jack Ryan, bass; George Pemberty, drums.

I Still Want You (LP, vocal)
    33:   >IAJRC IAJRC-28

NOTE: This is from the "Shell Chateau Show," a Red network broadcast. A large studio orchestra joins in on last chord.

Louis Prima And His New Orleans Gang
                                      Chicago, November 16, 1936

Louis Prima, trumpet, vocal; Gene Lafreniere, Denny Donaldson, trumpet; Bill Atkinson, trombone; Pee Wee Russell, clarinet, tenor; George Moore, Peyton Legare, alto; Joe Catalyne, tenor; Frank Pinero, piano; Garry McAdams, guitar; Jack Ryan, bass; Godfrey Hirsch, drums.

C 1675-1 Mr. Ghost Goes To Town (LP vocal)
    78:   Lucky (J) 60476, >Vocalion 3388
    33:   TOM-39
    CD: Jass J-CD-623

C 1676-1 Pennies From Heaven (LP vocal)
    78:    Brunswick (F) A-81100, Brunswick (G) A-81100, >Vocalion 3376
    33:    Historia (G) H-651, TOM-39

C-1677-1 The Goose Hangs High (LP vocal)
    78:    Lucky (J) 60476, >Vocalion 3388
    33:    TOM-39

C-1678-1 What Will Santa Claus Say? (When He Finds Everybody Swingin') (LP vocal)
    78:    Brunswick (F) A-81100, Brunswick (G) A-81100, >Vocalion 3376
    33:    Jass Number Eight, TOM-39
    CD: Jass J-CD-3

Teddy Wilson And His Orchestra

NYC, December 17, 1937

Hot Lips Page, trumpet; Pee Wee Russell, clarinet; Chu Berry, tenor; Teddy Wilson, piano; Allan Reuss, guitar; unknown bass and drums, Sally Gooding, vocal.

B-22192-2 My First Impression Of You (SG vocal)
    33:    >Meritt 21
    CD: Classics (F) 548

B-22193-1 With A Smile And A Song (SG vocal)
    33:    >Meritt 21
    CD: Classics (F) 548

B-22193-2 With A Smile And A Song (SG vocal)
    33:    >IAJRC-28, Meritt 21

B-22194-2 When You're Smiling
    33:    >Meritt 21
    CD: Classics (F) 548

B-22195-2 I Can't Believe That You're In Love With Me
    33:    >Meritt 21
    CD: Classics (F) 548

NOTE: Produced by John Hammond. IAJRC issue of matrix. 22193-2 is labeled "With A Song And A Smile." Meritt 21 is part of a two-LP set which also contains Meritt 22.

Eddie Condon And His Windy City Seven

NYC, January 17, 1938

Bobby Hackett, cornet; George Brunies, trombone; Pee Wee Russell, clarinet; Bud Freeman, tenor; Jess Stacy, piano; Eddie Condon, guitar; Artie Shapiro, bass; George Wettling, drums.

P-22306-1 Love Is Just Around The Corner
- 78: >Commodore 500
- 45: Commodore 45-500
- 33: Atlantic SD 2-309, Commodore CCL 7007, Commodore XFL 14427, Commodore (G) 6.24054 AG, Commodore (J) GXC 3150, Commodore (J) K23P-6618, Joker (I) SM 4023, Joker (I) C-76/6, London (E) DHMC 1, London (G) 6.24054 AG, London (J) SLC 442, Mosaic MR23-123, Time-Life STL-J17 (P 15733), Time-Life (Au) STL-J17, Time-Life (C) STL-J17
- TX: AFRS DB 299, VOA WOJ 19
- CD: Commodore CCD 7007, Commodore (G) 8.24054 ZP
- CT: Commodore CCK 7007, Time-Life 4TL-J17
- 8T: Time-Life 8TL-J17

P-22306-2 Love Is Just Around The Corner No. 2
- 33: Commodore XFL 14427, Commodore (G) 6.24054 AG, >London (E) DHMC 1, London (G) 6.24054 AG, Mosaic MR23-123, Time-Life STL-J17 P 15733), Time-Life (Au) STL-J17, Time-Life (C) STL-J17
- CD: Commodore (G) 8.24054 ZP
- CT: Time-Life 4TL-J17
- 8T: Time-Life 8TL-J17

P-22307-1 Beat To The Socks
- 78: >Commodore 502
- 33: Atlantic SD 2-309, Commodore CCL 7007, Commodore XFL 14427, Commodore (G) 6.24054 AG, Commodore (J) GXC 3149, Commodore (J) K23P 6618, London (E) DHMC 1, London (G) 6.24294 AG, London (J) SLC 442, Mosaic MR23-123
- CD: Commodore CCD 7007, Commodore (G) 8.24054 ZP
- CT: Commodore CCK 7007

XP-22308   Carnegie Drag
   78:   >Commodore 1500
   45:   Commodore 45-1500
   33:   Ace of Hearts (E) ZAHC 179, Commodore CCL 7007,
         Commodore FL 30,006, Commodore XFL 14427, London
         (G) 6.24054 AG, Commodore (J) GXC 3149, Commodore (J)
         K23P-6617, Jazztone J-1216, London (E) DHMC 1, London
         (G) 6.24054 AG, London (J) SLC 446, London (J) LAX
         3305, Mainstream S/6010, Mainstream 56010, Mainstream
         (J) XM 34 MSD, Mosaic MR23-123, Stateside (E) SL 10005,
         Top Rank (J) RANK 5033, Top Rank (H) HJA 16504
   CD: Commodore CCD 7007, Commodore (G) 8.24054 ZP
   CT: Commodore CCK 7007

XP-22309   Carnegie Jump
   78:   >Commodore 1500
   45:   Commodore 45-1500
   33:   Ace of Hearts (E) ZAHC 179, Commodore CCL 7007,
         Commodore FL 30,006, Commodore XFL 14427,
         Commodore (G) 6.24054 AG, Commodore (J) GXC 3149,
         Commodore (J) K23P-6617, Jazztone J-1216, London (E)
         DHMC 1, London (G) 6.24054 AG, London (J) LAX 3305,
         London (J) SLC 446, Mosaic MR23-123, Stateside (E) SL
         10005, Top Rank (J) RANK 5033, Top Rank (H) HJA 16504
   CD: Commodore CCD 7007, Commodore (G) 8.24054 ZP
   CT: Commodore CCK 7007

P-22310-1   Ja Da No. 2
   33:   Commodore XFL 14427, Commodore (G) 6.24054 AG,
         >London (E) DHMC 1, London (G) 6.24054 AG, Mosaic
         MR23-123
   CD: Commodore (G) 8.24054 ZP

P-22310-2 Ja Da
- 78: >Commodore 500
- 45: Commodore 45-500
- 33: Atlantic SD 2-309, Book of the Month Club 10-5557, Commodore CCL 7007, Commodore FL 20,016, Commodore XFL 14427, Commodore (G) 6.24054 AG, Commodore (J) GXC 3150, Commodore (J) K23P-6618, Franklin Mint 47, London (E) DHMC 1, London (G) 6.24054 AG, London (J) SLC 451, Mosaic MR23-123
- TX: AFRS DB 299, AFRS DB 348, AFRS DB 421
- CD: Commodore CCD 7007, Commodore (G) 8.24054 ZP
- CT: Book of the Month Club 60-5561, Commodore CCK 7007
- 8T: Book of the Month Club 50-5560

NOTE: Produced by Milt Gabler. Commodore 1500, a 12-inch disc, is labeled as "Jam Session At Commodore, No. 1." This session was recorded at Brunswick studios, 1776 Broadway. Commodore FL 20,016 issued as Bobby Hackett and His Orchestra. The 45 rpm discs probably were never issued. Pre-war Commodores were issued on laminated pressings. Later pressings were not laminated. London DHMC 1 is contained in a 2-LP set, London DHMC 1/2. Mosaic MR23-123 is a 23-LP boxed set.

Bobby Hackett And His Orchestra

NYC, February 16, 1938

Bobby Hackett, cornet; George Brunies, trombone; Pee Wee Russell, clarinet, tenor; Bernie Billings, tenor; Dave Bowman, piano; Eddie Condon, guitar; Clyde Newcombe, bass; Johnny Blowers, drums; Lola Bard, vocal.

M-754-1 You, You And Especially You (LB vocal)
- 78: Okeh V4142, >Vocalion V4142
- 33: CBS (Eu) M67273, Columbia KG 31564, Viking VLP 201

M-755-1 If Dreams Come True (LB vocal)
- 78: Okeh V4047, >Vocalion V4047
- 33: Columbia Special Products P5 14320 (P 14324), Viking VLP 201

Omit Billings, tenor.

M-756-1   At The Jazz Band Ball
　　78:　Biltmore 1026, Jay 3, Okeh V4047, >Vocalion V4047
　　45:　Columbia B-1868
　　33:　CBS (Eu) M67273, Columbia Special Products JEE 22003,
　　　　Epic EE 22003, Epic EE 22004, Viking VLP 201
　　CD:　CBS Portrait RK 44071, Epic (J) 25.8P-5128
　　CT:　CBS Portrait RJT 44071

M-757-1   That Da Da Strain
　　78:　Okeh V4142, >Vocalion V4142
　　45:　Epic EG 7074, Philips (E) 429264BE
　　33:　CBS (Eu) M67273, Columbia Special Products JEE 22003,
　　　　Epic LG 3106, Epic EE 22003, Epic EE 22004, Epic (J) NP
　　　　504, Viking VLP 201
　　CD:　CBS Portrait RK 44071, Epic (J) 25.8P-5128
　　CT:　CBS Portrait RJT 44071

NOTE: Pee Wee Russell plays tenor on matrix. M-754-1 and Billings
plays tenor on matrix. M-754-1 and M-755-l.

Teddy Wilson And His Orchestra

NYC, March 23, 1938

Bobby Hackett, cornet; Pee Wee Russell, clarinet; Tab Smith, alto;
Gene Sedric, tenor; Teddy Wilson, piano; Allan Reuss, guitar; Al Hall,
bass; Johnny Blowers, drums; Nan Wynn, vocal.

B-22610-1   Alone With You (NW vocal)
　　Unissued (test pressing exists)

B-22610-2   Alone With You (NW vocal)
　　33:　>IAJRC IAJRC-28

B-22611-2   Moments Like This (NW vocal)
　　78:　>Brunswick 8112, Brunswick (F) A-81592, Lucky (J) 60431
　　33:　Sony (J) 20AP-1839
　　CD:　Classics (F) 548

B-22612-2   I Can't Face The Music (Without Singin' The Blues) (NW
vocal)
　　78:　>Brunswick 8112, Brunswick (F) A-81592, Odeon (N) D-
　　　　3698, Parlophone (E) R-2553, Lucky (J) 60431
　　33:　Sony (J) 20AP-1839
　　CD:　Classics (F) 548

B-22613-1   Don't Be That Way
  78:   >Brunswick 8116, Brunswick (F) A-81589, Columbia 36335,
         Lucky (J) 60416, Odeon (N) D-3698, Parlophone (E) R-2553,
         Vocalion (E) S-188
  33:   CBS (C) GES 90054, CBS (Eu) 67289 (M65171), CBS (F)
         66274, CBS-Sony (J) SOPW-10, CBS-Sony (J) 20AP 1839,
         CBS-Sony (J) SONP 50333, Columbia KG 31617, Time-Life
         STL-J20 (P 15753), Time-Life (Au) STL-J20, Time-Life (C)
         STL-J20
  CD: Classics (F) 548
  CT: Time-Life 4TL-J20
  8T: Time-Life 8TL-J20

B-22613-2   Don't Be That Way
  33:   >Meritt 11, Everybody's (Sd) e-1003

NOTE: Produced by John Hammond.

*Personnel listings for the Teddy Wilson session of April 29, 1938,
usually include Pee Wee Russell but the clarinet is played by someone
else.*

Eddie Condon And His Windy City Seven

NYC, April 30, 1938

Bobby Hackett, cornet; Jack Teagarden, trombone, vocal; Pee Wee
Russell, clarinet; Bud Freeman, tenor; Jess Stacy, piano; Eddie Condon,
guitar; Artie Shapiro, bass; George Wettling, drums.

XP-22830-1   Embraceable You
  78:   >Commodore 1501
  45:   Commodore 45-1501, Commodore CRF-115, Commodore
         CRF-116, Commodore 45-1526
  33:   Atlantic SD 2-309, Commodore CCL 7007, Commodore FL
         20,016, Commodore XFL 14427, Commodore (G) 6.24054
         AG, Commodore (J) GXC 3149, Commodore (J) K23P-6617,
         Franklin Mint 47, London (E) DHMC 1, London (G) 6.24054
         AG, London (J) SLC 446, Mainstream S/6017, Mainstream
         56017, Mainstream (Arg) DPM 9048, Mosaic MR23-123,
         Vogue (F) INT 40025
  TX: AFRS DB 295
  CD: Commodore CCD 7007, Commodore (G) 8.24054 ZP

P-22831-1   Meet Me Tonight In Dreamland
  78:   >Commodore 505
  45:   Commodore 45-505, Commodore CRF 115
  33:   Atlantic SD 2-309, Book of the Month Club 10-5557,
        Commodore CCL 7007, Commodore FL 20,015,
        Commodore XFL 14427, Commodore (G) 6.24054 AG,
        Commodore (J) GXC 3150, Commodore (J) K23P-6618,
        London (E) DHMC 1; London HMC (E) 5007, London (G)
        6.24054 AG, London (J) SLC 452, Mosaic MR23-123
  TX: AFRS DB 349, AFRS DB 422
  CD: Commodore CCD 7007, Commodore (G) 8.24054 ZP
  CT: Book of the Month Club 60-5561, Commodore CCK 7007
  8T: Book of the Month Club 50-5560

P-22831-2   Meet Me Tonight In Dreamland No. 2
  33:   Commodore XFL 14427, Commodore (G) 6.24054 AG,
        >London (E) DHMC 1, London (G) 6.24054 AG, Mosaic
        MR23-123
  CD: Commodore (G) 8.24054 ZP

P-22832-1   Diane No. 2
  33:   Commodore XFL 14427, Commodore (G) 6.24054 AG,
        Commodore (J) GXC 3148, >London (E) DHMC 1, London
        (G) 6.24054 AG, Mosaic MR23-123
  CD: Commodore (G) 8.24054 ZP

P-22832-2   Diane
  78:   >Commodore 505
  45:   Commodore 45-505, Commodore CRF-115, Commodore
        CEP-30
  33:   Atlantic SD 2-309, Commodore CCL 7007, Commodore FL
        20,015, Commodore XFL 14427, Commodore (G) 6.24054
        AG, Commodore (J) GXC 3148, Commodore (J) K23P-6616,
        London (E) DHMC 1, London (E) HMC 5007, London (G)
        6.24054 AG, London (J) SLC 446, Mosaic MR23-123, Time-
        Life STL-J08 (P 15009), Time-Life (Au) STL-J08, Time-Life
        (C) STL-J08
  TX: AFRS DB 346, AFRS DB 419
  CD: Commodore CCD 7007, Commodore (G) 8.24054 ZP
  CT: Commodore CCK 7007, Time-Life 4TL-J08
  8T: Time-Life 8TL-J08

XP-22833-1   Serenade To A Shylock (JT vocal)
  78:   >Commodore 1501
  45:   Commodore 45-1501, Commodore CRF-115
  33:   Commodore CCL 7007, Commodore FL 20,015,
        Commodore XFL 14427, Commodore (G) 6.24054 AG,
        Commodore (J) GXC 3149, Commodore (J) K23P-6617,
        Guide de Jazz (F) J-100, Jazztone J-100, Jazztone (G) J-100,
        London (E) DHMC 2, London (G) 6.24054 AG, London (J)
        SLC 446, Mainstream S/6010, Mainstream 56010, Mosaic
        MR23-123, Time-Life STL-J08 (P 15009), Time-Life (Au)
        STL-J08, Time-Life (C) STL-J08
  TX: AFRS DB 243, AFRS DB 266, AFRS DB 319
  CD: Commodore CCD 7007, Commodore (G) 8.24054 ZP
  CT: Commodore CCK 7007, Time-Life 4TL-J08
  8T: Time-Life 8TL-J08

XP-22833-2   Serenade To A Shylock No. 2 (JT vocal)
  33:   Commodore XFL 14427, Commodore (G) 6.24054 AG,
        >Jazz Archives JA-1, London (E) DHMC 2, London (G)
        6.24054 AG, Mosaic MR23-123
  CD: Commodore (G) 8.24054 ZP

NOTE: Recorded at Brunswick studios, 1776 Broadway. Produced by
Milt Gabler. Commodore 1501, a 12-inch disc, issued as Jam Session
At Commodore No. 2. Matrix 22832-2 on Commodore 505 issued as
Jack Teagarden and His Trombone. Commodore FL 20,015 issued as
Jack Teagarden and His Swinging Gates. Commodore FL 20,016
issued as Bobby Hackett and His Orchestra. The 45 rpm discs were
scheduled but probably were never issued. An excerpt of XP-22833-1
appeared on a demonstration disc issued by Esquire Magazine in 1944.
London (E) DHMC 1 and London (E) DHMC 2 are contained in
London DHMC 1/2, a two-LP set. Mosaic MR23-123 is a 23-LP boxed
set. Photographs and article about this session were included in "Life"
magazine, August 8, 1938.

Bobby Hackett

NYC, June 25, 1938

Bobby Hackett, cornet; Brad Gowans, valve trombone; Pee Wee Russell, clarinet; Ernie Caceres, baritone sax; Dave Bowman, piano; Eddie Condon, guitar; Clyde Newcombe, bass; George Wettling, drums.

At The Jazz Band Ball
   33: >Fanfare 17-117

NOTE: This was from the second anniversary broadcast of "Saturday Night Swing Session" on CBS, produced by Phil Cohan.

The Saturday Night Swing Club

NYC, ? June, 1938

Bobby Hackett, cornet; George Brunies, trombone; Pee Wee Russell, clarinet; Dave Bowman, piano; Eddie Condon, guitar; Clyde Newcombe, bass; Johnny Blowers, drums.

At The Jazz Band Ball
   Unissued

Add The Saturday Night Swing Club Orchestra, conducted by Leith Stevens. Lloyd Williams, Robert Johnson, Russ Case, Nat Natoli, trumpet; Will Bradley, Joe Vargas, trombone; Toots Mondello, Artie Manners, alto sax; George Tudor, Hank Ross, tenor; Walter Gross, piano; Frank Worrell, guitar; Bobby Michaelson, bass; Bobby Gussak, drums; Edith Dick, vocal.

Dipsy Doodle

   Unissued

NOTE: This film short, entitled "The Saturday Night Swing Club," was released by Warner Brothers and copyrighted December 21, 1938. It was directed by Lloyd French, and Paul Douglas was the announcer. Other selections from the film do not include Pee Wee Russell.

Bud Freeman & His Gang

NYC, July 12, 1938

Bobby Hackett, cornet; Pee Wee Russell, clarinet; Dave Matthews, alto; Bud Freeman, tenor; Jess Stacy, piano; Eddie Condon, guitar; Artie Shapiro, bass; Dave Tough, drums.

P-23233-1 Tappin' The Commodore Till
78: >Commodore 508
33: Atlantic SD 2-309, Commodore CCL 7007, Commodore (G) 6.25894 AG, London (J) SLC 442, London (G) 6.25894, Mosaic MR23-123, Time-Life STL-J17 (P 15733), Time-Life (Au) STL-J17, Time-Life (C) STL-J17
CD: Commodore CCD 7007
CT: Commodore CCK 7007, Time-Life 4TL-J17
8T: Time-Life 8TL-J17

P-23233-2 Tappin' The Commodore Till No. 2
33: >Commodore (G) 6.25894 AG, London (G) 6.25894, Mosaic MR23-123

P-23234-1 Memories Of You
78: >Commodore 508
33: Atlantic SD 2-309, Commodore CCL 7007, Commodore (G) 6.25894 AG, Commodore (J) GXC 3154, Commodore (J) K23P-6622, London (J) SLC 442, London (G) 6.25894, Mosaic MR23-123
CD: Commodore CCD 7007
CT: Commodore CCK 7007

P-23234-2 Memories Of You No. 2
33: >Commodore (G) 6.25894 AG, London (G) 6.25894, Mosaic MR23-123

P-23234-NG Memories Of You #3
33: >Mosaic MR20-134

P-23234-PB Memories Of You #4
33: >Mosaic MR20-134

Marty Marsala replaces Tough on drums.

P-23235-BD "LIFE" Spears A Jitterbug (breakdown)
33: >Mosaic MR20-134

P-23235-1 'LIFE' Spears A Jitterbug
　78:　>Commodore 507
　33:　Atlantic SD 2-309, Commodore CCL 7007, Commodore (G)
　　　　6.25894 AG, London (G) 6.25894, Mosaic MR23-123
　CD:　Commodore CCD 7007
　CT:　Commodore CCK 7007

P-23236-PB What's The Use?
　33:　>Mosaic MR20-134

P-23236-1 What's The Use? No 2
　33:　>Commodore (G) 6.25894 AG, London (G) 6.25894, Mosaic
　　　　MR23-123

P-23236-2 What's The Use?
　78:　>Commodore 507
　33:　Atlantic SD 2-309, Commodore CCL 7007, Commodore (G)
　　　　6.25894 AG, Commodore (J) GXC 3154, Commodore (J)
　　　　K23P-6622, London (G) 6.25894, Mosaic MR23-123
　CD:　Commodore CCD 7007
　CT:　Commodore CCK 7007

NOTE: Produced by Milt Gabler. Recorded at Brunswick studios,
1776 Broadway. Time-Life (C) P 15733 is part of album STL-J17.
Mosaic MR23-123 is a 23-LP boxed set. It claims to include three
takes of "Memories of You," but the takes listed as P-23234-1 and P-
23234 are identical. MR20-134 is a 20-LP boxed set.

Bobby Hackett And His Jazz Band

NYC, August 17, 1938

Bobby Hackett, cornet; Brad Gowans, valve trombone; Pee Wee
Russell, clarinet; unknown piano, Eddie Condon, guitar; unknown bass
and drums.

Embraceable You
　Unissued

Muskrat Ramble
　Unissued

NOTE: From a Paul Whiteman Chesterfield broadcast.

Pee Wee Russell's Rhythmakers

NYC, August 31, 1938

Max Kaminsky, trumpet; Dickie Wells, trombone; Pee Wee Russell, clarinet; Al Gold, tenor; James P. Johnson, piano; Freddie Green, guitar; Wellman Braud, bass; Zutty Singleton, drums, vocal.

P-23391-1   Baby, Won't You Please Come Home
    78:   >HRS 1000, Melodisc (E) 1137
    45:   Atlantic EP 529
    33:   Atlantic ALR 126, BYG (F) 529.066, Joker (I) SM 3096, Original Jazz Classics OJC-1708, Riverside RLP 141, Time-Life STL-J17 (P 15733), Time-Life (Au) STL-J17, Time-Life (C) STL-J17
    TX: AFRS DB 347, AFRS DB 420
    CD: Original Jazz Classics OJCCD-1708-2
    CT: Time-Life 4TL-J17
    8T: Time-Life 8TL-J17

P-23391-2   Baby, Won't You Please Come Home
    78:   >HRS 17

P-23392-1   There'll Be Some Changes Made
    78:   Esquire (E) 10-051, >HRS 1001, Jazz Selection (F) 524
    33:   BYG (F) 529.066, Joker (I) SM 3096, Meritt 9, Original Jazz Classics OJC-1708, Riverside RLP 141
    CD: Original Jazz Classics OJCCD-1708-2

P-23392-2   There'll Be Some Changes Made
    78:   >HRS 1001
    45:   Atlantic EP 529
    33:   Atlantic ALR 126
    TX: AFRS DB 299

P-23393-1   Zutty's Hootie Blues (Horn of Plenty Blues) (ZS, vocal)
    78:   Esquire (E) 10-051, >HRS 1001, Jazz Selection (F) 524
    45:   Fratelli (I) SdMJ-022
    33:   Atlantic ALR 126, BYG (F) 529.066, ESC 101, Joker (I) SM 3096, Original Jazz Classics OJC-1708, Riverside RLP 141
    TX: AFRS DB 357
    CD: Original Jazz Classics OJCCD-1708-2

P-23394-1   Dinah
  78: >HRS 1000, Melodisc (E) 1137
  33: Atlantic ALR 126, BYG (F) 529.066, BYG (F) DALP 2
      1910, Original Jazz Classics OJC-1708, Riverside RLP 141,
      Time-Life STL-J18 (P 15523), Time-Life (Au) STL-J18, (C)
      STL-J18
  TX: AFRS DB 372
  CD: Original Jazz Classics OJCCD-1708-2
  CT: Time-Life 4TL-J18
  8T: Time-Life 8TL-J18

Pee Wee Russell, clarinet; James P. Johnson, piano; Zutty Singleton, drums. Same session.

P-23395-1   I've Found A New Baby
  78: >HRS 1002, Melodisc (E) 1144
  45: Atlantic EP 529
  33: Atlantic ALR 126, BYG (F) 529.066, Joker (I) SM 3096,
      Original Jazz Classics OJC-1708, Riverside RLP 141, Time-
      Life STL-J17 (P 15734), Time-Life (Au) STL-J17, Time-Life
      (C) STL-J17
  TX: AFRS DB 298, AFRS DB 345, AFRS DB 417
  CD: Original Jazz Classics OJCCD-1708-2
  CT: Time-Life 4TL-J17
  8T: Time-Life 8TL-J17

P-23396-2   Everybody Loves My Baby
  78: >HRS 1002, Melodisc (E) 1144
  45: Atlantic EP 529, Fratelli (I) SdMJ-022
  33: Atlantic ALR 126, BYG (F) 529.066, Joker (I) SM 3096,
      Original Jazz Classics OJC-1708, Riverside RLP 141, Time-
      Life STL-J18 (P 15523), Time-Life (Au) STL-J18, Time-Life
      (C) STL-J18
  CD: Original Jazz Classics OJCCD-1708-2
  CT: Time-Life 4TL-J18
  8T: Time-Life 8TL-J18

NOTE: Produced by Steve Smith, this is the first session to appear under Pee Wee Russell's name. HRS 1002 issued as Pee Wee, Zutty and James P. Melodisc 1144 and matrix 23395 on Time-Life as James P. Johnson Trio. P-23395 and P-23396 issued as The Rhythmakers on Jazz Selection. P-23393 titled as "Zutty's Hootie Blues" on the brown issue of HRS 1001 and microgrooves. P-23392-1, issued on the red HRS label, contains a trumpet solo following the opening ensemble while P-23392-2, issued on the brown HRS label, contains a piano solo in place of the trumpet solo. Later issues of HRS 1002 show P-23395-2 in the wax, but performance is identical. The red HRS labels are original pressings, the brown label issues are dubs.

Vic Lewis And His American Jazzmen

NYC, October 19, 1938

Bobby Hackett, cornet, guitar; Brad Gowans, valve trombone; Pee Wee Russell, clarinet; Bernie Billings, tenor; Ernie Caceres, baritone; Dave Bowman, piano; Eddie Condon, guitar, speech; Vic Lewis, guitar; Zutty Singleton, drums; Josie Carole, vocal.

M-7-299 Tiger Rag (EC speech)
    78: >Esquire (E) 10-251
    33: Esquire (E) ESQ 313

M-7-300 Leader's Headache Blues (JC vocal)
    78: >Esquire (E) 10-251
    33: Esquire (E) ESQ 313

M-7-301 Basin Street Blues
    78: >Esquire (E) 10-241
    33: DJM (E) SPECB 103, Esquire (E) ESQ 313

George Wettling replaces Singleton.

M-7-302 Wrap Your Troubles In Dreams
    78: >Esquire (E) 10-241
    33: Esquire (E) ESQ 313

M-7-303 That's A Plenty
    78: >Esquire (E) 10-231
    33: Esquire (E) ESQ 313

M-7-304   Muskrat Ramble
    78:   >Esquire (E) 10-231
    33:   Esquire (E) ESQ 313

NOTE: The matrix numbers quoted are from the Esquire issues. There are none on the original acetates from which these issues are dubbed. The recording was done at the Baldwin Company studios.

Bobby Hackett And His Orchestra
NYC, November 4, 1938

Bobby Hackett, cornet; Brad Gowans, valve trombone, alto sax; Pee Wee Russell, clarinet; Ernie Caceres, baritone; Dave Bowman, piano; Eddie Condon, guitar; Clyde Newcombe, bass; Andy Picard, drums; Linda Keene, vocal.

M-916-1   Blue And Disillusioned (LK vocal)
    78:   Okeh V4499, >Vocalion V4499
    45:   Epic EG 7106
    33:   Columbia Special Products JEE 22003, Epic LG 3106, Epic
          EE 22003, Epic EE 22004, Epic (J) NP 504
    CD: CBS Portrait RK 44071, Epic (J) 25.8P-5128
    CT: CBS Portrait RJT 44071

M-917-1   A Ghost Of A Chance
    78:   Columbia (Sd) DS 1695, Okeh V4565, Parlophone (E) DP
          240, >Vocalion V4565
    45:   Epic EG 7089
    33:   Columbia Special Products JEE 22003, Epic LG 3106, Epic
          EE 22003, Epic EE 22004, Epic (J) NP 504, Viking VLP 201
    CD: CBS Portrait RK 44071, Epic (J) 25.8P-5128
    CT: CBS Portrait RJT 44071

M-918-1   Poor Butterfly
    78:   Biltmore 1026, Columbia (Sd) DS 1695, Okeh V4499,
          Parlophone (E) DP 240, >Vocalion V4499
    45:   Epic EG 7106
    33:   Columbia Special Products JEE 22003, Epic LG 3106, Epic
          EE 22003, Epic EE 22004, Epic (J) NP 504
    TX: AFRS APM 553
    CD: CBS Portrait RK 44071, Epic (J) 25.8P-5128
    CT: CBS Portrait RJT 44071

M-919-1   Doin' The New Low-Down
   78:   Okeh V4565, >Vocalion V4565
   45:   Epic EG 7089, Philips (E) 429134BE, Philips (E) BBE12026
   33:   Columbia Special Products JEE 22003, Epic LG 3106, Epic
         EE 22003, Epic EE 22004, Epic (J) NP 504, Franklin Mint
         47, Viking VLP 201
   CD: CBS Portrait RK 44071, Epic (J) 25.8P-5128
   CT: CBS Portrait RJT 44071

NOTE: A vinyl pressing, coupling M-917-1 and M-918-1, exists.

St. Regis Hotel Jam Session

NYC, November 5, 1938

Bobby Hackett, cornet; Marty Marsala, trumpet; Pee Wee Russell,
clarinet; Bud Freeman, tenor; Joe Bushkin, piano; Eddie Condon,
guitar; Artie Shapiro, bass; Dave Tough, drums, Alistair Cooke,
narration.

Keep Smiling At Trouble
   33:   Alamac QSR 2445, Elec (J) KV-124, >Jazz Panorama (Sd)
         LP-9

Bobby Hackett, cornet; Pee Wee Russell, clarinet; Bud Freeman, tenor;
Jess Stacy, piano; Eddie Condon, guitar; Artie Shapiro, bass; Zutty
Singleton, drums; Lee Wiley, vocal.

Sugar (LW vocal)
   33:   Alamac QSR 2445, >Black Jack (G) LP 3003, Elec (J) KV
         124, Jass Nineteen
   CD: Jass Compact Disc Fifteen
   CT: Jass J-C-19

NOTE: This was a direct broadcast, via short-wave to England,
originating from the roof of the St. Regis Hotel. Although Pee Wee
Russell is announced on "You Took Advantage of Me," the clarinet is
played by Joe Marsala.

Eddie Condon And His Band

NYC, November 12, 1938

Bobby Hackett, cornet; Vernon Brown, trombone; Pee Wee Russell, clarinet; Bud Freeman, tenor; Joe Bushkin, piano; Eddie Condon, guitar; Artie Shapiro, bass; Lionel Hampton, drums.

P-23706-1 Sunday
   78: >Commodore 515
   33: Atlantic SD 2-309, Commodore CCL 7007, Commodore XFL 16568, Commodore (G) 6.25526 AG, Commodore (J) GXC 3150, Commodore (J) K23P-6618, London (E) DHMC 2, London (G) 6.25526, London (J) SLC 442, Mosaic MR23-123
   CD: Commodore CCD 7007
   CT: Commodore CCK 7007

P-23706-2 Sunday No. 2
   33: Commodore XFL 16568, Commodore (G) 6.25526 AG, >London (E) DHMC 2, London (G) 6.25526, Mosaic MR23-123

P-23707-1A California, Here I Come No. 2
   33: Commodore XFL 16568, Commodore (G) 6.25526 AG, >London (E) DHMC 2, London (G) 6.25526, Mosaic MR23-123

P-23707-2 California, Here I Come
   78: >Commodore 515
   33: Atlantic SD 2-309, Commodore CCL 7007, Commodore XFL 16568, Commodore (G) 6.25526 AG, Commodore (J) GXC 3150, Commodore (J) K23P-6618, London (E) DHMC 2, London (G) 6.25526, London (J) SLC 442, Mosaic MR23-123, Time-Life STL-J17 (P 15734), Time-Life (Au) STL-J17, Time-Life (C) STL-J17
   CD: BBC RPCD 852; Commodore CCD 7007
   CT: BBC RPMC 852; Commodore CCK 7007, Time-Life 4TL-J17
   8T: Time-Life 8TL-J17

NOTE: This session was recorded at Brunswick studios, 1776 Broadway. Produced by Milt Gabler. London (E) DHMC 2 is part of London (E) DHMC 1/2, a two-LP set. Mosaic MR23-123 is a 23-LP boxed set.

The Rhythm Cats

NYC, December 21, 1938

Bobby Hackett, cornet; Brad Gowans, valve trombone; Pee Wee Russell, clarinet; Ernie Caceres, baritone; Dave Bowman, piano; Andy Picard, drums.

MS 030738 A   Sensation Rag
    33:   Musica Jazz (I) 2MJP 1042, Shoestring SS-109
    TX: >Thesaurus 686, Thesaurus 1186

MS 030738 B Muskrat Ramble
    33:   Shoestring SS-109
    TX: >Thesaurus 686, Thesaurus 1149

MS 030738 C After You've Gone
    33:   Shoestring SS-109
    TX: >Thesaurus 686, Thesaurus 1149

MS 030738 D There'll Be Some Changes Made
    33:   Shoestring SS-109
    TX: >Thesaurus 686

MS 030739 H Love Is Just Around The Corner
    33:   Shoestring SS-109
    TX: >Thesaurus 615

MS 030739 J Jazz Me Blues
    33:   Musica Jazz (I) 2MJP 1042, Shoestring SS-109
    TX: >Thesaurus 615

MS 030739 K Jazz Band Ball (sic)
    33:   Musica Jazz (I) 2MJP 1042, Shoestring SS-109
    TX: >Thesaurus 615, Thesaurus 1186
    CD: Deja Vu (I) DVRECD 20

MS 030739 L Skeleton Jangle
    33:   IAJRC IAJRC-1, Musica Jazz (I) 2MJP 1042, Shoestring SS-109
    TX: >Thesaurus 615, Thesaurus 1186

MS 030740 A Royal Garden Blues
   33:   Shoestring SS-109
   TX: >Thesaurus 646, Thesaurus 796-646

MS 030740 B Thinking Of You
   33:   Deja Vu (I) DVLP 2119, Musica Jazz (I) MJP 1042,
         Shoestring SS-109
   TX: >Thesaurus 646, Thesaurus 796-646, Thesaurus 1186
   CT: Deja Vu (I) DVMC 2119

MS 030740 C Singing The Blues
   33:   IAJRC IAJRC-28, Shoestring SS-109
   TX: >Thesaurus 646, Thesaurus 796-646, Thesaurus 1149

MS 030740 D Sweet Georgia Brown
   33:   Shoestring SS-109
   TX: >Thesaurus 646, Thesaurus 796-646, Thesaurus 1149

NOTE: Matrix numbers are as shown on the original red-label Thesaurus issues, with the letter indicating the track number on the 16-inch disc. Shoestring SS 109 issued as by Pee Wee Russell and the Rhythm Cats. The following additional titles were listed by Carey and McCarthy in *Jazz Directory, Volume Four*: "Someday Sweetheart," "Crazy Rhythm," "Alice Blue Gown," "How Am I To Know," "Wolverine Blues" and "You Go To My Head." None of these titles have come to light.

Bobby Hackett And His Orchestra

NYC, April 10, 1939

Bobby Hackett, cornet; Sterling Bose, Frankie West, trumpet; George Troup, trombone; Brad Gowans, valve trombone; Pee Wee Russell, clarinet; Bernie Billings, tenor; Ernie Caceres, baritone; Dave Bowman, piano; Eddie Condon, guitar; Sid Jacobs, bass; Don Carter, drums.

   King Arthur
      Unissued

   World's Fair Shuffle
      Unissued

NOTE: Reportedly, this session was recorded for Vocalion. No other information is known and the recordings have not been found.

Bobby Hackett And His Orchestra

NYC, April 13, 1939

Bobby Hackett, cornet; Sterling Bose, Jack Thompson, trumpet; George Troup, trombone; Brad Gowans, valve trombone, alto sax; Pee Wee Russell, clarinet; Louis Columbo, alto; Bernie Billings, tenor; Ernie Caceres, baritone; Dave Bowman, piano; Eddie Condon, guitar; Sid Jacobs, bass; Don Carter, drums.

WM-1017-A That's How Dreams Should End
   78: Okeh 4806, >Vocalion V4806
   45: Epic EG 7089
   33: Columbia Special Products JEE 22003, Epic LG 3106, Epic EE 22003, Epic EE 22004, Epic (J) NP 504
   CD: CBS Portrait RK 44071, Epic (J) 25.8P-5128
   CT: CBS Portrait RJT 44071, MP (H) 3019/3 (47002)

WM-1018-A Ain't Misbehavin'
   78: Okeh 4877, Parlophone (E) DP 241, >Vocalion V4877
   45: Epic EG 7089
   33: Columbia Special Products JEE 22003, Epic LG 3106, Epic EE 22003, Epic EE 22004, Epic (J) NP 504, Philips (H) BO 7109L, Viking VLP 201
   CD: CBS Portrait RK 44071, Epic (J) 25.8P-5128
   CT: CBS Portrait RJT 44071

WM-1019-A Sunrise Serenade
   78: Conqueror 9270, Conqueror 9530, Okeh 4806, Parlophone (E) DP 241, >Vocalion V4806
   45: Epic EG 7106
   33: Columbia Special Products JEE 22003, Epic LG 3106, Epic EE 22003, Epic EE 22004, Epic (J) NP 504, Viking VLP 201
   CD: CBS Portrait RK 44071, Epic (J) 25.8P-5128
   CT: CBS Portrait RJT 44071

WM-1020-A Embraceable You
   78: Jay 3, Odeon (N) D-5045-S, Okeh 4877, Parlophone (E) DP 242, >Vocalion V4877
   33: Columbia Special Products JEE 22003, Epic LG 3106, Epic EE 22003, Epic EE 22004, Epic (J) NP 504, Reader's Digest RD 4-206-1, Smithsonian P6-19881, Viking VLP 201
   CD: CBS Portrait RK 44071, Epic (J) 25.8P-5128
   CT: CBS Portrait RJT 44071, Smithsonian 1P4T-19881

NOTE: Bobby Hackett arranged WM 1020-A, Brad Gowans arranged WM 1018-A, and Buck Ram arranged WM 1017-A and WM 1019-A. Smithsonian P6-19881 is part of a six-LP set, R 035 and IP4T-19881 is part of a cassette set, RC 035. MP (H) 3019/3 is the full label name, and is a 3-cassette boxed set.

Bud Freeman And His Summa Cum Laude Orchestra
NYC, July 19, 1939

Max Kaminsky, trumpet; Brad Gowans, valve trombone, arranger; Pee Wee Russell, clarinet; Bud Freeman, tenor; Dave Bowman, piano; Eddie Condon, guitar; Clyde Newcombe, bass; Danny Alvin, drums.

BS-038291-1 I've Found A New Baby
  78: >Bluebird B-10370, HMV (E) JO-113, HMV (E) B-9029, HMV (Sd) X-6824, Montgomery Ward M-8339
  45: RCA WEJ 4
  33: Bluebird 6752-1-RB, Bluebird (E) NL 86752, Dawn Club (G) 12009, Jazz Panorama 1819, RCA (F) PM 43267, RCA (F) 86583, RCA (F) 741.103, RCA (J) RA 88, RCA (J) RA 5381
  CD: Affinity (E) AFS 1008, Bluebird 6752-2-RB, Bluebird (E) ND 86752
  CT: Bluebird 6752-4-RB, Bluebird (E) NK 86752

BS-038291-2 I've Found A New Baby
  33: >Camden CAL 339, Camden (C) CDN 139, RCA LEJ-4, RCA (NZ) RPL 3063, Victor LPM 1373, Victor (Arg) LPM 1373, Victor (J) AX 5001
  CD: Affinity (E) AFS 1008

BS-038292-1 Easy To Get
  78: >Bluebird B-10370, HMV (E) JO-113, HMV (E) B-9029, HMV (Sd) X-6824, Montgomery Ward M-8339
  33: Bluebird 6752-1-RB, Bluebird (E) NL 86752, Dawn Club (G) 12009, Jazz Panorama 1819, RCA (F) 86583, RCA (F) 741.103, RCA (J) RA 88, RCA (NZ) RPL 3063, Victor LPM 1373, Victor (Arg) LPM 1373, Victor (J) AX 5001
  CD: Affinity (E) AFS 1008, Bluebird 6752-2-RB, Bluebird (E) ND 86752
  CT: Bluebird 6752-4-RB, Bluebird (E) NK 86752

BS-038293-1 China Boy
　　78: >Bluebird B-10386, HMV (E) B-9007, HMV (Sw) JK 2021,
　　　　　Montgomery Ward M-8338
　　33: Bluebird 6752-1-RB, Bluebird (E) NL 86752, Dawn Club (G)
　　　　　12009, Holy Hawk (Taiwan) 4042, Jazz Panorama 1819,
　　　　　RCA (F) 86583, RCA (F) 741.103, RCA (J) RA 88, Reader's
　　　　　Digest RD 3-45-3, Reader's Digest (C) 627-EM-2, Reader's
　　　　　Digest RD4A-017-3, Reader's Digest (E) RDS 6653
　　CD: Affinity (E) AFS 1008, Bluebird 6752-2-RB, Bluebird (E)
　　　　　ND 86752
　　CT: Bluebird 6752-4-RB, Bluebird (E) NK 86752

BS-038293-2 China Boy
　　33: RCA (NZ) RPL 3063, >Victor LPM 1373, Victor (Arg) LPM
　　　　　1373, Victor (J) AX 5001
　　CD: Affinity (E) AFS 1008

BS-038294-1 The Eel
　　78: >Bluebird B-10386, HMV (E) B-9007, HMV (Sw) JK-2021,
　　　　　Montgomery Ward M-8338, Victor (27-0140), Victor (J) A-
　　　　　1451
　　45: Victor WPT 36 (27-0140)
　　33: Bluebird 6752-1-RB, Bluebird (E) NL 86752, Dawn Club (G)
　　　　　12009, Holy Hawk (Taiwan) 4042, Jazz Panorama 1819,
　　　　　Neiman Marcus Third Series (RCA Special Products DMM4-
　　　　　0405), RCA (F) 86583, RCA (F) 741.103, RCA (J) RA 88,
　　　　　RCA (NZ) RPL 3063, Reader's Digest RD 3-45-5, Reader's
　　　　　Digest (C) 627-EM-5, Reader's Digest RD4A-017-3, Reader's
　　　　　Digest (E) RDS 6655, Shinseido (J) RCA 8227, Victor LPT-
　　　　　27, Victor WPT-36, Victor LPM 1373, Victor (Arg) LPM
　　　　　1373, Victor (J) AX 5001, Victor (J) RA 5359
　　CD: Affinity (E) AFS 1008, Bluebird 6752-2-RB, Bluebird (E)
　　　　　ND 86752
　　CT: Bluebird 6752-4-RB, Bluebird (E) ND 86752

NOTE: Recorded in RCA studio 2. Victor (27-0140) is a vinyl "Record
Preview" dubbed pressing.

Eddie Condon And His Chicagoans

NYC, August 11, 1939

Max Kaminsky, trumpet; Brad Gowans, valve trombone; Pee Wee Russell, clarinet; Bud Freeman, tenor; Joe Sullivan, piano; Eddie Condon, guitar; Clyde Newcombe, bass; Dave Tough, drums.

66072-A   There'll Be Some Changes Made
  78:   Brunswick (E) 03056, Brunswick (E) 284572, >Decca 18041, Decca (Au) Y-5850, Decca (C) 18041, Odeon (Arg) 286124
  45:   Brunswick (E) oe 9152, Decca SEP 4, Decca ED 2053, Decca (Arg) DIM/E, Decca (J) DEP 4
  33:   Affinity (E) AFS 1021, Brunswick (E) LAT 8042, Brunswick (E) CE 9152, Coral (E) CP 38, Coral (F) COPS 1625, Decca DL 8029, Decca (Arg) LTM 9279, Decca (J) JDL 5072, MCA (J) MCL-1033, MCA (J) MCA 3034, Time-Life STL-J27 (P 15967), Time-Life (Au) STL-J27, Time-Life (C) STL-J27
  TX: AFRS DB 325
  CT: Time-Life 4TL-J27
  8T: Time-Life 8TL-J27

66072-B   There'll Be Some Changes Made
  33:   >Meritt 11, Musica Jazz (I) 2MJP 1042

66073-A   Nobody's Sweetheart
  78:   Brunswick (E) 03055, >Decca 18040, Decca (Au) Y-5610, Decca (C) 18040, Odeon (Arg) 286123
  45:   Brunswick (E) oe 9152, Decca SEP 4, Decca ED 2053, Decca (Arg) DIM/E, Decca (J) DEP 4
  33:   Affinity (E) AFS 1021, Brunswick (E) LAT 8042, Brunswick (E) CE 9152, Coral (E) CP 38, Coral (F) COPS 1625, Decca DL 8029, Decca (Arg) LTM 9279, Decca (J) JDL 5072, MCA (J) MCL-1033, MCA (J) MCA 3034
  TX: AFRS DB 304

66073-B   Nobody's Sweetheart
  33:   >Meritt 19, Musica Jazz (I) 2MJP 1042

66074-A Friar's Point Shuffle
- 78: Brunswick (E) 03055, >Decca 18040, Decca (Au) Y-5610, Decca (C) 18040, Odeon (Arg) 286123
- 33: Affinity (E) AFS 1021, MCA (J) VIM 18, MCA (J) MCA 3002, Time-Life STL-J17 (P 15734), Time-Life (Au) STL-J17, Time-Life (C) STL-J17
- CT: Time-Life 4TL-J17
- 8T: Time-Life 8TL-J17

66074-B Friar's Point Shuffle
- 78: >Decca (C) 18040
- 45: Brunswick (E) oe 9152, Decca SEP 4, Decca ED 2053, Decca (Arg) DIM/E, Decca (J) DEP 4
- 33: Brunswick (E) LAT 8042, Brunswick (E) CE 9152, Coral CP (E) 38, Coral (F) COPS 1625, Decca DL 8029, Decca DL 34313, Decca (Arg) LTM 9279, Decca (J) JDL 5072, MCA (J) MCL-1033, MCA (J) MCA 3034

66075-X Someday Sweetheart (rehearsal take)
- 33: >Jazz Archives JA-40

66075-A Someday Sweetheart
- 78: Brunswick (E) 03056, >Decca 18041, Decca (Au) Y-5850, Decca (C) 18041, Odeon (Arg) 286124
- 45: Brunswick (E) oe 9152, Decca SEP 4, Decca ED 2053, Decca (Arg) DIM/E, Decca (J) DEP 4
- 33: Brunswick (E) LAT 8042, Brunswick (E) CE 9152, Coral CP (E) 38, Coral (F) COPS 1625, Decca DL 8029, Decca (Arg) LTM 9279, Decca (J) JDL 5072, MCA (J) MCL-1033, MCA (J) MCA 3034, Time-Life STL-J17 (P 15734), Time-Life (Au) STL-J17, Time-Life (C) STL-J17
- CT: Time-Life 4TL-J17
- 8T: Time-Life 8TL-J17

66075-B Someday Sweetheart
- 33: >Blu-Disc T-1005

NOTE: Produced by George Avakian. Decca 18040 and 18041 are part of Decca album 121, with the title "Chicago Jazz Album." This was the first set of new jazz recordings issued in an album format.

Bud Freeman And His Summa Cum Laude Orchestra

NYC, September 18, 1939

Max Kaminsky, trumpet; Brad Gowans, valve trombone, arranger; Pee Wee Russell, clarinet; Bud Freeman, tenor; Dave Bowman, piano; Eddie Condon, guitar; Clyde Newcombe, bass; Al Sidell, drums.

66603-A   As Long As I Live
- 78:   Brunswick (E) 02968, >Decca 2849, Decca 3885, Decca (C) 3885, Decca (C) M30307, Odeon (Arg) 286309
- CD: Affinity (E) AFS 1008

66603-B   As Long As I Live
- 33:   Affinity (E) AFS 1036, >Brunswick BL 58037, Dawn Club (G) 12009, MCA (J) MCA 3082, Swaggie (Au) S 1216, Time-Life STL-J17 (P 15734), Time-Life (Au) STL-J17, Time-Life (C) STL-J17
- CD: Affinity (E) AFS 1008
- CT: Time-Life 4TL-J17
- 8T: Time-Life 8TL-J17

66604-A   The Sail Fish
- 78:   Brunswick (E) 02998, >Decca 2781, Decca (Au) Y-5465
- 33:   Affinity (E) AFS 1036, Brunswick BL 58037, MCA (J) MCA 3082, Swaggie (Au) S-1216
- CD: Affinity (E) AFS 1008

66604-B   The Sail Fish
- 78:   >Decca 2781

66605-A   Sunday
- 78:   >Decca 2849, Decca 3865, Decca (C) M30307, Decca (E) 02968, Odeon (Arg) 286309
- 33:   Affinity (E) AFS 1036, Brunswick BL 58037, MCA (J) MCA 3082, Swaggie (Au) S-1216
- CD: Affinity (E) AFS 1008

66606-A   Satanic Blues
  78:   Brunswick (E) 02998,>Decca 2781, Decca 3525, Decca (Au)
        Y-5465
  33:   Affinity (E) AFS 1036, Brunswick BL 58037, MCA (J) MCA
        3082, Swaggie (Au) S-1216, Time-Life STL-J17 (P 15734),
        Time-Life (Au) STL-J17, Time-Life (C) STL-J17
  CD: Affinity (E) AFS 1008
  CT: Time-Life 4TL-J17
  8T: Time-Life 8TL-J17
NOTE: Despite liner notes on all LP issues of 66603, which indicate
take A was used, it is take B.

Lee Wiley With Max Kaminsky's Orchestra
NYC, November 15, 1939

Max Kaminsky, trumpet; Pee Wee Russell, clarinet; Bud Freeman,
tenor; Fats Waller, piano, celeste on mx. 26272; Eddie Condon, guitar;
Artie Shapiro, bass; George Wettling, drums; Lee Wiley, vocal; Brad
Gowans, arranger.

wp 26270-A   I've Got A Crush On You
  78:   >LMS L 282
  33:   Audiophile AP-1, Halcyon (E) HAL-6, LMS 1004,
        Monmouth-Evergreen MES 7034, RIC M 2002, RIC ST
        2002, Victor (J) SMJX 10151
  CD: Audiophile ACD-1

wp 26272-A   How Long Has This Been Going On?
  78:   >LMS L 281
  33:   Audiophile AP-1, Halcyon (E) HAL 6, LMS 1004,
        Monmouth-Evergreen MES 7034, RIC M 2002, RIC ST
        2002, Victor (J) SMJX 10151
  CD: Audiophile ACD-1

wp 26273-A   But Not For Me
  78:   >LMS L 284
  33:   Audiophile AP-1, Halcyon (E) HAL 6, LMS 1004,
        Monmouth-Evergreen MES 7034, Victor (J) SMJX 10151
  CD: Audiophile ACD-1

NOTE: The Monmouth-Evergreen and Halcyon issues of 26273-A
have the piano solo edited out. Mx. 26271, also cut at this session, has
accompaniment by "Maurice" (Fats Waller) on organ only. The 78
discs were issued in an unnumbered album.

Eddie Condon And His Band

NYC, November 30, 1939

Max Kaminsky, trumpet; Brad Gowans, valve trombone; Pee Wee
Russell, clarinet; Joe Bushkin, piano; Eddie Condon, guitar; Artie
Shapiro, bass; George Wettling, drums.

P-25706-TK1 I Ain't Gonna Give Nobody None of My Jelly Roll
    33:   >Mosaic MR23-123

P-25706-TK2 I Ain't Gonna Give Nobody None of My Jelly Roll
    33:   Commodore XFL 15355, Commodore (G) 6.24295 AG,
        >London (E) DHCM 2, London (G) 6.24295 AG, Mosaic
        MR23-123

P-25706-1 I Ain't Gonna Give Nobody None Of My Jelly Roll
    78:   >Commodore 531
    45:   Commodore CEP 42
    33:   Ace of Hearts (E) AH 178, Book of the Month Club 10-5557,
        Commodore CCL 7015, Commodore FL 20,022,
        Commodore FL 30,010, Commodore XFL 15355,
        Commodore (G) 6.24295 AG, Commodore (J) GXC 3150,
        Commodore (J) K23P-6618, Decca (G) ND 476, London (E)
        DHCM 2, London (G) 6.24295 AG, London (J) LAX 3307,
        Mainstream S/6024, Mainstream 56024, Mainstream (Arg)
        DPM 9050, Mainstream (J) XM 34 MSD, Mosaic MR23-
        123, Stateside (E) SL 10010, Top Rank (H) HJA 16507
    CD: Commodore CCD 7015
    CT: Book of the Month Club 60-5561, Commodore CCK 7015
    8T: Book of the Month Club 50-5560

P-25707-1 Strut Miss Lizzie
    78:   >Commodore 530
    45:   Commodore CEP 42
    33:   Ace of Hearts (E) AH 178, Commodore CCL 7015,
        Commodore FL 20,022, Commodore FL 30,010, Commodore
        XFL 15355, Commodore (G) 6.24295 AG, Commodore (J)
        GXC 3150, Commodore (J) K23P-6618, Decca (G) ND 476,
        London (E) DHCM 2, London (G) 6.24295 AG, London (J)
        LAX 3307, Mosaic MR23-123, Stateside (E) SL 10010, Top
        Rank (H) HJA 16507
    CD: Commodore CCD 7015
    CT: Commodore CCK 7015

P-25707-2 Strut Miss Lizzie No. 2
  33:   Commodore XFL 15355, Commodore (G) 6.24295 AG,
        >London (E) DHCM 2, London (G) 6.24295 AG, Mosaic
        MR23-123

P-25708-1 It's All Right Here For You
  78:   >Commodore 530
  45:   Commodore CEP 42
  33:   Ace of Hearts (E) AH 178, Commodore CCL 7015,
        Commodore FL 20,022, Commodore FL 30,010, Commodore
        XFL 15355, Commodore (G) 6.24295 AG, Commodore (J)
        GXC 3150, Commodore (J) K23P-6618, Decca (G) ND 476,
        London (E) DHCM 2, London (G) 6.24295 AG, London (J)
        LAX 3307, London (J) SLC 456, Mainstream S/6024,
        Mainstream 56024, Mainstream (Arg) DPM 9050, Mosaic
        MR23-123, Stateside (E) SL 10010, Time-Life STL-J17 (P
        15734), Time-Life (Au) STL-J17, Time-Life (C) STL-J17,
        Top Rank (H) HJA 16507
  CD: Commodore CCD 7015
  CT: Commodore CCK 7015, Time-Life 4TL-J17
  8T: Time-Life 8TL-J17

P-25708-2 It's Right Here For You No. 2
  33:   Commodore XFL 15355, Commodore (G) 6.24295 AG,
        >London (E) DHCM 2, London (G) 6.24295 AG, Mosaic
        MR23-123

P-25709-1 Ballin' The Jack
  78:   >Commodore 531
  45:   Commodore CEP 42
  33:   Ace of Hearts (E) AH 178, Book of the Month Club 10-5557,
        Commodore CCL 7015, Commodore FL 20,022,
        Commodore FL 30,010, Commodore XFL 15355,
        Commodore (G) 6.24295 AG, Commodore (J) GXC 3150,
        Commodore (J) K23P-6618, Decca (G) ND 476, London (E)
        DHCM 2, London (G) 6.24295 AG, London (J) LAX 3307,
        Mosaic MR23-123, Stateside (E) SL 10010, Top Rank (H)
        HJA 16507
  CD: Commodore CCD 7015
  CT: Book of the Month Club 60-5561, Commodore CCK 7015
  8T: Book of the Month Club 50-5560

NOTE: Produced by Milt Gabler. Recorded at Columbia studios, Liederkranz Hall, E. 58th Street. Commodore (J) GXC 3150 shows P-25707-1 as "Strut Miss Lissie." Original pressings of Commodore 530, and Time-Life issues, show P-25708-1 titled as indicated; later Commodore pressings, however, have the title corrected to "It's Right Here For You." London (E) DHCM 2 is part of a two-LP set, London DHCM 1/2. Mosaic MR23-123 is a 23-LP boxed set.

Buddy Clark With Orchestra

NYC, March, 1940

Marty Marsala, trumpet; Brad Gowans, valve trombone; Pee Wee Russell, clarinet; Bud Freeman, tenor; Jess Stacy, piano; Sid Weiss, bass; Morey Feld, drums; Buddy Clark, vocal.

US 1457-1 Nothing But You (Nada Sino Tu)
    78:   >Varsity 8230
    33:   IAJRC 53

US 1458-1 From Another World (De Autro Mundo)
    78:   >Varsity 8230
    33:   IAJRC 53

US 1459-1 I Walk With Music
    78:   Montgomery Ward M 10059, >Varsity 8233
    33:   IAJRC 53

US 1460-1 This Is The Beginning Of The End
    78:   Montgomery Ward M 10059, >Varsity 8233
    33:   IAJRC 53

US 1460-2 This Is The Beginning Of The End
    78:   >Varsity 8233
    33:   IAJRC 53

Jam Session At Commodore

NYC, March 23, 1940

Max Kaminsky, trumpet; Brad Gowans, valve trombone; Pee Wee
Russell, Joe Marsala, clarinet; Jess Stacy, piano; Eddie Condon, guitar;
Sid Weiss, bass; George Wettling, drums.

76329-AA A Good Man Is Hard To Find, part 1
    78:   >Commodore 1504
    45:   Commodore 45-1504
    33:   Ace of Hearts (E) AH 179, Commodore FL 30,006,
          Commodore XFL 16568, Commodore (G) 6.25526 AG,
          Commodore (J) GXC 3149, Commodore (J) K23P-6617,
          Fontana (E) TL 5271, Fontana (H) 687 708TL, London (G)
          6.25526, London (J) SLC 446, London (J) LAX 3305,
          Mainstream S/6024, Mainstream 56024, Mosaic MR23-123,
          Stateside (E) SL 10005, Top Rank (H) HJA 16504, Top Rank
          (J) RANK 5033

Muggsy Spanier, cornet; Max Kaminsky, trumpet; Brad Gowans, Miff
Mole, trombone; Pee Wee Russell, clarinet; Joe Marsala, alto, clarinet;
Bud Freeman, tenor, Jess Stacy, piano; Eddie Condon, guitar; Sid
Weiss, bass; George Wettling, drums.

76330-A A Good Man Is Hard To Find, part 4
    78:   >Commodore 1505
    45:   Commodore 45-1505
    33:   Ace of Hearts (E) AH 179, Commodore FL 30,006,
          Commodore XFL 16568, Commodore (G) 6.25526 AG,
          Commodore (J) GXC 3149, Commodore (J) K23P-6617,
          London (G) 6.25526, London (J) SLC 446, London (J) LAX
          3305, Mainstream S/6024, Mainstream 56024, Mosaic
          MR23-123, Stateside (E) SL 10005, Top Rank (H) HJA
          16504, Top Rank (J) RANK 5033

Muggsy Spanier, cornet; Max Kaminsky, trumpet; Brad Gowans, valve trombone; Pee Wee Russell, clarinet; Jess Stacy, piano; Eddie Condon, guitar; Sid Weiss, bass; George Wettling, drums.

76332-A   A Good Man Is Hard To Find, part 3
   78:   >Commodore 1505
   45:   Commodore 45-1505
   33:   Ace of Hearts (E) AH 179, Commodore FL 30,006, Commodore XFL 16568, Commodore (G) 6.25526 AG, Commodore (J) GXC 3149, Commodore (J) K23P-6617, London (G) 6.25526, London (J) SLC 446, London (J) LAX 3305, Mainstream S/6024, Mainstream 56024, Mosaic MR23-123 Stateside (E) SL 10005, Top Rank (H) HJA 16504, Top Rank (J) RANK 5033

NOTE: Produced by Milt Gabler. Recorded at Decca studios, West 57th Street. Commodore 1504 is issued as Jam Session At Commodore, No. 3 and Commodore 1505 as Jam Session At Commodore, No. 4. Both are 12-inch discs. It is possible that the collective personnel may play a few notes on each of the selections as background chords, but soloing personnel are listed as above. Russell is not audible on matrix 76331. Part 4 was recorded prior to part 3. Mosaic MR23-123 is a 23-LP boxed set.

Bud Freeman And His Summa Cum Laude Orchestra
NYC, March 25, 1940

Max Kaminsky, trumpet; Brad Gowans, valve trombone, arranger; Pee Wee Russell, clarinet; Bud Freeman, tenor; Dave Bowman, piano; Eddie Condon, guitar; Pete Peterson, bass; Morey Feld, drums.

67391-A   Oh, Baby
   78:   Brunswick (E) 03226, Brunswick (In) 03226, >Decca 18065, Decca (Au) Y-5922, Decca (Cz) 03226, Odeon (Arg) 286254
   33:   Affinity (E) AFS 1036, Brunswick (E) LA 8526, Decca DL 5213, Franklin Mint 66, MCA (J) MCA 3082, Swaggie (Au) S-1216
   CD: Affinity (E) AFS 1008

67392-A   I Need Some Pettin'
   78:   Brunswick (E) 03227, Brunswick (In) 03227, >Decca 18066,
         Decca (Au) Y-5966, Odeon (Arg) 286255
   33:   Affinity (E) AFS 1036, Brunswick (E) LA 8526, Decca DL
         5213, MCA (J) MCA 3082, Swaggie (Au) S-1216
   CD: Affinity (E) AFS 1008

67393-A   Susie
   78:   Brunswick (E) 03228, Brunswick (In) 03228, >Decca 18067,
         Odeon (Arg) 286256
   33:   Affinity (E) AFS 1036, Brunswick (E) LA 8526, Decca DL
         5213, MCA (J) MCA 3082, MK 1001, Swaggie S-1216
   CD: Affinity (E) AFS 1008

67393-B   Susie
   78:   >Decca 18067

67394-A   Big Boy
   78:   Brunswick (E) 03225, Brunswick (In) 03225, >Decca 18064,
         Decca (Au) Y-6022, Decca (Cz) 03225, Odeon (Arg) 286253
   33:   Affinity (E) AFS 1036, Brunswick (E) LA 8526, Decca DL
         5213, MCA (J) MCA 3082, Swaggie (Au) S-1216
   CD: Affinity (E) AFS 1008

NOTE: Decca 18065, 18066 and 18067 are contained in Decca album
133.

Doris Rhodes, Orchestra Under Direction Of Joe Sullivan
                                              NYC, March 26, 1940

Max Kaminsky, trumpet; Brad Gowans, valve trombone, Pee Wee
Russell, clarinet; Bud Freeman, tenor; Joe Sullivan, piano; Eddie
Condon, guitar; Billy Taylor, bass; Sid Catlett, drums; Doris Rhodes,
vocal.

CO-27092-   Let There Be Love
   33:   >IAJRC 53

CO-27092-   Let There Be Love (breakdown)
   33:   >IAJRC 53

CO-27092-   Let There Be Love (breakdown)
   33:   >IAJRC 53

CO-27092-1 Let There Be Love
    78: >Columbia 35449
    33: IAJRC 53

CO-27093- Melancholy Baby
    33: >IAJRC 53

CO-27093-1 Melancholy Baby
    78: >Columbia 35548
    33: IAJRC 53

CO-27094-1 Sierra Sue
    78: >Columbia 35449
    33: IAJRC 53

CO-27095- Lorelei
    33: >IAJRC 53

CO-27095- Lorelei (breakdown)
    33: >IAJRC 53

CO-27095-1 Lorelei
    78: >Columbia 35548
    33: IAJRC 53

NOTE: Produced by John Hammond. The above sequence of recording is according to the acetate safety disc, which exists. Although the 78 rpm issues show take 1 for all titles, that is merely an indication of the take being first choice for issue.

Bud Freeman And His Summa Cum Laude Orchestra
NYC, April 4, 1940

Max Kaminsky, trumpet; Brad Gowans, valve trombone, arranger; Pee
Wee Russell, clarinet; Bud Freeman, tenor; Eddie Condon, guitar; Dave
Bowman, piano; Pete Peterson, bass; Morey Feld, drums.

67477-A   Sensation
    78:   Brunswick (E) 03226, Brunswick (In) 03226, >Decca 18065,
          Decca (Au) Y-5922, Decca (Cz) 03226, Odeon (Arg) 286254
    33:   Affinity (E) AFS 1036, Brunswick (E) LA 8526, Decca DL
          5213, MCA (J) MCA 3082, Swaggie (Au) S 1216
    CD: Affinity (E) AFS 1008

67478-A   Fidgety Feet
    78:   Brunswick (E) 03228, Brunswick (In) 03228, >Decca 18067,
          Odeon (Arg) 286256
    33:   Affinity (E) AFS 1036, Brunswick (E) LA 8526, Decca DL
          5213, MCA (J) MCA 3082, Swaggie (Au) S 1216
    CD: Affinity (E) AFS 1008

67479-A   Tia Juana
    78:   Brunswick (E) 03227, Brunswick (In) 03227, >Decca 18066,
          Decca (Au) Y-5966, Odeon (Arg) 286255
    33:   Affinity (E) AFS 1036, Brunswick (E) LA 8526, Decca DL
          5213, MCA (J) MCA 3082, Swaggie (Au) S-1216
    CD: Affinity (E) AFS 1008

67480-A   Copenhagen
    78:   Brunswick (E) 03225, Brunswick (In) 03225, >Decca 18064,
          Decca (Au) Y-6022, Decca (Cz) 03226, Odeon (Arg) 286253
    33:   Affinity (E) AFS 1036, Brunswick (E) LA 8526, Decca DL
          5213, MCA (J) MCA 3082, Swaggie (Au) S-1216
    CD: Affinity (E) AFS 1008

NOTE: Decca 18064, 18065, 18066 and 18067 are contained in Decca
album 133, Wolverine Jazz..

Squirrel Ashcraft

Evanston, Illinois, c. May, 1940

Jimmy McPartland, cornet; Brad Gowans, valve trombone; Pee Wee Russell, clarinet; Joe Rushton, bass sax; Dave Bowman, piano; unknown drums.

Royal Garden Blues
    Unissued

Pee Wee Russell, clarinet; Dave Bowman, piano.

Blues
    Unissued

Bud Freeman, "moderator," Dave Bowman, Fred Moynahan, Brad Gowans, Pee Wee Russell, Jimmy McPartland, Gloria Faye, Jane Ashcraft, Max Kaminsky, speech.

Information, My Ahss
    Unissued

NOTE: These are private recordings made at Squirrel Ashcraft's house. The last title is a satire on the popular radio program, "Information, Please."

Bud Freeman And His Summa Cum Laude Orchestra

Chicago, May, 1940

Max Kaminsky, trumpet; Brad Gowans, valve trombone; Pee Wee Russell, clarinet; Bud Freeman, tenor; Dave Bowman, piano; Eddie Condon, guitar; possibly Mort Stuhlmaker, bass; probably Fred Moynahan, drums.

China Boy
    33:   >Blue Rhythm (G) 12-3

Strut Miss Lizzie
    33:   >Blue Rhythm (G) 12-3

Big Boy
    Unissued

NOTE: NBC broadcasts from The Panther Room, Hotel Sherman.

Bud Freeman And His Summa Cum Laude Orchestra

Chicago, May 5, 1940

Same personnel.

China Boy
    Unissued

NOTE: NBC broadcast from The Panther Room, Hotel Sherman.

Bud Freeman And His Summa Cum Laude Orchestra

Chicago, May 10, 1940

Same Personnel.

What Can I Say, Dear, After I Say I'm Sorry (partial)
    33:    Blue Rhythm (G) 12-3, >Ristic (E) SAE

NOTE: NBC broadcast from The Panther Room, Hotel Sherman

Bud Freeman And His Summa Cum Laude Orchestra

Chicago, May 11, 1940

Same Personnel.

What Can I Say, Dear, After I Say I'm Sorry
    33:    Blue Rhythm (G) 12-3, >Ristic (E) SAE

Oh, Baby!
    33:    Blue Rhythm (G) 12-3, >Ristic (E) SAE

NOTE: NBC broadcast from The Panther Room, Hotel Sherman.

Bud Freeman And His Summa Cum Laude Orchestra

Chicago, May 14, 1940

Same Personnel.

Tia Juana
    Unissued

One O'Clock Jump (partial)
    Unissued

NOTE: NBC broadcast from The Panther Room, Hotel Sherman.

85

Bud Freeman And His Summa Cum Laude Orchestra
Chicago, May 15, 1940

Same Personnel
I Ain't Gonna Give Nobody None of My Jelly Roll
    Unissued

April Played The Fiddle (partial)
    Unissued

Royal Garden Blues (partial)
    Unissued

Sunday (partial)
    Unissued

Sierra Sue
    Unissued

One O'Clock Jump
    Unissued

Theme (Easy to Get) (partial)
    Unissued
NOTE: NBC broadcast from The Panther Room, Hotel Sherman.

Bud Freeman And His Summa Cum Laude Orchestra
Chicago, May 16, 1940

Same personnel, with Lee Wiley, vocal.
Imagination (LW, vocal) (partial)
    Unissued

Sierra Sue (partial)
    Unissued

April Played The Fiddle (partial)
    Unissued

Where Was It? (partial)
    Unissued

Medley: Ma, He's Makin' Eyes At Me; Cherry; I Haven't Time To Be A
Millionaire; It's A Wonderful World; My, My (partial)
    Unissued
NOTE: NBC broadcast from The Panther Room, Hotel Sherman.

86

Bud Freeman And His Summa Cum Laude Orchestra
Chicago, May 18, 1940

Same personnel.

I Need Some Pettin' (partial)
    33:   Blue Rhythm (G) 12-3, >Ristic (E) SAE

Fast Blues (partial)
    33:   Blue Rhythm (G) 12-3, >Ristic (E) SAE

I Got Rhythm
    33:   Blue Rhythm (G) 12-3, >Ristic (E) SAE

Wrap Your Troubles In Dreams (partial)
    33:   Blue Rhythm (G) 12-3, >Ristic (E) SAE

I Ain't Gonna Give Nobody None Of My Jelly Roll
    33:   Blue Rhythm (G) 12-3, >Ristic (E) SAE

One O'Clock Jump (partial)
    33:   >IAJRC IAJRC-28

NOTE: NBC broadcast from The Panther Room, Hotel Sherman.

Bud Freeman And His Summa Cum Laude Orchestra
Chicago, May 20, 1940

Same personnel.

Theme (Easy to Get)
    33:   Fanfare 15-115

I Ain't Gonna Give Nobody None Of My Jelly Roll
    33:   >Fanfare 15-115

Medley: Secrets in the Moonlight; Shake Down The Stars; Out Of This
World; Yours Is My Heart Alone; I Love You Much Too Much
    33:   >Fanfare 15-115

Sierra Sue
    33:   >Fanfare 15-115

One O'Clock Jump
    33:   >Fanfare 15-115

Theme (Easy to Get)
    33:   >Fanfare 15-115

NOTE: NBC broaccast from The Panther Room, Hotel Sherman. A
few bars of "Easy To Get" are used to connect each of the tunes in the
medley.

Bud Freeman And His Summa Cum Laude Orchestra
                                        Chicago, May 24, 1940

Same personnel.

Ja Da
    33:   Blue Rhythm (G) 12-3, >Ristic (E) SAE

I Ain't Gonna Give Nobody None Of My Jelly Roll
    Unissued

NOTE: NBC broadcast from The Panther Room, Hotel Sherman.

Bud Freeman And His Summa Cum Laude Orchestra
                                        Chicago, May 25, 1940

Same personnel.

Susie
    33:   >Fanfare 15-115

Copenhagen (partial)
    33:   >Fanfare 15-115

Tia Juana (partial)
    33:   >Fanfare 15-115

I Need Some Pettin' (partial)
    33:   >Fanfare 15-115

NOTE: NBC broadcast from The Panther Room, Hotel Sherman.
Fanfare 15-115 labels "Susie" as "Sussie."

Bud Freeman And His Summa Cum Laude Orchestra
Chicago, May 31, 1940

Same personnel.

Honeysuckle Rose (partial)
   Unissued

NOTE: NBC broadcast from The Panther Room, Hotel Sherman.

Bud Freeman And His Famous Chicagoans
NYC, July 24, 1940

Jack Teagarden, trombone, vocal; Pee Wee Russell, clarinet; Bud Freeman, tenor; Dave Bowman, piano; Eddie Condon, guitar; Mort Stuhlmaker, bass; Dave Tough, drums.

CO-27684-1   Jack Hits The Road (JT, vocal)
   78:   >Columbia 35854, Columbia (Sd) DS-1433, Parlophone (Au) A-7455, Parlophone (E) R-2820
   45:   Epic "Memory Lane" 5-2211
   33:   CBS (SA) ASK 3028, Columbia CL 2558, Columbia CL 6107, Columbia CJ 40652, Columbia (Arg) 6016, Columbia (Au) OS 1016, Columbia (C) CL 2558, Columbia (E) 33SX 1016, Columbia Special Products JLN 6044, Dawn Club (G) 12009, Epic SN 6042 (LN 24029), Epic (C) SN 6042 (LN 24029), Family (I) SFR 742, Harmony HL 7046, Philips (E) 07224L, Philips (E) BO 7226L, Time-Life STL-J08 (P 15009), Time-Life (Au) STL-J08, Time-Life (C) STL-J08
   TX: AFRS P-1843, VOA JS 31, VOA WOJ 7
   CD: Columbia CK 40652, Jazzman (G) 625.50.008, Phontastic (Sd) 7668
   CT: Columbia CJT 40652, Time-Life 4TL-J08,
   8T: Time-Life 8TL-J08

CO-27685-1   Forty-Seventh And State
    78:   >Columbia 35855, Columbia (Sd) DS-1491, Parlophone (Au)
          A-7454
    33:   CBS Sony (J) SOPB 55016, Columbia CL 6107, Columbia
          (Arg) 6016, Columbia (Au) OS 1016, Columbia (E) 33SX
          1016, Columbia (E) 33SX 1573, Columbia (G) 33WS 1016,
          Columbia Special Products JLN 6044, Dawn Club (G) 12009,
          Epic SN 6044 (LN 24047), Epic (C) SN 6044 (LN 24047),
          Family (I) SFR 742, Harmony HL 7046, Philips (E) BO
          7224L
    TX: AFRS P-1843

Add Max Kaminsky, trumpet.

CO-27686-1   Muskrat Ramble
    78:   >Columbia 35855, Columbia (Sd) DS 1424, Columbia (J) M-
          635, Parlophone (E) R-2809, Parlophone (I) B-71150
    33:   CBS (SA) ASK 3028, Columbia CL 2558, Columbia CL
          6107, Columbia (Arg) 6016, Columbia (Au) OS 1016,
          Columbia (C) CL 2558, Columbia (E) 33SX 1016, Columbia
          (G) 33WS 1016, Columbia (J) PL 5064, Dawn Club (G)
          12009, Family (I) SFR 742, Harmony HL 7046, MK 1001
    TX: AFRS P-1843

CO-27686-2   Muskrat Ramble
    33:   CBS Sony (J) SOPB 55016, Columbia (E) 33SX 1573,
          Columbia Special Products JLN 6044, Dawn Club (G) 12009,
          >Epic SN 6044 (LN 24047), Epic (C) SN 6044 (LN 24047),
          Family (I) SFR 742

CO-27687-1   That Da Da Strain
    78:   >Columbia 35854, Columbia (Sd) DS 1433, Columbia (J) M-
          635, Parlophone (E) R-2820
    45:   Fontana (E) TFE 17082
    33:   CBS (SA) ASK 3028, Columbia CL 2558, Columbia CL
          6107, Columbia (Arg) 6016, Columbia (Au) OS 1016,
          Columbia (C) CL 2558, Columbia (E) 33SX 1016, Columbia
          (E) 1499, Columbia (E) 1511, Columbia (G) 33WS 1016,
          Columbia Special Products JLN 6042, Epic SN 6042 (LN
          24029), Epic (C) SN 6042 (LN 24049), Dawn Club (G)
          12009, Family (I) SFR 742, Harmony HL 7046, Philips (E)
          072241
    TX: VOA AJ 31

CO-27688-1   Shim-Me-Sha-Wabble
  78:   >Columbia 35856, Parlophone (Au) A-7474
  45:   Fontana (E) TFE 17082
  33:   Columbia CL 2558, Columbia CL 6107, Columbia (Arg)
        6016, Columbia (Au) OS 1016, Columbia (C) CL 2558,
        Columbia (E) 33SX 1016, Columbia (G) 33WS 1016, Dawn
        Club (G) 12009, Family (I) SFR 742, Harmony HL 7046,
        Time-Life STL-J17 (P 15734), Time-Life (Au) STL-J17,
        Time-Life (C) STL-J17
  TX: AFRS P-1843
  CT: Time-Life 4TL-J17
  8T: Time-Life 8TL-J17
CO-27688-2   Shim-Me-Sha-Wabble
  33:   CBS Sony (J) SOPB 55016, Columbia (E) 33SX 1573,
        Columbia Special Products JLN 6044, Dawn Club (G) 12009,
        >Epic SN 6044 (LN 24047), Epic (C) SN 6044 (LN 24047),
        Family (I) SFR 742

CO-27689-1   At The Jazz Band Ball
  78:   >Columbia 35853, Columbia (Arg) 291620, Columbia (Sd)
        DS 1491, Columbia (Sp) 291620, Parlophone (E) R-2877,
        Parlophone (In) DPE 81, Parlophone (Sw) PZ-11016
  45:   Fontana (E) TFE 17082
  33:   CBS (SA) ASK 3028, Columbia CL 2558, Columbia CL
        6107, Columbia (Arg) 6016, Columbia (Au) OS 1016,
        Columbia (C) CL 2558, Columbia (E) 33SX 1016, Columbia
        (G) 33WS 1016, Columbia (J) PL 5064, Dawn Club (G)
        12009, Family (I) SFR 742, Harmony HL 7046
  TX: VOA AJ 31

CO-27690-1   After Awhile
  78:   >Columbia 35856, Columbia (Arg) 291620, Columbia (Sp)
        291620, Parlophone (Au) A-7474, Parlophone (E) R-2877,
        Parlophone (In) DPE 81, Parlophone (Sw) PZ-11016
  45:   Fontana (E) TFE 17082
  33:   CBS (SA) ASK 3028, Columbia CL 2558, Columbia 6107,
        Columbia (Arg) 6016, Columbia (Au) OS 1016, Columbia
        (C) CL 2558, Columbia (E) 33SX 1016, Columbia (G) 33WS
        1016, Dawn Club (G) 12009, Family (I) SFR 742, Harmony
        HL 7046, Time-Life STL-J08 (P 15009), Time-Life (Au)
        STL-J08, Time-Life (C) STL-J08
  TX: AFRS P-1843
  CT: Time-Life 4TL-J08
  8T: Time-Life 8TL-J08

CO-27690-2   After Awhile
   33:   Columbia JSN 6044, Columbia (E) 33SX 1573, Columbia
         Special Products JLN 6044, Dawn Club (G) 12009, >Epic SN
         6044 (LN 24047), Epic (C) SN 6044 (LN 24047), Family (I)
         SFR 742

CO-27691-1   Prince Of Wails
   78:   >Columbia 35853, Columbia (Sd) DS 1424, Parlophone (E)
         R-2809, Parlophone (I) B-71150
   33:   CBS (SA) ASK 3028, Columbia CL 6107, Columbia (Arg)
         6016, Columbia (Au) OS 1016, Columbia (E) 33SX 1016,
         Columbia (G) 33WS 1016, Dawn Club (G) 12009, Family (I)
         SFR 742, Franklin Mint 66, Harmony HL 7046, Reader's
         Digest RD-4-206
   TX: AFRS P-1843

NOTE: Session recorded 9:30 a.m. to 1:45 p.m. Date from Columbia
files. Columbia 35853, 35854, 35855 and 35856 were issued in
Columbia album A-40. Parlophone (In) DPE 81 shows 2T1 in the wax
on both sides of the disc, but both are identical to take 1 of the original
issues. Produced by Morty Palitz.

**Teddy Grace With Bud Freeman And The Summa Cum Laude
Orchestra**

NYC, September 26, 1940

Max Kaminsky, trumpet; Brad Gowans, valve trombone; Pee Wee
Russell, clarinet; Bud Freeman, tenor; Dave Bowman, piano; Eddie
Condon, guitar; Pete Peterson, bass; Morey Feld, drums; Teddy Grace,
vocal.

68153-A   Gee, But I Hate To Go Home Alone
   78:   >Decca 3463
   33:   IAJRC 53
   CD: Affinity (E) AFS 1008

68154-A   Sing (It's Good For Ya!)
   78:   >Decca 3463
   33:   IAJRC 53
   CD: Affinity (E) AFS 1008

68155-A See What The Boys In The Back Room Will Have
    78: >Decca 3428
    33: IAJRC 53
    CD: Affinity (E) AFS 1008

68156-A I'm The Lonesomest Gal In Town
    78: >Decca 3428
    33: IAJRC 53
    CD: Affinity (E) AFS 1008

Eddie Condon And His Band

NYC, November 11, 1940

Marty Marsala, cornet; George Brunies, trombone; Pee Wee Russell, clarinet; Fats Waller (as Maurice on labels), piano; Eddie Condon, guitar; Artie Shapiro, bass; George Wettling, drums.

P-29054-TK1 Georgia Grind
    33: Mosaic MR23-123, >Rarest Fats Waller RFW-4 (track 2), TOM-61
P-29054-TK2 Georgia Grind No. 2
    33: Commodore XFL 15355, Commodore (G) 6.24295 AG, London (G) 6.24295 AG, Mosaic MR23-123, >Rarest Fats Waller RFW-4 (track 3), TOM-61

P-29054-1b Georgia Grind
    78: >Commodore 536
    45: Commodore CEP 43, Guilde du Jazz (F) J 727, Jazztone J 727
    33: Ace of Hearts (E) AHC 178, Book of the Month Club 10-5557, Commodore CCL 7015, Commodore FL 20,022, Commodore FL 30,010, Commodore XFL 15355, Commodore (G) 6.24295 AG, Commodore (J) GXC 3150, Commodore (J) K23P-6618, Decca (G) ND 476, Jazztone J-1216, London (G) 6.24295 AG, London (J) SLC 442, London (J) LAX 3307, Mainstream S/6008, Mainstream 56008, Mainstream (J) PS 1240, Mosaic MR23-123, Stateside (E) SL 10010, Time-Life STL-J15 (STLJ-5015-F), Time-Life (Au) STL-J15, Time-Life (C) STL-J15, Top Rank (H) HJA 16507, Vogue (F) INT 40015
    CD: Commodore CCD 7000, Commodore CCD 7015
    CT: Book of the Month Club 60-5561, Commodore CCK 7015, Time-Life 4TL-J15
    8T: Book of the Month Club 50-5560, Time-Life 8TL-J15

93

P-29055-BD   Oh, Sister, Ain't That Hot! (incomplete take)
  33: >Jazz Archives JA-15, Mosaic MR23-123

P-29055-1 Oh, Sister, Ain't That Hot! No. 2
  33:   Commodore XFL 15355, Commodore (G) 6.24295 AG,
       London (G) 6.24295 AG, Mosaic MR23-123, >Rarest Fats
       Waller RFW-4 (track 7), TOM-61

P-29055-2 Oh, Sister, Ain't That Hot!
  78: >Commodore 535
  45:   Commodore CEP 43, Guilde du Jazz (F) J 727, Jazztone J
       727
  33:   Ace of Hearts (E) AHC 178, Commodore CCL 7015,
       Commodore 20,022, Commodore FL 30,010, Commodore
       XFL 15355, Commodore (G) 6.24295 AG, Commodore (J)
       GXC 3150, Commodore (J) K23P-6618, Decca (G) ND 476,
       Jazztone J-1216, London (G) 6.24295 AG, London (J) SLC
       442, London (J) LAX 3307, Mosaic MR23-123, Stateside (E)
       SL 10010, Time-Life STL-J17 (P 15734), Time-Life (Au)
       STL-J17, Time-Life (C) STL-J17, Top Rank (H) HJA 16507
  TX: AFRS DB 339
  CD: Commodore CCD 7015
  CT: Commodore CCK 7015, Time-Life 4TL-J17
  8T: Time-Life 8TL-J17

P-29055-TK3 Oh, Sister, Ain't That Hot!
  33:   Mosaic MR23-123, >Rarest Fats Waller RFW-4 (track 6),
       TOM-61

P-29056-TK1 Dancing Fool
  33:   >Jazz Archives JA-1, Mosaic MR23-123, Rarest Fats Waller
       RFW-4 (track 3), TOM-61

P-29056-TK2 Dancing Fool No. 2
  33:   Commodore XFL 15355, Commodore (G) 6.24295 AG,
       >Jazz Archives JA-1, London (G) 6.24295 AG, Mosaic
       MR23-123

P-29056-1 Dancing Fool
    78:   >Commodore 536
    45:   Commodore CEP 43, Guilde du Jazz (F) J727, Jazztone J 727
    33:   Ace of Hearts (E) AHC 178, Commodore CCL 7015,
          Commodore 20,022, Commodore FL 30,010, Commodore
          XFL 15355, Commodore (G) 6.24295 AG, Commodore (J)
          GXC 3150, Commodore (J) K23P-6618, Decca (G) ND 476,
          Jazztone J-1216, London (G) 6.24295 AG, London (J) SLC
          442, London (J) LAX 3307, Mainstream S/6008, Mainstream
          56008, Mainstream (J) PS 1240, Mosaic MR23-123,
          Stateside (E) SL 10010, Top Rank (H) HJA 16507, Vogue
          (F) INT 40015
    CD: Commodore CCD 7015
    CT: Commodore CCK 7015

P-29057-TK1 (You're Some) Pretty Doll No. 2
    33:   Commodore XFL 15355, Commodore (G) 6.24295 AG,
          >Jazz Archives JA-1, London (G) 6.24295 AG, Mosaic
          MR23-123, Rarest Fats Waller RFW-4 (track 5), Time-Life
          STL-J17 (P 15734), Time-Life (Au) STL-J17, Time-Life (C)
          STL-J17, TOM-61
    CT: Time-Life 4TL-J17
    8T: Time-Life 8TL-J17

P-29057-TK2 (You're Some) Pretty Doll
    33:   >Jazz Archives JA-1, Mosaic MR23-123

P-29057-1 (You're Some) Pretty Doll
    78:   >Commodore 535
    45:   Commodore CEP 43, Guilde du Jazz (F) J727, Jazztone J 727
    33:   Ace of Hearts (E) AHC 178, Commodore CCL 7015,
          Commodore FL 20,022, Commodore FL 30,010, Commodore
          XFL 15355, Commodore (G) 6.24295 AG, Commodore (J)
          GXC 3150, Commodore (J) K23P-6618, Decca (G) ND 476,
          Jazztone J 1216, London (G) 6.24295 AG, London (J) SLC
          442, London (J) LAX 3307, Mosaic MR23-123, Stateside (E)
          SL 10010, Time-Life STL-J15 (STLJ-5015-F), Time-Life
          (Au) STL-J15, Time-Life (C) STL-J15, Top Rank (H) HJA
          16507
    CD: Commodore CCD 7015
    CT: Commodore CCK 7015, Time-Life 4TL-J15
    8T: Time-Life 8TL-J15

NOTE: Produced by Milt Gabler. Recorded at Brunswick studios, 1776 Broadway. This session probably exists on safeties. The various take designations on the Commodore original issues refer to the choice for issue, rather than actual recording sequence. Matrix 29054-1B on Mainstream S/6008 and Mainstream 56008 has had the piano introduction edited out. Pre-war laminated pressings of Commodore 535 and Commodore 536 indicate the session was "sponsored by Colin Campbell" while post-war pressings do not. TOM-61 is identical to Rarest Fats Waller RFW-4 (both are dubbed off-speed). Mosaic MR23-123 is a 23-LP boxed set.

Eddie Condon

NYC, January 6, 1941

Pee Wee Russell, clarinet; Joe Sullivan, piano; Eddie Condon, guitar; Dave Tough, drums.

Monday Night Special
    33: Fanfare 23-123, Kings of Jazz (I) KLJ 20028, >Spook Jazz
           (D) SPJ 6607
    CT: Holmia (Sd) HM 106

The Blues
    33: Fanfare 23-123, Kings of Jazz (I) KLJ 20028, >Spook Jazz
           (D) SPJ 6607
    CT: Holmia (Sd) HM 106
NOTE: NBC broadcast of the Chamber Music Society of Lower Basin Street.

The Three Deuces

NYC, March 25, 1941

Pee Wee Russell, clarinet; Joe Sullivan, piano; Zutty Singleton, drums.

R-4049 Jig Walk
    78: >Commodore 539
    45: Commodore 45-539, Commodore CEP-28
    33: Commodore FL 20,014, Commodore XFL 16440,
           Commodore (G) 6.25490 AG, London (G) 6.25490, London
           (J) SLC 459, Mosaic MR23-123, Time-Life STL-J17
           (P15734), Time-Life (Au) STL-J17, Time-Life (C) STL-J17
    CT: Time-Life 4TL-J17
    8T: Time-Life 8TL-J17

R-4050   Deuces Wild
   78:   >Commodore 537
   45:   Commodore 45-537, CEP-28
   33:   Commodore FL 20,014, Commodore XFL 16440,
         Commodore (G) 6.25490 AG, ESC 101, Fontana (E) TL
         5271, London (G) 6.25490, London (J) SLC 459, Mainstream
         S/6026, Mainstream 56026, Mainstream (J) XM 33 MSD,
         Mosaic MR23-123, Time-Life STL-J27 (P 15967), Time-Life
         (Au) STL-J27, Time-Life (C) STL-J27
   TX: AFRS DB 426
   CT: Time-Life 4TL-J27
   8T: Time-Life 8TL-J27

R-4050-2 Deuces Wild No. 2
   33:   >Commodore XFL 16440, Commodore (G) 6.25490 AG,
         London (G) 6.25490, Mosaic MR23-123

R-4051-1 The Last Time I Saw Chicago No. 2
   33:   >Commodore XFL 16440, Commodore (G) 6.25490 AG,
         London (G) 6.25490, Mosaic MR23-123

R-4051-2 The Last Time I Saw Chicago
   78:   >Commodore 537
   45:   Commodore 45-537, Commodore CEP-28
   33:   Commodore FL 20,014, Commodore XFL 16440,
         Commodore (G) 6.25490 AG, Fontana (E) TL 5271, Fontana
         (H) 687 708TL, London (G) 6.25490, London (J) SLC 459,
         Mainstream S/6026, Mainstream 56026, Mainstream (J) XM
         33 MSD, Mosaic MR23-123, Time-Life STL-J17 (P 15734),
         Time-Life (Au) STL-J17, Time-Life (C) STL-J17
   CT: Time-Life 4TL-J17
   8T: Time-Life 8TL-J17

R-4052   About Face
   78:   >Commodore 539
   45:   Commodore 45-539, Commodore CEP-28
   33:   Commodore FL 20,014, Commodore XFL 16440,
         Commodore (G) 6.25490 AG, Franklin Mint 73, London (G)
         6.25490, London (J) SLC 459, Mosaic MR23-123, Time-Life
         STL-J27 (P 15967), Time-Life (Au) STL-J27 (P 15734),
         Time-Life (C) STL-J27
   TX: OWI MJ8 Disc 11 (Show 21)
   CT: Time-Life 4TL-J27
   8T: Time-Life 8TL-J27

R-4052-1 About Face No. 2
33:    >Commodore XFL 16440, Commodore (G) 6.25490 AG,
       London (G) 6.25490, Mosaic MR23-123

NOTE: Produced by Milt Gabler. Recorded at Reeves Sound studios,
1600 Broadway. "The Last Time I Saw Chicago" was composed by
Pee Wee Russell. Mosaic MR23-123 is a 23-LP boxed set.

Jimmy McPartland

Chicago, July, 1941

Jimmy McPartland, cornet; George Brunies, trombone, vocal; Pee Wee
Russell, clarinet; Joe Sullivan, piano; Eddie Condon, guitar; Hank
Isaacs, drums.

Angry (GB, vocal)
    Unissued

I'm Comin' Virginia
    Unissued

The Jazz Me Blues (partial)
    Unissued

At The Jazz Band Ball
    Unissued

Squeeze Me (partial)
    Unissued

NOTE: The July 15, 1941, edition of Down Beat reported that this
band, led by McPartland, opened at the Brass Rail on July 6 for a four-
week stint. The article noted that the club had a nightly CBS radio
hook-up.   "Angry" may be from a broadcast. The other titles were
recorded privately.

The Three Deuces

NYC, December 3, 1941

Pee Wee Russell, clarinet; Joe Sullivan, piano; Zutty Singleton, drums.

Deuces Wild
  Unissued

The Last Time I Saw Chicago
  Unissued

NOTE: From the NBC broadcast of the Chamber Music Society of Lower Basin Street.

Fats Waller And His Orchestra

NYC, January 14, 1942

Max Kaminsky, trumpet; Pee Wee Russell, clarinet; Bud Freeman, tenor; Fats Waller, piano; Eddie Condon, guitar; John Kirby, bass; Gene Krupa, drums.

Honeysuckle Rose
  33: >Jazz Archives JA-1

NOTE: Recorded at a Carnegie Hall concert featuring Waller, produced by Ernest Anderson. Other selections issued from this concert do not include Russell.

Eddie Condon And His Band

NYC, January 28, 1942

Max Kaminsky, trumpet; Brad Gowans, valve trombone; Pee Wee Russell, clarinet; Joe Sullivan, piano; Eddie Condon, guitar; Al Morgan, bass; George Wettling, drums.

R-4305-3 Don't Leave Me Daddy
  78: >Commodore 542
  45: Commodore 45-542, Commodore CEP 37
  33: Commodore CCL 7015, Commodore FL 20,019, Commodore FL 30,013, Commodore XFL 16568, Commodore (G) 6.25526 AG, London (G) 6.25526, London (J) LAX 3309, Melodisc (E) MLP 12-126, Mosaic MR23-123
  CD: Commodore CCD 7015
  CT: Commodore CCK 7015

R-4306-3 Fidgety Feet No. 2
  33: >Commodore XFL 16568, Commodore (G) 6.25526 AG, London (G) 6.25526, Mosaic MR23-123

R-4306-4 Fidgety Feet
  78: >Commodore 542
  45: Commodore 45-542, Commodore CEP 36
  33: Commodore CCL 7015, Commodore FL 20,019, Commodore FL 30,013, Commodore XFL 16568, Commodore (G) 6.25526 AG, London (G) 6.25526, London (J) LAX 3309, Mainstream S/6024, Mainstream 56024, Mainstream (Arg) DPM 9050, Melodisc (E) MLP 12-126, Mosaic MR23-123
  TX: VOA WOJ 71
  CD: Commodore CCD 7015
  CT: Commodore CCK 7015

R-4306-5 Fidgety Feet #3
  33: Mosaic MR23-123

R-4307-1 Mammy O' Mine
  78: >Commodore 1509
  33: Commodore CCL 7015, Commodore XFL 16568, Commodore (G) 6.25526 AG, London (G) 6.25526, London (J) SLC 446, Mosaic MR23-123, Time-Life STL-J27 (P 15968), Time-Life (Au) STL-J27 (P 15968), Time-Life (C) STL-J27
  CD: Commodore CCD 7015
  CT: Commodore CCK 7015, Time-Life 4TL-J27
  8T: Time-Life 8TL-J27

R-4307-2 Mammy O' Mine No. 2
  33: >Commodore XFL 16568, Commodore (G) 6.25526 AG, London (G) 6.25526, Mosaic MR23-123

R-4308-1 Lonesome Tag Blues
  78: >Commodore 1510
  33: Commodore CCL 7015, Commodore XFL 16568, Commodore (G) 6.25526, Commodore (J) GXC 3149, Commodore (J) K23P-6617, London (J) SLC 446, London (G) 6.25526, Mosaic MR23-123
  CD: Commodore CCD 7015
  CT: Commodore CCK 7015

R-4308-2 Tortilla B Flat
   78:   >Commodore 1509
   33:   Commodore CCL 7015, Commodore XFL 16568,
         Commodore (G) 6.25526 AG, London (G) 6.25526, London
         (J) SLC 446, Mosaic MR23-123
   CD: Commodore CCD 7015
   CT: Commodore CCK 7015

R-4308-4 More Tortilla In B Flat
   78:   >Commodore 1510
   33:   Commodore CCL 7015, Commodore (J) GXC 3149,
         Commodore (J) K23P-6617, Mosaic MR23-123
   CD: Commodore CCD 7015
   CT: Commodore CCK 7015

NOTE: Produced by Milt Gabler. Recorded at Reeves Sound studios,
1600 Broadway. Commodore 1509 and 1510 are 12-inch discs. Early
pressings of Commodore 1510 issued as Jam Session at Commodore
No. 4, later pressings as Eddie Condon and His Band. Commodore 45-
542 was scheduled for release but never appeared. Mosaic MR23-123
is a 23-LP boxed set.

*During 1942, Eddie Condon conducted four concerts at Town Hall.
They all were recorded by the Rockefeller Committee which was
established to develop an educational radio system for Latin America.
According to a contemporary report, a set of the recordings was
presented to the Library of Congress, but a search of the Library's
holdings has failed to produce any evidence of their existence.
Pressings of the concerts with dubbed-in announcements in Spanish
and Portugese were to be sent by the Rockefeller Committee to 300
radio stations throughout Latin America, but may never have been
distributed, due to World War II.*

*The first concert took place on February 21, 1942, starting at 5:30
p.m., and included Hot Lips Page, Max Kaminsky, Bobby Hackett,
trumpets; J.C. Higginbotham, Brad Gowans, trombones; Sidney
Bechet, clarinet, soprano sax; Pee Wee Russell, clarinet; Willie "The
Lion" Smith, Joe Sullivan, Mel Powell, pianos; Eddie Condon, guitar;
Sid Weiss, John Simmons, bass; Zutty Singleton, George Wettling, Carl
"Kansas" Fields, Sid Catlett, drums.*

The second concert was held on March 7, 1942, at 5:30 p.m., and included Red Allen, Max Kaminsky, Muggsy Spanier, trumpets; Higginbotham, Gowans and George Brunies, trombones; Pee Wee Russell, Ed Hall and Irving Fazola, clarinets; Billy Kyle, Joe Sullivan, Mel Powell, pianos; Eddie Condon, guitar; John Kirby, bass; Zutty Singleton, Kansas Fields and Cozy Cole, drums.

The third concert was on March 21, 1942 at 5:30 p.m. and included Hot Lips Page, Max Kaminsky, trumpets; J.C. Higginbotham, Brad Gowans, Benny Morton, trombones; Pee Wee Russell, clarinet; Earl Hines, Joe Sullivan, pianos; Eddie Condon, guitar; Al Morgan, bass; Ray McKinley, Zutty Singleton, drums, and the piano-dance team of Buck Washington and John "Bubbles" Sublett.

The fourth concert was on April 11, 1942, at 5:30 p.m. and included Hot Lips Page, Red Allen, trumpets; Benny Morton, trombone; Pee Wee Russell, clarinet; Bud Freeman, tenor; Al Morgan, bass; Kansas Fields, Zutty Singleton, drums.

None of these concert recordings have been available for examination.

Eddie Condon's Barrelhouse Gang
NYC, November 20, 1943

Yank Lawson, trumpet; Brad Gowans, valide trombone; Pee Wee Russell, clarinet; James P. Johnson, piano; Eddie Condon, guitar; Bob Haggart, bass; Tony Spargo, drums.

T1901   Squeeze Me
   78:    >Signature 28130
   33:    Bob Thiele BBM1-0941, Doctor Jazz FW 40064, Doctor Jazz (E) ASLP 812, Joker (I) SM 3244, Riverside RLP 2509
   CT: Doctor Jazz FWT 40064

T1902   That's A Plenty
   78:    >Signature 28130
   33:    Bob Thiele BBM1-0941, Doctor Jazz FW 40064, Doctor Jazz (E) ASLP 812, Joker (I) SM 3244, Riverside RLP 2509
   CT: Doctor Jazz FWT 40064

Yank Lawson's Jazz Doctors

Same session

Same personnel.

T1903   Yank's Blues
    33: Bob Thiele BBM1-0941, Doctor Jazz FW 40064, Doctor Jazz
          (E) ASLP-812, Joker (I) SM 3244, >Riverside RLP 2509,
          Riverside RLP 12-116, Riverside SPD-11, Riverside (J)
          R5015
    CT: Doctor Jazz FWT 40064

Add Ray Eckstrand, clarinet.

T1904   Old Fashioned Love
    33: Bob Thiele BBM1-0941, Doctor Jazz FW 40064, Doctor Jazz
          (E) ASLP-812, Joker (I) SM 3244, >Riverside RLP 2509
    CT: Doctor Jazz FWT 40064

NOTE: A 78 rpm test pressing of T1903 reveals that an unaccompanied trumpet introduction is omitted from all issues. All microgroove issues of T1901 and T1902 as Yank Lawson. The valide trombone was a combination slide and valve trombone invented by Gowans. Riverside SPD-11 is a 5-LP boxed set including Riverside RLP 12-116, which was also issued as a single album.

Wild Bill Davison And His Commodores

NYC, November 27, 1943

Wild Bill Davison, cornet; George Brunies, trombone; Pee Wee Russell, clarinet; Gene Schroeder, piano; Eddie Condon, guitar; Bob Casey, bass; George Wettling, drums.

A 4675 That's A Plenty
- 78: >Commodore 1511
- 45: Commodore 45-1511, Commodore CEP 1
- 33: Ancient Age no # (excerpt), Book of the Month Club 10-5557, Commodore CCL 7011, Commodore FL 20,000, Commodore FL 30,009, Commodore XFL 14939, Commodore (G) 6.24059 AG, Decca London (F) 180.016, Dial (Arg) DPM 9059, Dial (Arg) DPE 10059, London (E) HMC 5011, London (G) 6.24059 AG, London (J) SLC 452, London (J) LAX 3306, Mainstream S/6003, Mainstream 56003, Mainstream (J) XM 34 MSD, Melodisc (E) MLP 12-127, Mosaic MR23-123, Time-Life STL-J17 (P 15734), Time-Life (Au) STL-J17, Time-Life (C) STL-J17, Top Rank (J) RANK 5014, Top Rank (H) HJA 16506
- TX: AFRTS World of Jazz 48
- CD: Commodore CCD 7011
- CT: Book of the Month Club 60-5561, Commodore CCK 7015, Time-Life 4TL-J17
- 8T: Book of the Month Club 50-5560, Time-Life 8TL-J17

A 4675-2 That's A Plenty No. 2
- 33: >Commodore XFL 14939, Commodore (G) 6.24059 AG, Decca London (F) 180.016, London (G) 6.24059 AG, Mosaic MR23-123

A 4676-1 Panama
- 78: >Commodore 1511
- 45: Commodore 45-1511, Commodore CEP 2
- 33: Commodore CCL 7000, Commodore CCL 7011, Commodore FL 20,000, Commodore FL 30,009, Commodore XFL 14939, Commodore (G) 6.24059 AG, Decca London (F) 180.016, London (E) HMC 5011, London (G) 6.24059 AG, London (J) LAX 3306, Mainstream S/6003, Mainstream 56003, Mainstream (J) XM 34 MSD, Melodisc (E) MLP 12-127, Mosaic MR23-123, Top Rank (J) RANK 5014, Top Rank (H) HJA 16506
- CD: Commodore CCD 7000, Commodore CCD 7011
- CT: Commodore CCK 7000, Commodore CCK 7011

A 4676-2/1/2 Panama No. 2
33:   >Commodore XFL 14939, Commodore (G) 6.24059 AG,
      Decca London (F) 180.016, London (G) 6.24059, Mosaic
      MR23-123

A 4677-1 Riverboat Shuffle
78:   >Commodore 618
45:   Commodore 45-618, Commodore CEP 2
33:   Book of the Month Club 10-5557, Commodore CCL 7011,
      Commodore FL 20,000, Commodore FL 30,009, Commodore
      XFL 14939, Commodore (G) 6.24059 AG, Decca London (F)
      180.016, Dial (Arg) DPM 9059, Dial (Arg) DPE 10059,
      London (E) HMC 5011, London (G) 6.24059 AG, London (J)
      LAX 3306, Mainstream 56003, Mainstream S/6003,
      Melodisc (E) MLP 12-127, Mosaic MR23-123, Top Rank (J)
      RANK 5014, Top Rank (H) HJA 16506
CD: Commodore CCD 7011
CT: Book of the Month Club 60-5561, Commodore CCK 7011
8T: Book of the Month Club 50-5560

A 4677-2 Riverboat Shuffle No. 2
33:   >Commodore XFL 14939, Commodore (G) 6.24059 AG,
      Decca London (F) 180.016, London (G) 6.24059 AG, Mosaic
      MR23-123

A 4678-1 Muskrat Ramble No. 2
33:   >Commodore XFL 14939, Commodore (G) 6.24059 AG,
      Decca London (F) 180.016, London (G) 6.24059 AG, Mosaic
      MR23-123

A 4678-2 Muskrat Ramble
78:   >Commodore 618
45:   Commodore 45-618, Commodore CEP 1
33:   Book of the Month Club 10-5557, Commodore CCL 7011,
      Commodore FL 20,000, Commodore FL 30,015, Commodore
      XFL 14939, Commodore (G) 6.24059 AG, Decca London (F)
      180.016, London (E) HMC 5011, London (G) 6.24059,
      Mainstream S/6010, Mainstream 56010, Mosaic MR23-123,
      Stateside (E) SL 10022
CD: Commodore CCD 7011
CT: Book of the Month Club 60-5561, Commodore CCK 7011
8T: Book of the Month Club 50-5560

NOTE: Produced by Milt Gabler. Recorded at WOR studios, 1440 Broadway. Commodore 1511 is a 12-inch disc. The Ancient Age disc is a paper promotional issue. Commodore 45-618 and 45-1511 were issued in a boxed set with the number CRF-100 appearing only on the box. Mosaic MR23-123 is a 23-LP boxed set. P-4676-2/1/2 indicates a spliced take, using a portion of take 1 spliced into take 2.

George Brunies Jazz Band

NYC, November 29, 1943

Wild Bill Davison, cornet; George Brunies, trombone, vocal; Pee Wee Russell, clarinet; Gene Schroeder, piano; Eddie Condon, guitar; Bob Casey, bass; George Wettling, drums.

A 4976-TK1 Royal Garden Blues No. 2
    33:   >Commodore XFL 15354, Commodore (G) 6.24294 AG,
          London (G) 6.24294 AG, Mosaic MR23-123
A 4976-1 Royal Garden Blues
    78:   >Commodore 556
    45:   Commodore 45-556, Commodore CEP-21
    33:   Book of the Month Club 10-5557, Commodore CCL 7011,
          Commodore FL 20,010, Commodore FL 30,015, Commodore
          XFL 15354, Commodore (G) 6.24294 AG, Commodore (J)
          GXC 3148, Commodore (J) K23P-6616, Decca London (F)
          180.016, Dial (Arg) DPM 9059, Dial (Arg) DPE 10059,
          London (G) 6.24294 AG, Mainstream S/6003, Mainstream
          56003, Mainstream (J) XM 34 MSD, Mosaic MR23-123,
          Stateside (E) SL 10022
    TX: VOA Jam Session 13
    CD: Commodore CCD 7011
    CT: Book of the Month Club 60-5561, Commodore CCK 7011
    8T: Book of the Month Club 50-5560

A 4680-TK1 Ugly Child No. 2 (GB vocal)
    33:   >Commodore XFL 15354, Commodore (G) 6.24294 AG,
          London (G) 6.24294 AG, Mosaic MR23-123

A 4680-1 Ugly Chile (sic) (GB vocal)
  78: >Commodore 546
  45: Commodore 45-546, Commodore CEP-16
  33: Commodore CCL 7011, Commodore FL 20,010,
       Commodore FL 30,015, Commodore XFL 15354,
       Commodore (G) 6.24294 AG, Commodore (J) GXC 3148,
       Commodore (J) K23P-6616, London (E) HMC 5011, London
       (G) 6.24294 AG, London (J) SLC 442, Mainstream S/6003,
       Mainstream 56003, Mosaic MR23-123, Stateside (E) SL
       10022
  CD: Commodore CCD 7011
  CT: Commodore CCK 7011

A 4681-TK1 Tin Roof Blues #3
  33: >Mosaic MR23-123

A 4681-1 Tin Roof Blues
  78: >Commodore 556
  45: Commodore 45-556, Commodore CEP-20
  33: Book of the Month Club 10-5557, Commodore CCL 7011,
       Commodore FL 20,010, Commodore FL 30,015, Commodore
       XFL 15354, Commodore (G) 6.24294 AG, Commodore (J)
       GXC 3148, Commodore (J) K23P-6616, Decca London (F)
       180.007, Franklin Mint 91, London (E) HMC 5011, London
       (G) 6.24294 AG, London (J) SLC 452; Mainstream S/6010,
       Mainstream 56010, Mainstream (J) XM-34-MSD, Mosaic
       MR23-123, Stateside (E) SL 10022, World Record Club (Au)
       R-04657
  TX: VOA Jam Session 14
  CD: Commodore CCD 7011
  CT: Book of the Month Club 60-5561, Commodore CCK 7011
  8T: Book of the Month Club 50-5560

A 4681-2 Tin Roof Blues No. 2
  33: >Commodore XFL 15354, Commodore (G) 6.24294 AG,
       Decca London (F) 180.016, London (E) HMC 5007, London
       (G) 6.24294, Mosaic MR23-123

A 4682-1 That Da Da Strain No. 2
  33: >Commodore XFL 15354, Commodore (G) 6.24294 AG,
       Decca London (F) 180.016, London (E) HMC 5011, London
       (G) 6.24294 AG, Mosaic MR23-123

A 4682-2 That Da Da Strain
   78: >Commodore 546
   33: Commodore CCL 7011, Commodore FL 20008, Commodore FL 30015, Commodore XFL 15354, Commodore (G) 6.24294, Commodore (J) GMC 3148, Commodore (J) K23P-6616, Decca London (F) 180.007, Dial (Arg) DPM 9050, Dial (Arg) DPE 10050, London (E) HMV 5007, London (G) 6.24294, London (J) SLC 452, Mainstream S/6024, Mainstream 56024, Mainstream (Arg) DPM 9050, Mainstream (J) XM 34 MSD, Mosaic MR23-123, Stateside (E) SL 10022, World Record Club (Au) R-04657
   TX: VOA Jazz Club USA 11, part 1
   CD: Commodore CCD 7011
   CT: Commodore CCK 7011

NOTE: Produced by Milt Gabler. Recorded at WOR studios, 1440 Broadway. Commodore 45-546 and 45-556 were scheduled for issue but never appeared. Mosaic MR23-123 is a 23-LP boxed set. Takes indicated in the notes of London (E) HMC 5007 and HMC 5011 are in error for "Tin Roof Blues" and "That Da Da Strain."

Eddie Condon And His Band
NYC, December 2, 1943

Max Kaminsky, trumpet; Benny Morton, trombone; Pee Wee Russell, clarinet; Joe Bushkin, piano; Eddie Condon, guitar; Bob Casey, bass; Sidney Catlett, drums.

A 4687-1 Nobody Knows You When You're Down and Out #2
   33: >Mosaic MR23-123

A 4687-2 Nobody Knows You
   78: >Commodore 603
   45: Commodore 45-603, Commodore CEP-33
   33: Ace of Hearts (E) AHC 178, Commodore FL 20,017, Commodore FL 30,010, Commodore (J) GXC 3150, Commodore (J) K23P-6618, Decca (G) ND 476, London (J) SLC 442, London (J) LAX 3305, Mosaic MR23-123, Stateside (E) SL 10010, Top Rank (H) HJA 16507

A 4688-1   Rose Room
    78:   >Commodore 603
    45:   Commodore 45-603, Commodore CEP-32
    33:   Commodore FL 20,017, Commodore FL 30,013, Commodore
          (J) GXC 3150, Commodore (J) K23P-6618, London (J) SLC
          442, London (J) LAX 3309, Melodisc (E) 12-126, Mosaic
          MR23-123

A-4688-2 Rose Room #2
    33:   >Mosaic MR23-123

A 4689-BD Basin Street Blues #2
    33:   >Mosaic MR23-123
A 4689   Basin Street Blues
    78:   >Commodore 1513
    45:   Commodore 45-1513
    33:   Ace of Hearts (E) AHC 178, Book of the Month Club 10-
          5557, Commodore FL 30,006, Commodore (J) GXC 3149,
          Commodore (J) K23P-6617, London (J) SLC 446, London (J)
          LAX 3305, Mainstream S/6024, Mainstream 56024,
          Mainstream (Arg) DPM 9050, MK 1001, Mosaic MR23-123,
          Stateside (E) SL 10005, Top Rank (J) RANK 5033, Top
          Rank (H) HJA 16504
    TX: AFRS DB 328
    CT: Book of the Month Club 60-5561
    8T: Book of the Month Club 50-5560

A 4690-1   Oh Katharina
    78:   >Commodore 1513
    45:   Commodore 45-1513
    33:   Ace of Hearts (E) AHC 178, Commodore FL 30,006,
          Commodore (J) GXC 3149, Commodore (J) K23P-6617,
          London (J) SLC 446, London (J) LAX 3305, Mainstream
          S/6024, Mainstream 56024, Mosaic MR23-123, Stateside (E)
          SL 10005, Top Rank (J) RANK 5033, Top Rank (H) HJA
          16504

A-4690-2 Oh Katharina #2
    33:   >Mosaic MR23-123
 NOTE: Produced by Milt Gabler. Recorded at Brunswick studios,
1776 Broadway. Commodore 1513, a 12-inch disc, issued as Jam
Session At Commodore No. 5. Commodore 603 is included in album
CR-12. Commodore 45-603 and Commodore 45-1513 were scheduled
for issue but never appeared. Mosaic MR23-123 is a 23-LP boxed set.

Wild Bill Davison

Wild Bill Davison, cornet; George Brunies, trombone; Pee Wee Russell, clarinet; Gene Schroeder, piano; Eddie Condon, guitar; Bob Casey, bass; George Wettling, drums.

N 1075-1 Muskrat Ramble
    33: >Jazzology J-103
    CD: Jazzology JCD-103

N 1075-2 Muskrat Ramble
    33: Jazzology J 103
    TX: World Disc 531, >World Feature JS 14, World Program
          Service (Au) Disc 581
    CD: Jazzology JCD-103

N 1076-1 Squeeze Me (false start)
    33: >Jazzology J 103
    CD: Jazzology JCD-103

N 1076-2 Squeeze Me
    33: Jazzology J 103
    TX: World Disc 531, >World Feature JS 14, World Program
          Service (Au) Disc 581
    CD: Jazzology JCD-103

N 1077-1 Royal Garden Blues
    33: >Jazzology J 103
    CD: Jazzology JCD-103

N 1077-2 Royal Garden Blues (incomplete)
    33: >Jazzology J 103
    CD: Jazzology JCD-103

N 1077-3 Royal Garden Blues
    33: >Jazzology J 103
    CD: Jazzology JCD-103

N 1077-4 Royal Garden Blues
    33: >Jazzology J 103
    CD: Jazzology JCD-103

N 1077-5 Royal Garden Blues
    33:   Jazzology J 103
    TX: World Disc 531, >World Feature JS 14, World Program
           Service (Au) Disc 581
    CD: Jazzology JCD-103

N 1078-1 That Da Da Strain
    33:   >Jazzology J 103
    CD: Jazzology JCD-103

N 1078-2 That Da Da Strain
    33:   Jazzology J 103
    TX: World Disc 531, >World Feature JS 14, World Program
           Service (Au) Disc 581
    CD: Jazzology JCD-103

N 1079-1 That's A Plenty
    33:   Jazzology J 103
    TX: World Disc 531, >World Feature JS 14, World Program
           Service (Au) Disc 581
    CD: Jazzology JCD-103

NOTE: Produced by Milt Gabler. World Feature transcriptions were issued in both lateral and vertical cut versions. World studio acetates of this session show "That Da Da Strain" in the wax as "Dhat-Dhat-Dhat Strain." Commodore 45-603 and 45-1513 were scheduled, but probably never issued.

Eddie Condon And His Band

NYC, December 8, 1943

Max Kaminsky, trumpet; Brad Gowans, valide trombone; Pee Wee Russell, clarinet; Joe Bushkin, piano; Eddie Condon, guitar; Bob Casey, bass; Tony Spargo, drums.

A 4695 Pray For The Lights To Go Out #3
    33:   >Mosaic MR23-123

A-4695-1 Pray For The Lights To Go Out #2
    33:   >Mosaic MR23-123

A 4695-2 Pray For The Lights To Go Out
   78:   >Commodore 568
   45:   Commodore 45-568, Commodore CEP 33
   33:   Ace of Hearts (E) AHC 178, Commodore FL 20,017, Commodore FL 30,010, Decca (G) ND 476, London (J) LAX 3307, Mosaic MR23-123, Stateside (E) SL 10010, Top Rank (H) HJA 16507

A 4696-1 Tell 'Em 'Bout Me #2
   33:   >Mosaic MR23-123

A 4696-2 Tell 'Em About Me
   78:   >Commodore 604
   45:   Commodore 45-604, Commodore CEP 33
   33:   Ace of Hearts (E) AHC 178, Commodore FL 20,017, Commodore FL 30,010, Decca (G) ND 476, London (J) LAX 3307, Mosaic MR23-123, Stateside (E) SL 10010, Top Rank (H) HJA 16507

A 4697-1 Mandy, Make Up Your Mind #2
   33:   >Mosaic MR23-123

A 4697-2 Mandy, Make Up Your Mind
   78:   >Commodore 604
   45:   Commodore 45-604, Commodore CEP 32
   33:   Commodore FL 20,017, Commodore FL 30,013, London (J) LAX 3309, Melodisc (E) MLP 12-126, Mosaic MR23-123

A 4698-1 Singin' The Blues
   45:   Commodore 45-568, Commodore CEP-32
   33:   >Commodore FL 20017, Commodore FL 30013, London (J) LAX 3309, Mainstream S/6003, Mainstream 56003, Melodisc (E) MLP 12-126, Mosaic MR23-123

A 4698-2 Singin' The Blues
   78:   >Commodore 568
   33:   Mosaic MR23-123

A 4698 Singin' The Blues #3
   33:   >Mosaic MR23-123

NOTE: Produced by Milt Gabler. Recorded at WOR studios, 1440 Broadway. It is not known which take of A 4698 was used on Melodisc. Commodore 604 is included in Commodore album CR-12. Commodore 45-568 and Commodore 45-604 were scheduled for issue but never appeared. Mosaic MR23-123 is a 23-LP boxed set. Mosaic titles both takes of A-4696 as "Tell 'Em 'Bout Me," but the Commodore issues of A-4696-2 are titled as shown.

Eddie Condon And His Band

NYC, December 11, 1943

Max Kaminsky, trumpet; Lou McGarity, trombone; Pee Wee Russell, clarinet; Gene Schroeder, piano; Eddie Condon, guitar; Bob Casey, bass; George Wettling, drums.

A 4699   Back In Your Own Backyard #3
   33:   >Mosaic MR23-123

A 4699-1   Back In Your Own Backyard #2
   33:   >Mosaic MR23-123

A 4699-2   Back In Your Own Backyard
   78:   >Commodore 551
   45:   Commodore 45-551, Commodore CEP 36
   33:   Commodore FL 20,019, Commodore FL 30,013, Fontana (E) TL 5271, Fontana (H) 687 708TL, London (J) SLC 456, London (J) LAX 3309, Mainstream S/6026, Mainstream 56026, Melodisc (E) MLP 12-126, Mosaic MR23-123

A 4700   All The Wrongs You've Done To Me
   78:   >Commodore 551
   45:   Commodore 45-551, Commodore CEP-37
   33:   Commodore FL 20,019, Commodore FL 30,013, London (J) SLC 456, London (J) LAX 3309, Melodisc (E) MLP 12-126, Mosaic MR23-123

A 4700-1   All The Wrongs You've Done To Me #2
   33:   >Mosaic MR23-123

A 4701   You Can't Cheat A Cheater
   78:   >Commodore 605
   45:   Commodore 45-605, Commodore CEP 32
   33:   Commodore FL 20017, Commodore FL 30013, London (J)
         SLC 456, London (J) LAX 3307, Melodisc (E) MLP 12-126,
         Mosaic MR23-123

A 4701-1 You Can't Cheat A Cheater #2
   33:   >Mosaic MR23-123

A 4702-1 Save Your Sorrow
   78:   >Commodore 605
   45:   Commodore 45-605, Commodore CEP 33
   33:   Ace of Hearts (E) AHC 178, Commodore FL 20017,
         Commodore FL 30010, Decca (G) ND 476, London (J) LAX
         3307, Mainstream S/6024, Mainstream 56024, Mainstream
         (Arg) DPM 9050, Mosaic MR23-123, Stateside (E) SL
         10010, Top Rank (Sd) HJA 16507

A 4702   Save Your Sorrow #2
   33:   >Mosaic MR23-123

NOTE: Produced by Milt Gabler. Recorded at WOR studios, 1440
Broadway.   Commodore 45-551 and Commodore 45-605 were
scheduled for issue but never appeared. Commodore 605 is included in
Commodore album CR-12. Mosaic MR23-123 is a 23-LP boxed set.

*On December 18, 1943, Ernest Anderson produced the first of that
season's Town Hall concerts with Eddie Condon as master of
ceremonies. It was a tribute to Fats Waller who had died a few days
earlier. Anderson and Condon continued the series with concerts on
January 8, February 19, March 11, April 8, April 29 and May 13,
1944. The May 20 concert was broadcast nationally over the Blue
network. The concerts were then held weekly through April 7, 1945.
Pee Wee Russell's contributions to the broadcasts are all documented
below under the appropriate dates. The material listed in the following
session, however, was issued on transcriptions for which the exact
dates remain unknown. They were undoubtedly drawn from the
concerts preceding the first network broadcast, all of which were
recorded by Columbia's transcription service and portions of which
were broadcast locally in New York by WHN.*

Eddie Condon

NYC, c. December, 1943 - May, 1944

Sterling Bose, trumpet; Miff Mole, trombone; Pee Wee Russell, clarinet; unknown piano; Eddie Condon, guitar; unknown bass; possibly Sidney Catlett, drums.

Easter Parade
    TX: >Columbia BRA 2-4327 (Concertos de Musica Popular, Programma No. 11)

Peg O' My Heart
    TX: >Columbia BRA 2-4327 (Concertos de Musica Popular, Programma No. 13)

Art Hodes, piano, replaces unknown.

Sometimes I'm Happy
    TX: >Columbia BRA 2-4327 (Concertos de Musica Popular, Programma No. 12)

Jam On Jazz
    TX: >Columbia BRA 2-4327 (Concertos de Musica Popular, Programma No. 12)

Max Kaminsky, trumpet; Miff Mole, trombone; Pee Wee Russell, clarinet; Joe Bushkin, piano; Eddie Condon, guitar; unknown bass; unknown drums.

The World Is Waiting For The Sunrise
    TX: >VOA NOJ 13-A

Max Kaminsky, trumpet; Benny Morton, trombone; Pee Wee Russell, clarinet; Jess Stacy, piano; Eddie Condon, guitar; unknown bass; George Wettling, drums.

Improvisation ("Cheri")
    TX: >VOA NOJ 16-A

Max Kaminsky, trumpet; Benny Morton, trombone; Pee Wee Russell, clarinet; Ernie Caceres, baritone; Eddie Condon, guitar; Jess Stacy, piano; Bob Casey, bass; George Wettling, drums.

Squeeze Me
    TX: >VOA NOJ 16-A

Max Kaminsky, trumpet; Brad Gowans, valide trombone; Pee Wee Russell, clarinet; unknown piano; unknown bass; possibly Dave Tough, drums.

I Got Rhythm
    TX: VOA NOJ 18-A

NOTE: "Cheri" is Don Redman's "Cherry"; and "Jam on Jazz" is "At the Jazz Band Ball."

Miff Mole And His Dixieland Orchestra
NYC, February 9, 1944

Sterling Bose, trumpet; Miff Mole, trombone; Pee Wee Russell, clarinet; Gene Schroeder, piano; Eddie Condon, guitar; Bob Casey, bass; Joe Grauso, drums.

N 1652-1   Ballin' the Jack (incomplete)
    33: >Jazzology J-105

N 1652-2   Ballin' the Jack (false start)
    33: >Jazzology J-105

N 1652-3   Ballin' the Jack
    33: >Jazzology J-105

N 1652-4 Ballin' the Jack
    78: Brunswick 80105, Brunswick (C) 80105
    33: Brunswick BL 58042, Jazzology J-105
    TX: AFRS MD 19, AFRS MD 29, AFRS MD 95, World Disc 398, >World Feature JS-26

N 1653-1   Peg O' My Heart
    33: Jazzology J 105
    TX: World Audition, >World Feature JS-26

N 1654-1 At the Jazz Band Ball (incomplete)
33: >Jazzology J-105

N 1654-2 At the Jazz Band Ball
33: Jazzology J-105
TX: World Audition, World Disc 391, >World Feature JS-26

N 1655-1 At Sundown
33: Jazzology J-105
TX: World Disc 384, >World Feature JS-25

N 1656-1 How Come You Do Me Like You Do? (false start)
33: >Jazzology J-105

N 1656-2 How Come You Do Me Like You Do? (incomplete)
33: >Jazzology J-105

N 1656-3 How Come You Do Me Like You Do? (false start)
33: >Jazzology J-105

N 1656-4 How Come You Do Me Like You Do?
78: Brunswick 80105, Brunswick (C) 80105
33: Brunswick BL 58042, Jazzology J-105
TX: AFRS MD 24, AFRS MD 81, AFRS MD 96, AFRS MD 115,
      >World Feature JS 26

N 1657-1 (I Would Do) Anything For You (incomplete)
33: >Jazzology J-105

N 1657-2 (I Would Do) Anything For You
33: Brunswick BL 58042, Jazzology J 105
TX: World Disc 398, World Disc R-678, >World Feature JS-25

N 1658-1 I Ain't Gonna Give Nobody None Of This Jelly Role
33: Jazzology J-105
TX: World Audition, World Disc R-678, >World Feature JS-25

N 1659-1 If I Had You (false start)
33: >Jazzology J-105

N 1659-2 If I Had You (false start)
33: >Jazzology J-105

117

N 1659-3   If I Had You
    33:   Jazzology J 105
    TX: World Disc R-678, >World Feature JS-25

N 1660-1   Beale Street Blues (false start)
    33:   >Jazzology J-105

N 1660-2   Beale Street Blues
    33:   Jazzology J 105
    TX: World Disc 391, World Disc R-678, >World Feature JS-25

N 1661-1   Barnyard Blues (false start)
    33:   >Jazzology J-105

N 1661-2   Barnyard Blues
    33:   >Jazzology J-105

N 1661-3   Barnyard Blues
    33:   Jazzology J-105
    TX: World Disc 384, World Disc R-678, >World Feature JS-26

NOTE: Produced by Milt Gabler. World Feature transcriptions were issued in both lateral and vertical cut versions. World JS 25, JS 26, World Audition, World Disc 384, 389 and 398 are 16-inch transcriptions but World Disc R-678 is a standard groove, 12-inch pressing. World Audition has no issue number and contains narration between selections. It lists N 1658-1 as "Ain't Gonna Give Nobody None of My Jelly Roll."

Cliff Jackson Quartet

NYC, March 4, 1944

Pee Wee Russell, clarinet; Cliff Jackson, piano; Bob Casey, bass; Jack "The Bear" Parker, drums.

HS-1206   Quiet Please
    78:   >Black & White 3
    CD: Pickwick PJFD 15001
    CT: Pickwick PJFT 15001

HS-1207   Squeeze Me
    78:   >Black & White 3
    CD: Pickwick PJFD 15001
    CT: Pickwick PJFT 15001

BW-6   If I Could Be With You
  78:    >Black & White 4
  33:    IAJRC IAJRC-28
  CD: Pickwick PJFD 15001
  CT: Pickwick PJFT 15001

BW-7   Weary Blues
  78:    >Black & White 4
  CD: Pickwick PJFD 15001
  CT: Pickwick PJFT 15001
NOTE: Black & White 4 labeled "Cliff Jackson's Black & White
Stompers." BW-7 as "Weary Lonesome Blues" on Pickwick issues.

Eddie Condon

                                                    NYC, March 8, 1944

Hot Lips Page, trumpet, vocal; Sterling Bose, trumpet; Miff Mole,
trombone; Pee Wee Russell, clarinet; Gene Schroeder, piano; Eddie
Condon, guitar; Bob Casey, bass; Joe Grauso, drums.

VP 542 D4TC 89 Uncle Sam Blues (HLP vocal)
  78:    >V-Disc 191
  33:    Fonit Cetra (I) VDL 1018, Foxy (F) 9005, Palm Club (F) 09

Omit Page.

VP 543 D4TC 90 Tin Roof Blues/Ballin' The Jack
  78:    >V-Disc 211
  33:    Fonit Cetra (I) VDL 1018, Ariston (I) 12030, FDC (I) 1020

Peg O' My Heart
  Unissued

Fidgety Feet
  Unissued

Royal Garden Blues
  Unissued

Ain't Gonna Give Nobody None Of My Jelly Roll
  Unissued
NOTE: V-Disc 191 and 211 are 12-inch discs. "Uncle Sam Blues" on
Palm Club (F) 09 as "Uncle Sam Ain't No Woman." The unissued
titles are not known to exist.

119

Eddie Condon

NYC, March 11, 1944

Max Kaminsky, trumpet; Miff Mole, trombone; Pee Wee Russell, clarinet; Cliff Jackson, piano; Eddie Condon, guitar; Pops Foster, bass; George Wettling, drums.

Darktown Strutters' Ball
    TX: >Columbia BRA 2-4327 (Concertos de Musica Popular, Programma No. 8)
    CD: Jass J-CD-634

Dear Old Southland
    TX: >Columbia BRA 2-4327 (Concertos de Musica Popular, Programma No. 14)
    CD: Jass J-CD-634

Add Bobby Hackett, cornet.

Ja Da
    CD: >Jass J-CD-634

Muskrat Ramble
    TX: >Columbia BRA 2-4327 (Concertos de Musica Popular, Programma No. 10)
    CD: Jass J-CD-634

Hot Lips Page, trumpet, vocal; Max Kaminsky, Billy Butterfield, trumpet; Bobby Hackett, cornet; Miff Mole, trombone; Pee Wee Russell, Ed Hall, clarinet; Cliff Jackson, Joe Bushkin, piano; Pops Foster, bass; George Wettling, drums.

El Tio Sam No Es Una Muchacha; pero te puede quitar el novio (HLP, vocal)
    33: Foxy (F) 9005, Palm Club (F) 09
    TX: >Columbia BRA 2-4327 (Concertos de Musica Popular, Programma No. 9)
    CD: Jass J-CD-634

Impromptu Ensemble
    CD: >Jass J-CD-634

120

NOTE: "El Tio..." is titled "Uncle Sam Ain't No Woman" on Foxy and Palm Club, and as "Uncle Sam Blues" on Jass. Columbia BRA 2-4327 has Portuguese announcements dubbed in. This concert from Town Hall, 123 West 43rd Street, was not part of the Blue network series listed below; however, a portion of the concert was broadcast on WHN in New York City.

Eddie Condon

March 12, 1944

Wild Bill Davison, cornet; George Lugg, trombone; Ed Hall, Pee Wee Russell, clarinet; James P. Johnson, piano; Eddie Condon, guitar; Pops Foster, bass; Kansas Fields, drums, Jimmy Rushing, vocal.

Blues (J.R., vocal)
    33:   >Aircheck 31

I Ain't Gonna Give Nobody None Of My Jelly Roll #1
    33:   >Aircheck 31

I Ain't Gonna Give Nobody None Of My Jelly Roll #2
    33:   >Aircheck 31

Joe Bushkin, piano, replaces James P. Johnson.

Honeysuckle Rose (false start)
    Unissued
Honeysuckle Rose
    33:   Aircheck 31, >IAJRC 28

NOTE: Recorded at Liederkrantz Hall, supervised by Morty Palitz for V-Disc. It has been reported that "Baby, Won't You Please Come Home," "Someday Sweetheart" and "Old Fashioned Love" were also recorded at this session.

Eddie Condon

NYC, March 30, 1944

Max Kaminsky, trumpet; Wilbur De Paris, trombone; Pee Wee Russell, clarinet; Joe Bushkin, piano; Eddie Condon, guitar; Bob Casey, bass; George Wettling, drums; Red McKenzie, vocal.

N 2023-1 Save Your Sorrow (false start)
    33:   >Jazzology J 101

N 2023-2 Save Your Sorrow (false start)
    33: >Jazzology J 101
N 2023-3 Save Your Sorrow
    33: Jazum 77, Jazzology J 101
    TX: >World Feature JS-12

N 2024-1 Rose Room
    33: >Jazzology J 101

N 2024-2 Rose Room
    33: >Jazzology J 101

N 2024-3 Rose Room (false start)
    33: >Jazzology J 102

N 2024-4 Rose Room
    33: Jazum 77, Jazzology J 102
    TX: World Disc 358, >World Feature JS-12

N 2025-1 Back In Your Own Backyard (RMcK vocal)
    33: >Jazzology J 101

N 2025-2 Back In Your Own Backyard (RMcK vocal)
    33: >Jazzology J 101

N 2025-3 Back In Your Own Backyard (RMcK vocal) (false start)
    33: >Jazzology J 102

N 2025-4 Back In Your Own Backyard (RMcK vocal)
    33: Jazum 77, Jazzology J 102
    TX: World Disc 358, >World Feature JS-12

N 2026-1 Darktown Strutters' Ball (RMcK vocal) (incomplete take)
    33: >Jazzology J 101

N 2026-2 Darktown Strutters' Ball (RMcK vocal)
    33: >Jazzology J 101

N 2026-3 Darktown Strutters' Ball (RMcK vocal) (false start)
    33: >Jazzology J 102

N 2026-4 Darktown Strutters' Ball (RMcK vocal)
    33: Jazum 78, Jazzology J 102
    TX: World Disc R-564, >World Feature JS-13

N 2027-1 Everybody Loves My Baby (false start)
    33:   >Jazzology J 101

N 2027-2 Everybody Loves My Baby
    33:   >Jazzology J 101

N 2027-3 Everybody Loves My Baby (false start)
    33:   >Jazzology J 101

N 2027-4 Everybody Loves My Baby (incomplete take)
    33:   >Jazzology J 101

N 2027-5 Everybody Loves My Baby (incomplete take)
    33:   >Jazzology J 101

N 2027-6 Everybody Loves My Baby
    33:   Jazum 78, Jazzology J 101
    TX: World Disc 398, World Disc R-564, >World Feature JS-13

N 2028-1 Of All The Wrongs You've Done To Me
    33:   >Jazzology J 101

N 2028-2 Of All The Wrongs You've Done To Me (incomplete take)
33:   >Jazzology J 102

N 2028-3 Of All The Wrongs You've Done To Me
    33:   Jazum 78, Jazzology J 102
    TX: World Disc R-564, >World Feature JS-13

N 2029-1 Mandy
    33:   Jazum 78, Jazzology J 102
    TX: World Disc R-564, >World Feature JS-13

N 2030-1 Blues For Pee Wee
    33:   Jazum 77, Jazzology J 102
    TX: World Disc R-564, >World Feature JS-13

NOTE: Produced by Milt Gabler. World Feature transcriptions were issued in both lateral and vertical cut versions. World Feature JS 12, World Feature JS 13, World Disc 358 and World Disc 398 are 16-inch transcriptions but World Disc R-564 is a standard 12-inch microgroove issue. Jazzology J 101/102 is a two record set.

Muggsy Spanier's Sheridan Squares

NYC, April 4, 1944

Muggsy Spanier, cornet; Pee Wee Russell, clarinet; Ernie Caceres, baritone; Dick Cary, piano; Eddie Condon, guitar; Bob Casey or Sid Weiss, bass; Joe Grauso, drums.

N 2156- Sugar
   TX: >World Feature JS-31

N 2157- Oh! Lady Be Good
   TX: >World Feature JS-31

N 2158- Sweet Lorraine
   TX: World Disc R-530, >World Feature JS-30

N-2159- September In The Rain
   TX: >World Feature JS-30

N 2160- I Wish I Could Shimmy Like My Sister Kate
   TX: >World Feature JS-30

NOTE: Produced by Milt Gabler. World Feature transcriptions were issued in both lateral and vertical cut versions. World JS-30 and JS-31 are 16-inch transcriptions but World Disc R-530 is a standard 12-inch LP.

Muggsy Spanier And His Ragtimers

NYC, April 15, 1944

Muggsy Spanier, cornet; Miff Mole, trombone; Pee Wee Russell, clarinet; Dick Cary, piano; Eddie Condon, guitar; Bob Casey, bass; Joe Grauso, drums.

A 4762-TK1 Angry #3
   33: >Mosaic MR23-128

A 4762-1 Angry No. 2
   33: >Commodore XFL 15777, Commodore (G) 6.25494 AG, London (G) 6.25494, Mosaic MR23-128

A 4762-2 Angry
   78:   >Commodore 616
   45:   Commodore 45-616, Commodore CEP 19
   33:   Commodore CCL 7009, Commodore FL 20,009,
         Commodore FL 30,016, Commodore XFL 15777,
         Commodore (G) 6.25494 AG, Fontana (E) FL 5271, Fontana
         (H) 687 708TL, Jazztone J-1216, London (E) HMC 5025,
         London (G) 6.25494, London (J) LAX 3311, Mainstream
         S/6026, Mainstream 56026, Mainstream (J) XM 33 MSD,
         Mosaic MR23-128, Stateside (E) SL 10004
   TX: AFRS MD40, AFRS TBC 953
   CD: Commodore CCD 7009
   CT: Commodore CCK 7009

A 4763-TK1 Weary Blues No. 2
   33:   >Commodore XFL 15777, Commodore (G) 6.25494 AG,
         London (G) 6.25494, Mosaic MR23-128

A 4763-1 Weary Blues
   78:   >Commodore 625
   45:   Commodore 45-625, Commodore CEP 24
   33:   Book of the Month Club 10-5557, Commodore CCL 7009,
         Commodore FL 20012, Commodore XFL 15777,
         Commodore (G) 6.25494 AG, Commodore (J) GXC 3154,
         Commodore (J) K23P-6622, London (E) HMC 5025, London
         (G) 6.25494, London (J) SLC 451, Mosaic MR23-128
   CD: Commodore CCD 7009
   CT: Book of the Month Club 60-5561, Commodore CCK 7009
   8T: Book of the Month Club 50-5560

A 4764-TK1 Snag It #3
   33:   >Mosaic MR23-128

A 4764-1 Snag It No. 2
   33:   >Commodore XFL 15777, Commodore (G) 6.25494 AG,
         London (G) 6.25494, Mosaic MR23-128

A 4764-2 Snag It
    78:   >Commodore 616
    45:   Commodore 45-616, Commodore CEP 19
    33:   Commodore 7000, Commodore CCL 7009, Commodore FL 20,009, Commodore FL 30,016, Commodore XFL 15777, Commodore (G) 6.25494 AG, Commodore (J) GXC 3148, Commodore (J) K23P-6616, Fontana (E) FL 5271, Fontana (H) 687 708TL, Jazztone J-1216, London (E) HMC 5025, London (G) 6.25494, London (J) LAX 3311, Mainstream S/6026, Mainstream 56026, Mosaic MR23-128, Stateside (E) SL 10004
    CD: Commodore CCD 7000, Commodore CCK 7009
    CT: Commodore 7000, Commodore 7009

A 4765-1 Alice Blue Gown
    78:   >Commodore 625
    45:   Commodore 45-625, Commodore CEP 25
    33:   Commodore CCL 7009, Commodore FL 20,012, Commodore XFL 15777, Commodore (G) 6.25494 AG, Commodore (J) GXC 3154, Commodore (J) K23P-6622, London (E) HMC 5025, London (G) 6.25494, London (J) SLC 451, Mosaic MR23-128
    CD: Commodore CCD 7009
    CT: Commodore CCK 7009

A 4765-2 Alice Blue Gown #3
    33:   >Mosaic MR23-128

A 4765-3 Alice Blue Gown No. 2
    33:   >Commodore XFL 15777, Commodore (G) 6.25494 AG, London (G) 6.25494, Mosaic MR23-128

NOTE: Produced by Milt Gabler. Recorded at WOR studios, 1440 Broadway. Commodore 45-616 and 45-625 were scheduled for issue but never appeared.

Muggsy Spanier And His Ragtimers

NYC, April 22, 1944

Muggsy Spanier, cornet; Ernie Caceres, baritone; Pee Wee Russell, clarinet; Dick Cary, piano; Eddie Condon, guitar; Sid Weiss, bass; Joe Grauso, drums.

A 4766-TK1 Sweet Lorraine No. 2
    33:   >Commodore XFL 15777, Commodore (G) 6.25494 AG, London (G) 6.25494, Mosaic MR23-128

A 4766-1 Sweet Lorraine
    78:   >Commodore 1517
    45:   Commodore 45-1517, Commodore CEP 18
    33:   Commodore FL 20,009, Commodore FL 30,016, Commodore XFL 15777, Commodore (G) 6.25494 AG, Dial (Arg) DPM 9053, London (E) HMC 5025, London (G) 6.25494, London (J) LAX 3311, Mainstream S/6011, Mainstream 56011, Mainstream (Arg) DPM 9053, Mainstream (J) PS 1307, Mosaic MR23-128, Stateside (E) SL 10004, Vogue (F) INT 40026
    TX: AFRS MD 35, AFRS MD 102, AFRS MD 119

A 4767-TK1 Oh, Lady Be Good #3
    33:   >Mosaic MR23-128

A 4767-1 Oh, Lady Be Good
    78   >Commodore 629
    45   Commodore 45-629, Commodore CEP 25
    33   Commodore FL 20,012, Commodore FL 30,016, Commodore XFL 15777, Commodore (G) 6.25494 AG, Giants of Jazz (E) LPJT 16, London (E) HMC 5025, London (G) 6.25494, London (J) LAX 3311, Mainstream S/6024, Mainstream 56024, Mainstream (Arg) DPM 9050, Mainstream (J) XM 34 MSD, Mosaic MR23-128, Stateside (E) SL 10004

A 4767-2 Oh, Lady Be Good No. 2
    33   >Commodore XFL 15777, Commodore (G) 6.25494 AG, London (G) 6.25494, Mosaic MR23-128

A 4768-TK1 Sugar No. 2
    33   >Commodore XFL 15777, Commodore (G) 6.25494 AG, London (G) 6.25494, Mosaic MR23-128

A 4768-1 Sugar
  78:   >Commodore 629
  45:   Commodore 45-629, Commodore CEP 24
  33:   Commodore FL 20,012, Commodore FL 30,016, Commodore
        XFL 15777, Commodore (G) 6.25494 AG, Dial (Arg) DPM
        9053, London (E) HMC 5025, London (G) 6.25494, London
        (J) LAX 3311, Mainstream S/6011, Mainstream 56011,
        Mainstream (Arg) DPM 9053, Mainstream (J) PS 1307,
        Mosaic MR23-128, Stateside (E) SL 10004, Vogue (F) INT
        40026

A 4769-1 September In The Rain
  78:   >Commodore 1517
  45:   Commodore 45-1517, Commodore CEP 19
  33:   Commodore FL 20,009, Commodore FL 30,016, Commodore
        XFL 15777, Commodore (G) 6.25494 AG, London (E) HMC
        5025, London (G) 6.25494, London (J) LAX 3311, Mosaic
        MR23-128, Stateside (E) SL 10004
  TX: AFRS MD 39, AFRS MD 80, AFRS MD 84

A 4769-2 September In The Rain #2
  33:   >Mosaic MR23-128

NOTE: Produced by Milt Gabler. Recorded at WOR studios, 1440
Broadway. Commodore 1517 is a 12-inch disc. Commodore 45-629
and 45-1517 were scheduled for issue but never appeared.

Miff Mole And His Nicksieland Band
                                                    NYC, April 28, 1944

Bobby Hackett, cornet; Miff Mole, trombone; Pee Wee Russell,
clarinet; Ernie Caceres, baritone; Gene Schroeder, piano; Eddie
Condon, guitar; Bob Casey, bass; Joe Grauso, drums.

A 4770-TK1 St. Louis Blues No. 2
  33:   >Commodore (G) 6.26171 AG, Mosaic MR23-128

A 4770-1 St. Louis Blues
   78:   >Commodore 1518
   45:   Commodore CEP-20, Commodore 45-1518
   33:   Commodore CCL 7009, Commodore FL 20,010, Commodore (G) 6.26171 AG, Commodore (J) GXC 3148, Commodore (J) K23P-6616, London (E) HMC 5007, London (G) 6.26171, London (J) SLC 452, Mosaic MR23-128
  TX: AFRS DB 351, AFRS DB 424
  CD: Commodore CCD 7009
  CT: Commodore CCK 7009

A 4771-TK1 Peg O' My Heart #2
   33:   >Mosaic MR23-128

A 4771-1 Peg O' My Heart
   78:   >Commodore 1518
   45:   Commodore CEP-20, Commodore 45-1518
   33:   Commodore CCL 7009, Commodore FL 20,010, Commodore (G) 6.26171 AG, Commodore (J) GXC 3148, Commodore (J) K23P-6616, London (E) HMC 5007, London (G) 6.26171, London (J) SLC 452, Mosaic MR23-128
  TX: AFRS DB 350, AFRS DB 423, AFRS MD 61, AFRS MD 74
  CD: Commodore CCD 7009
  CT: Commodore CCK 7009

A 4772-TK1 Beale Street Blues #2
   33:   >Mosaic MR23-128

A 4772-1 Beale Street Blues
   78:   >Commodore 620
   45:   Commodore CEP-21, Commodore CEP-31, Commodore 45-620
   33:   Commodore CCL 7009, Commodore FL 20,010, Commodore FL 20,016, Commodore (G) 6.26171 AG, London (E) HMC 5007, London (G) 6.26171, London (J) SLC 442, Mosaic MR23-128
  CD: Commodore CCD 7009
  CT: Commodore CCK 7009

A 4773-BD I Must Have That Man No. 2 (breakdown)
   33:   >Commodore (G) 6.26171 AG, London (G) 6.26171, Mosaic MR23-128

A 4773-1 I Must Have That Man
- 78: >Commodore 620
- 45: Commodore CEP-21, Commodore CEP-31, Commodore 45-620
- 33: Commodore CCL 7009, Commodore FL 20,010, Commodore FL 20,016, Commodore (G) 6.26171 AG, Commodore (J) GXC 3154, Commodore (J) K23P-6622, Franklin Mint 48, London (E) HMC 5007, London (G) 6.26171, London (J) SLC 451, Mainstream S/6017, Mainstream 56017, Mainstream (Arg) DPM 9048, Mosaic MR23-128, Vogue (F) INT 40025
- TX: AFRS MD 106
- CD: Commodore CCD 7009
- CT: Commodore CCK 7009

NOTE: Produced by Milt Gabler. Recorded at WOR studios, 1440 Broadway. Commodore 1518 is a 12-inch disc. Commodore FL 20,016 issued as Bobby Hackett and his Orchestra. Commodore 45-1518 and 45-620 were scheduled to be issued but never appeared.

Eddie Condon

NYC, probably May, 1944

Max Kaminsky, trumpet; Miff Mole, trombone; Pee Wee Russell, clarinet; Ernie Caceres, baritone; Jess Stacy, piano; unknown bass and drums; Lee Wiley, vocal.

Easter Parade
- 33: Jazum 66
- TX: >World Chesterfield Audition #1

Old Folks (LW vocal)
- TX: >World Chesterfield Audition #1

On the Sunny Side Of The Street
- TX: >World Chesterfield Audition #1

On the Sunny Side Of The Street
- TX: >World Chesterfield Audition #1

'S Wonderful
- 33: Jazum 66
- TX: >World Chesterfield Audition #2

Jess Stacy, arranger.

Someone To Watch Over Me (LW vocal)
   TX: >World Chesterfield Audition #2

Somebody Loves Me (LW vocal)
   33:   Jazum 66
   TX: >World Chesterfield Audition #2

Somebody Loves Me (reprise)
   33:   Jazum 66
   TX: >World Chesterfield Audition #2

NOTE: The Chesterfield Audition discs are 16-inch transcriptions and were recorded to demonstrate the format of the show to a potential sponsor of the Blue network broadcasts of the Eddie Condon concerts from Town Hall. "Easter Parade" and "'S Wonderful" were reissued on another Chesterfield Audition disc that combined selections from the two programs. Fred Robbins is the announcer.

Eddie Condon

NYC, May 20, 1944

Max Kaminsky, trumpet; Miff Mole, trombone; Pee Wee Russell, clarinet; Gene Schroeder, piano; Bob Casey, bass; Joe Grauso, drums.

Sweet Georgia Brown
   33: >Jazzology JCE 1001
   CD: >Jazzology JCECD 1001

Add Billy Butterfield, trumpet

Wherever There's Love
   33: >Jazzology JCE 1001
   CD: >Jazzology JCECD 1001

Peg O' My Heart
   33: >Jazzology JCE 1001
   CD: >Jazzology JCECD 1001

Add Hot Lips Page, trumpet and vocal, omit Butterfield

Uncle Sam Blues (HLP, vocal)
    33: >Jazzology JCE 1001
    CD: >Jazzology JCECD 1001

Bobby Hackett, cornet and arranger; Pee Wee Russell, clarinet; Gene Schroeder, piano; Bob Casey, bass; Joe Grauso, drums; Liza Morrow, vocal.

Someone To Watch Over Me (LM, vocal)
    33: >Jazzology JCE 1001
    CD: >Jazzology JCECD 1001

Max Kaminsky, Bobby Hackett, Billy Butterfield, possibly Hot Lips Page, trumpets; Miff Mole, trombone; Pee Wee Russell, clarinet; Gene Schroeder, James P. Johnson, piano; Bob Casey, bass; Joe Grauso, drums.

Impromptu Ensemble
    33: >Jazzology JCE 1001
    CD: >Jazzology JCECD 1001

NOTE: Other titles from this broadcast do not include Pee Wee Russell. This was the first in the series of Eddie Condon concerts to be broadcast by the Blue network from Town Hall, 3:30 to 4 P.M., and produced by Ernest Anderson. The Jazzology issues contain the complete program, including narration, as broadcast by the Blue network.

Eddie Condon
NYC, May 27, 1944

Max Kaminsky, trumpet; Miff Mole, trombone; Pee Wee Russell, clarinet; Ernie Caceres, baritone sax; Gene Schroeder, piano; John Kirby, bass; Sonny Greer, drums.

At The Jazz Band Ball
    33: Baybridge (J) UPS 2255, Baybridge (J) UXP 126, Jazum 4,
          Jazum 10, Jazzology JCE 1001, Kings of Jazz (I) KLJ 20018
    TX: >AFRS EC1, AFRS EC 5, AFRS EC 6, AFRS EC 12
    CD: Baybridge (J) 30CP-136, Jazzology JCECD 1001

Add Bobby Hackett, cornet, arranger

I Must Have That Man
    33:    Baybridge (J) UPS 2255, Good Music JRR-3, Jazum 4,
           Jazzology JCE 1001, Kings of Jazz (I) KLJ 20018
    TX: >AFRS EC 1
    CD: Jazzology JCECD 1001

Bobby Hackett, cornet; Hot Lips Page, trumpet, vocal; Max Kaminsky,
trumpet; Miff Mole, trombone; Pee Wee Russell, clarinet; Ernie
Caceres, baritone; Gene Schroeder, piano; John Kirby, bass; Sonny
Greer, drums.

The Sheik Of Araby (HLP vocal)
    33:    Baybridge (J) UXP 126, Baybridge (J) UPS 2255, Foxy (F)
           9007, Good Music JRR-3, Jazum 4, Jazzology JCE 1001,
           Kings of Jazz (I) KLJ 20018
    TX: >AFRS EC 1
    CD: Baybridge (J) 30CP-136, Jazzology JCECD 1001

Bobby Hackett, cornet; possibly Max Kaminsky, trumpet; Miff Mole,
trombone; Pee Wee Russell, clarinet; Ernie Caceres, baritone; Gene
Schroeder, piano; John Kirby, bass; Sonny Greer, drums.

Time On My Hands
    33:    Baybridge (J) UPS 2255, Jazum 4, Jazzlogy JCE 1001, Kings
           of Jazz (I) KLJ 20018
    TX: >AFRS EC 1, AFRS EC 25, AFRS EC 47
    CD: Jazzology JCECD 1001

Bobby Hackett, Rex Stewart, cornets, Max Kaminsky, Hot Lips Page,
trumpet; Miff Mole, trombone; Pee Wee Russell, clarinet; Ernie
Caceres, baritone; Gene Schroeder, piano; John Kirby, bass; Sonny
Greer, drums.

Impromptu Ensemble
    33:    Baybridge (J) UPS 2255, Foxy (F) 9007, Good Music JRR-
           3, Jazum 4, Jazzology JCE 1001, Kings of Jazz (I) KLJ
           20018,
    TX: >AFRS EC 1
    CD: Jazzology JCECD 1001

NOTE: Produced by Ernest Anderson. Blue network broadcast #2 from Town Hall. Other selections from this concert do not include Pee Wee Russell. "Impromptu Ensemble" titled "Ole Miss" on Foxy 9007. The Jazzology issues contain the complete program, including narration, as broadcast by the Blue network, 3:30 to 4 P.M.

Eddie Condon

NYC, June 3, 1944

Max Kaminsky, trumpet, Benny Morton, trombone, Pee Wee Russell, clarinet; Ernie Caceres, baritone; Gene Schroeder, piano; Eddie Condon, guitar; Bob Casey, bass; Joe Grauso, drums.

Ballin' The Jack
    33:   Jazum 4, Jazzology JCE 1002, Kings of Jazz (I) KLJ 20018
    TX: >AFRS EC 1
    CD: Jazzology JCECD 1002

Bobby Hackett, cornet; Hot Lips Page, trumpet, vocal; Pee Wee Russell, clarinet; Ernie Caceres, baritone; Gene Schroeder, piano; Bob Casey, bass; Joe Grauso, drums.

Whatcha Doin' After The War (HLP, vocal)
    33:   Jazum 10, Jazzology JCE 1002
    TX: >AFRS EC 4
    CD: Jazzology JCECD 1002

Bobby Hackett, cornet; Billy Butterfield, trumpet; Benny Morton, trombone; Pee Wee Russell, clarinet; Ernie Caceres, baritone; Gene Schroeder, piano; Eddie Condon, guitar; Bob Casey, bass; Joe Grauso, drums.

What's New
    33:   Jazum 10, Jazzology JCE 1002
    TX: >AFRS EC 5
    CD: Jazzology JCECD 1002

The One I Love Belongs To Somebody Else (LM vocal)
    33:   >Jazzology JCE 1002
    CD: >Jazzology JCECD 1002

Bobby Hackett, cornet; Billy Butterfield, Max Kaminsky, Hot Lips Page, trumpet; Benny Morton, trombone; Ernie Caceres, Ed Hall, Pee Wee Russell, clarinet; Gene Schroeder, piano; Eddie Condon, guitar; Bob Casey, bass; Joe Grauso, drums.

Impromptu Ensemble
    33:   >Jazzology JCE 1002
    CD: >Jazzology JCECD 1002

NOTE: Produced by Ernest Anderson. This concert was presented at Town Hall. The Jazzology issues contain the complete program, including narration, as broadcast by the Blue network, 3:30 to 4 P.M.

Eddie Condon and His Orchestra
NYC, June 8, 1944

Bobby Hackett, cornet; Pee Wee Russell, clarinet; Ernie Caceres, baritone; Gene Schroeder, piano; Bob Haggart, bass; Joe Grauso, drums.

zz-3905-1 Ballin' The Jack
    33:   Allegro (E) ALL 791, Design DLP-47, Design DLP 148, Design SDLP 148, DJM DJML 065, Everest FS 274, Everest 924730, Gala GLP 342, Jazz Bird (I) JAZ 2012, Jazz Club (F) 1652.371025, Murray Hill S 53968/5, Music For Pleasure (E) 165.237, Olympic OL-7122, Pickwick PR 111, SP 47, Trip TLP 5800, Vogue DP 35
    TX: >Associated A 60,598
    CD: Pickwick PJFD 15000, Stash ST-CD-530
    CT: Everest FS-274, Pickwick PJFT 15000

zz-3905-2 That's A Plenty
    33:   Allegro (E) ALL 791, Design DLP-47, Design DLP 148, Design SDLP 148, DJM DJML 065, Everest FS 274, Everest 924730, Gala GLP 342, Jazz Bird (I) JAZ-2012, Jazz Club (F) 1652.371, Murray Hill S 53968/5, Music For Pleasure (E) 165.237, Olympic OL-7122, Pickwick PR 111, Trip TLP 5800, Vogue DP 35
    TX: >Associated A 60,598
    CD: Pickwick PJFJ 15000, Stash ST-CD-530
    CT: Everest FS-274, Pickwick PJFT 15000

Billy Butterfield, trumpet, replaces Hackett, cornet.

zz-3905-3   Cherry
    CD: >Stash ST-CD-530

zz-3905-4   Cherry (breakdown)
    CD: >Stash ST-CD-530

zz-3905-5   Cherry
    33:   Design DLP-47, DJM DJML 065, Everest FS 274, Everest
           924730, Gala GLP 342, Jazz Bird (I) JAZ-2012, Jazz Club
           (F) 1652.371, Murray Hill S 53968/5, Music for Pleasure
           165.237, Olympic OL-7122, Trip TLP 5800, Vogue DP 35
    TX: AFRS BML P-369, >Associated A 60,598
    CD: Stash ST-CD-530
    CT: Everest FS-274

Bobby Hackett, cornet, replaces Butterfield, trumpet.

zz-3906-1   Sweet Georgia Brown
    33:   Design DLP-47, DJM DJML 065, DGR (H) DGR2004,
           Everest 1001/5, Gala GLP 342, Jazz Bird (I) JAZ-2012,
           Olympic OL-7122, Trip TLP 5800, Vogue DP 35
    TX: AFRS BML P-368, >Associated A 60,598
    CD: Stash ST-CD-530

zz-3906-2   At The Jazz Band Ball
    TX: >Associated A 60,802, Muzak M-2425
    CD: Stash ST-CD-530

Add Hot Lips Page, trumpet, vocal; possibly Billy Butterfield, trumpet;
Eddie Condon, guitar.

zz-3906-3   When My Sugar Walks Down The Street (HLP vocal)
    CD: >Stash ST-CD-530

zz-3906-4   When My Sugar Walks Down The Street (HLP vocal)
    33:   DJM DJML 065, Jazz Bird (I) JAZ-2012, Murray Hill S
           53968/5, Olympic OL-7122, Trip TLP 5800
    TX: AFRS BML P-369, >Associated A 60,598
    CD: Stash ST-CD-530

Add Benny Morton, trombone.

zz-3906-5 Uncle Sam Blues (HLP vocal)
   CD: >Stash ST-CD-530

zz-3907-1 Uncle Sam Blues (HLP vocal)
   33: DJM DJML 065, Jazz Bird (I) JAZ-2012, Foxy (F) 9007,
        Olympic OL-7122, Trip TLP 5800
   TX: AFRS BML P-368, >Associated A 60,598
   CD: Stash ST-CD-530, VJC 1036

Bobby Hackett, cornet; possibly Billy Butterfield, trumpet; possibly
Pee Wee Russell, clarinet; Ernie Caceres, baritone; Gene Schroeder,
piano; Eddie Condon, guitar; Bob Haggart, bass; Joe Grauso, drums;
Liza Morrow, vocal.

zz-3907-2 Someone To Watch Over Me (LM vocal)
   33: DJM DJML 065, Jazz Bird (I) JAZ-2012, Olympic OL-7122,
        Trip TLP 5800
   TX: >Associated A 60,598
   CD: Stash ST-CD-530

zz-3907-3 The One I Love Belongs To Somebody Else (LM, vocal)
   33: DJM DJML 065, Jazz Bird (I) JAZ-2012, Olympic OL-7122,
        Trip TLP 5800, Vogue DP 35
   TX: AFRS Just Jazz, >Associated A 60,598
   CD: Stash ST-CD-530

Possibly Bobby Hackett, cornet; Billy Butterfield, trumpet; Benny
Morton, trombone; Pee Wee Russell, clarinet; Ernie Caceres, baritone;
Gene Schroeder, piano; Eddie Condon, guitar; Bob Haggart, bass; Joe
Grauso, drums.

zz-3907-4 Wherever There's Love
   33: Allegro (E) ALL 791, Design DLP-47, Design DLP 148,
        Design SDLP 148, DJM DJML-065, Everest FS 274, Everest
        924730, Gala GLP 342, Jazz Club (F) 1652.371, Music for
        Pleasure 165.237, Murry Hill S-53968/5, Olympic OL-7122,
        Pickwick PR 111, Trip TLP 5800, Vogue (F) DP-35
   TX: AFRS BML P-397, >Associated A 60,645, Associated A
        61,105
   CD: Stash ST-CD-530
   CT: Everest FS-274

137

Bobby Hackett, cornet; Billy Butterfield, trumpet; possibly Benny Morton, trombone; Pee Wee Russell, clarinet; Ernie Caceres, baritone; Gene Schroeder, piano; Eddie Condon, guitar, Bob Haggart, bass; Joe Grauso, drums.

zz-3908-1   What's New (breakdown)
   CD: >Stash ST-CD-530

zz-3908-2 What's New
   33:   Design DLP 47, Palm 30 (E) P.30:08
   TX: >Associated A 60,634, Associated A 61,018, Associated A 61,246
   CD: Stash ST-CD-530

zz-3908-3 Ja-Da
   CD: >Stash ST-CD-530

zz-3908-4 Ja-Da
   33:   Design DLP-47, Everest FS 274, Everest 924730, Gala GLP 342, Jazz Club (F) 1652.371, Murray Hill S53968/5
   TX: AFRS BML P-397, >Associated A 60,645, Associated A 61,105
   CD: Pickwick PJFD 15000, Stash ST-CD-530
   CT: Everest FS-274, Murray Hill C55175/5, Pickwick PJFT 15000

zz-3909-1 Time On My Hands (breakdown)
   CD: >Stash ST-CD-530

zz-3909-2 Time On My Hands (breakdown)
   Unissued

zz-3909-3 Time On My Hands
   33:   Palm 30 (E) P.30:08
   TX: >Associated A 60,635, Associated A 61,105
   CD: Stash ST-CD-530

zz-3909-4   Royal Garden Blues
   78:   Wax Shop 105
   33:   Allegro (E) ALL 79l, Design DLP-47, Design DLP 148,
         Design SDLP 148, Design DLP-213, Everest FS 274, Everest
         924730, Gala GLP 342, Jazz Club (F) 1652.371, Murray Hill
         S53968/5, Music for Pleasure 165.237, Pickwick PR 111
   TX: AFRS BML P-397, >Associated A 60,645, Associated A
         61,105
   CD: Stash ST-CD-530

Add Hot Lips Page, trumpet.

zz-3909-5   Muskrat Ramble
   TX: AFRS BML P-397, >Associated A 60,645, Associated A
         61,105
   CD: Stash ST-CD-530

NOTE: This session was recorded from 4:30 to 7:30 p.m. Matrix
numbers listed are from the original studio acetates of this session. The
titles grouped under each matrix number are as they appear on the
acetates, with several performances being recorded on one side of the
16-inch, 33 1/3 discs. The matrix numbers on the issued Associated
transcriptions, all 16-inch discs, do not correspond in all cases since
they were dubbed from the acetates. Muzak M-2425 is a standard 12-
inch disc. Wax Shop 105 is credited to "Eddie's Hot Shots."

Eddie Condon

                                                    NYC, June 10, 1944

Max Kaminsky, trumpet; Bill Harris, valve trombone; Pee Wee Russell,
clarinet; Ernie Caceres, baritone; Clyde Hart, piano; Eddie Condon,
guitar; Bob Haggart, bass; Joe Grauso, drums.

Muskrat Ramble
   33:   Baybridge (J) UPS 2255, Jazum 25, Jazum 72, Jazzology JCE
         1002
   TX: >AFRS EC 2, AFRS EC 13, AFRS EC 14
   CD: Jazzology JCECD 1002

Mean To Me
   33:   Baybridge (J) UPS 2255, Jazum 72, Jazzology JCE 1002
   TX: >AFRS EC 2
   CD: Jazzology JCECD 1002

Hot Lips Page, trumpet, vocal, added.

When My Sugar Walks Down The Street (HLP, vocal)
> 33: Baybridge (J) UPS 2255, Chiaroscuro CR 113, Foxy (F)
> 9007, Jazzology JCE 1002, Overseas (J) ULX-54-V
> TX: >AFRS EC 2
> CD: Jazzology JCECD 1002

Omit Page.

Body And Soul
> 33: Baybridge (J) UPS 2255, Jazum 72, Jazzology JCE 1002
> TX: >AFRS EC 2
> CD: Jazzology JCECD 1002

Bobby Hackett, cornet and arranger, added.

Ja Da
> 33: Baybridge (J) UXP 126, Baybridge (J) UPS 2255, Jazum 72,
> Jazzology JCE 1002
> TX: >AFRS EC 2, AFRS EC 25
> CD: Baybridge (J) 30CP-136, Jazzology JCECD 1002

Omit Hackett, cornet.

Back In Your Own Backyard
> 33: Baybridge (J) UPS 2255, Jazum 72, Jazzology JCE 1002
> TX: >AFRS EC 2, AFRS EC 7, AFRS EC 25
> CD: Jazzology JCECD 1002

Add Bobby Hackett, cornet and arranger, Liza Morrow, vocal.

You Don't Know What Love Is (LM vocal)
> 33: Baybridge (J) UPS 2255, Jazum 72, Jazzology JCE 1002
> TX: >AFRS EC 2
> CD: Jazzology JCECD 1002

Bobby Hackett, cornet; Max Kaminsky, Hot Lips Page, trumpet; Bill Harris, valve trombone; Pee Wee Russell, clarinet; Ernie Caceres, baritone; Clyde Hart, piano; Bob Haggart, bass; Joe Grauso, drums.

Impromptu Ensemble
    33:    Baybridge (J) UPS 2255, Jazum 72, Jazzology JCE 1002
    TX: >AFRS EC 2
    CD: Jazzology JCECD 1002

NOTE: Produced by Ernest Anderson. From a Town Hall concert, broadcast by the Blue network, 3:30 to 4 p.m. "Muskrat Ramble" is repeated on AFRS EC 2 at the end of the program. The Jazzology issues contain the complete program, including narration, as broadcast by the Blue network.

Eddie Condon
                                                    NYC, June 17, 1944

Bobby Hackett, cornet; Hot Lips Page, trumpet, vocal; Bill Harris, valve trombone; Pee Wee Russell, clarinet; Ernie Caceres, baritone; James P. Johnson, piano; unknown bass; Joe Grauso, drums.

The Joint Is Jumpin' (HLP vocal)
    33:    Jazzology JCE-1003, >Pumpkin 117
    CD: Jazzology JCE-CD-1003

Omit Hot Lips Page.

Squeeze Me
    33:    >Jazzology JCE-1003
    CD: Jazzology JCE-CD-1003

Gene Schroeder, piano, replaces Johnson.

Ain't Misbehavin'
    33:    >Jazzology JCE-1003
    CD: Jazzology JCE-CD-1003

Omit Hackett, add Page.

Honeysuckle Rose
    33:    >Jazzology JCE-1003
    CD: Jazzology JCE-CD-1003

Hackett replaces Page.

If It Ain't Love
    33: >Jazzology JCE-1003
    CD: Jazzology JCE-CD-1003

Same personnel as The Joint Is Jumpin'.

Buy Bonds Blues; Ensemble Blues; Old Miss Blues
    33: >Jazzology JCE-1003
    CD: Jazzology JCE-CD-1003

NOTE: Produced by Ernest Anderson. From a Town Hall concert.
Blue network broadcast #5. No AFRS transcription has been located
for this show. Other selections do not include Pee Wee Russell. The
Jazzology issues contain the complete program, including narration, as
broadcast by the Blue network.

Eddie Condon
                                                    NYC, June 24, 1944
Max Kaminsky, trumpet; Pee Wee Russell, clarinet; Ernie Caceres,
baritone; Gene Schroeder, piano; Eddie Condon, guitar, Bob Haggart,
bass; Joe Grauso, drums.

I've Found A New Baby
    33: Baybridge (J) UPS 2256, Good Music JRR3, Jazum 4,
         Jazzology JCE-1003, Kings of Jazz (I) KLJ 20018
    TX: >AFRS EC 4
    CD: Jazzology JCE-CD-1003

Hot Lips Page, trumpet, vocal; possibly Bobby Hackett, cornet, added.

Chinatown, My Chinatown (HLP vocal)
    33: Baybridge (J) UPS 2256, Jazum 10, Jazzology JCE-1003
    TX: >AFRS EC 4
    CD: Jazzology JCE-CD-1003

Omit Page and Kaminsky.

Cherry
    33: Baybridge (J) UPS 2256, Jazum 10, Jazzology JCE-1003,
         Rhapsody (E) RHA 6028
    TX: >AFRS EC 4
    CD: Jazzology JCE-CD-1003

Kaminsky replaces Hackett.

Jazz Me Blues
   33:   Baybridge (J) UPS 2256, Good Music JRR3, Jazum 4,
         Jazzology JCE-1003, Kings of Jazz (I) KLJ 20018
   TX: >AFRS EC 4
   CD: Jazzology JCE-CD-1003

Add Hot Lips Page, vocal only.

Keepin' Out Of Mischief Now (HLP vocal)
   33:   Baybridge (J) UPS 2256, Jazum 10, Jazzology JCE-1003
   TX: >AFRS EC 4
   CD: Jazzology JCE-CD-1003

Add Page, trumpet.

Ensemble Blues
   33:   Jazum 10, Jazzology JCE-1003
   TX: >AFRS EC 4
   CD: Jazzology JCE-CD-1003

NOTE: Produced by Ernest Anderson. From a Town Hall concert,
Blue network broadcast #6. Other titles recorded at this concert do not
include Pee Wee Russell. The Jazzology issues contain the complete
program, including narration, as broadcast by the Blue network.

Eddie Condon

NYC, July 1, 1944.

Bobby Hackett, cornet; Pee Wee Russell, clarinet; Ernie Caceres,
baritone; Gene Schroeder, piano; Eddie Condon, guitar; Sid Weiss,
bass; Gene Krupa, drums.

The Lady's In Love With You
   33:   Chiaroscuro CR 108, Jazzology JCE-1004, Overseas (J)
         ULX-53-V, Storyville (D) SLP 509
   TX: >AFRS EC 5
   CD: Jazzology JCE-CD-1004

Max Kaminsky, trumpet; Benny Morton, trombone, added.

China Boy
    33:   Chiaroscuro CR 108, Jazzology JCE-1004, Overseas (J)
          ULX-53-V, Storyville (D) SLP 509
    TX: >AFRS EC 5
    CD: Jazzology JCE-CD-1004

Bobby Hackett, cornet; Benny Morton, trombone; Ernie Caceres, Pee
Wee Russell, Joe Marsala, clarinet; Gene Schroeder, piano; Sid Weiss,
bass; Gene Krupa, drums.

Clarinet Chase
    33:   Chiaroscuro CR 108, Jazzology JCE-1004, Overseas (J)
          ULX-53-V, Storyville (D) SLP 509, Swaggie (Au) JCS
          33776
    TX: >AFRS EC 5
    CD: Jazzology JCE-CD-1004

Jonah Jones, trumpet, vocal; Bobby Hackett or Max Kaminsky,
trumpet; possibly Benny Morton, trombone; Pee Wee Russell, clarinet;
Ernie Caceres, baritone; Gene Schroeder, piano; Sid Weiss, bass; Gene
Krupa, drums.

Baby, Won't You Please Come Home (JJ vocal)
    33:   >Jazzology JCE-1004
    CD: Jazzology JCE-CD-1004

Bobby Hackett, cornet; either Max Kaminsky or Jonah Jones, trumpet;
Benny Morton, trombone; Pee Wee Russell, clarinet; Ernie Caceres,
baritone; Gene Schroeder, piano; Sid Weiss, bass; Gene Krupa, drums.

Pennies from Heaven
    33:   Chiaroscuro CR 108, Jazzology JCE-1004, Overseas (J)
          ULX-53-V, Storyville (D) SLP 509
    TX: >AFRS EC 5
    CD: Jazzology JCE-CD-1004

Bobby Hackett, cornet; Max Kaminsky, Jonah Jones, trumpet; Benny Morton, trombone; Pee Wee Russell, Joe Marsala, clarinet; Ernie Caceres, baritone; Gene Schroeder, piano; Sid Weiss, bass; Gene Krupa, drums.

Impromptu Ensemble
    33:   Baybridge (J) LPE 1, Chiaroscuro CR 108, Overseas (J)
          ULX-53-V, Storyville (D) SLP 509
    TX: >AFRS EC 5, AFRS EC 16
    CD: Jazzology JCE-CD-1004
NOTE: Produced by Ernest Anderson. From a Town Hall concert, Blue network broadcast #7. Other selections from this concert do not include Pee Wee Russell. "Impromptu Ensemble" issued as "Impromptu Ensemble #2" on Chiaroscuro CR 108 with the Jonah Jones solo edited out, and as "Ensemble Blues; Carnegie Leap" on Jazzology JCE-1004. The Jazzology issues contain the complete program, including narration, as broadcast by the Blue network.

Eddie Condon
                                      NYC, July 8, 1944
Bobby Hackett, cornet; Benny Morton, trombone; Pee Wee Russell, clarinet; Ernie Caceres, baritone; Gene Schroeder, piano; possibly Eddie Condon, guitar; Johnny Williams, bass; Joe Grauso, drums.

Struttin' With Some Barbecue
    33:   Baybridge (J) LPE 1, Good Music JRR 3, Jazum 72,
          Jazzology JCE-1004, Swaggie (Au) JCS 33776
    TX: >AFRS EC 6
    CD: Jazzology JCE-CD-1004

Add Jonah Jones, trumpet, vocal.
You Can Depend On Me (JJ vocal)
    33:   Jazum 72, Jazzology JCE-1004
    TX: >AFRS EC 6
    CD: Jazzology JCE-CD-1004

Bobby Hackett, cornet; Benny Morton, trombone; Pee Wee Russell, clarinet; Ernie Caceres, baritone; Gene Schroeder, piano; Johnny Williams, bass; Joe Grauso, drums.

Singin' The Blues
    33:   Good Music JRR 3, Jazum 26, Jazzology JCE-1004
    TX: >AFRS EC 6, AFRS EC 16
    CD: Jazzology JCE-CD-1004

Bobby Hackett, cornet; Jonah Jones, Billy Butterfield, trumpets; Benny Morton, trombone; Pee Wee Russell, Ed Hall, clarinet; Ernie Caceres, baritone; Gene Schroeder, piano; Johnny Williams, bass; Joe Grauso, drums.

Impromptu Ensemble
    33:   Jazum 73, Jazzology JCE-1004
    TX: >AFRS EC 6, AFRS EC 29
    CD: Jazzology JCE-CD-1004

NOTE: Produced by Ernest Anderson. From a Town Hall concert, Blue network broadcast #8. Other selections from this concert do not include Pee Wee Russell. On AFRS EC 29, the first 20 seconds of Schroeder's piano solo on "Impromptu Ensemble" have been edited out. "Impromtu Ensemble" issued as "Blues Ensemble" on Jazzology JCE-1004. The Jazzology issues contain the complete program, including narration, as broadcast by the Blue network.

Eddie Condon
NYC, July 15, 1944

Max Kaminsky, trumpet; Benny Morton, trombone; Pee Wee Russell, clarinet; Ernie Caceres, baritone; Gene Schroeder, piano; Bob Haggart, bass; George Wettling, drums.

That's A Plenty
    33:   Baybridge (J) UXP 126, Baybridge (J) UPS 2256, Jazum 52,
          Jazzology JCE-1005
    TX: >AFRS EC 7, AFRS EC 9, AFRS EC 11 (incomplete)
    CD: Baybridge (J) 30CP-136, Jazzology JCECD-1005

Add Jonah Jones, trumpet, vocal. Omit Kaminsky.

I'm A Ding Dong Daddy (JJ vocal)
    33:   Baybridge (J) UPS 2256, Jazum 73, Jazzology JCE-1005
    TX: >AFRS EC 7
    CD: Jazzology JCECD-1005

Bobby Hackett, cornet; Benny Morton, trombone; Pee Wee Russell, clarinet; Ernie Caceres, baritone; Gene Schroeder, piano; Bob Haggart, bass; George Wettling, drums.

New Orleans
- 33: Baybridge (J) UXP 126, Baybridge (J) UPS 2256, Jazum 24, Jazzology JCE-1005
- TX: >AFRS EC 7, AFRS EC 11
- CD: Baybridge (J) 30CP-136, Jazzology JCECD-1005

Wolverine Blues
- 78: Gazell (Sd) 1045
- 33: Baybridge (J) UPS 2256, Good Music JRR 3, Jazum 11, Jazum 26, Jazzology JCE-1005, Spook Jazz (D) SPJ 6607, Swaggie (Au) JCS 33776
- TX: >AFRS EC 7, AFRS EC 8, AFRS EC 16, AFRS EC 45
- CD: Jazzology JCECD-1005

Add Jonah Jones, Max Kaminsky, trumpet.

Impromptu Ensemble
- 33: Baybridge (J) UPS 2256, Jazum 73, Jazzology JCE-1005
- TX: >AFRS EC 7
- CD: Jazzology JCECD-1005

NOTE: Produced by Ernest Anderson. From a Town Hall concert, Blue network broadcast #9. Other selections from this broadcast do not include Pee Wee Russell. The Jazzology issues contain the complete program, including narration, as broadcast by the Blue network.

Eddie Condon
                                                    NYC, July 22, 1944

Sterling Bose, trumpet; Benny Morton, trombone; Pee Wee Russell, clarinet; Ernie Caceres, baritone; Gene Schroeder, piano; Bob Haggart, bass; Gene Krupa, drums.

Fidgety Feet
- 33: Jazum 10, Jazzology JCE-1005, Rare Broadcast 479, Storyville (D) SLP 133, Storyville - Teichiku (J) ULS-1564R, Swaggie (Au) JCS 33776
- TX: >AFRS EC 8
- CD: Jazzology JCECD-1005

Max Kaminsky, trumpet, replaces Bose

Oh, Katharina
   33:   Jazum 10, Jazzology JCE-1005, Rare Broadcast 479,
         Rhapsody (E) RHA 6028
   TX: >AFRS EC 8
   CD: Jazzology JCECD-1005

Pee Wee Russell, clarinet; Gene Schroeder, piano; Bob Haggart, bass;
Joe Grauso, drums.

I'd Climb The Highest Mountain
   33:   Chiaroscuro CR-113, Jazum 24, Jazzology JCE-1005,
         Overseas (J) ULX-54-V, Rare Broadcast 479
   TX: >AFRS EC 8, AFRS EC 16
   CD: Jazzology JCECD-1005

Sterling Bose, Max Kaminsky, trumpet; Benny Morton, trombone; Pee
Wee Russell, clarinet; Ernie Caceres, baritone; Gene Schroeder, piano;
Bob Haggart, bass; Joe Grauso, drums.

Jazz Me Blues
   33:   Jazum 10, Jazzology JCE-1005, Rare Broadcast 479,
         Rhapsody (E) RHA 6028
   TX: >AFRS EC 8
   CD: Jazzology JCECD-1005

NOTE: Produced by Ernest Anderson. From a Town Hall concert,
Blue network broadcast #10. Other selections from this concert do not
include Pee Wee Russell. The Jazzology issues contain the complete
program, including narration, as broadcast by the Blue network.

Eddie Condon
                                              NYC, July 29, 1944
Max Kaminsky, trumpet; Benny Morton, trombone; Pee Wee Russell,
clarinet; Ernie Caceres, baritone; possibly Eddie Condon, guitar,
possibly Bob Haggart, bass; Gene Krupa, drums.

Swing That Music
   33:   Good Music JRR 3, Jazum 11, Jazzology JCE-1006, Radiola
         MR 1042
   TX: >AFRS EC 10, AFRS EC 15 (incomplete)
   CD: Jazzology JCECD-1006

148

Joe Grauso, drums, replaces Krupa.

Big Boy
    33:    Good Music JRR 3, Jazum 11, Jazzology JCE-1006, Radiola
            MR 1042
    TX: >AFRS EC 10, AFRS EC 15
    CD: Jazzology JCECD-1006

I Ain't Gonna Give Nobody None Of My Jelly Roll
    33:    Jazum 11, Jazzology JCE-1006, Spook Jazz (E) SPJ 6607
    TX: >AFRS EC 10
    CD: Jazzology JCECD-1006

Bobby Hackett, cornet; Max Kaminsky, trumpet; Benny Morton, trombone; Pee Wee Russell, Ed Hall, clarinet; Ernie Caceres, baritone; Gene Schroeder, piano; Bob Haggart, bass; Joe Grauso, drums.

Impromptu Ensemble
    33:    Baybridge (J) LPE 1, Jazum 11, Jazzology JCE-1006
    TX: >AFRS EC 10, AFRS EC 26 (incomplete)
    CD: Jazzology JCECD-1006

NOTE: Produced by Ernest Anderson. From a Town Hall concert, Blue network broadcast #11. Other selections from this broadcast do not include Pee Wee Russell. "Impromptu Ensemble" entitled "Ensemble Blues" on Jazum 11. The Jazzology issues contain the complete program, including narration, as broadcast by the Blue network.

Eddie Condon
                                     NYC, August 5, 1944

Max Kaminsky, trumpet; Benny Morton, trombone; Pee Wee Russell, clarinet; Ernie Caceres, baritone; Jess Stacy, piano; unknown bass; Gene Krupa, drums.

I Got Rhythm
    33:    Jazum 26, Jazzology JCE-1006
    TX: >AFRS EC 9, AFRS EC 18, AFRS EC 20 (incomplete)
    CD: Jazzology JCECD-1006

Max Kaminsky, trumpet; Benny Morton, trombone; Pee Wee Russell, clarinet; Ernie Caceres, baritone; Jess Stacy, piano; unknown bass; Gene Krupa, drums; Lee Wiley, vocal.

I've Got A Crush On You (LW vocal)
    33:   Baybridge (J) UPS 2280, Jazum 52, Jazzology JCE-1006,
           Totem 1033
    TX: >AFRS EC 9
    CD: Baybridge (J) 30CP-135, Jazzology JCECD-1006

Bobby Hackett, cornet; Max Kaminsky, trumpet; Benny Morton, trombone; Pee Wee Russell, clarinet; Ernie Caceres, baritone; Gene Schroeder, piano; unknown bass; Joe Grauso, drums.

Soon
    33:   Jazum 52, Jazzology JCE-1006
    TX: >AFRS EC 9
    CD: Jazzology JCECD-1006

Add Lee Wiley, vocal; omit Kaminsky. Stacy replaces Schroeder, piano.

Sweet And Lowdown (LW vocal)
    33:   Baybridge (J) UPS 2280, Jazum 52, Jazzology JCE-1006,
           Totem 1033
    TX: >AFRS EC 9
    CD: Baybridge (J) 30CP-135, Jazzology JCECD-1006

NOTE: Produced by Ernest Anderson. From a Town Hall concert, Blue network broadcast #12. Other selections from this broadcast do not include Pee Wee Russell. The Jazzology issues contain the complete program, including narration, as broadcast by the Blue network.

Eddie Condon

Muggsy Spanier, cornet; Benny Morton, trombone; Pee Wee Russell, clarinet; Ernie Caceres, baritone; Gene Schroeder, piano; Bob Haggart, bass; Gene Krupa, drums.

Everybody Loves My Baby
- 45: Gazell (Sd) gep 8, Storyville (D) SEP 14
- 33: Good Music JRR 3, Jazum 11, Jazzology JCE 1007, Spook Jazz (D) SPJ 6607
- TX: >AFRS EC 11
- CD: Jazzology JCD 1007

Add Bobby Hackett, cornet; Lee Wiley, vocal.

You're Lucky To Me (LW vocal)
- 33: Baybridge (J) UPS 2280, Dan (J) VC-5020, Jazum 11, Jazzology JCE 1007, Kings of Jazz (I) KLJ 20036, Totem 1033
- TX: >AFRS EC 11
- CD: Baybridge (J) 30CP-135, Jazzology JCD 1007
- CT: Jazz Connoisseur Cassettes (E) J.C.C. 114

Same personnel as "Everybody Loves My Baby," except Joe Grauso probably replaces Krupa.

Black And Blue
- 45: Gazell (Sd) gep 8, Storyville (D) SEP 515
- 33: Chiaroscuro CR 108, Jazum 24, Jazzology JCE 1007, Overseas (J) ULX-53-V, Storyville (D) SLP 133, Storyville (D) SLP 509, Storyville - Teichiku (J) ULS-1564(R)
- TX: >AFRS EC 11, AFRS EC 16, AFRS EC 25
- CD: Jazzology JCD 1007

Muggsy Spanier, Bobby Hackett, cornet; Benny Morton, trombone; Pee Wee Russell, clarinet; Ernie Caceres, baritone; Gene Schroeder, piano; Bob Haggart, bass; possibly Joe Grauso, drums.

Impromptu Ensemble
- 33: Jazum 24, Jazzology JCE 1007
- TX: >AFRS EC 11
- CD: Jazzology JCD 1007

NOTE: Produced by Ernest Anderson. From a Town Hall concert, Blue network broadcast #13. Other selections from this broadcast do not include Pee Wee Russell. "Impromptu Ensemble" entitled "Ensemble Blues" on Jazum 24. The Jazzology issues contain the complete program, including narration, as broadcast by the Blue network.

Eddie Condon

NYC, August 19, 1944

Bobby Hackett, cornet; Benny Morton, trombone; Pee Wee Russell, clarinet; Ernie Caceres, baritone; Gene Schroeder, piano; possibly Eddie Condon, guitar; Bob Casey, bass; Gene Krupa, drums.

Clarinet Marmalade
  33: Jazum 24, Jazzology JCE 1007, Storyville (D) SLP 133, Storyville-Teichiku (J) ULS-1564-R, Swaggie (Au) JSC 33776
  TX: >AFRS EC 12
  CD: Jazzology JCD 1007

Lee Wiley, vocal; Billy Butterfield, trumpet, added.

On The Sunny Side Of The Street (LW vocal)
  33: Baybridge (J) UPS 2280, Dan (J) VC-5020, Jazum 24, Jazzology JCE 1007, Kings of Jazz (I) KLJ 20036, Napoleon (F) NLP 11091, Totem 1033
  TX: >AFRS EC 12
  CD: Baybridge (J) 30CP-135, Jazzology JCD 1007

Billy Butterfield, trumpet; Benny Morton, trombone; Pee Wee Russell, clarinet; Ernie Caceres, baritone; Gene Schroeder, piano; Bob Casey, bass; Joe Grauso, drums.

Muskrat Ramble
  33: Jazum 24, Jazzology JCE 1007, King of Jazz (I) KLJ 20028
  TX: >AFRS EC 12
  CD: Jazzology JCD 1007

Bobby Hackett, cornet; Billy Butterfield, trumpet; Benny Morton, trombone; Ed Hall, Pee Wee Russell, clarinet; Ernie Caceres, baritone; Gene Schroeder, piano; Bob Casey, bass; Joe Grauso, drums.

Impromptu Ensemble
    33:   Chiaroscuro CR 113, Jazzology JCE 1007, Overseas (J)
         ULX-54-V
    TX: >AFRS EC 12
    CD: Jazzology JCD 1007

NOTE: Produced by Ernest Anderson. From a Town Hall concert, Blue network broadcast #14. Other selections from this broadcast do not include Pee Wee Russell. "Impromptu Ensemble" entitled "Impromptu Ensemble #2" on Chiaroscuro CR 113. Totem 1033 was issued as by Lee Wiley. The Jazzology issues contain the complete program, including narration, as broadcast by the Blue network.

Eddie Condon
NYC, August 26, 1944

Max Kaminsky, trumpet; Bill Harris, valve trombone; Pee Wee Russell, clarinet; Ernie Caceres, baritone; Gene Schroeder, piano; Bob Haggart, bass; Gene Krupa, drums.

California, Here I Come
    33:   Baybridge (J) UPS 2257, Jazum 24, Jazzology JCE 1008
    TX: >AFRS EC 13
    CD: Jazzology JCD 1008

Muggsy Spanier, cornet, replaces Kaminsky.

Dinah
    33:   Baybridge (J) UXP 126, Baybridge (J) UPS 2257, Jazum 25,
         Jazzology JCE 1008, Rhapsody (E) RHA 6029
    TX: >AFRS EC 13
    CD: Baybridge (J) 30CP-136, Jazzology JCD 1008

Possibly Bobby Hackett or Muggsy Spanier, cornet; Max Kaminsky, trumpet; Bill Harris, valve trombone; Pee Wee Russell, Joe Marsala, Ernie Caceres, clarinet; Gene Schroeder, piano; Bob Haggart, bass; Gene Krupa, drums.

Untitled Three Clarinet Improvisation
    33:   Baybridge (J) UPS 2257, Jazum 25, Jazzology JCE 1008
    TX: >AFRS EC 13
    CD: Jazzology JCD 1008

Bobby Hackett, cornet; Max Kaminsky, trumpet; Bill Harris, valve trombone; Pee Wee Russell, clarinet; Ernie Caceres, baritone; Gene Schroeder, piano; Bob Haggart, bass; Gene Krupa, drums.

Soon
    33:   Baybridge (J) UPS 2257, Jazum 25, Jazzology JCE 1008
    TX: >AFRS EC 13
    CD: Jazzology JCD 1008

Add Muggsy Spanier, cornet; Joe Marsala, clarinet.

Impromptu Ensemble
    33:   Baybridge (J) UPS 2257, Jazum 25, Jazzology JCE 1008,
          Rhapsody (E) RHA 6028
    TX: >AFRS EC 13
    CD: Jazzology JCD 1008

NOTE: Produced by Ernest Anderson. From a Town Hall concert, Blue network broadcast # 15. Other selections from this broadcast do not include Pee Wee Russell. "Impromptu Ensemble" entitled "Ensemble Blues" on Jazum 25.   "Untitled Three Clarinet Improvisation" is entitled "Clarinet Jam" on Jazum 25 and Baybridge UPS 2257, and "Clarinet Chase" on Jazzology J (and JCD) 1008. The Jazzology issues contain the complete program, including narration, as broadcast by the Blue network.

Eddie Condon

NYC, September 2, 1944

Bobby Hackett, cornet; Miff Mole, trombone; Pee Wee Russell, clarinet; Gene Schroeder, piano; Eddie Condon, guitar; Sid Weiss, bass; Gene Krupa, drums.

Walkin' The Dog
>   33:   Jazum 73, Jazzology JCE 1008
>   TX: >AFRS EC 14
>   CD: Jazzology JCD 1008

Add Jonah Jones, trumpet, vocal; Bobby Hackett, arranger.

I Can't Give You Anything But Love, Baby (JJ vocal)
>   33:   Good Music JRR 3, Jazum 73, Jazzology JCE 1008
>   TX: >AFRS EC 14
>   CD: Jazzology JCD 1008

Omit Jones, trumpet. Add Ernie Caceres, baritone. Joe Grauso replaces Krupa.

Peg O' My Heart
>   33:   Jazum 73, Jazzology JCE 1008
>   TX: >AFRS EC 14
>   CD: Jazzology JCD 1008

Ja Da
>   33:   Jazum 73, Jazzology JCE 1008
>   TX: >AFRS EC 14
>   CD: Jazzology JCD 1008

Impromptu Ensemble
>   33:   Jazzology JCE 1008
>   TX: >AFRS EC 14
>   CD: Jazzology JCD 1008

NOTE: Produced by Ernest Anderson. From a Town Hall concert, Blue network broadcast #16. Other selections from this broadcast do not include Pee Wee Russell. The Jazzology issues contain the complete program, including narration, as broadcast by the Blue network.

Eddie Condon

Max Kaminsky, trumpet; Miff Mole, trombone; Pee Wee Russell, clarinet; Ernie Caceres, baritone; Gene Schroeder, piano; Bob Haggart, bass; Gene Krupa, drums.

Love Nest
- 78: Gazel (Sd) 1015
- 33: Good Music JRR 3, Jazum 25, Jazzology JCE 1009, Radiola MR 1042, Rhapsody (E) RHA 6028, Spook Jazz (D) SPJ 6607
- TX: >AFRS EC 15
- CD: Jazzology JCD-1009
- CT: Holmia (Sd) HM 06

Muggsy Spanier, cornet; Miff Mole, trombone; Pee Wee Russell, clarinet; Ernie Caceres, baritone; Gene Schroeder, piano; Bob Haggart, bass; Gene Krupa, drums.

Big Butter And Egg Man
- 33: Baybridge (J) LPE-1, Good Music JRR 3, Jazum 25, Jazzology JCE 1009, Radiola MR 1042, Rhapsody (E) RHA 6028
- TX: >AFRS EC 15
- CD: Jazzology JCD-1009

Pee Wee Russell, clarinet; Gene Schroeder, piano; Bob Haggart, bass; Gene Krupa, drums.

The Blues By Pee Wee Russell
- 33: Chiaroscuro CR 108, Jazzology JCE 1009, Overseas (J) ULX-53-V, Radiola MR 1042, Storyville (D) SLP 509, Storyville-Teichiku (J) ULS 1564-R
- TX: >AFRS EC 15
- CD: Jazzology JCD-1009

Billy Butterfield, trumpet; Miff Mole, trombone; Pee Wee Russell, clarinet; Ernie Caceres, baritone; Gene Schroeder, piano; Bob Haggart, bass; Joe Grauso, drums.

Heebie Jeebies
    45:   Gazel (Sd) gep 6
    33:   Jazum 25, Jazzology JCE 1009, Radiola MR 1042
    TX: >AFRS EC 15
    CD: Jazzology JCD-1009

Add Muggsy Spanier, cornet; Max Kaminsky, trumpet.

Impromptu Ensemble
    33:   Jazum 25, Jazzology JCE 1009, Radiola MR 1042, Storyville
          (D) SLP 133, Storyville-Teichiku (J) ULS-1564-R
    TX: >AFRS EC 15
    CD: Jazzology JCD-1009

NOTE: Produced by Ernest Anderson. From a Town Hall concert, Blue network broadcast #17. Other selections from this broadcast do not include Pee Wee Russell. "Impromptu Ensemble" is entitled "Presenting the Blues" on Storyville (D) SLP 133 and "Ensemble Blues" on Jazum 25. The Jazzology issues contain the complete program, including narration, as broadcast by the Blue network.

Eddie Condon

NYC, September 16, 1944

Muggsy Spanier, cornet; Miff Mole, trombone; Pee Wee Russell, clarinet; Ernie Caceres, baritone; Gene Schroeder, piano; Eddie Condon, guitar; Jack Lesberg, bass; Gene Krupa, drums.

Rosetta
    33:   Chiaroscuro CR 108, Jazzology JCE 1010, Overseas (J)
          ULX-53-V, Storyville (D) SLP 509
    TX: >AFRS EC 16
    CD: Jazzology JCD-1010

Memphis Blues
    33:   Chiaroscuro CR 108, Jazzology JCE 1010, Overseas (J)
          ULX-53-V, Storyville (D) SLP 509
    TX: >AFRS EC 16
    CD: Jazzology JCD-1010

157

Red McKenzie, vocal, added.

There'll Be Some Changes Made (RMcK vocal)
    33:   >Jazzology JCE 1010
    CD: >Jazzology JCD-1010

Omit McKenzie.

I Would Do Anything For You
    33:   Jazum 26, Jazzology JCE 1010
    TX: >AFRS EC 16
    CD: Jazzology JCD-1010

NOTE: Produced by Ernest Anderson. From a Town Hall concert, Blue network broadcast #18. "There'll Be Some Changes Made" was interrupted for a network news bulletin. The Jazzology issues contain the complete program, including narration, as broadcast by the Blue network.

Eddie Condon
NYC, September 23, 1944

Max Kaminsky, trumpet; Miff Mole, trombone; Pee Wee Russell, clarinet; Ernie Caceres, baritone; Jess Stacy, piano; Sid Weiss, bass; Gene Krupa, drums.

That's A Plenty
    33:   Jazum 78, Jazzology JCE 1010
    TX: >AFRS EC 17
    CD: Jazzology JCD-1010

Bobby Hackett, cornet, replaces Kaminsky.

Easter Parade
    33:   >Jazzology JCE 1010
    CD: >Jazzology JCD 1010

Muggsy Spanier, cornet, replaces Hackett.

Relaxin' At The Touro
   33:   Jazum 52, Jazum 78, Jazzology JCE 1010, Rhapsody (E)
         RHA 6029
   TX: >AFRS EC 17, AFRS EC 33
   CD: Jazzology JCD-1010

Poor As A Churchmouse
   33:   Jazum 78, Jazzology JCE 1010
   TX: >AFRS EC 17
   CD: Jazzology JCD 1010

Bobby Hackett, cornet; Max Kaminsky, trumpet; Miff Mole, trombone;
Pee Wee Russell, clarinet; Ernie Caceres, baritone; Jess Stacy, piano;
Sid Weiss, bass; Gene Krupa, drums; Lee Wiley, vocal.

Wherever There's Love (LW vocal)
   33:   Jazum 78, Jazzology JCE 1010
   TX: >AFRS EC 17
   CD: Jazzology JCD-1010

Muggsy Spanier, cornet; Max Kaminsky, trumpet; replace Hackett.

Impromptu Ensemble
   33:   Jazum 78, Jazzology JCE 1010
   TX: >AFRS EC 17
   CD: Jazzology JCD-1010

NOTE: Produced by Ernest Anderson. From a Town Hall concert,
Blue network broadcast #19. Other selections from this broadcast do
not include Pee Wee Russell. "That's A Plenty" titled "Muskrat
Ramble" on Jazum 78. The Jazzology issues contain the complete
program, including narration, as broadcast by the Blue network.

Bobby Hackett And His Orchestra

NYC, September 23, 1944

Bobby Hackett, cornet; Lou McGarity, trombone; Pee Wee Russell, clarinet; Ernie Caceres, baritone; Jess Stacy, piano, Eddie Condon, guitar; Bob Casey, bass; George Wettling, drums.

A 4805   At Sundown
    78:   >Commodore 1523
    45:   Commodore 45-1523
    33:   Book of the Month Club 10-5557, Commodore CCL 7009, Commodore (G) 6.26171 AG, Commodore (J) GXC 3154, Commodore (J) K23P-6622, London (G) 6.26171, London (J) SLC 451, Mosaic MR23-128
    CD: Commodore CCD 7009
    CT: Book of the Month Club 60-5561, Commodore CCK 7009
    8T: Book of the Month Club 50-5560

A 4806-1 New Orleans
    78:   >Commodore 622
    45:   Commodore CEP 31, Commodore 45-622
    33:   Commodore CCL 7009, Commodore FL 20,016, Commodore (G) 6.26171 AG, Commodore (J) GXC 3154, Commodore (J) K23P-6622, London (G) 6.26171, London (J) SLC 451, Mosaic MR23-128
    CD: Commodore CCD 7009
    CT: Commodore CCK 7009

A 4807-TK1 Skeleton Jangle No. 2
    33:   >Commodore (G) 6.26171 AG, London (G) 6.26171, Mosaic MR23-128

A 4807   Skeleton Jangle
    78:   >Commodore 622
    45:   Commodore CEP 31, Commodore 45-622
    33:   Commodore CCL 7009, Commodore FL 20016, Commodore (G) 6.26171 AG, Commodore (J) GXC 3154, Commodore (J) K23P-6622, London (G) 6.26171, London (J) SLC 451, Mosaic MR23-128
    CD: Commodore CCD 7009
    CT: Commodore CCK 7009

A 4808-1 When Day Is Done No. 2
   33: >Commodore (G) 6.26171 AG, London (G) 6.26171, Mosaic
         MR23-128

A 4808   When Day Is Done
   78: >Commodore 1523
   45: Commodore 45-1523
   33: Commodore CCL 7009, Commodore FL 20016, Commodore
         (G) 6.26171 AG, Commodore (J) GXC 3154, Commodore (J)
         K23P-6622, London (G) 6.26171, London (J) SLC 451,
         Mosaic MR23-128
   CD: Commodore CCD 7009
   CT: Commodore CCK 7009

A 4809T Soon
   33: Commodore CCL 7009, Commodore (G) 6.26171 AG,
         >Commodore (J) GXC 3154, Commodore (J) K23P-6622,
         London (G) 6.26171, London (J) SLC 451, Mosaic MR23-
         128
   CD: Commodore CCD 7009
   CT: Commodore CCK 7009

NOTE: Produced by Milt Gabler. Recorded at WOR studios, 1440
Broadway. Commodore 1523, a 12-inch disc, was issued as Jam
Session at Commodore No. 6. Commodore 45-622 and 45-1523 were
scheduled for issue but never appeared.

Muggsy Spanier And His Ragtimers
                                    NYC, September 27, 1944

Muggsy Spanier, cornet; Miff Mole, trombone; Pee Wee Russell,
clarinet; Boomie Richmond, tenor; Gene Schroeder, piano; Eddie
Condon, guitar; Bob Haggart, bass; George Wettling, drums.

A 4810-1 Sweet Sue
   78: >Commodore 1519
   45: Commodore CEP 25, Commodore 45-1519
   33: Commodore FL 20,012, Commodore (G) 6.26167 AG,
         Commodore (J) GXC 3154, Commodore (J) K23P-6622,
         London (E) HMC 5025, London (G) 6.26167, London (J)
         SLC 451, Mosaic MR23-128
   TX: AFRS DB 427

A 4811-1   Memphis Blues
   78:   >Commodore 1519
   45:   Commodore CEP 24, Commodore 45-1519
   33:   Book of the Month Club 10-5557, Commodore FL 20,012,
        Commodore (G) 6.26167 AG, Commodore (J) GXC 3154,
        Commodore (J) K23P-6622, Franklin Mint 66, London (E)
        HMC 5025, London (G) 6.26167, London (J) SLC 451,
        Mosaic MR23-128
   CT: Book of the Month Club 60-5561
   8T: Book of the Month Club 50-5560

A 4812-TK1 Riverside Blues #3
   33:   >Mosaic MR23-128

A 4812-1   Riverside Blues No 2
   33:   >Commodore (G) 6.26167 AG, London (G) 6.26167, Mosaic
        MR23-128

A 4812-2   Riverside Blues
   78:   >Commodore 586
   45:   Commodore CEP 19, Commodore 45-586
   33:   Commodore FL 20,009, Commodore FL 30,016, Commodore
        (G) 6.26167 AG, Commodore (J) GXC 3154, Commodore (J)
        K23P-6622, London (E) HMC 5025, London (G) 6.26167,
        London (J) LAX 3311, Mosaic MR23-128, Stateside (E) SL
        10004

A 4813-TK 1 Rosetta #4
   33:   >Mosaic MR23-128

A 4813-TK2 Rosetta #5
   33:   >Mosaic MR23-128

A 4813-1   Rosetta No. 2
   33:   >Commodore (G) 6.26167 AG, London (G) 6.26167, Mosaic
        MR23-128

A 4813-2   Rosetta
    78:   >Commodore 586
    45:   Commodore CEP 18
    33:   Book of the Month Club 10-5557, Commodore FL 20,009,
          Commodore FL 30,016, Commodore (G) 6.26167 AG,
          Commodore (J) GXC 3148, Commodore (J) K23P-6616,
          London (E) HMC 5025, London (G) 6.26167, London (J)
          LAX 331, London (J) SLC 452, Mainstream S/6010,
          Mainstream 56010, Mainstream (J) XM 33 MSD, Mosaic
          MR23-128, Stateside (E) SL 10004
    TX: AFRS MD 38
    CT: Book of the Month Club 60-5561
    8T: Book of the Month Club 50-5560

A 4813-3 Rosetta #3
    33:   >Mosaic MR23-128

NOTE: Produced by Milt Gabler. Recorded at WOR studios, 1440
Broadway.   Commodore 1519 is a 12-inch disc. Commodore 45-586
and 45-1519 were scheduled for issue but never appeared.

Pee Wee Russell's Hot Four

NYC, September 30, 1944

Pee Wee Russell, clarinet; Jess Stacy, piano; Sid Weiss, bass; George
Wettling, drums.

A 4818-TK1 Take Me To The Land Of Jazz #3
    33:   >Mosaic MR23-128

A 4818-1 Take Me To The Land Of Jazz No. 2
    33:   >Commodore XFL 16440, Commodore (G) 6.25490 AG,
          London (G) 6.25490, Mosaic MR23-128

A 4818-2 Take Me To The Land Of Jazz
- 78: >Commodore 596
- 45: Commodore 45-596
- 33: Commodore FL 20,014, Commodore XFL 16440, Commodore (G) 6.25490 AG, Fontana (E) TL 5271, Fontana (H) 687 708TL, London (E) HMC 5005, London (F) 180.005, London (G) 6.25490, London (J) SLC 459, Mainstream S/6026, Mainstream 56026, Mainstream (J) XM 33 MSD, Mosaic MR23-128, Time-Life STL-J17 (P 15734), Time-Life (Au) STL-J17, Time-Life (C) STL-J17
- CT: Time-Life 4TL-J17
- 8T: Time-Life 8TL-J17

A 4819-TK1 Rose Of Washington Square #3
- 33: >Mosaic MR23-128

A 4819-1 Rose Of Washington Square No. 2
- 33: >Commodore XFL 16440, Commodore (G) 6.25490 AG, London (G) 6.25490, Mosaic MR23-128

A 4819-2 Rose Of Washington Square
- 78: >Commodore 627
- 45: Commodore 45-627
- 33: Commodore FL 20,014, Commodore XFL 16440, Commodore (G) 6.25490 AG, Fontana (E) TL 5271, Fontana (H) 687 708TL, London (E) HMC 5005, London (F) 180.005, London (G) 6.25490, London (J) SLC 459, Mainstream S/6026, Mainstream 56026, Mainstream (J) XM 33 MSD, Mosaic MR23-128

A 4820-TK1 Keepin' Out Of Mischief Now
- 33: >Commodore XFL 16440, Commodore (G) 6.25490 AG, London (G) 6.25490, Mosaic MR23-128

A 4820-1 Keepin' Out Of Mischief Now
- 78: >Commodore 627
- 45: Commodore 45-627
- 33: Commodore FL 20,014, Commodore XFL 16440, Commodore (G) 6.25490 AG, Fontana (E) TL 5271, Fontana (H) 687 708TL, London (E) HMC 5005, London (F) 180.005, London (G) 6.25490, London (J) SLC 459, Mainstream S/6026, Mainstream 56026, Mainstream (J) XM 33 MSD, Mosaic MR23-128

A 4821-TK1 Wailing D.A. Blues
  33: >Mosaic MR23-128

A 4821-TK2 D.A. Blues No. 2
  33: >Commodore XFL 16440, Commodore (G) 6.25490 AG,
        London (G) 6.25490, Mosaic MR23-128

A 4821-1 D.A. Blues
  78: >Commodore 596
  45: Commodore 45-596
  33: Commodore FL 20014, Commodore XFL 16440,
        Commodore (G) 6.25490 AG, Fontana (E) TL 5271, Fontana
        (H) 687 708TL, London (E) HMC 5005, London (F)
        180.005, London (G) 6.25490, London (J) SLC 459,
        Mainstream S/6026, Mainstream 56026, Mainstream (J) XM
        33 MSD, Mosaic MR 23-128

NOTE: Produced by Milt Gabler. Recorded at WOR studios, 1440
Broadway. The 45 rpm issues were scheduled but never appeared.

Eddie Condon
                                        NYC, October 14, 1944.

Billy Butterfield, trumpet; Benny Morton, trombone; Pee Wee Russell,
clarinet; Ernie Caceres, baritone; Gene Schroeder, piano; Bob Casey,
bass; George Wettling, drums.

Muskrat Ramble
  33: Baybridge (J) UXP 126, Baybridge (J) UPS 2257, Good
        Music JRR 3, Jazum 26, Jazzology JCE 1011
  TX: >AFRS EC 20, AFRS EC 21
  CD: Baybridge (J) 30CP-136, Jazzology JCD-1011

Add Red McKenzie, vocal.

Sweet Lorraine (RMcK vocal)
  33: Baybridge (J) UPS 2257, Jazum 26, Jazzology JCE 1011
  TX: >AFRS EC 20
  CD: Jazzology JCD-1011

Max Kaminsky, trumpet; Benny Morton, trombone; Pee Wee Russell, clarinet; Ernie Caceres, baritone; Jess Stacy, piano; Bob Casey, bass; George Wettling, drums.

Sugar
33: Baybridge (J) UPS 2257, Jazum 26, Jazzology JCE-1011, Palm 30 (E) P.30:08, Rhapsody (E) RHA 6028
TX: >AFRS EC 20, AFRS EC 33
CD: Jazzology JCD-1011

Add Lee Wiley, vocal.

Don't Blame Me (LW vocal)
33: Baybridge (J) UPS 2257, Baybridge (J) UPS 2280, Jazum 36, Jazzology JCE 1011, Totem 1033
TX: >AFRS EC 20, AFRS EC 33
CD: Baybridge (J) 30CP-135, Jazzology JCD 1011

Billy Butterfield, Max Kaminsky, trumpet; Benny Morton, trombone; Pee Wee Russell, possibly Ed Hall, clarinet; Ernie Caceres, baritone; probably Gene Schroeder, piano; Bob Casey, bass; George Wettling, drums.

Impromptu Ensemble
33: Baybridge (J) UPS 2257, Jazum 26, Jazzology JCE 1011
TX: >AFRS EC 20
CD: Jazzology JCD 1011

NOTE: Produced by Ernest Anderson. From a concert at the Ritz Theater, 48th Street and Broadway, Blue network broadcast #22. Other selections from this broadcast do not included Pee Wee Russell. "Impromptu Ensemble" entitled "Ensemble Blues" on Jazum 26. The Jazzology issues contain the complete program, including narration, as broadcast by the Blue network.

Muggsy Spanier And His V-Disc All Stars

NYC, October 17, 1944.

Muggsy Spanier, cornet; Lou McGarity, trombone; Pee Wee Russell, clarinet, vocal; Boomie Richmond, tenor; Jess Stacy, piano; Hy White, guitar; Bob Haggart, bass, whistling; George Wettling, drums.

VP 971-D4TC 469 That's A Plenty
- 78: >V-Disc 424, >V-Disc (Navy) 204
- 33: Connoisseur (Sw) CR 552, Elec (J) KV 121, Everybodys (Sd) 1020, Joker (I) SM 3575, FDC (I) 1020, Saga (E) PAN 6917, Spook Jazz (E) SPJ 6603
- CD: Panassie (F) CTPL 003
- CT: Holmia (Sd) HM 06, Jazz Connoisseur Cassettes (E) JCC 90, Saga (E) 6917

VP 972-D4TC 470 Squeeze Me
- 78: >V-Disc 475, >V-Disc (Navy) 255
- 33: Connoisseur (Sw) CR 522, Elec (J) KV 121, Everybodys (Sd) 1020, FDC (I) 1020, Joker (I) SM 3575, Saga (E) PAN 6917, Spook Jazz (E) SPJ 6603, V-Disc (I) VDL 1006
- CT: Holmia (Sd) HM 06, Jazz Connoisseur Cassettes (E) JCC 90, Saga (E) 6917

VP 973-D4TC 471 Jazz Me Blues
- 78: >V-Disc 507, >V-Disc (Navy) 267, >V-Disc (Special Services) 267
- 33: Connoisseur (Sw) CR 522, Dan (J) VC 5008, Elec (J) KV 121, Everybodys (Sd) 1020, FDC (I) 1020, Joker (I) SM 3575, Redwood (C) RWJ 1001, Saga (E) PAN 6917, Spook Jazz (E) SPJ 6603
- CT: Holmia (Sd) HM 06, Jazz Connoisseur Cassettes (E) JCC 90, Saga (E) 6917

VP 974-D4TC 472 Pee Wee Speaks (PWR, vocal)
- 78: >V-Disc 344, >V-Disc (Navy) l35
- 33: Connoisseur (Sw) CR 522, Discomania (J) 101, Elec (J) KV 121, Everybodys (Sd) 1020, FDC (I) 1020, Joker (I) SM 3575, Saga (E) PAN 6917, Spook Jazz (E) SPJ 6603
- CT: Holmia (Sd) HM 06, Jazz Connoisseur Cassettes (E) JCC 90, Saga (E) 6917

VP 975-D4TC 473 Pat's Blues (BH, whistling)
    78:   >V-Disc 394, >V-Disc (Navy) 174
    33:   Connoisseur (Sw) CR 522, Discomania (J) 101, Elec (J) KV
          121, Everybodys (Sd) 1020, FDC (I) 1020, Joker (I) SM
          3575, Saga (E) PAN 6917, Spook Jazz (E) SPJ 6603
    CT: Holmia (Sd) HM 06, Jazz Connoisseur Cassettes (E) JCC 90,
          Saga (E) 6917

NOTE: Supervised by George Simon. Recorded in RCA studios. At least one additional title was cut at this session, according to Simon. V-Disc issues are 12-inch discs. FDC (I) 1020 may never have been issued. Pee Wee Speaks issued as Pee Wee Blues on Jazz Connoisseur Cassettes JCC 90. A spoken introduction by Muggsy Spanier to Jazz Me Blues and a dialog by Spanier and Pee Wee Russell preceeding Pee Wee Speaks are included on the original V-Disc issues, but omitted from most other releases. Alternate takes of both introductions were recorded but not issued.

Eddie Condon
NYC, October 21, 1944

Max Kaminsky, trumpet; Miff Mole, trombone; Pee Wee Russell, clarinet; Ernie Caceres, baritone; Gene Schroeder, piano; Bob Casey, bass; Joe Grauso, drums.

Royal Garden Blues
    33:   Baybridge (J) UXP 126, Baybridge (J) UPS 2258, Jazum 37,
          Jazzology JCE 1012
    TX: >AFRS EC 21
    CD: Baybridge (J) 30CP-136, Jazzology JCD 1012

Billy Butterfield, Dick Cary, trumpet; Miff Mole, trombone; Pee Wee Russell, clarinet; Ernie Caceres, baritone; Gene Schroeder, piano; Bob Casey, bass; Joe Grauso, drums; Red McKenzie, vocal.

Little High Chairman (RMcK vocal)
    33:   Baybridge (J) JPS 2258, Jazum 37, Jazzology JCE 1012
    TX: >AFRS EC 21
    CD: Jazzology JCD 1012

Billy Butterfield, trumpet; Miff Mole, trombone; Pee Wee Russell, clarinet; Ernie Caceres, baritone; Jess Stacy or Gene Schroeder, piano; Bob Casey, bass; Joe Grauso, drums.

Struttin' With Some Barbecue
    45:   Gazel (Sd) gep 7
    33:   Baybridge (J) UXP 126, Baybridge (J) UPS 2258, Jazum 37,
           Jazzology JCE 1012, Storyville (D) SLP 133, Teichiku (J)
           ULS-1564(R)
    TX: >AFRS EC 21
    CD: Baybridge (J) 30CP-136, Jazzology JCD 1012

Dick Cary, Billy Butterfield, trumpet; Miff Mole, trombone; Pee Wee Russell, clarinet; Ernie Caceres, baritone; Jess Stacy, piano; Bob Casey, bass; Joe Grauso, drums; Dick Cary, arranger; Lee Wiley, vocal.

Old Folks (LW vocal)
    33:   Baybridge (J) UPS 2258, Baybridge (J) UPS 2280, Dan (J)
           VC 5020, Jazum 38, Jazzology JCE 1012
    TX: >AFRS EC 21
    CD: Baybridge (J) 30CP-135, Jazzology JCD 1012

Max Kaminsky, Billy Butterfield, trumpet, Miff Mole, trombone; Pee Wee Russell, clarinet; Ernie Caceres, baritone; Jess Stacy, Gene Schroeder, piano; Bob Casey, bass; Joe Grauso, drums.

Impromptu Ensemble
    33:   Baybridge (J) UPS 2258, Jazum 38, Jazum 66, Jazzology JCE
           1012
    TX: >AFRS EC 21, AFRS EC 44 (incomplete)
    CD: Jazzology JCD 1012

NOTE: Produced by Ernest Anderson. From a concert at the Ritz Theater, Blue network broadcast #23. Other selections from this broadcast do not include Pee Wee Russell. "Impromptu Ensemble" entitled "Ensemble Blues" on Jazum 38 and 66. The Jazzology issues contain the complete program, including narration, as broadcast by the Blue network.

Eddie Condon And His Orchestra

NYC, October 24, 1944

Billy Butterfield, Max Kaminsky, trumpet; Lou McGarity, trombone; Pee Wee Russell, clarinet; Ernie Caceres, baritone; Jess Stacy, piano; Eddie Condon, guitar; Bob Haggart, bass; George Wettling, drums; Lee Wiley, vocal.

zz-4167-4   You're Lucky To Me (LW, vocal)
    33:   Palm 30 (E) P.30:08, Tono TJ-6004
    TX: >Associated A 60,635, Associated A 61,015
    CD: Stash ST-CD-530

Muggsy Spanier, cornet; Lou McGarity, trombone; Pee Wee Russell, clarinet; Jess Stacy, piano; Eddie Condon, guitar; Bob Haggart, bass; George Wettling, drums.

zz-4167-5   I Want A Big Butter And Egg Man (breakdown)
    Unissued

zz-4168-1   I Want A Big Butter And Egg Man (breakdown)
    Unissued

zz-4168-2   I Want A Big Butter And Egg Man (breakdown)
    Unissued

zz-4168-3   I Want A Big Butter And Egg Man
    TX: >Associated A 60,802, Muzak M-2425

Add Max Kaminsky, trumpet; Ed Hall, clarinet.

zz-4168-4   Carnegie Leap (false start)
    Unissued

zz-4168-5   Carnegie Leap
    78:   Wax Shop 105
    33:   Palm 30 (E) P.30:08
    TX: AFRS BML P-368, >Associated A 60,635, Associated A 61,018, Associated A 61,246

Omit Spanier, cornet; and Hall, clarinet.

zz-4168-6 At Sundown
   TX: >Associated A 60,802

zz-4169-1 Sugar
   Unissued

zz-4169-2 Sugar
   33: Design DLP 47, Gala GLP 342, Palm 30 (E) P.30:08, Sp 47
   TX: >Associated A 60,636, Associated A 61,015, Muzak M-2425

Muggsy Spanier, cornet; Billy Butterfield, Max Kaminsky, trumpet; Lou McGarity, trombone; Pee Wee Russell, clarinet; Ernie Caceres, clarinet, baritone; Jess Stacy, piano; Eddie Condon, guitar; Bob Haggart, bass; George Wettling, drums.

zz-4169-3 Muggsy's Serenade (breakdown)
   Unissued

zz-4169-4 Muggsy's Serenade
   33: Palm 30 (E) P.30:08
   TX: AFRS BML P-369, >Associated A 60,635, Associated A 61,015

NOTE: Recorded at Muzak studios from 4:30 p.m. to 7:30 p.m. Matrix numbers are from the original Associated acetates. The matrix numbers on the issued transcriptions do not correspond to the above in all cases. Other selections recorded at this session do not include Pee Wee Russell. All Associated and AFRS transcriptions are 16-inch discs. Muzak M-2425 is a standard 12-inch disc. Wax Shop 105 issued by "Eddie's Hot Shots."

Eddie Condon

NYC, October 28, 1944

Max Kaminsky; trumpet; Lou McGarity, trombone; Pee Wee Russell, clarinet; Ernie Caceres, baritone; Jess Stacy, piano; Sid Weiss, bass; George Wettling, drums.

Sweet Georgia Brown
    33:   Jazum 52, Jazzology JCE 1012, Storyville (D) SLP 133
    TX: >AFRS EC 33
    CD: Jazzology JCD 1012

I Ain't Gonna Give Nobody None Of My Jelly Roll
    33:   Chiaroscuro CR 108, Jazzology JCE 1012, Overseas (J)
          ULX-53-V, Spook Jazz (E) SPJ 6607
    TX: >AFRS EC 33
    CD: Jazzology JCD 1012

Max Kaminsky, Dick Cary, trumpet; Lou McGarity, trombone; Pee Wee Russell, Joe Marsala, clarinet; Ernie Caceres, baritone; Jess Stacy, piano; Sid Weiss, bass; George Wettling, drums.

Impromptu Ensemble
    33:   IAJRC IAJRC-38, Jazzology JCE 1012
    TX: >AFRS EC 33
    CD: Jazzology JCD 1012

NOTE: Produced by Ernest Anderson. From a concert at the Ritz Theater, Blue network broadcast #24. Other selections from this broadcast do not include Pee Wee Russell. The Jazzology issues contain the complete program, including narration, as broadcast by the Blue network.

Miff Mole And His Nicksieland Band

NYC, October 30, 1944

Muggsy Spanier, cornet; Miff Mole, trombone; Pee Wee Russell, clarinet; Gene Schroeder, piano; Bert Naser, bass; Joe Grauso, drums.

Peg O' My Heart
    33:   Fanfare 15-115, Joyce 1062
    TX: >AFRS FTR 14, AFRS P-625

Big Butter And Egg Man
    33:    Fanfare 15-115, Joyce 1062
    TX: >AFRS FTR 14, AFRS P-625

NOTE: From a "For the Record" broadcast, NBC studios. Other titles from this broadcast do not include Pee Wee Russell. The program was announced as a V-Disc recording session but none of the selections appeared on that label.

Eddie Condon

NYC, November 4, 1944

Billy Butterfield, trumpet; Lou McGarity, trombone; Pee Wee Russell, clarinet; Ernie Caceres, baritone; Gene Schroeder, piano; Bob Casey, bass; George Wettling, drums.

My Blue Heaven
    33:    Jazum 53, Jazzology JCE-1013, Rarities (E) 44
    TX: >AFRS EC 23, AFRS EC 25, AFRS EC 30
    CD: Jazzology JCD-1013

Dick Cary, trumpet and arranger, Red McKenzie, vocal, added.

Through A Veil Of Indifference (RMcK, vocal)
    33:    Jazzology JCE-1013, Rarities (E) 44
    TX: >AFRS EC 23
    CD: Jazzology JCD-1013

Pee Wee Russell, clarinet; Jess Stacy, piano; Bob Casey, bass; George Wettling, drums.

Untitled Improvisation
    33:    Chiaroscuro CR 108, Jazzology JCE-1013, Overseas (J)
           ULX-53-V, Rarities (E) 44, Storyville (D) SLP 509
    TX: >AFRS EC 23
    CD: Jazzology JCD-1013

Muggsy Spanier, cornet; Billy Butterfield, trumpet; Lou McGarity, trombone; Pee Wee Russell, clarinet; Ernie Caceres, baritone; Gene Schroeder, piano; Bob Casey, bass; George Wettling, drums.

Riverside Blues
    33:   Jazzology JCE-1013, Rarities (E) 44
    TX: >AFRS EC 23
    CD: Jazzology JCD-1013

Billy Butterfield, Dick Cary, trumpet; Lou McGarity, trombone; Pee Wee Russell, Ernie Caceres, clarinet; Jess Stacy, piano; Bob Casey, bass; George Wettling, drums; Lee Wiley, vocal.

Wherever There's Love (LW vocal)
    33:   Jazum 63, Jazzology JCE-1013, Rarities (E) 44
    TX: >AFRS EC 23, AFRS EC 36
    CD: Jazzology JCD-1013

Muggsy Spanier, cornet; Billy Butterfield, Dick Cary, trumpet; Lou McGarity, trombone; Pee Wee Russell, clarinet; Ernie Caceres, baritone; Jess Stacy, Gene Schroeder, piano; Bob Casey, bass; George Wettling, drums.

Impromptu Ensemble
    33:   Jazzology JCE-1013, Rarities (E) 44
    TX: >AFRS EC 23
    CD: Jazzology JCD-1013

NOTE: Produced by Ernest Anderson. From a Ritz Theater concert, Blue network #25. "Untitled Improvisation" entitled "Pee Wee's Town Hall Stomp," on Chiaroscuro CR 108, Overseas (J) ULX-53-V and Jazzology JCD-1013, and entitled "Pee Wee Original" on Rarities 44. Other selections from this broadcast do not include Pee Wee Russell. The Jazzology issues contain the complete program, including narration, as broadcast by the Blue network.

Eddie Condon

NYC, November 11, 1944

Max Kaminsky, trumpet; Pee Wee Russell, clarinet; Ernie Caceres, baritone; Jess Stacy, piano; Bob Casey, bass; Joe Grauso, drums.

Easter Parade
    33: >Jazzology JCE-1013
    CD: >Jazzology JCD-1013

Someday Sweetheart
    33: >Jazzology JCE-1013
    CD: >Jazzology JCD-1013

Impromptu Ensemble
    33: >Jazzology JCE-1013
    CD: >Jazzology JCE-1013

NOTE: Produced by Ernest Anderson. From a Ritz Theater concert, Blue network broadcast #26. No AFRS transcription was issued. One other selection known to exist from this show does not include Pee Wee Russell. No trombone was present on this broadcast. The Jazzology issues contain the complete program, including narration, as broadcast by the Blue network.

Eddie Condon

NYC, November 18, 1944

Billy Butterfield, trumpet; Lou McGarity, trombone; Pee Wee Russell, clarinet; Ernie Caceres, baritone; Jess Stacy, piano; Bob Casey, bass; George Wettling, drums.

Way Down Yonder In New Orleans
    33: >Jazum 74, Jazzology JCE-1013
    CD: Jazzology JCD-1013

Song Of The Wanderer
    33: >Jazum 74, Jazzology JCE-1013
    CD: Jazzology JCD-1013

Impromptu Ensemble
    33:   >Jazum 74, Jazzology JCE-1013
    CD: Jazzology JCD-1013

NOTE: Produced by Ernest Anderson. From a concert at the Ritz Theater, Blue network broadcast #27. No AFRS transcription is known to exist of this broadcast. One other selection does not include Pee Wee Russell. The Jazzology issues contain the complete program, including narration, as broadcast by the Blue network.

Eddie Condon
NYC, November 25, 1944

Billy Butterfield, trumpet; Lou McGarity, trombone; Pee Wee Russell, clarinet; Ernie Caceres, baritone; Jess Stacy, piano; Bob Casey, bass; Johnny Blowers, drums.

September In The Rain
    33:   Jazum 38, Jazzology JCE-1014, Rhapsody (E) RHA 6028
    TX: >AFRS EC 24
    CD: Jazzology JCD-1014

Muggsy Spanier, cornet, replaces Butterfield.

The Lady's In Love With You
    33:   Jazum 38, Jazzology JCE-1014
    TX: >AFRS EC 24
    CD: Jazzology JCD-1014

Dick Cary, trumpet and arranger; probably Billy Butterfield, trumpet; Lou McGarity, trombone; Pee Wee Russell, clarinet; Ernie Caceres, baritone; Jess Stacy, piano; Bob Casey, bass; Johnny Blowers, drums, Lee Wiley, vocal.

Old Folks (LW vocal)
    33:   Dan (J) VC 5020, Jazzology JCE-1014, Palm 30 (E) P.30:08
    TX: >AFRS EC 24
    CD: Jazzology JCD-1014

Muggsy Spanier, cornet; Hot Lips Page, trumpet, vocal; Billy Butterfield, Dick Cary, trumpet; Lou McGarity, trombone; Pee Wee Russell, clarinet; Ernie Caceres, baritone; Jess Stacy, piano; Bob Casey, bass; Johnny Blowers, drums.

Uncle Sam Blues (HLP vocal)
- 33: Chiaroscuro CR 113, Foxy (F) 9007, Jazzology JCE-1014,
  Overseas (J) ULX-54-V
- TX: >AFRS EC 24
- CD: Jazzology JCE-1014

NOTE: Produced by Ernest Anderson. From a Ritz Theater concert, Blue network broadcast 28. The Jazzology issues contain the complete program, including narration, as broadcast by the Blue network.

Eddie Condon

NYC, December 2, 1944

Max Kaminsky, trumpet; Jack Teagarden, trombone; Pee Wee Russell, clarinet; Ernie Caceres, baritone; Cliff Jackson, piano; Jack Lesberg, bass; George Wettling, drums.

I've Found A New Baby
- 33: Baybridge (J) UXP 126, Baybridge (J) UPS 2258, Good
  Music JRR 3, Jazzology JCE-1014, Pumpkin 106
- TX: >AFRS EC 26
- CD: Baybridge (J) 30CP-136, Jazzology JCE-1014

Norma Teagarden, piano, replaces Jackson.

Little Rock Getaway
- 33: Baybridge (J) UPS 2258, Jazzology JCE-1014, Pumpkin 106
- TX: >AFRS EC 26
- CD: Jazzology JCE-1014

Wingy Manone, trumpet, replaces Kaminsky. Jackson, piano, replaces Norma Teagarden.

The Sheik of Araby
- 33: Baybridge (J) UPS 2258, Jazzology JCE-1014, Pumpkin 106
- TX: >AFRS EC 26
- CD: Jazzology JCD-1014

Bobby Hackett, cornet; Max Kaminsky, trumpet, replace Manone.

Baby, Won't You Please Come Home
    33: Baybridge (J) UXP 126, Baybridge (J) UPS 2258, Jazzology
          JCE-1014, Pumpkin 106
    TX: >AFRS EC 26
    CD: Baybridge (J) 30CP-136, Jazzology JCD-1014
    CT: Jazz Connoisseur Cassettes (E) J.C.C. 41

Bobby Hackett, cornet; Wingy Manone, trumpet, vocal; Max
Kaminsky, trumpet; Jack Teagarden, trombone, vocal; Pee Wee
Russell, clarinet; Ernie Caceres, baritone; Cliff Jackson, Norma
Teagarden, piano; Jack Lesberg, bass; George Wettling, drums.

Impromptu Ensemble (WM & JT vocal)
    33: Baybridge (J) UPS 2258, Jazzology JCE-1014, Pumpkin 106
    TX: AFRS EC 26
    CD: Jazzology JCD-1014
    CT: Jazz Connoisseur Cassettes (E) J.C.C. 41

NOTE: Produced by Ernest Anderson. From a concert at the Ritz
Theatre, Blue network broadcast #29. "Impromptu Ensemble" entitled
"Big T and Wingy Blues" on Pumpkin 106. Other selections from this
broadcast do not include Pee Wee Russell. The Jazzology issues
contain the complete program, including narration, as broadcast by the
Blue network.

Muggsy Spanier And His Ragtimers

                              NYC, December 7, 1944

Muggsy Spanier, cornet; Lou McGarity, trombone; Pee Wee Russell,
clarinet; Gene Schroeder, piano; Eddie Condon, guitar; Bob Haggart,
bass, whistling; Joe Grauso, drums.

A 4835-1 Sobbin' Blues No. 2
    33: >Commodore (G) 6.26167 AG, London (G) 6.26167, Mosaic
          MR23-128

A 4835-2   Sobbin' Blues
   78:   >Commodore 621
   45:   Commodore CEP-25, Commodore 45-621
   33:   Commodore FL 20,012, Commodore FL 30,016, Commodore
         (G) 6.26167 AG, London (E) HMC 5025, London (G)
         6.26167, London (J) LAX 3311, Mainstream S/6010,
         Mainstream 56010, Mainstream (J) XM 33 MSD, Mosaic
         MR23-128, Stateside (E) SL 10004

A 4836-1   Darktown Strutters' Ball
   78:   >Commodore 621
   45:   Commodore CEP 24, Commodore 45-621
   33:   Book of the Month Club 10-5557, Commodore FL 20,012,
         Commodore FL 30,016, Commodore (G) 6.26167 AG,
         London (E) HMC 5025, London (G) 6.26167, London (J)
         LAX 3311, Mainstream S/6010, Mainstream 56010,
         Mainstream (J) XM 33 MSD, Mosaic MR23-128, Stateside
         (E) SL 10004
   CT: Book of the Month Club 60-5561
   8T: Book of the Month Club 50-5560

A 4836-2   Darktown Strutters' Ball No. 2
   33   >Commodore (G) 6.26167 AG, London (G) 6.26167, Mosaic
         MR23-128

A 4837-1   The Lady's In Love With You
   78:   >Commodore 576
   45:   Commodore CEP 18, Commodore 45-576
   33:   Commodore FL 20,009, Commodore FL 30,016, Commodore
         (G) 6.26167 AG, London (E) HMC 5025, London (G)
         6.26167, London (J) LAX 3311, Mosaic MR23-128,
         Stateside (E) SL 10004
   TX: AFRS MD 87

A 4838-TK1 Whistlin' The Blues #3 (BH whistling)
   33:   >Mosaic MR23-128

A 4838-1   Whistlin' The Blues No. 2 (BH whistling)
   33:   >Commodore (G) 6.26167 AG, London (G) 6.26167, Mosaic
         MR23-128

A-4838-2   Whistlin' The Blues #4 (BH whistling)
   33:   >Mosaic MR23-128

179

A 4838-3   Whistlin' The Blues (BH whistling)
  78: >Commodore 576
  45: Commodore CEP 18, Commodore 45-576
  33: Commodore FL 20,009, Commodore FL 30,016,
      Commodore (G) 6.26167 AG, Commodore (J) GXC 3154,
      Commodore (J) K23P-6622, Giants of Jazz (E) LPJT 16,
      London (E) HMC 5025, London (G) 6.26167, London (J)
      SLC 442, London (J) LAX 3311, Mainstream S/6010,
      Mainstream 56010, Mainstream (J) XM 33 MSD, Mosaic
      MR23-128, Stateside (E) SL 10004

NOTE: Produced by Milt Gabler. Recorded at WOR studios, 1440
Broadway. Commodore 45-576 and 45-621 were scheduled for release
but never appeared.

Red McKenzie And The Eddie Condon Band

NYC, December 8, 1944

Max Kaminsky, trumpet; Jack Teagarden, trombone; Pee Wee Russell,
clarinet; Gene Schroeder, piano; Eddie Condon, guitar; Bob Casey,
bass; Joe Grauso, drums; Red McKenzie, vocal.

N 2914-1 Ida, Sweet As Apple Cider (false start)
  33: >Jazzology J-110

N 2914-2 Ida, Sweet As Apple Cider
  33: >Jazzology J-110

N 2914-3 Ida, Sweet As Apple Cider
  33: >Jazzology J-110

N 2914-4 Ida, Sweet As Apple Cider
  33: Jazzology J-110
  TX: >World Feature JS 41

N 2915-1 I Would Do Anything For You (false start)
  33: >Jazzology J-110

N 2915-2 I Would Do Anything For You (false start)
  33: >Jazzology J-110

N 2915-3 I Would Do Anything For You (incomplete)
  33: >Jazzology J-110

N 2915-4 I Would Do Anything For You (false start)
    33:   >Jazzology J-110

N 2915-5 I Would Do Anything For You
    33:   Jazzology J-110
    TX: >World Feature JS 40

N 2916-1 I've Got the World On A String
    33:   Jazzology J-110
    TX: >World Feature JS 41

N 2916-2 I've Got the World On A String
    33:   Jazzology J-110
    TX: >World Feature JS 41

N 2917-1 Exactly Like You
    33:   Jazzology J-110
    TX: >World Feature JS 41

N 2918-1 Basin Street Blues
    33:   >Jazzology J-110

N 2918-2 Basin Street Blues (incomplete)
    33:   >Jazzology J-110

N 2918-3 Basin Street Blues
    33:   Jazzology J 110
    TX: World Disc R-585, >World Feature JS 40

N 2919-1 Baby, Won't You Please Come Home
    33:   >Jazzology J-110

N 2919-2 Baby, Won't You Please Come Home
    33:   Jazzology J 110
    TX: World Disc R-585, >World Feature JS 40

N 2920-1 Sweet Lorraine (false start)
    33:   >Jazzology J-110

N 2920-2 Sweet Lorraine (false start)
    33:   >Jazzology J-110

N 2920-3 Sweet Lorraine
    33:   >Jazzology J-110

N 2920-4 Sweet Lorraine
    33:   Jazzology J 110
    TX: World Disc R-585, >World Feature JS 41

N 2921-1 Dinah (false start)
    33:   >Jazzology J-110

N 2921-2 Dinah
    33:   Jazzology J 110
    TX: World Disc R-585, >World Feature JS 40

N 2922-1 After You've Gone (incomplete)
    33:   >Jazzology J-110

N 2922-2 After You've Gone (false start)
    33:   >Jazzology J-110

N 2922-3 After You've Gone
    33:   Jazzology J-110
    TX: >World Feature JS 40

N 2923-1 Way Down Yonder In New Orleans
    33:   Jazzology J-110
    TX: >World Feature JS 40

N 2923-2 Way Down Yonder In New Orleans
    33:   >Jazzology J-110

N 2923-3 Way Down Yonder In New Orleans (false start)
    33:   >Jazzology J-110

N 2923-4 Way Down Yonder In New Orleans (false start)
    33:   >Jazzology J-110

N 2923-5 Way Down Yonder In New Orleans
    33:   >Jazzology J-110

NOTE: Produced by Milt Gabler. World Feature transcriptions were issued in both lateral and vertical cut versions. This session was recorded from 2 p.m. to 5:30 p.m. World Disc 585, a 12-inch disc, is labeled as Eddie Condon, vocal by Red McKenzie. Other World transcriptions are 16-inch discs.

182

Eddie Condon
                                    NYC, December 10, 1944
Bobby Hackett, cornet; Jack Teagarden, trombone; Pee Wee Russell,
clarinet; Ernie Caceres, baritone; Norma Teagarden, piano; Bob
Haggart, bass; George Wettling, drums; Lowell Thomas, announcer.

Honeysuckle Rose (LT voice over)
    Unissued

Reader's Digest Blues
    Unissued

NOTE: From the 118th broadcast of Radio Reader's Digest.

Eddie Condon and His Orchestra
                                    NYC, December 13, 1944
Bobby Hackett, cornet; Billy Butterfield, Max Kaminsky, trumpet; Jack
Teagarden, trombone, vocal; Pee Wee Russell, clarinet; Ernie Caceres,
baritone; Gene Schroeder, piano; Eddie Condon, guitar; Bob Haggart,
bass; George Wettling, drums; Lee Wiley, vocal.

W-72621-A Impromptu Ensemble No. 1 (JT vocal)
    78: Brunswick (E) 04306, >Decca 23718, Decca (E) M 30464,
         Decca (F) MU 60234
    45: Decca ED 722, Decca ED 843, Decca 91527, Decca 91713
    33: Ace of Hearts (E) AH 100, Affinity (E) AFS 1021,
         Brunswick (E) LAT 8124, Brunswick (E) LA 8577,
         Brunswick (F) LPBM 87003, Brunswick (F) LPBM 87008,
         Brunswick (G) LPBM 87003, Brunswick (G) LPBM 87008,
         Decca DL 5218, Decca DL 8244, Decca DL 8281, Decca
         (Arg) LTM 9291, Decca (J) JDL 2060, Decca (J) JDL 6013,
         Decca (J) JDL 6037, Decca (Sc) BKL 8124, Decca (Sc)
         BML8577, MCA 2-4071, MCA (F) 510 206, MCA (J) MCA
         3100

W-72622-A The Man I Love (LW vocal)
    78: >Decca 23432, Decca (C) 23432
    45: Decca ED 539, Decca 91051
    33: Brunswick (E) LA 8518, Compagnie Ind. du Disque (F) UM
         233043, Decca DL 5137, Decca DL 9234, Decca DL 79234,
         Decca (C) DL 5137, Decca (Sc) BML 8518, Decca (J) JDL 7,
         MCA (J) MCA 3019, MCA (J) MCA 3100, MCA (J) MCA
         3160, Tono TJ 6004

Omit Hackett, cornet, and Kaminsky, trumpet.

W-72623-A   'S Wonderful
  78: Brunswick (E) 04304, >Decca 23430, Decca (C) 23430
  45: Decca ED 539, Decca 91050
  33: Brunswick (E) LA 8518, Compagnie Ind. du Disque (F) UM
       233043, Decca DL 5137, Decca DL 9234, Decca DL 79234,
       Decca (C) DL 5137, Decca (Sc) BML 8518, Decca (J) JDL 7,
       MCA (J) MCA 3019, MCA (J) MCA 3100

NOTE: Produced by Milt Gabler. Two additional titles, W 72619-A, "When Your Lover Has Gone," and W 72620-A, "Wherever There's Love," cut at this session, do not include Russell.

Eddie Condon and His Orchestra

NYC, December 14, 1944

Bobby Hackett, cornet; Billy Butterfield, Max Kaminsky, trumpet; Jack Teagarden, trombone, vocal; Pee Wee Russell, clarinet; Ernie Caceres, baritone; Gene Schroeder, piano; Eddie Condon, guitar; Bob Haggart, bass; George Wettling, drums; Lee Wiley, vocal.

N 2944-1 Jam Session Jump (false start)
  33: >Jazzology J 101

N 2944-2 Jam Session Jump
  33: >Jazzology J 101

N 2944-3 Jam Session Jump
  33: Jazum 78, Jazzology J 102
  TX: World Disc 358, >World Feature JS 44

N 2945-1 Jam Session Blues (false start)
  33: >Jazzology J 101

N 2945-2 Jam Session Blues
  33: >Jazzology J 101

N 2945-3 Jam Session Blues
  33: >Jazzology J 101

N 2945-4 Jam Session Blues
  33: Jazzology J 102
  TX: World Disc 358, >World Feature JS 44

N 2946- Someone To Watch Over Me (LW, vocal)
  78: Decca 23422, Decca (C) 23422
  45: Decca ED 539, Decca 91051
  33: Brunswick (E) LA 8518, Compagnie Ind. du Disque (F) UM
      233043, Decca DL 5137, Decca DL 9234, Decca DL 79234,
      Decca (Sc) BML 8518, Decca (J) JDL 7, Jazzology J 102,
      MCA (J) VIM 8, MCA (J) MCA 3005, MCA (J) MCA 3019,
      MCA (J) MCA 3100, MCA (J) MCA 3160, Tono TJ 6004
  TX: >World Feature JS 42

N 2947- Sheik Of Araby (JT & EC vocal)
  78: Decca 23718, Decca BM 30464
  45: Decca ED 722, Decca 91527
  33: Ace of Hearts (E) AH 28, Affinity (E) AFS 1021, Brunswick
      (E) LAT 8229, Brunswick (E) LA 8577, Coral (E) COPS
      3442, Coral 6.21851, Coral (E) CB 20013, Decca DL 4540,
      Decca DL 5218, Decca DL 8281, Decca DL 8304, Decca
      (Arg) LTM 9291, Decca (J) JDL 2060, Decca (J) JDL 2066,
      Decca (J) JDL 5082, Decca (J) JDL 6037, Decca (J) JDL
      6077, Decca (Sc) BKL 8229, Decca (Sc) BML 8577,
      Jazzology J 102, MCA (Arg) MCAB 5062, MCA (F) 510
      206, MCA (J) 227, MCA (J) 3100
  TX: >World Feature JS 42

N 2948- The Man I Love (LW vocal)
  33: Jazzology J 102
  TX: >World Feature JS 42

N 2949-   Somebody Loves Me (JT vocal)
   78:    Brunswick (E) 04305, Decca 23430
   45:    Decca ED 539
   33:    Ace of Hearts (E) AH 28, Affinity (E) AFS 1021, Brunswick (F) LPB 87016, Brunswick (G) LPB 87016, Brunswick (E) LAT 8168, Brunswick (E) LAT 8229, Brunswick (E) LA 8518, Compaigne Ind. du Disque UM 233043, Coral (E) COPS 3442, Coral 6.21851, Decca DL 4540, Decca DL 5137, Decca DL 8304, Decca DL 8400, Decca DL 9234, Decca DL 79234, Decca (C) DL 5137, Decca (J) JDL 7, Decca (J) JDL 5082, Decca (J) JDL 6025, Decca (J) JDL 6077, Decca (Sc) BKL 8168, Decca (Sc) BML 8518, Decca (Sc) BKL 8229, Festival (Au) FAL 3, Jazzology J 102, MCA 227, MCA 2-4062, MCA (Arg) MCAB 5062, MCA (C) 2-4062, MCA (F) 510 206, MCA (J) MCA 3019, MCA (J) MCA 3100
   TX: World Disc 494, >World Feature JS 42

NOTE: Produced by Milt Gabler. World Feature transcriptions were issued in both lateral and vertical cut versions. Matrix numbers shown on Decca 78 issues are as follows: W-72630-A (N 2946), W-72631-A (N 2947), W-72632- (N 2948) and W-72633- (N 2949). Decca 23422 and 23430 were issued in album A-398 as "George Gershwin Jazz Concert." Decca 23718 was issued in album A-490 as "A Night at Eddie Condon's." Decca DL 8400 was issued both singly and as part of an album with the overall number of DXF-140.

Eddie Condon

                                       NYC, December 16, 1944

Max Kaminsky, trumpet; Jack Teagarden, trombone, vocal; Pee Wee Russell, clarinet; Ernie Caceres, baritone; Gene Schroeder, piano; Eddie Condon, guitar, vocal; Sid Weiss, bass; Johnny Blowers, drums.

Ballin' The Jack
   33:    Baybridge (J) UPS 2259, Pumpkin 106
   TX: >AFRS EC 28

The Sheik Of Araby (JT & EC vocals)
   33:    Baybridge (J) UPS 2259, Pumpkin 106
   TX: >AFRS EC 28

One of the bands in JAM SESSION

Eddie Condon, guitar • Pee Wee Russell, clarinet • Bob Casey, bass • Gene Schroeder, piano • "Wild Bill" Davison, trumpet • George Brunis, trombone • George Wettling, drums

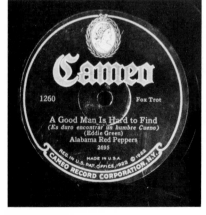

POLYDOR
SÉRIE
RYTHME
A.C.L.   580.009
MÉDIUM
BASIN STREET BLUES
(Sp Williams)
Louis PRIMA
and his New Orléans Gang
B 17 615

Brunswick   Recording
Lucky
Fox Trot (Mid-Step)
Vocal Refrain
THE LADY IN RED
From the Warner Picture "In Caliente"
(Dixon & Wrubel)   (Tempo 45)
LOUIS PRIMA and HIS
NEW ORLEANS GANG
(B 17612) B   60144

COMMODORE
CLASSICS IN SWING
500 B
Eddie Condon & His Windy City Seven
Bobby Hackett   Bud Freeman
Cornet   Tenor Sax
Pee-Wee Russell   George Brunies
Clarinet   Trombone
Love Is Just Around The Corner
(Robin—Gensler)
Jess Stacy   Eddie Condon
Piano   Tenor Guitar
George Wettling   Drums
Artie Shapiro, Bass
Wax Licensed for Radio Broadcast Jan. 1938
Published by Commodore Music Shop, 144 East 42nd Street, New York City
Commodore Music Shop, 144 East 42nd Street, New York City

10-251
(M-7-300)
Esquire
COPYRIGHT
CONTROL
Complimentary Copy
LEADERS HEADACHE BLUES
(The Gang)
VIC LEWIS AND HIS AMERICAN JAZZMEN
Bobby Hackett, cornet.   Brad Gowans, valve trombone.
Pee Wee Russell, clarinet.   Bernie Billings, tenor sax.
Ernie Caceres, baritone sax.   Dave Bowman,
piano.   Zutty Singleton, drums.
Eddie Condon, Vic Lewis, guitars.
Josie Carole, vocal.
19.10.38.

HOT RECORD SOCIETY
Originals

HRS 1000
(P23391-1)

BABY WON'T YOU PLEASE COME HOME
(Warfield-Williams)
PEE-WEE RUSSELL'S RHYTHMAKERS

Pee-Wee Russell, clarinet; Max Kaminsky, trumpet
Dicky Wells, trombone; Al Gold, tenor sax
Jimmy Johnson, piano; Freddie Green, guitar
Zutty Singleton, drums; Wellman Braud, bass
Released by
H. R. S. RECORD SHOP
827 Seventh Ave.
N. Y. C.

WAR DEPARTMENT
187 B

THE ARMED FORCES RADIO SERVICE
Presents

PART 1   Prog. Time & Fill 30:00

EDDIE CONDON

2 9

This transcription is the property of the War Department of the United States Government and use
for commercial purposes is prohibited.

No. 394B
PAT'S BLUES
Spanier
Muggsy Spanier and his V-DISC All Stars

Muggsy Spanier, Cornet; Lou McGarity, Trom-
bone; Peewee Russell, Clarinet; Bonnie Richmond,
Tenor Sax; Jess Stacy, Piano; George Wettling,
Drums; Hi White, Guitar; Bob Haggart,
Bass and Whistling

Hot Jazz

This record is the property of the War Department
of the United States and use for radio or
commercial purposes is prohibited.

WAR DEPARTMENT-MUSIC SECTION-ENTERTAINMENT & RECREATION BRANCH-SPECIAL SERVICES DIVISION-A.S.F.

OUTSIDE START · 78 RPM

BREAKABLE IN NORMAL USE

Bird Cage

1601-A

FEATHER BRAIN BLUES
(KATE SPANIER, P. DANIEL)
MUGGSY SPANIER'S JAZZ BAND

Muggsy Spanier, Pee Wee Russell, Bob Haggart,
Ernie Caceres, Chas. Carol, Gene Schroeder,
Lou McGarrity, Karl Kress

PRESSED BY CIRCLE RECORD COMPANY, SAN FRANCISCO

COLUMBIA

ELECTRICAL TRANSCRIPTION

LATERAL CUT   PLAYING SPEED 33⅓ R.P.M.

CONCÉRTOS DE MÚSICA POPULAR
De Town Hall
em Nova York

BRA 2-4327 (Portuguese)   Programa No. 9

1. She Is Funny That Way
2. El Tio Sam no es una muchacha;
pero te puede quitar el novio

RECORDED AND PRESSED BY

COLUMBIA RECORDING CORPORATION

NEW YORK – BRIDGEPORT – HOLLYWOOD – CHICAGO

MADE IN U.S.A.
YTNY 2996

DISC
NEW YORK

6032A

PEE WEE SQUAWKS
(Spanier-Russell)

Muggsy Spanier, cornet; Pee Wee Russell,
clarinet; Vernon Brown, trombone; Nick
Ciazzo, tenor sax; Gene Schroeder,
piano; Bob Haggart, bass;
George Wettling, drums.

519

HOLIDAY
RECORD CO.
NEW YORK

4002 B   Instrumental

SENTIMENTAL JOURNEY
(Green, Brown, Homer)

Muggsy Spanier Orchestra
MUGGSY SPENIER, Cornet; VERNON BROWN, Trombone;
NICK CIAZZA, Tenor Sax; PEE WEE RUSSELL,
Clarinet; GENE SCHROEDER, Piano; BOB
HAGGART, Bass; GEORGE WETTLING,
Drums
520-H

MANUFACTURER ONLY FOR NON-COMMERCIAL USE FOR PHONOGRAMS IN HOMES

the WAX shop

139 east 47th street, new york 17

105 A

CARNEGIE LEAP
EDDIE'S HOT SHOTS

Feat: Muggsy Spanier, Max Kaminsky, cornets;
Lou McGarity, trombone; Pee Wee
Russell, Edmond Hall, clarinets.

for sale exclusively at the wax shop

Bobby Hackett, cornet, added. Dick Cary, arranger.

There's A Small Hotel
    33:   Baybridge (J) UPS 2259
    TX: >AFRS EC 28

Billy Butterfield, trumpet, replaces Kaminsky. Hackett omitted.

Royal Garden Blues
    33:   Baybridge (J) UPS 2259, Pumpkin 106
    TX: >AFRS EC 28

Add Bobby Hackett, cornet; Lee Wiley, vocal.

Wherever There's Love (LW vocal)
    33:   Baybridge (J) UPS 2259, Dan (J) VC 5020, Pumpkin 106
    TX: >AFRS EC 28
    CT: Jazz Connoisseur Cassettes (E) J.C.C. 41, Jazz Connoisseur
           Cassettes (E) J.C.C. 114

Add Max Kaminsky, trumpet; Sidney Bechet, soprano.

Impromptu Ensemble
    33:   Baybridge (J) UPS 2259, Pumpkin 106
    TX: >AFRS EC 28
    CT: Jazz Connoisseur Cassettes (E) J.C.C. 41

NOTE: Produced by Ernest Anderson. From a concert at the Ritz
Theater, Blue network broadcast #30. "Impromptu Ensemble" entitled
"Christmas at Carnegie" on Pumpkin. Other selections from this
broadcast do not include Pee Wee Russell. The complete broadcast,
including narration, is scheduled to be issued on Jazzology JCE 1015
and Jazzology JCD 1015.

Eddie Condon

                        NYC, December 23, 1944

Max Kaminsky, Wingy Manone, trumpet; Pee Wee Russell, clarinet;
Jess Stacy, piano; Bob Casey, bass; George Wettling, drums.

Jingle Bells
    Unissued

On The Sunny Side Of The Street
    33:    Baybridge (J) LPE-1, Jazum 74
    TX: >AFRS EC 29

Pee Wee Russell, clarinet; Jess Stacy, piano; Bob Casey, bass; George Wettling, drums.

D.A. Blues
    33:    Aircheck 26, Chiaroscuro CR 108, Overseas (J) ULX-53-V, Storyville (D) SLP 509
    TX: >AFRS EC 29

Same personnel as for "Jingle Bells."

Blue Skies
    33:    Jazum 74
    TX: >AFRS EC 29

Bobby Hackett, cornet; Wingy Manone, trumpet; Pee Wee Russell, clarinet; Ernie Caceres, baritone; Gene Schroeder, piano; Bob Casey, bass; George Wettling, drums. Max Kaminsky, trumpet, may also be present on this title.

Exactly Like You
    33:    Baybridge (J) LPE 1, Jazum 74
    TX: >AFRS EC 29

Omit Manone, trumpet.

Ja Da
    33:    Jazum 74
    TX: >AFRS EC 29

Add Lee Wiley, vocal; omit Manone, trumpet.

You're Lucky To Me (LW, vocal)
    33:    Jazum 74
    TX: >AFRS EC 29

Bobby Hackett, cornet; Max Kaminsky, Wingy Manone, trumpet; Pee Wee Russell, clarinet; Ernie Caceres, baritone; Gene Schroeder and possibly Jess Stacy, piano; Bob Casey, bass; George Wettling, drums.

Impromptu Ensemble
    Unissued

NOTE: Produced by Ernest Anderson. From a concert at the Ritz Theater, Blue network broadcast #31. Other selections from this broadcast do not include Pee Wee Russell. The complete broadcast, including narration, is scheduled to be issued on Jazzology JCE 1015 and Jazzology JCD 1015.

Eddie Condon
                                        NYC, December 30, 1944

Max Kaminsky, trumpet; Benny Morton, trombone; Pee Wee Russell, clarinet; Ernie Caceres, baritone; Jess Stacy, piano; possibly Eddie Condon, guitar; Jack Lesberg, bass; George Wettling, drums.

Walkin' The Dog
    33:   Baybridge (J) UPS 2259, Good Music JRR 3, Jazum 53,
          Rhapsody (E) RHA 6028
    TX: >AFRS EC 30, AFRS EC 48

Strut Miss Lizzie
    33:   Baybridge (J) UPS 2259, Jazum 53, Rhapsody (E) RHA 6029
    TX: >AFRS EC 30

Add Sidney Bechet, soprano.

Sweet Georgia Brown
    33:   Baybridge (J) UPS 2259, Good Music JRR 3, FDC (I) 1012,
          Jazum 53, Jazum 65, Mus 2522
    TX: >AFRS EC 30, AFRS EC 44

Add Lee Wiley, vocal; omit Bechet.

When Your Lover Has Gone (LW vocal)
    33:   Baybridge (J) UPS 2259, Baybridge (J) UPS 2280, Good
          Music JRR 3, Jazum 53, Totem 1033
    TX: >AFRS EC 30
    CD: Baybridge (J) 30CP-135

Omit Wiley; add Bechet, soprano.

Impromptu Ensemble
  33: Baybridge (J) UPS 2259, Good Music JRR 3, Jazum 53,
       Jazum 64
  TX: >AFRS EC 30, AFRS EC 40

NOTE: Produced by Ernest Anderson. From a concert at the Ritz
Theater, Blue network broadcast #32. Other selections from this
broadcast do not include Pee Wee Russell. "Impromptu Ensemble"
entitled "Ensemble Blues" on Jazum 53 and 64. The complete
broadcast, including narration, is scheduled to be issued on Jazzology
JCE 1016 and Jazzology JCD 1016.

Eddie Condon

NYC, January 6, 1945

Billy Butterfield, trumpet; Tommy Dorsey, trombone; Pee Wee
Russell, clarinet; Ernie Caceres, baritone; Jess Stacy, piano; possibly
Eddie Condon, guitar; Sid Weiss, bass; George Wettling, drums.

Sunday
  45: Gazel (Sd) gep 5
  33: Baybridge (J) UPS 2260, Rarities (E) 37
  TX: >AFRS EC 31, AFRS EC 46 (incomplete)
  CD: Baybridge (J) 30CP-136

How Come You Do Me Like You Do
  45: Gazel (Sd) gep 5
  33: Baybridge (J) UPS 2260, Good Music JRR 3, Rarities (E) 37
  TX: >AFRS EC 31, AFRS EC 46

Max Kaminsky, trumpet, replaces Butterfield.

Keep Smiling At Trouble
  33: Baybridge (J) UPS 2260, Rarities (E) 37, Spook Jazz (D) SPJ
       6607
  TX: >AFRS EC 31

Add Billy Butterfield, trumpet.

That's A Plenty
  33: Baybridge (J) UPS 2260, Good Music JRR 3, Rarities (E) 37
  TX: >AFRS EC 31, AFRS EC 46

Probably Butterfield, Dick Cary, trumpet; Tommy Dorsey, trombone; Pee Wee Russell, Ernie Caceres, clarinet; Jess Stacy, piano; Sid Weiss, bass; George Wettling, drums; Bobby Hackett, arranger; Lee Wiley, vocal.

Sugar (LW vocal)
    33:   Baybridge (J) UPS 2260, Good Music JRR 3, Memories
          LWIL 403, Rarities (E) 37
    TX: >AFRS EC 32, AFRS EC 46
    CT: Jazz Connoisseur Cassettes (E) J.C.C. 114

Omit Wiley, add Kaminsky, trumpet.

Impromptu Ensemble
    33:   Baybridge (J) UPS 2260, Chiaroscuro CR 108, Chiaroscuro
          (J) ULX-53-V, Rarities (E) 37, Storyville (D) SLP 509
    TX: >AFRS EC 31

NOTE: Produced by Ernest Anderson. From a Ritz Theater concert, Blue network broadcast #31. Other selections from this broadcast do not include Pee Wee Russell. "Impromptu Ensemble" entitled "Impromptu Ensemble #1," on Chiaroscuro CR 108, and "Carnegie Leap" on Rarities 37. The complete broadcast, including narration, is scheduled to be issued on Jazzology JCE 1016 and Jazzology JCD 1016.

Eddie Condon

NYC, January 13, 1945.

Billy Butterfield, trumpet; Tommy Dorsey, trombone; Pee Wee Russell, clarinet; Ernie Caceres, baritone; Jess Stacy, piano; Sid Weiss, bass; George Wettling, drums.

September In The Rain
    33:   Baybridge (J) UPS 2260, Good Music JRR 3, Rarities (E) 37,
          Sunbeam SB-231
    TX: >AFRS EC 32, AFRS EC 34 (incomplete), AFRS EC 46

191

Muggsy Spanier, cornet, added.

Rose Room
    78: Gazel (Sd) 1044
    33: Baybridge (J) UXP 126, Baybridge (J) UPS 2260, Rarities
         (E) 37, Sunbeam SB-231
    TX: >AFRS EC 32, AFRS EC 46
    CD: Baybridge (J) 30CP-136

At The Jazz Band Ball
    78: Gazel (Sd) 1048
    45: Storyville (D) sep 506
    33: Baybridge (J) UPS 2260, Good Music JRR 3, Joker (I) SM
         3575, Rarities (E) 37, Saga (E) PAN 6917, Spook Jazz (E)
         SPJ 6603, Sunbeam SB 231
    TX: >AFRS EC 32, AFRS EC 46
    CT: Holmia (Sd) HM 06

Lee Wiley, vocal; Billy Butterfield and Dick Cary, trumpets; possibly
Tommy Dorsey, trombone; Pee Wee Russell, clarinet; Ernie Caceres,
baritone; Jess Stacy, piano; Sid Weiss, bass; George Wettling, drums.

How Long Has This Been Going On (LW vocal)
    33: Baybridge (J) UPS 2260, Dan (J) VC 5020, Rarities (E) 37,
         Sunbeam SB 231, Totem 1033
    TX: >AFRS EC 32

Muggsy Spanier, cornet; Billy Butterfield, possibly Dick Cary, trumpet;
Tommy Dorsey, trombone; Pee Wee Russell, clarinet; Ernie Caceres,
baritone; Jess Stacy, Earl Hines, piano; Sid Weiss, bass; George
Wettling, drums.

Impromptu Ensemble
    33: Baybridge (J) UPS 2260, Rarities (E) 37, Sunbeam SB 231
    TX: >AFRS EC 32

NOTE: Produced by Ernest Anderson. From a Ritz Theater concert,
Blue network broadcast #34. Other selections from this broadcast do
not include Pee Wee Russell. The complete broadcast, including
narration, is scheduled to be issued on Jazzology JCE 1017 and
Jazzology JCD 1017.

Wild Bill Davison And His Commodores

NYC, January 19, 1945

Wild Bill Davison, cornet; Lou McGarity, trombone; Pee Wee Russell, clarinet; George Zack or Dick Cary, piano; Eddie Condon, guitar; Bob Casey, bass; Danny Alvin, drums.

A 4843-   I Don't Stand A Ghost Of A Chance #3
    33:    >Mosaic MR23-128

A 4843-1   Ghost Of A Chance
    78:    >Commodore 635
    45:    Commodore CEP-26, Commodore 45-635
    33:    Commodore FL 20,013, Commodore FL 30,009, London (E) HMC 5012, London (F) 180.017, London (J) LAX-3306, Melodisc (E) MLP 12-127, Mosaic MR23-128, Top Rank (J) RANK 5014, Top Rank (H) HJA 16506

A 4843-2 I Don't Stand A Ghost Of A Chance #2
    33:    >Mosaic MR23-128

George Zack, piano.

A 4844-TK1 Jazz Me Blues #2
    33:    >Mosaic MR23-128

A 4844-1   Jazz Me Blues
    78:    >Commodore 623
    45:    Commodore CEP-26, Commodore 45-623
    33:    Book of the Month Club 10-5557, Commodore FL 20,013, London (E) HMC 5012, London (F) 180.017, Mosaic MR23-128
    CT: Book of the Month Club 60-5561
    8T: Book of the Month Club 50-5560

Dick Cary, piano, replaces Zack.

A 4845-TK1/1 Little Girl #2
    33:    >Mosaic MR23-128

A 4845-1   Little Girl
    78:   >Commodore 635
    45:   Commodore CEP-27, Commodore 45-635
    33:   Commodore FL 20,013, London (E) HMC 5012, London (F)
           180.017, London (J) SLC 456, Mosaic MR23-128

A 4846-1   Squeeze Me
    78:   >Commodore 623
    45:   Commodore CEP-27, Commodore 45-623
    33:   Commodore FL 20,013, London (E) HMC 5012, London (F)
           180.017, London (J) SLC 456, Mosaic MR23-128

A 4846-2   Squeeze Me #2
    33:   >Mosaic MR23-128
NOTE: Produced by Milt Gabler. Recorded at WOR studios, 1440
Broadway. Commodore 45-623 and Commodore 45-635 were
scheduled for release but never appeared.

Eddie Condon
                                       NYC, January 20, 1945
Wild Bill Davison, cornet; Tommy Dorsey, trombone; Pee Wee
Russell, clarinet; Ernie Caceres, baritone; Jess Stacy, piano; Sid Weiss,
bass; George Wettling, drums.

Jazz Me Blues
    Unissued

Max Kaminsky, trumpet, replaces Davison.

At Sundown
    Unissued

Earl Hines, piano, replaces Stacy.

Rosetta
    Unissued

Wild Bill Davison, cornet; Tommy Dorsey, trombone; Pee Wee
Russell, clarinet; Sidney Bechet, soprano; Ernie Caceres, baritone; Earl
Hines, piano; Sid Weiss, bass; George Wettling, drums.

The Sheik Of Araby
    33:   Baybridge (J) UXP 126
    CD: Baybridge (J) 30CP-136

Omit Davison, Bechet and Hines. Add Kaminsky, trumpet; Jess Stacy, piano; Lee Wiley, vocal.

Don't Blame Me
    Unissued

Probably collective personnel:

Impromptu Ensemble
    Unissued

NOTE: Produced by Ernest Anderson. From a Ritz Theater concert, Blue network broadcast #35. This was the annual Downbeat awards show and Lee Wiley presented Pee Wee Russell with his trophy for winning first place in the clarinet category. No AFRS transcription of this broadcast is known to exist. Other selections do not include Pee Wee Russell. The complete broadcast, including narration, is scheduled to be issued on Jazzology JCE 1017 and Jazzology JCD 1017.

Eddie Condon
                                                        NYC, February 17, 1945

Max Kaminsky, trumpet; Lou McGarity, trombone; Pee Wee Russell, clarinet; Ernie Caceres, baritone; Jess Stacy, piano; Jack Lesberg, bass; George Wettling, drums.

Strut Miss Lizzie
    33:    Baybridge (J) UPS 2261, Jazum 75
    TX: >AFRS EC 37, AFRS EC 47

Dick Cary, Billy Butterfield, trumpet; possibly Lou McGarity, trombone; possibly Pee Wee Russell, clarinet; Ernie Caceres, baritone; Jess Stacy, piano; Jack Lesberg, bass; George Wettling, drums; Dick Cary, arranger; Red McKenzie, vocal.

Time On My Hands (RMcK vocal)
    33:    Baybridge (J) UPS 2261, Jazum 75, Palm 30 (E) P.30:08
    TX: >AFRS EC 37

Billy Butterfield, trumpet; Lou McGarity, trombone; Pee Wee Russell, clarinet; Ernie Caceres, baritone; Jess Stacy, piano; Jack Lesberg, bass; George Wettling, drums.

Ain't Misbehavin'
78: Gazel (Sd) 1050
33: Baybridge (J) UXP 126, Baybridge (J) UPS 2261, Jazum 76, Spook Jazz (D) SPJ 6007
TX: >AFRS EC 37, AFRS EC 47
CD: Baybridge (J) 30CP-136

Add Max Kaminsky, trumpet, Sidney Bechet, soprano.

At The Jazz Band Ball
33: Baybridge (J) UPS 2261
TX: >AFRS EC 37

Add Lee Wiley, vocal, Omit Kaminsky and Bechet. Bobby Hackett, arranger.

Someone To Watch Over Me (LW vocal)
33: Baybridge (J) UPS 2261, Dan (J) VC 5020, Jazum 63, Totem 1033
TX: >AFRS EC 37, AFRS EC 40

Omit Wiley, vocal. Add Max Kaminsky, trumpet; Sidney Bechet, soprano.

Impromptu Ensemble
33: Baybridge (J) UPS 2261, Jazum 76, Spook Jazz (D) SPJ 6007
TX: >AFRS EC 37

NOTE: Produced by Ernest Anderson. From a Ritz Theater concert, Blue network broadcast #39. Other selections from this broadcast do not include Pee Wee Russell. The complete broadcast, including narration, is scheduled to be issued on Jazzology JCE 1019 and Jazzology JCD 1019.

Nick Presents His Dixieland Band under the direction of Muggsy Spanier

NYC, March 1, 1945

Muggsy Spanier, cornet; Lou McGarity, trombone; Pee Wee Russell, clarinet; Gene Schroeder, piano; Carl Kress, guitar; Bob Casey, bass; Joe Grauso, drums.

Tin Roof Blues
- 78: >Manhattan (C) A 20-1, Tempo (E) A 36
- 45: Storyville (D) SEP 323, Tempo (E) EXA 3
- 33: Storyville SLP 4020, Storyville (D) 671.206, Storyville (J) ULS 1599R, Telefunken (G) UX 4733
- CT: Jazz Connoisseur Cassettes (E) J.C.C. 90

Muskrat Ramble
- 78: >Manhattan (C) A 20-1, Tempo (E) A 36
- 45: Storyville (D) SEP 323, Tempo (E) EXA 3
- 33: Storyville SLP 4020, Storyville (D) 671.206, Storyville (J) ULS 1599R, Telefunken (G) UX 4733
- CT: Jazz Connoisseur Cassettes (E) J.C.C. 90

NOTE: The Manhattans were issued in album A-20. They were pressed by Compo in Montreal.

Nick Presents His Dixieland Band under the direction of Miff Mole

NYC, March 2, 1945

Muggsy Spanier, cornet; Miff Mole, trombone; Pee Wee Russell, clarinet; Gene Schroeder, piano; Fred Sharp, guitar; Jack Lesberg, bass; Charles Carroll, drums.

Original Dixieland One-Step
- 78: >Manhattan (C) A 10-1
- 33: Storyville SLP 4020, Storyville (D) 671.206, Storyville (J) ULS 1599R

I Can't Give You Anything But Love
- 78: >Manhattan (C) A 10-1
- 33: Storyville SLP 4020, Storyville (D) 671.206, Storyville (J) ULS 1599R

Three Little Words
  78:   >Manhattan (C) A 10-2
  33:   Storyville SLP 4020, Storyville (D) 671.206, Storyville (J)
        ULS 1599R

Allen Hanlon, guitar, replaces Sharp.

Livery Stable Blues
  78:   >Manhattan (C) A 10-2
  33:   Storyville SLP 4020, Storyville (D) 671.206, Storyville (J)
        ULS 1599R

I'm Sorry I Made You Cry
  78:   >Manhattan (C) A 10-3
  33:   Storyville SLP 4020, Storyville (D) 671.206, Storyville (J)
        ULS 1599R

Miff's Blues
  78:   >Manhattan (C) A 10-3
  33:   Storyville SLP 4053, Storyville (D) SLP 826

NOTE: The Manhattans were issued in album A-10. They were
pressed by Compo in Montreal.

Nick Presents his Dixieland Band under the direction of Muggsy Spanier

NYC, March 2, 1945

Muggsy Spanier, cornet; Lou McGarity, trombone; Pee Wee Russell,
clarinet; Ernie Caceres, baritone; Gene Schroeder, piano; Carl Kress,
guitar; Bob Haggart, bass, whistling; Charlie Carroll, drums.

M 289   Bugle Call Rag
  78:   >Manhattan (C) A 20-3, Tempo (E) A 64
  45:   Storyville (D) SEP 323, Tempo (E) EXA 3
  33:   Storyville SLP 4020, Storyville (D) 671.206, Storyville (J)
        ULS 1599R, Telefunken (G) UX 4733
  CT: Jazz Connoisseur Cassettes (E) J.C.C. 90

Nick Rongetti, piano, replaces Schroeder on the following title only.

M 290   That's A Plenty
   78: >Manhattan (C) A 20-3, Tempo (E) A 64
   45: Storyville (D) SEP 323, Tempo (E) EXA 3
   33: Storyville SLP 4053, Storyville (D) 826, Telefunken (G) UX
      4733
   CT: Jazz Connoisseur Cassettes (E) J.C.C. 90

Gene Schroeder, piano, replaces Rongetti.

Feather Brain Blues (BH whistling)
   78: Bird Cage 1601, >Manhattan (C) A 20-2, Tempo (E) A 51
   33: Storyville SLP 4020, Storyville (D) 671.206, Storyville (J)
      ULS 1599R

You're Lucky To Me
   78: >Manhattan (C) A 20-2, Tempo (E) A 51
   33: Saga (E) 6917, Spook Jazz (E) SPJ 6603, Storyville SLP
      4020, Storyville (D) 671.206, Storyville (J) ULS 1599R
   CT: Holmia (Sd) HM 06, Saga (E) 6917

NOTE: The Manhattans were issued in album A-20. They were
pressed by Compo in Montreal and were initially sold only at Nick's by
the hat check girl. "You're Lucky to Me" issued as "Lucky To Me" on
Manhattan A20-2. Bird Cage 1601 by Muggsy Spanier's Jazz Band.
Nick Rongetti, who replaces Schroeder on matrix M290, was the owner
of Nick's. This is his only recording.

**Nick Presents his Dixieland Band under the direction of Pee Wee
Russell.**
                                       NYC, March 2, 1945

Muggsy Spanier, cornet; Lou McGarity, trombone; Pee Wee Russell,
clarinet; Gene Schroeder, piano; Carl Kress, guitar; Bob Casey, bass;
Joe Grauso, drums.

Indiana
   78: >Manhattan (C) A 30-1
   33: Storyville SLP 4020, Storyville (D) 671.206, Storyville (J)
      ULS 1599R

Jelly Roll
>   78:   Bird Cage 1601, >Manhattan (Can) A 30-1
>   33:   Storyville SLP 4020, Storyville (D) 671.206, Storyville (J)
>   ULS 1599R

Bob Haggart, bass, replaces Casey; Charlie Carroll, drums, replaces Grauso. Add Ernie Caceres, baritone.

Clarinet Marmalade
>   78:   >Manhattan (C) A 30-2
>   33:   Storyville SLP 4053, Storyville (D) SLP 826

Mama's In The Groove
>   78:   >Manhattan (C) A 30-2
>   33:   Storyville SLP 4053, Storyville (D) SLP 826

My Honey's Lovin' Arms
>   78:   >Manhattan (C) A 30-3
>   33:   Storyville SLP 4020, Storyville (D) 671.206, Storyville (J)
>   ULS 1599R

Fidgety Feet
>   78:   >Manhattan (C) A 30-3
>   33:   Storyville SLP 4020, Storyville (D) 671.206, Storyville (J)
>   ULS 1599R

NOTE: The Manhattans were issued in album A-30. They were pressed by Compo in Montreal. Bird Cage 1601 issued as Muggsy Spanier's Jazz Band. "Mama's In the Groove" was composed by Pee Wee Russell.

Eddie Condon
                                                      NYC, March 10, 1945

Billy Butterfield, trumpet; Lou McGarity, trombone; Pee Wee Russell, clarinet; Ernie Caceres, baritone; Joe Bushkin, piano; Jack Lesberg, bass; Rollo Laylan, drums.

Sweet Georgia Brown
>   45:   Gazel (Sd) gep 6
>   33:   Baybridge (J) UXP 126, Baybridge (J) UPS 2263, Jazum 64,
>   Storyville (D) SLP 133, Storyville-Teichiku (J) ULS-1564(R)
>   TX: >AFRS EC 41
>   CD: Baybridge (J) 30CP-136

Max Kaminsky, trumpet, replaces Butterfield.

Sugar
    33:   Baybridge (J) UXP 126, Baybridge (J) UPS 2263, Jazum 64,
           Storyville (J) UXP 126
    TX: >AFRS EC 41, AFRS EC 48
    CD: Baybridge (J) 30CP-136

Billy Butterfield, trumpet, replaces Kaminsky.

Love Is Just Around The Corner
    33:   Baybridge (J) UPS 2263, Jazum 64, Storyville (D) SLP 133,
           Storyville-Teichiku (J) ULS-1564(R)
    TX: >AFRS EC 41

Dick Cary, trumpet and arranger; Red McKenzie, vocal, added.

Can't We Be Friends? (RMcK vocal)
    33:   Baybridge (J) UPS 2263, Jazum 64
    TX: >AFRS EC 41, AFRS EC 48

Max Kaminsky, trumpet, added. Omit McKenzie and possibly Cary.

Impromptu Ensemble
    33:   Baybridge (J) UPS 2263, Jazum 64
    TX: >AFRS EC 41

NOTE: Produced by Ernest Anderson. From a Ritz Theater concert, Blue network broadcast #42. Other selections from this broadcast do not include Pee Wee Russell. "Impromptu Ensemble" entitled "Ensemble Blues" on Jazum 64. The complete broadcast, including narration, is scheduled to be issued on Jazzology JCE 1021 and Jazzology JCD 1021.

Eddie Condon

                                       NYC, March 17, 1945

Billy Butterfield, trumpet; Lou McGarity, trombone; Pee Wee Russell, clarinet; Ernie Caceres, baritone; Joe Bushkin, piano; Sid Weiss, bass; Johnny Blowers, drums.

When Irish Eyes Are Smiling
    33: Baybridge (J) UPS 2263, Jazum 66
    TX: >AFRS EC 42

As Long As I Live
    33:   Baybridge (J) UPS 2263, Jazum 66
    TX: >AFRS EC 42, AFRS EC 48

Muggsy Spanier, cornet, replaces Butterfield.

Tin Roof Blues
    33:   Baybridge (J) UXP 126, Baybridge (J) UPS 2263, Jazum 66
    TX: >AFRS EC 42, AFRS EC 48
    CD: Baybridge (J) 30CP-136

Butterfield, trumpet, replaces Spanier.

Three Little Words
    33:   Baybridge (J) UPS 2263, Jazum 65
    TX: >AFRS EC 42, AFRS EC 43, AFRS EC 48

Culver City Suite
    33:   Baybridge (J) UPS 2263, Jazum 76
    TX: >AFRS EC 42

Spanier, cornet, replaces Butterfield.

My Honey's Lovin' Arms
    33:   Baybridge (J) UPS 2263, Jazum 76
    TX: >AFRS EC 42

Butterfield, trumpet, replaces Spanier.

The Lady's In Love With You
    33:   Baybridge (J) UPS 2263, Jazum 76
    TX: >AFRS EC 42

Add Spanier, cornet.

Impromptu Ensemble
    33:   Baybridge (J) UPS 2263, Jazum 76
    TX: >AFRS EC 42

NOTE: Produced by Ernest Anderson. From a Ritz Theater concert, Blue network broadcast #43. Other selections from this broadcast do not include Pee Wee Russell. "Impromptu Ensemble" entitled "Ensemble Blues," and "Culver City Suite" entitled "Culver City Blues" on Jazum 76. The complete broadcast, including narration, is scheduled to be issued on Jazzology JCE 1021 and Jazzology JCD 1021.

Eddie Condon

NYC, March 24, 1945

Billy Butterfield, trumpet; Lou McGarity, trombone; Pee Wee Russell, clarinet; Ernie Caceres, baritone; Joe Bushkin, piano; Jack Lesberg, bass; Danny Alvin, drums.

Struttin' With Some Barbecue
    33:   Baybridge (J) UPS 2264, Jazum 65
    TX: >AFRS EC 43

Joe Bushkin switches to trumpet and is replaced on piano by Jess Stacy. Bobby Hackett, arranger.

When Your Lover Has Gone
    33:   Baybridge (J) UPS 2264, Jazum 65
    TX: >AFRS EC 43

Max Kaminsky, trumpet, replaces Bushkin. Jess Stacy, piano.

Jazz Me Blues
    33:   Baybridge (J) UPS 2264, Jazum 65
    TX: >AFRS EC 43

Billy Butterfield, trumpet, omitted. Add Joe Bushkin, Jess Stacy, piano.

Clarinet Marmalade
    33:   Baybridge (J) UPS 2264, Jazum 65, Rhapsody (E) RHA 6029
    TX: >AFRS EC 43

Billy Butterfield, Max Kaminsky, trumpet; Lou McGarity, trombone; Pee Wee Russell, Ernie Caceres, clarinet; Jess Stacy, piano; Jack Lesberg, bass; Danny Alvin, drums; Bobby Hackett, arranger; Lee Wiley, vocal.

Wherever There's Love (LW vocal)
    33:   Baybridge (J) UPS 2264
    TX: >AFRS EC 43

Add Joe Bushkin, who plays both trumpet and piano. Omit Wiley and Hackett. Caceres switches to baritone.

Impromptu Ensemble
    TX: >AFRS EC 43

NOTE: Produced by Ernest Anderson. From a Ritz Theater concert, Blue network broadcast #44. Other selections from this broadcast do not include Pee Wee Russell. The complete broadcast, including narration, is scheduled to be issued on Jazzology JCE 1022 and Jazzology JCD 1022.

Eddie Condon

NYC, March 31, 1945

Billy Butterfield, trumpet; Lou McGarity, trombone; Pee Wee Russell, clarinet; Ernie Caceres, baritone; Gene Schroeder, piano; Sid Weiss, bass; Sid Catlett, drums.

Easter Parade
    Unissued

Muggsy Spanier, cornet, replaces Butterfield.

I Ain't Gonna Give Nobody None Of My Jelly Roll
    33:   Baybridge (J) UPS 2264, Jazum 65, Rhapsody (E) RHA 6029
    TX: >AFRS EC 44

You're Lucky To Me
    78:   Gazel (Sd) 1045
    33:   Baybridge (J) UPS 2264, Jazum 65, Spook Jazz (E) SPJ 6603
    TX: >AFRS EC 44
    CT: Holmia (Sd) HM 06

Butterfield, trumpet, replaces Spanier.

California, Here I Come
    33: Baybridge (J) UPS 2264, Jazum 66
    TX: >AFRS EC 44

Muggsy Spanier, cornet; Billy Butterfield, trumpet; Lou McGarity, trombone; Pee Wee Russell, clarinet; Ernie Caceres, baritone; Gene Schroeder, piano; Sid Weiss, bass; Sid Catlett, drums.

Impromptu Ensemble
    33: Baybridge (J) UPS 2264, Jazum 66
    TX: >AFRS EC 44

NOTE: Produced by Ernest Anderson. From a Ritz Theater concert, Blue network broadcast #45. Other selections from this broadcast do not include Pee Wee Russell. "Impromptu Ensemble" entitled "Ensemble Blues" on Jazum 66. "I Ain't Gonna Give Nobody None of My Jelly Roll" entitled "None of My Jelly Roll" on Rhapsody (E) RHA 6029. The complete broadcast, including narration, is scheduled to be issued on Jazzology JCE 1022 and Jazzology JCD 1022.

Max Kaminsky

Boston, Mass., November, 1945

Max Kaminsky, trumpet; Brad Gowans, valaide trombone; Pee Wee Russell, clarinet; Teddy Roy, piano; John Field, bass; Buzzy Drootin, drums.

Love Is Just Around The Corner (incomplete)
    Unissued

Love Is Just Around The Corner (incomplete)
    Unissued

The World Is Waiting For The Sunrise (incomplete)
    Unissued

Tin Roof Blues (incomplete)
    Unissued

Tin Roof Blues (incomplete)
    Unissued

Ja Da
    Unissued

Honeysuckle Rose
    Unissued

Sugar
    Unissued

Royal Garden Blues (incomplete)
    Unissued

Royal Garden Blues (incomplete)
    Unissued

Royal Garden Blues (incomplete)
    Unissued

Sweet Georgia Brown (incomplete)
    Unissued

I Can't Give You Anything But Love (incomplete)
    Unissued

The Sheik Of Araby (incomplete)
    Unissued

I Can't Say (incomplete)
    Unissued

The following, all issued on a cassette tape, may be performances listed
above or from the following sessions:

Fidgety Feet (incomplete)
    CT: >Fat Cat FCJ 018

The World Is Waiting For The Sunrise
    CT: >Fat Cat FCJ 018

Copley Terrace Blues
    CT: >Fat Cat FCJ 018

Squeeze Me
    CT: >Fat Cat FCJ 018

206

Someday Sweetheart
    CT: >Fat Cat FCJ 018

Basin Street Blues
    CT: >Fat Cat FCJ 018

That's A Plenty
    CT: >Fat Cat FCJ 018

NOTE: From WHJN broadcasts from the Copley Terrace. Specific
dates are unknown.

Max Kaminsky

Boston, Mass., November 2, 1945

Same personnel.

Love Is Just Around The Corner
    CT: >Fat Cat FCJ 018

The World Is Waiting For The Sunrise
    Unissued

St. Louis Blues
    Unissued

At The Jazz Band Ball
    Unissued

Tin Roof Blues
    Unissued

NOTE: From a WHJN broadcast from the Copley Terrace.

Max Kaminsky

Boston, Mass., November 3, 1945

Same personnel.

At The Jazz Band Ball
    CT: >Fat Cat FCJ 017

The World Is Waiting For The Sunrise
    Unissued

Ja Da
    Unissued

St. Louis Blues
    CT: >Fat Cat FCJ 017

NOTE: From a WHJN broadcast from the Copley Terrace. The issue on Fat Cat FCJ 017 of "At the Jazz Band Ball" is spliced with part of the November 9, 1945, performance.

Max Kaminsky   Boston, Mass., November 5, 1945

Same personnel

Basin Street Blues
    Unissued

Muskrat Ramble
    CT: >Fat Cat FCJ 017

NOTE: From a WHJN broadcast from the Copley Terrace.

Max Kaminsky
                                         Boston, Mass., November 6, 1945

Same personnel

That's A Plenty
    Unissued

Sugar
    Unissued

Love Is Just Around The Corner
    Unissued

NOTE: From a WHJN broadcast from the Copley Terrace.

Max Kaminsky

Boston, Mass., November 7, 1945

Same personnel

Sunday (incomplete)
CT: >Fat Cat FCJ 017

Dippermouth Blues
CT: >Fat Cat FCJ 017

Royal Garden Blues
Unissued

The World Is Waiting For The Sunrise
Unissued

That's A Plenty
Unissued

Royal Garden Blues
Unissued

Squeeze Me
Unissued

NOTE: From a WHJN broadcast from the Copley Terrace. The issue
on Fat Cat FCJ 017 of "Sunday" is spliced with part of the November
20, 1945, performance.

Max Kaminsky

Boston, Mass., November 8, 1945

Same personnel

Wrap Your Troubles In Dreams
CT: Fat Cat FCJ 017

Squeeze Me
Unissued

NOTE: From a WHJN broadcast from the Copley Terrace.

Max Kaminsky

Boston, Mass., November 9, 1945

Same personnel

Someday Sweetheart
    Unissued

At The Jazz Band Ball (incomplete)
    CT: >Fat Cat FCJ 017

Jazz Me Blues
    CT: >Fat Cat FCJ 018

Tin Roof Blues
    CT: >Fat Cat FCJ 017

NOTE: From a WHJN broadcast from the Copley Terrace. See November 3, 1945, note regarding the issue of "At The Jazz Band Ball."

Max Kaminsky

Boston, Mass., November 10, 1945

Same personnel

At Sundown
    CT: >Fat Cat FCJ 017

NOTE: From a WHJN broadcast from the Copley Terrace.

Max Kaminsky

Boston, Mass., November 13, 1945

Same personnel

I'm Confessin'
    CT: >Fat Cat FCJ 017

NOTE: From a WHJN broadcast from the Copley Terrace.

Max Kaminsky

Boston, Mass., November 15, 1945

Same personnel

Someday Sweetheart
    Unissued

Fidgety Feet
    Unissued

NOTE: From a WHJN broadcast from the Copley Terrace.

Max Kaminsky

Boston, Mass., November 16, 1945

Same personnel

Original Dixieland One-Step
    CT: >Fat Cat FCJ 017

It Had To Be You (incomplete)
    CT: >Fat Cat FCJ 018

NOTE: From a WHJN broadcast from the Copley Terrace.

Max Kaminsky

Boston, Mass., November 17, 1945

Same personnel

Mammy O' Mine
    CT: >Fat Cat FCJ 017

NOTE: From a WHJN broadcast from the Copley Terrace. The issue on Fat Cat FCJ 017 is spliced with part of the November 24, 1945, performance.

Max Kaminsky

Boston, Mass., November 20, 1945

Same personnel

Sunday
    CT: >Fat Cat FCJ 017

NOTE: See November 7, 1945, note. From a WHJN broadcast from the Copley Terrace.

Max Kaminsky

Boston, Mass., November 21, 1945

Same personnel

Blues
    Unissued

Exactly Like You
    33:   >Fat Cat FCJ 018

NOTE: From a WHJN broadcast from the Copley Terrace.

Max Kaminsky

Boston, Mass., November 24, 1945

Same personnel

Mammy O' Mine
    CT: >Fat Cat FCJ 017

NOTE: From a WHJN broadcast from the Copley Terrace. See November 17, 1945, note.

Pee Wee Russell Jazz Ensemble

NYC, May 27, 1946

Muggsy Spanier, cornet; Vic Dickenson, trombone; Pee Wee Russell, clarinet, vocal; Cliff Jackson, piano, vocal; Bob Casey, bass; Joe Grauso, drums.

CD 415   Since My Best Gal Turned Me Down
- 78:   Baronet (Sd) B 49510, >Disc 5053
- 45:   Melodisc (E) EPM 7-104
- 33:   Folkways FJ 2853, Stinson LP 30, Time-Life STL-J17 (P 15735), Time-Life (Au) STL-J17, Time-Life (C) STL-J17
- CT: Jazz Connoisseur Cassettes (E) J.C.C. 90, Time-Life 4TL-J17
- 8T: Time-Life 8TL-J17

CD 416   Muskogee Blue
- 78:   >Disc 5053
- 45:   Melodisc (E) EPM 7-104
- 33:   Folkways FJ 2853, Musica Jazz Presenta (I) 2MJP 1071, Stinson LP 30, Time-Life STL-J17 (P 15735), Time-Life (Au) STL-J17, Time-Life (C) STL-J17
- TX: AFRS JS 31
- CT: Jazz Connoisseur Cassettes (E) J.C.C. 90, Time-Life 4TL-J17
- 8T: Time-Life 8TL-J17

CD 417   Rosie (CJ vocal)
- 78:   >Disc 5054
- 33:   Folkways FJ 2853, Stinson LP 30

Francis Palmer, bass, replaces Casey.

CD 418   Take Me Back To The Land Of Jazz (PWR vocal)
- 78:   >Disc 5054
- 45:   Fratelli (I) SdMJ-022
- 33:   Asch AA 2, Folkways FJ 2853, Stinson LP 30
- TX: AFRS JS 32

CD 419   I'd Climb The Highest Mountain
- 78:   Baronet (Sd) B 48503, >Disc 5055
- 45:   Fratelli SdMJ-022, Melodisc (E) EPM 7-104
- 33:   Asch AA 2, Folkways FJ 2853, Stinson LP 30
- CT: Jazz Connoisseur Cassettes (E) J.C.C. 90

CD 420   Red Hot Mama
    78:   >Disc 5055
    45:   Melodisc (E) EPM 7-104
    33:   Folkways FJ 2853, Stinson LP 30
    TX: AFRS JS 32
    CT: Jazz Connoisseur Cassettes (E) J.C.C. 90

NOTE: Produced by Charles Edward Smith. Stinson LP 30 was issued
on both 10 and 12-inch discs with the same contents. The notes on
these issues list Francis Palmer as the bass player. Asch AA 2 was
issued as a single LP and also as part of a boxed set, Asch AA 1/2. The
notes to Asch AA 1/2 include a photograph of Pee Wee Russell and
Moses Asch, presumably taken at this or the following session.
Folkways FJ 2853 issued as by Muggsy Spanier. Disc 78 rpm records
issued in album 632B. Copies of the Disc 78's exist without band
names. LP issues of CD 416 show the title correctly as "Muskogee
Blues."

Muggsy Spanier And His Orchestra
                                                NYC, September 9, 1946

Muggsy Spanier, cornet, vocal; Vernon Brown, trombone; Pee Wee
Russell, clarinet, vocal; Nick Caiazza, tenor; Gene Schroeder, piano;
Bob Haggart, bass, whistling; George Wettling, drums.

CD 519   Pee Wee Squawks (MS & PWR vocal)
    78:   Disc 816, >Disc 6032
    33:   Stinson LP 31

CD 520   Sentimental Journey (BH whistling)
    78:   Disc 815, >Disc 6031
    33:   Stinson LP 31

CD 520-   Sentimental Journey (BH whistling)
    78:   >Holiday 4002
    33:   Meritt 9

CD 521   Muggsy Special
    78:   Disc 816, >Disc 6032
    33:   Stinson LP 31

CD 522   You're Driving Me Crazy
   78:   Baronet (Sd) A 48504, Disc 815, >Disc 6031, Holiday 4002,
        New York 108
   33:   Asch AA 2, Stinson LP 31

CD 523   Am I Blue?
   78:   Baronet (Sd) A 48503, Disc 8l4, >Disc 6030, New York 108
   33:   Stinson LP 31

CD 524   How Come You Do Me Like You Do
   78:   Baronet (Sd) 495l0, Disc 814, >Disc 6030
   33:   Stinson LP 31

NOTE: Produced by Charles Edward Smith. Stinson LP 31 was issued
on both l0 and 12-inch discs with the same contents. Asch AA 2 was
issued as a single LP and also as part of a boxed set, Asch AA 1/2.
Disc 6030, 6031 and 6032 issued in Disc album 711. Copies of the
Disc 78s exist without band names.

Jazz At The Town Hall

NYC, September 21, 1946

Muggsy Spanier, cornet; Miff Mole, trombone; Pee Wee Russell,
clarinet; Art Hodes, piano; Pops Foster, bass; George Wettling, drums.

Royal Garden Blues
   45:   Storyville (D) SEP 380
   33:   >Folkways FJ 284l (edited), HMV (Au) OXLP 7503, >Xtra
        (E) XTR 1003

How Come You Do Me Like You Do
   33:   >Folkways FJ 2841 (edited), HMV (Au) OXLP 7503, >Xtra
        (E) XTR 1003

Relaxin' At The Touro
   45:   Storyville (D) SEP 380
   33:   >Folkways FJ 284l (edited), HMV (Au) OXLP 7503, >Xtra
        (E) XTR 1003

Add Wild Bill Davison, cornet; Johnny Windhurst, trumpet; Vernon Brown, trombone; Mezz Mezzrow, clarinet; James P. Johnson, piano; possibly Baby Dodds, drums.

The Blues
    33:   >Folkways FJ 2841 (edited), >Xtra (E) XTR 1043

NOTE: Recorded at a Town Hall concert. The above titles on Folkways are heavily edited as follows:

Royal Garden Blues: Xtra, 3:52; Folkways, 3:32. The Hodes piano solo is deleted.

How Come You Do Me Like You Do: Xtra, 4:05; Folkways 3:25. The Pee Wee Russell solo is deleted.

Relaxin' At The Touro: Xtra, 2:29; Folkways 2:18. The piano intro is deleted.

The Blues: Xtra 13:40; Folkways 5:14. Solos deleted are in this order: Mezzrow, Mole; Mezzrow-Russell duet; Mezzrow, Johnson; Windhurst and the ensemble going into double time.

Other selections from this concert as issued on Xtra and Folkways do not include Pee Wee Russell. Xtra 1003 and HMV OXLP 7503 list the date of the concert as October, 1948. Date listed above is from the Folkways LP. "Relaxin' at the Touro" is not listed on the cover and label of Xtra 1003 and HMV (Au) OXLP 7503, although it appears as the last track on side two.

Eddie Condon
NYC, December 25, 1946

Max Kaminsky, Joe Thomas, trumpets; Fred Ohms, George Brunies, trombone; Pee Wee Russell, Joe Dixon, clarinet; Gene Schroeder, piano; Jack Lesberg, bass; Morey Feld, drums.

Bugle Call Blues
    Unissued

NOTE: Recorded in the early morning hours at Eddie Condon's.

WNYC Jazz Festival

NYC, February 22, 1947

Wild Bill Davison, cornet; Pee Wee Russell, clarinet; Peanuts Hucko, tenor; Joe Sullivan, piano; Sid Weiss, bass; Danny Alvin, drums; Red McKenzie, vocal.

There'll Be Some Changes Made (RMcK, vocal)
   Unissued

China Boy
   Unissued

NOTE: From a WNYC broadcast.

Eddie Condon And His Orchestra

NYC, August 6, 1947

Wild Bill Davison, cornet; Jack Teagarden, trombone, vocal; Pee Wee Russell, clarinet; Gene Schroeder, piano; Eddie Condon, guitar; Morey Rayman, bass; Johnny Blowers, drums.

W-74030-A   Aunt Hagar's Blues (JT vocal)
   78: Brunswick (E) 04303, >Decca 24220, Decca (C) 24220, Decca (Sw) 30823
   33: Ace of Hearts (E) AH 28, Affinity (E) AFS 1021, Brunswick (Au) LA 8542, Brunswick (E) LAT 8229, Brunswick (E) LA 8542, Brunswick (F) 87008, Brunswick (G) 87008LPBM, Decca DL 5246, Decca DL 8281, Decca DL 8304, Decca (Arg) LTM-9289, Decca (Arg) LTM-9291, Decca (C) DL 8281, Decca (E) BML 8542, Decca (J) JDL-5082, Decca (J) JDL-6027, Decca (J) JDL-6077, Decca (J) JDL 8077, Decca (J) AL 12044, Decca (Sc) BKL 8229, Decca (Sp) LTM-9291, Franklin Mint 48, MCA 2-4064, MCA 2-4071, MCA (Au) 2-4071, MCA (C) 2-4071, MCA (C) 2-4064, MCA (F) 510.206, MCA (J) MCA 3101
   TX: AFRS P-980

W-74031-A   Down Among The Sheltering Palms (JT vocal)
    78:   Brunswick (E) 03964, >Decca 24219, Decca (C) 24219, Decca (I) BM 1386
    33:   Ace of Hearts (E) AH 100, Brunswick (Au) LA 8542, Decca DL 5246, Decca DL 8282, Decca (Arg) LTM-9247, Decca (B) UDL 8282, Decca (C) 8282, Decca (G) BM 30821, Decca (J) JDL 6013, Decca (J) SDL 10293, Decca (J) AL 12044, Decca (Sc) BML-8542, Decca (Sw) 30821, Decca (Ur) UDL-8282, Fonit (I) DL 8282, MCA 2-4071, MCA (Au) 24071, MCA (C) MCA 2-4071, MCA (F) 510.206, MCA (J) MCA 3101
    TX: AFRS P-979

W-74032-A   Rose Of The Rio Grande
    78:   >Decca 24220, Decca (C) 24220
    33:   Ace of Hearts (E) AH 28, Brunswick (Au) LA 8542, Brunswick (E) LAT 8229, Brunswick (F) 87008, Brunswick (G) 87008LPBM, Calendar (Au) R66-160, Calendar (Au) R66-9160, Coral (G) COPS 3442, Coral (G) 6.21851, Decca DL 4540, Decca DL 5246, Decca DL 8281, Decca DL 8304, Decca DL 74540, Decca (Arg) LTM-9289, Decca (Arg) LTM-9291, Decca (C) DL 4540, Decca (C) DL 8281, Decca (C) DL 74540, Decca (E) M32469, Decca (G) BM 30821, Decca (H) M32469, Decca (J) JDL 6077, Decca (Sp) LTM-9291, Decca (Sw) 30821, Decca BKL 8229, Decca BML 8542, Festival (Au) SFL-931,404, MCA 227, MCA (Arg) MCAB 5062, MCA (Au) MCA-227, MCA (Can) MCA 227, MCA (F) 510.206, MCA (J) MCA 3102, MCA Coral CB-20013, MCA Coral (C) CB-20013
    TX: AFRTS Turn Back the Clock 262, part 2

W-74033-A   Ida, Sweet As Apple Cider
    78:   Brunswick (E) 03964, >Decca 24219, Decca (C) 24219, Decca (E) M 32469, Decca (H) M 32469, Decca (I) BM 1386
    45:   Decca ED 413
    33:   Brunswick (Au) LA 8542, Brunswick (E) LA 8542, Decca DL 5246, Decca DL 8282, Decca (Arg) LTM-9247, Decca (B) UDL 8282, Decca (C) DL 8282, Decca (E) M32469, Decca (H) M32469, Decca (J) JDL-6013, Decca (J) SDL 10293, Decca (J) AL 12044, Decca (Sc) BM 1386, Decca (Sc) BML 8542, Decca (Ur) UDL-8282, Fonit (I) DL 8282, MCA (J) MCA 3102, MCA Coral CB-20013, MCA Coral (C) CB-20013
    TX: AFRS P-980

NOTE: Produced by Milt Gabler. Test pressings containing alternate takes of each of the four titles are reported to exist. Decca 24219 and 24220 (both U.S. and Canadian issues) were released in album A-604 entitled "We Called It Music." AFRS P-979, P-980 were issued as Eddie Condon Jazz Concert.

Eddie Condon

NYC, c. 1948

Hot Lips Page, trumpet; Lou McGarity, trombone; Pee Wee Russell, clarinet; unknown piano; probably George Wettling, drums.

Honeysuckle Rose
    Unissued

After You've Gone
    Unissued

NOTE: Probably from a Stuyvesant Casino broadcast, although this might be from a Dr. Jazz broadcast which would place it in the 1951-52 period.

Eddie Condon

NYC, December 16, 1948

Wild Bill Davison, cornet; Brad Gowans, valide trombone; Pee Wee Russell, clarinet; Dick Cary, piano; Eddie Condon, guitar; Jack Lesberg, bass; George Wettling, drums; Johnny Mercer, vocal.

I Ain't Gonna Give Nobody None Of My Jelly Roll (JM vocal)
    Unissued

Add Sidney Bechet, soprano.

Happy Birthday To Eddie
    Unissued

Omit Bechet. Add Henry "Red" Allen, trumpet, vocal.

I Told Ya, I Love Ya, Now Get Out (HA vocal)
    Unissued

Omit Allen. Add Teddy Hale, tap dancing.

Big Fine Mama
   Unissued

Omit Hale.

I'm Confessin'
   Unissued

Down Among The Sheltering Palms (JM vocal)
   Unissued

Add Sidney Bechet, soprano; Mary Lou Williams, piano.

Anniversary Blues
   Unissued.

NOTE: From Eddie Condon's "Floor Show" television series, telecast by WPIX-TV. Other selections do not include Pee Wee Russell.

Eddie Condon

NYC, January 15, 1949

Roy Eldridge, Billy Butterfield, trumpet; Cutty Cutshall, trombone; Pee Wee Russell, Peanuts Hucko, clarinet; Freddie Slack, piano; Jack Lesberg, bass; Gene Krupa, drums.

Slow Blues
   33: >Broadcast Tributes BTRIB 0001

NOTE: From Eddie Condon's "Floor Show" television series, telecast by WPIX-TV. Other selections from the broadcast do not include Russell.

Art Hodes Trio

NYC, February 15, 1949

Pee Wee Russell, clarinet; Art Hodes, piano; Shelly Manne, drums.

Four Or Five Times
   33: Shoestring SS 109
   TX: >VOA 38

Eddie Condon

NYC, August 20, 1949

Bobby Hackett, cornet; Cutty Cutshall, trombone; Pee Wee Russell, clarinet; Joe Bushkin, piano; Eddie Condon, guitar; Jack Lesberg, bass; George Wettling, drums.

Love Is Just Around The Corner
    Unissued

Jammin' At The Three Deuces
    Unissued

NOTE: From Eddie Condon's "Floor Show," television series, telecast by WPIX-TV. Other selections from the broadcast do not include Russell.

Eddie Condon

NYC, August 27, 1949

Bobby Hackett, cornet; Cutty Cutshall, trombone; Pee Wee Russell, clarinet; Joe Bushkin, piano; Eddie Condon, guitar, vocal; Jack Lesberg, bass; George Wettling, drums.

One Hour (EC vocal)
    33: FDC (I) 1014, >Palm 30 (E) P.30:17, SagaPan (E) PAN
          6916, Saga World Wide (E) 6916
    CT: Saga (E) 6916

Mandy, Make Up Your Mind
    33: FDC (I) 1014, >Palm 30 (E) P.30:17, Saga Pan (E) PAN
          6916, Saga World Wide (E) 6916
    CT: Saga (E) 6916

I Got Rhythm
    33: FDC (I) 1014, >Palm 30 (E) P.30:17, SagaPan (E) PAN
          6916, Saga World Wide (E) 6916
    CT: Saga (E) 6916

Add Hot Lips Page, trumpet.

Jam Session
    33: FDC (I) 1014, >Palm 30 (E) P.30:17, SagaPan (E) PAN
          6916, Saga World Wide (E) 6916
    CT: Saga (E) 6916

Bobby Hackett, cornet; Louis Armstrong, trumpet, vocal; Jack
Teagarden, trombone, vocal; Pee Wee Russell, clarinet; Joe Bushkin,
piano; Eddie Condon, guitar; Jack Lesberg, bass; George Wettling,
drums.

We Called It Music (JT vocal)
    33: FDC (I) 1014, Palm 30 (E) P.30:17, SagaPan (E) PAN 6916,
          Saga World Wide (E) 6916
    TX: >AFRS 302
    CT: Saga (E) 6916

Omit Hackett and Bushkin. Add Earl Hines, piano.

Chinatown, My Chinatown (LA vocal)
    78: Jazz Society (F) AA 551
    33: Alamac 2436, Alamac (F) 180053, Ariston (I) ARI 12010,
          Bulldog BDL 2007, Discophon (Sp) S 4.271, DJM (E)
          DJLMD 8001, Ember (E) CJS 838, Everest EK-3, Everest FS
          312, Everest 3312, FDC (I) 1014, Forlane (I) 19.001, Jazz
          Anthology (F) 30-JA 5155, Jazz Society (F) LP 7, Jazz
          Society (F) 67401, Jazz Society (F) 67414, Jazz Trip 10, Jazz
          Trip JT X (2), Metronome (G) DALP 2/1969, Music for
          Pleasure (SA) MFP 3518, Quadrifoglio (I) VDS 282, Palm
          Club (F) PC-23, Sagapan (E) PAN 6904, Saga World Wide
          (E) 6904, Trip TLX 5814
    TX: >AFRS 302
    CD: Forlane (F) UCD 19002
    CT: Bulldog BDL-2007

NOTE: From Eddie Condon's television series, "Floor Show," telecast
by WPIX-TV. Pee Wee Russell does not appear on other titles from
this telecast.

Pee Wee Russell

Chicago, June 20, 1950

Jimmy James, trombone; Pee Wee Russell, Bud Jacobson, clarinet; Jack Gardner, piano.

Louise
    Unissued

Jacobson omitted; Mike Snow replaces Gardner.

Ja Da
    Unissued

NOTE: These are private acetates, recorded by John Steiner at his home, 1637 North Ashland. At least two additional titles, "You Took Advantage of Me," and a blues were recorded but they do not include Pee Wee Russell.

George Wettling's Stuyvesant Stompers

NYC, January 4, 1952

Wild Bill Davison, cornet; Hot Lips Page, trumpet, vocal; Lou McGarity, trombone; Pee Wee Russell, clarinet; Dick Cary, piano; George Wettling, drums.

How Come You Do Me Like You Do? (HLP vocal)
    Unissued

You're Driving Me Crazy
    33: >IAJRC IAJRC-36

NOTE: From a "Dr. Jazz" broadcast, WMGM, from Stuyvesant Casino, 140 Second Avenue, 10:30 to 11 P.M. Other tunes from this broadcast do not include Pee Wee Russell.

223

Pee Wee Russell

Boston, Mass., January 14, 1952

Ruby Braff, cornet; Eph Resnick, trombone; Pee Wee Russell, clarinet; Red Richards, piano; John Field, bass; Kenny John, drums.

Struttin' With Some Barbecue
  Unissued

Basin Street Blues
  Unissued

'S Wonderful
  Unissued

Someday Sweetheart
  Unissued

Ballin' The Jack
  Unissued

At The Jazz Band Ball
  Unissued

NOTE: From a WMEX broadcast from the Storyville Club, Buckminster Hotel.

Pee Wee Russell

Boston, Mass., January 16, 1952

Same personnel

Way Down Yonder In New Orleans
  Unissued

Sentimental Journey
  Unissued

Sunday
  Unissued

Wrap Your Troubles In Dreams
  Unissued

224

St. Louis Blues
  Unissued

Muskrat Ramble
  Unissued

NOTE: From a WMEX broadcast from the Storyville Club, Buckminster Hotel.

Pee Wee Russell

Boston, Mass., January 21, 1952

Same personnel

Muskrat Ramble
  Unissued

Squeeze Me
  Unissued

Blue Room
  Unissued

The Lady's In Love With You
  Unissued

I Can't Give You Anything But Love
  Unissued

Original Dixieland One-Step
  Unissued

NOTE: From a WMEX broadcast from the Storyville Club, Buckminster Hotel.

Jazz At Storyville

Same personnel

Love Is Just Around The Corner
  45: Royale EP 387, Savoy XP 8070
  33: Allegro LP 1633, Allegro 1745, CBS Realm (E) RM 151,
       Ember (E) CJS 806, Galaxy 4802, London (E) LTZ-C15061,
       London Savoy (C) MG 12034, Manhattan (Au) LMS 48,
       Pickwick PTP 2026, Pickwick SPC 3152, Rondolette LP A2,
       Royale LP 18158, Savoy SJL 2228, Savoy MG 12034,
       >Savoy MG 15014, Savoy (F) WL-70538

Squeeze Me
  45: Savoy XP 8070
  33: Allegro LP 1745, CBS Realm (E) RM 151, London (E) LTZ-
       C15061, London Savoy (Can) MG 12034, Manhattan (Au)
       LMS 50, Pickwick PTP 2026, Pickwick SPC 3152, Savoy
       SJL 2228, Savoy MG 12034, >Savoy MG 15016, Savoy (F)
       WL-70538

Ballin' The Four Bar Break
  45: Savoy XP 8070
  33: CBS Realm (E) RM 151, London (E) LTZ-C15061, London
       Savoy (C) MG 12034, Manhattan (Au) LMS 50, Savoy SJL
       2228, Savoy MG 12034, >Savoy MG 15016, Savoy (F) WL-
       70538

I Would Do Anything For You
  45: Savoy XP 8071
  33: Allegro LP 1745, CBS Realm (E) RM 151, London (E) LTZ-
       C15061, London Savoy (C) MG 12034, Manhattan (Au)
       LMS 52, Pickwick PTP 2026, Pickwick SPC 3152, Savoy
       SJL 2228, Savoy MG 12034, >Savoy MG 15020, Savoy (F)
       WL-70538

The Lady Is A Tramp
  45: Savoy XP 8073
  33: Allegro LP 1633, Ember (E) CJS 806, Galaxy 4802, London
       Savoy (C) MG 12041, Manhattan (Au) LMS 48, Royale LP
       18158, Savoy SJL 2228, Savoy MG 12041, >Savoy MG
       15014, Savoy (F) WL-70538

California, Here I Come
  45: Savoy XP 8071
  33: Allegro LP 1633, CBS Realm (E) RM 151, Ember (E) CJS
      806, Galaxy 4802, London (E) LTZ-C15061, London Savoy
      (C) MG 12034, Manhattan (Au) LMS 48, Rondolette LP A2,
      Royale 18l58, Savoy SJL 2228, Savoy MG 12034, >Savoy
      MG 15014

Baby, Won't You Please Come Home
  45: Savoy XP 8071
  33: Allegro LP 1745, CBS Realm (E) RM 151, London (E) LTZ-
      C15061, London Savoy (C) MG 12034, Manhattan (Au)
      LMS 50, Pickwick PTP 2026, Pickwick SPC 3152, Savoy
      SJL 2228, Savoy MG 12034, >Savoy MG 15016, Savoy (F)
      WL-70538

St. James Infirmary
  45: Royale EP 387, Savoy XP 8071
  33: Allegro LP 1633, CBS Realm (E) RM 151, Ember (E) NR
      5002, Ember (E) CJS 806, Galaxy 4802, Halo 50268, Hudson
      265, Jonaplay (J) RCA 50268, London (E) LTZ-C15061,
      London Savoy (C) MG 12034, Manhattan (Au) LMS 48,
      Rondolette LP A2, Savoy SJL 2228, Savoy MG 12034,
      >Savoy MG 15014, Savoy (F) WL-70538, Ultraphonic 50268

The Lady's In Love With You
  45: Savoy XP 8072
  33: Allegro LP 1745, CBS Realm (E) RM 151, London (E) LTZ-
      C15061, London Savoy (C) MG 12034, Manhattan (Au)
      LMS 52, Rondolette LP A2, Savoy SJL 2228, Savoy MG
      12034, >Savoy MG 15020, Savoy (F) WL-70538

Struttin' With Some Barbecue
  45: Savoy XP 8072
  33: Allegro LP 1745, CBS Realm (E) RM 151, London (E) LTZ-
      C15061, London Savoy (C) MG 12034, Manhattan (Au)
      LMS 52, Pickwick PTP 2026, Pickwick SPC 3152, Savoy
      SJL 2228, Savoy MG 12034, >Savoy MG 15020, Savoy (F)
      WL-70538

St. Louis Blues
   45:   Savoy XP 8073
   33:   CBS Realm (E) RM 189, London Savoy (C) MG 12041,
         Manhattan (Au) LMS 52, Savoy SJL 2228, Savoy MG
         12041, >Savoy MG 15014, Savoy (F) WL-70538

Sweet Lorraine
   45:   Savoy XP 8074
   33:   Allegro LP 1745, CBS Realm (E) RM 189, London Savoy
         (C) MG 12041, Manhattan (Au) LMS 50, Pickwick PTP
         2026, Pickwick SPC 3152, Savoy SJL 2228, Savoy MG
         12041, >Savoy MG 15016, Savoy (F) WL-70538

Sentimental Journey
   45:   Savoy XP 8074
   33:   Allegro LP 1745, CBS Realm (E) RM 189, London Savoy
         (C) MG 12041, Manhattan (Au) LMS 52, Pickwick PTP
         2026, Pickwick SPC 3152, Savoy SJL 2228, Savoy MG
         12041, >Savoy MG 15020, Savoy (F) WL-70538

If I Had You
   45:   Savoy XP 8075
   33:   Allegro LP 1745, Brookville LCA 0002, CBS Realm (E) RM
         189, Everest 1001/5, London Savoy (C) MG 12041,
         Manhattan (Au) LMS 50, Pickwick PTP 2026, Pickwick SPC
         3152, Savoy SJL 2228, Savoy MG 12041, >Savoy MG 15016,

Coquette
   45:   Savoy XP 8075
   33:   Allego LP 1745, CBS Realm (E) RM 189, Ember (E) CJS
         806, Galaxy 4802, London Savoy (C) MG 12041, Manhattan
         (Au) LMS 48, Pickwick PTP 2026, Pickwick SPC 3152,
         Rondolette LP A2, Savoy SJL 2228, Savoy MG 12041,
         >Savoy MG 15014, Savoy (F) WL-70538

NOTE: Produced by Charles Bourgeois. Recorded at the Storyville
Club, Buckminster Hotel. "Love Is Just Around the Corner" entitled
"Love Is Here to Stay" on Galaxy 4802 and Royale LP 18158, and
"Euphoria Is Here To Stay" on Savoy XP 8070, Savoy MG 15014,
Allegro LP 1633, Rondolette LPA2, Manhattan (Au) LMS 48.
Brookville LCA 0002 is part of album LCA 5000 (5-LP set).

Stuyvesant Stompers

NYC, February 1, 1952.

Max Kaminsky, trumpet; Vic Dickenson, trombone; Pee Wee Russell, clarinet; Dick Cary, piano; Sonny Greer, drums.

That's A Plenty (incomplete)
    Unissued

NOTE: "Dr. Jazz" broadcast, WMGM, from the Stuyvesant Casino, 140 Second Avenue. Aime Gauvin is the announcer. Other selections from this broadcast do not include Pee Wee Russell.

Stuyvesant Stompers

NYC, February 8, 1952

Jimmy McPartland, Lee Castle, trumpets; Pee Wee Russell, clarinet; Ray McKinley, drums, others unknown.

The World Is Waiting For The Sunrise
    Unissued

Basin Street Blues
    Unissued

Sunny Side Of The Street
    Unissued

I Can't Get Started
    Unissued

I Got Rhythm
    Unissued

At The Jazz Band Ball
    Unissued

NOTE: "Dr. Jazz" broadcast, WMGM, from the Stuyvesant Casino, 140 Second Avenue. Aime Gauvin is the announcer. It is not known which of the titles from this broadcast Pee Wee Russell appears on.

Stuyvesant Stompers

Hot Lips Page, trumpet, vocal; Lou McGarity, trombone; Pee Wee Russell, clarinet; Joe Sullivan, piano; George Wettling, drums.

When The Saints Go Marching In
    33: >Stycon 200

Sweet Georgia Brown
    33: >Stycon 200

When My Sugar Walks Down The Street (HLP vocal)
    33: >Stycon 200

Sweet Sue
    33: >Stycon 200

NOTE: "Dr. Jazz" broadcast, WMGM, from the Stuyvesant Casino, 140 Second Avenue, 10:30 to 11 p.m. Other titles from this broadcast do not include Pee Wee Russell.

Stuyvesant Stompers

NYC, March 7, 1952

Hot Lips Page, trumpet; Lou McGarity, trombone; Pee Wee Russell, clarinet; Joe Sullivan, piano; George Wettling, drums.

When The Saints Go Marching In
    33: >Stycon 200

Honeysuckle Rose
    33: >Stycon 200

Margie
    33: >Stycon 200

Jimmy McPartland, trumpet, replaces Page. Add Bud Freeman, tenor.

Sugar
    33: >Stycon 200

China Boy
   33: >Stycon 200

NOTE: From a "Dr. Jazz" broadcast, WMGM, from Stuyvesant Casino, 140 Second Avenue, 10:30 to 11 p.m. Other titles from this broadcast do not include Pee Wee Russell.

Stuyvesant Stompers
NYC, March 21, 1952

Jimmy McPartland, trumpet and vocal; Pee Wee Russell, clarinet; Bud Freeman, tenor; Joe Sullivan, piano; George Wettling, drums.

When The Saints Go Marching In
   Unissued

That's A Plenty
   Unissued

Tin Roof Blues
   Unissued

Sister Kate (JMcP, vocal)
   Unissued

At The Jazz Band Ball
   Unissued

When The Saints Go Marching In
   Unissued

NOTE: From a "Dr. Jazz" broadcast, WMGM, from Stuyvesant Casino, 140 Second Avenue, 10:30 to 11 p.m.

Stuyvesant Stompers
NYC, March 28, 1952

Jimmy McPartland, trumpet; Ziggy Elmer, trombone; Pee Wee Russell, clarinet; Joe Sullivan, piano; Eddie Dougherty, drums.

When The Saints Go Marching In
   Unissued

231

At Sundown
 Unissued

Squeeze Me
 Unissued

Muskrat Ramble
 Unissued

Basin Street Blues
 Unissued

At The Jazz Band Ball
 Unissued

When The Saints Go Marching In
 Unissued

NOTE: "Dr. Jazz" broadcast, WMGM, from Stuyvesant Casino, 140 Second Avenue, 10:30 to 11 p.m.

Jimmy McPartland's Stompers

NYC, May 2, 1952

Jimmy McPartland, trumpet; Pee Wee Russell, clarinet; Bud Freeman, tenor; Ken Kersey, piano; Arnold Hyman, bass; Johnny Blowers, drums.

When The Saints Go Marching In
 Unissued

Muskrat Ramble
 Unissued

Ja Da
 Unissued

Way Down Yonder In New Orleans
 Unissued

Squeeze Me
 Unissued

232

That's A Plenty (incomplete)
    Unissued

NOTE: "Dr. Jazz" broadcast, WMGM, from Stuyvesant Casino, 140
Second Avenue, 10:30 to 11 p.m.

Ray McKinley's Sextet

NYC, summer, 1952

Lee Castle, trumpet; possibly Ray Diehl, trombone; Pee Wee Russell,
clarinet; possibly Joe Cribari, piano; possibly Jim Thorpe, bass; Ray
McKinley, drums and vocal.

Blues For Pee Wee (RMcK, vocal) (incomplete)
    Unissued

That's A Plenty (RMcK, vocal) (incomplete)
    Unissued

Hard Hearted Hannah (RMcK, vocal) (incomplete)
    Unissued

NOTE: From the NBC telecast, "Saturday Night Dancing Party."

Pee Wee Russell with John Dengler's Jazz Band

Mountainhome, Pennsylvania, August, 1952

John Dengler, trumpet; George Stell, trombone; Pee Wee Russell,
clarinet; Frank Thompson, piano; George Bineth, bass; Lee Kohler,
drums.

Squeeze Me
    Unissued

Strut Miss Lizzie
    Unissued

Clarinet Marmalade
    Unissued

Love Is Just Around The Corner
    Unissued

Blues (incomplete)
Unissued

NOTE: Recorded at Vogt's Tavern.

Pee Wee Russell And The Mahogany All Stars

Boston, 1953

Doc Cheatham, trumpet; Vic Dickenson, trombone; Pee Wee Russell, clarinet; George Wein, piano; John Field, bass; Buzzy Drootin, drums; Al Bandini, vocal.

We're In The Money
   45:   Storyville EP 407
   33:   Black Lion (G) BL 760 909, Jazztone J 1257, >Storyville LP
          308, Storyville STLP 909, Storyville (J) PA 6009
   CD: Black Lion (G) BLCD 760 909

Gabriel Found His Horn (AB vocal)
   45:   Storyville EP 407
   33:   Black Lion (G) BL 760 909, Jazztone J 1257, >Storyville LP
          308, Storyville STLP 909, Storyville (J) PA 6009
   CD: Black Lion (G) BLCD 760 909

Sugar
   45:   Storyville EP 408
   33:   Black Lion (G) BL 760 909, Jazztone J 1257, >Storyville LP
          308, Storyville STLP 909, Storyville (J) PA 6009
   CD: Black Lion (G) BLCD 760 909

Missy
   45:   Storyville EP 407
   33:   Black Lion (G) BL 760 909, Jazztone J 1257, >Storyville LP
          308, Storyville STLP 909, Storyville (J) PA 6009
   CD: Black Lion (G) BLCD 760 909

Sweet And Slow
   45:   Storyville EP 408
   33:   Black Lion (G) BL 760 909, Jazztone J 1257, >Storyville LP
          308, Storyville STLP 909, Storyville (J) PA 6009
   CD: Black Lion (G) BLCD 760 909

Lulu's Back In Town
    45: Storyville EP 408
    33: Black Lion (G) BLCD 760 909, Jazztone J 1257, >Storyville
          LP 308, Storyville STLP 909, Storyville (J) PA 6009
    CD: Black Lion (G) BLCD 760 909

NOTE: Produced by George Wein. Arrangements by Dick Cary. "Missy" was composed by Pee Wee Russell.

George Avakian

NYC, March 10, 1953

George Avakian interviews Jimmy McPartland and Pee Wee Russell
    Unissued

NOTE: Recorded at CBS studios for broadcast on a program hosted by Frank Trumbauer on WOC, Davenport, Iowa.

Charlie Fisk NBC Dixieland Jamboree

NYC, May 27, 1953

Charlie Fisk, trumpet; Pee Wee Russell, clarinet; possibly Herbie Nichols, piano; unknown bass sax; unknown bass; George Wettling, drums, Lee Sharmel, vocal

Down Yonder (LS vocal)
    TX: >AFRS ONS 3345

Basin Street Blues
    TX: >AFRS ONS 3345

Pagan Love Song
    33: IAJRC 28
    TX: >AFRS ONS 3345

NOTE: Broadcast from the Cafe Rouge, Hotel Statler.

Charlie Fisk NBC Dixieland Jamboree

NYC, June 16, 1953

Charlie Fisk, trumpet; Pee Wee Russell, clarinet; possibly Herbie Nichols, piano; unknown bass sax; unknown bass; George Wettling, drums.

Honeysuckle Rose
    TX: >AFRS ONS 3352

NOTE: Broadcast from the Cafe Rouge, Hotel Statler.

Max Kaminsky and His Windy City Six

NYC, 1954

Max Kaminsky, trumpet; Miff Mole, trombone; Pee Wee Russell, clarinet; Joe Sullivan, piano; Jack Lesberg, bass; George Wettling, drums.

Hot Time In The Old Town Tonight
    33: Concert Hall CHJ 1009, >Jazztone J 1009, Jazztone J 1208
    CT: Jazz Connoisseur Cassettes (E) J.C.C. 101

Tavern In The Town
    33: Concert Hall CHJ 1009, >Jazztone J 1009, Jazztone J 1208
    CT: Jazz Connoisseur Cassettes (E) J.C.C. 101

Del Mar Rag
    33: Concert Hall CHJ 1009, >Jazztone J 1009, Jazztone J 1208, Time-Life STL-J27 (P 15969), Time-Life (Au) STL-J27, Time-Life (C) STL-J27
    CT: Time-Life 4TL-J27, Jazz Connoisseur Cassettes (E) J.C.C. 101
    8T: Time-Life 8TL-J27

Stuyvesant Blues
    33: Concert Hall CHJ 1009, Hall of Fame JG-603, >Jazztone J 1009, Jazztone J 1208, Jazztone J 1258, MK 1001, Musica Jazz Presenta (I) 2MJP 1071
    CT: Jazz Connoisseur Cassettes (E) J.C.C. 101

Lonesome Road
   33:   Concert Hall CHJ 1009, Hall of Fame JG-603, >Jazztone J
          1009, Jazztone J 1208, Jazztone J 1278, MK 1001
   CT: Jazz Connoisseur Cassettes (E) J.C.C. 101

Never Touched Me
   33:   Concert Hall CHJ 1009, Hall of Fame JG-616, >Jazztone J
          1009, Jazztone J 1208, Jazztone J 1278, MK 1001
   CT: Jazz Connoisseur Cassettes (E) J.C.C. 101

Short Ties And Long Ties
   33:   Hall of Fame JG-616, >Jazztone J 1208, Jazztone J 1278
   CT: Jazz Connoisseur Cassettes (E) J.C.C. 101

At The Jazz Band Ball
   33:   Hall of Fame JG-616, >Jazztone J 1208, Jazztone J 1278
   CT: Jazz Connoisseur Cassettes (E) J.C.C. 101

Fidgety Feet
   33:   >Jazztone J 1208
   CT: Jazz Connoisseur Cassettes (E) J.C.C. 101

NOTE: "Never Touched Me" issued as "New Orleans Joys" and
"Stuyvesant Blues" issued as "Midnight Blues" on MK 1001. Pee Wee
Russell does not appear on "Mix Max," also recorded at this session.

Jazz Dance

NYC, early 1954

Jimmy McPartland, trumpet; Jimmy Archey, trombone; Pee Wee
Russell, clarinet; Willie "The Lion" Smith, piano, vocal; Pops Foster,
bass; George Wettling, drums.

Jazz Me Blues
   33:   >Jaguar LP 801, Melodisc (E) MLP 514
   VT: Jazz Pioneer (C) JMV 101691

Ballin' The Jack (W"TL"S vocal)
   33:   >Jaguar LP 801, Melodisc (E) MLP 514
   VT: Jazz Pioneer (C) JMV 101691

Royal Garden Blues
   33:   >Jaguar LP 801, Melodisc (E) MLP 514
   VT: Jazz Pioneer (C) JMV 101691

237

When The Saints Go Marching In
    33: >Jaguar LP 801, Melodisc (E) MLP 514
    VT: Jazz Pioneer (C) JMV 101691

NOTE: From the film "Jazz Dance," shot at Central Plaza, directed and produced by Roger Tilton. It was copyrighted on June 22, 1954.

Eddie Condon group

NYC, May 10, 1954

Wild Bill Davison, cornet; Cutty Cutshall, trombone; Pee Wee Russell, clarinet; others unknown.

Program 1:
The Blues
    Unissued

I Ain't Got Nobody
    Unissued

Medley: Sweet And Lovely; I'd Climb The Highest Mountain; I'm Comin' Virginia
    Unissued

Indiana
    Unissued

Yes Sir, That's My Baby
    Unissued

Squeeze Me
    Unissued

Program 2:
I Ain't Gonna Give Nobody None Of My Jelly Roll
    Unissued

Sweet Georgia Brown
    Unissued

Riverboat Shuffle
    Unissued

Medley: On The Alamo; Tenderly; I'm In The Market For You; All Of
Me; I Can't Give You Anything But Love
     Unissued

Program 3:
Big Eight Blues
     Unissued

I Gotta Right To Sing The Blues
     Unissued

That's A Plenty
     Unissued

Sunday
     Unissued

Program 4:
After You've Gone
     Unissued

When The Saints Go Marching In
     Unissued

Struttin' With Some Barbecue
     Unissued

Basin Street Blues
     Unissued

Dippermouth Blues
     Unissued

The World Is Waiting For The Sunrise
     Unissued

NOTE: This information comes from lists of acetates sold by
"Amalgamated Records." None of these programs have been available
for audition. Personnel of programs three and four is not certain.

Eddie Condon group

Wild Bill Davison, cornet; Pee Wee Russell, clarinet; Eddie Condon, guitar; others unknown.

Program 1:
I Can't Give You Anything But Love
  Unissued

Ja-Da
  Unissued

Medley: You Turned The Tables On Me; Ain't Misbehavin'; You Took Advantage Of Me
  Unissued

Indiana
  Unissued

Oh, Baby
  Unissued

September In The Rain
  Unissued

Sweet Georgia Brown
  Unissued

Program 2:
Beale Street Blues
  Unissued

It Had To Be You
  Unissued

Medley: unnamed tune; I'm In The Market For You; If I Had You
  Unissued

The World Is Waiting For The Sunrise
  Unissued

Bill Bailey, Won't You Please Come Home
  Unissued

Medley: Lover Man; Sweet And Lovely; I Surrender, Dear
   Unissued

Old Folks
   Unissued

Program 3:
I've Found A New Baby
   Unissued

Easy Stampede
   Unissued

Just Blues
   Unissued

More Blues
   Unissued

Bye And Bye
   Unissued

Squeeze Me
   Unissued

The Lady's In Love With You
   Unissued

NOTE: Above as listed on acetates by "Amalgamated Records."
None of this material has been available for audition.

Jazz At Storyville

Cambridge, Mass., October 2, 1954

Wild Bill Davison, cornet; Vic Dickenson, trombone; Pee Wee Russell,
clarinet; George Wein, piano; Stan Wheeler, bass; Buzzy Drootin,
drums.

Sweet Georgia Brown
   45:   Storyville EP 430
   33:   Black Lion (G) BL 760 909, Jazz Selection (F) JSLP 50.046,
         Jazztone J 1257, >Storyville LP 319, Storyville STLP 909,
         Storyville (J) PA-6009, Vogue (F) LDE 134
   CD: Black Lion (G) BLCD 760 909

The Lady's In Love With You
- 33: Black Lion (G) BL 760 909, Jazz Selection (F) JSLP 50.046, Jazztone J 1257, >Storyville LP 319, Storyville STLP 909, Storyville (J) PA-6009, Vogue (F) LDE 134
- CD: Black Lion (G) BLCD 760 909

Louise
- 45: Storyville EP 431
- 33: Black Lion (G) BL 760 909, Jazz Selection (F) JSLP 50.046, Jazztone J 1257, >Storyville LP 319, Storyville STLP 909, Storyville (J) PA-6009, Vogue (F) LDE 134, Vogue (F) V.2325
- CD: Black Lion (G) BLCD 760 909

She's Funny That Way
- 45: Storyville EP 430
- 33: Black Lion (G) BL 760 909, Jazz Selection (F) JSLP 50.046, Jazztone J 1257, >Storyville LP 319, Storyville STLP 909, Storyville (J) PA-6009, Vogue (F) LDE 134, Vogue (F) V.2325
- CD: Black Lion (G) BLCD 760 909

If I Had You
- 45: Storyville EP 431
- 33: Black Lion (G) BL 760 909, Jazz Selection (F) JSLP 50.046, Jazztone J 1257, >Storyville LP 319, Storyville STLP 909, Storyville (J) PA-6009, Vogue (F) LDE 134, Vogue (F) V.2325
- CD: Black Lion (G) BLCD 760 909

Back In Your Own Backyard
- 45: Storyville EP 431
- 33: Black Lion (G) BL 760 909, Jazz Selection (F) JSLP 50.046, Jazztone J 1257, >Storyville LP 319, Storyville STLP 909, Storyville (J) PA-6009, Vogue (F) LDE 134, Vogue (F) V.2325
- CD: Black Lion (G) BLCD 760 909

I Want A Little Girl
   45:   Storyville EP 430
   33:   Black Lion (G) BL 760 909, Jazz Selection (F) JSLP 50.046,
         Jazztone J 1257, >Storyville LP 319, Storyville STLP 909,
         Storyville (J) PA-6009, Vogue (F) LDE 134, Vogue (F)
         V.2325
   CD: Black Lion (G) BLCD 760 909

Note: Produced by George Wein. Recorded at Rockwell Film studio,
Harvard Square. Although this date is given on the record jacket and in
all other sources, it may actually have been recorded around the time of
the second Newport Jazz Festival in July, 1955.

*In mid-November, Pee Wee Russell participated in a Hot Lips Page
memorial jam session which was broadcast from the Stuyvesant Casino
beginning at 8 p.m. No recording is known to exist of this concert.*

Newport All Stars
                              Newport, Rhode Island, July 16, 1955

Wild Bill Davison, cornet; Vic Dickenson, trombone; Pee Wee Russell,
clarinet; Bud Freeman, tenor; George Wein, piano; Milt Hinton, bass;
Buzzy Drootin, drums.

At The Jazz Band Ball (incomplete)
   Unissued

NOTE: Recorded from a radio broadcast of the second Newport Jazz
Festival. Al "Jazzbo" Collins announced the selection.

Eddie Condon And His All Stars

                              Miami, Florida, November 27, 1955

Wild Bill Davison, cornet; Lou McGarity, trombone; Pee Wee Russell,
clarinet; Gene Schroeder, piano; Eddie Condon, guitar; Walter Page,
bass; George Wettling, drums.

If I Had You
   Unissued

Medley: Peg O' My Heart; Old Folks; I'm Comin' Virginia
   Unissued

I Ain't Gonna Give Nobody None Of My Jelly Roll
     33:   >Pumpkin 111

That's A Plenty
     Unissued

Fidgety Feet
     Unissued

Squeeze Me
     33:   >Pumpkin 111

Beale Street Blues
     33:   >Pumpkin 111

Add Preacher Rollo and The Saints: Tommy Justice, cornet; Jerry
Gorman, trombone; Ernie Goodson, clarinet; Bobby Rosen, piano; Al
Mattucci, bass; Rollo Laylan, drums.

Blues/Ole Miss (incomplete performance)
     Unissued

Blues/Ole Miss (final two choruses)
     Unissued

Tin Roof Blues
     Unissued

NOTE: From a concert at the Dade County Auditorium. In the
medley, Pee Wee Russell solos on "Old Folks" and can be heard in the
closing ensemble on "I'm Coming Virginia."

Eddie Condon And His All Stars

                              Miami Beach, Florida, November 27, 1955

Wild Bill Davison, cornet; Lou McGarity, trombone; Pee Wee Russell,
clarinet; Gene Schroeder, piano; Eddie Condon, guitar; Walter Page,
bass; George Wettling, drums.

Dippermouth Blues
     33:   >Pumpkin 111

Medley: Peg O' My Heart; Judy; I'm In the Market For You; It's The Talk Of The Town; Rockin' Chair
    33: >Pumpkin 111

Struttin' With Some Barbecue
    33: >Pumpkin 111

NOTE: Recorded at the Shoremede Hotel following the concert at the Dade County Auditorium. The medley as issued on Pumpkin 111 has been edited to omit "Peg O' My Heart" and "It's the Talk of the Town." Pee Wee Russell solos on "I'm In the Market for You."

Eddie Condon And his All Stars

Miami Beach, Florida, November 29, 1955

Wild Bill Davison, cornet; Lou McGarity, trombone; Pee Wee Russell, clarinet; Gene Schroeder, piano; Eddie Condon, guitar; Walter Page, bass; George Wettling, drums.

Beale Street Blues
    Unissued

The One I Love Belongs To Somebody Else
    Unissued

Medley: How Deep Is The Ocean; Ain't Misbehavin'; Old Man River
    Unissued

Fidgety Feet
    Unissued

Singin' the Blues
    33: >Pumpkin 111

I Want To Be Happy
    33: >Pumpkin 111

Note: Recorded at the Shoremede Hotel. In the medley, Pee Wee Russell solos on "Ain't Misbehavin'."

George Wettling Trio

Englewood, New Jersey, February 11, 1956

Pee Wee Russell, clarinet; Gene Schroeder, piano; George Wettling, drums.

1390 Old Folks
    33: >Kapp KL 1028, Time-Life STL J-17 (P 15735), Time-Life
           (Au) STL-J17, Time-Life (C) STL J-17
    CT: Holmia (E) HM 03, Time-Life 4TL-J17
    8T: Time-Life 8TL-J17

1391 Louise
    33: Kapp KS 1, >Kapp KL 1028
    CT: Holmia (E) HM 03

1392 I'm In The Market for You
    33: >Kapp KL 1028
    CT: Holmia (E) HM 03

1393 I Would Do Anything For You
    33: >Kapp KL 1028
    CT: Holmia (E) HM 03

Eddie Condon And His All Stars

NYC, February 16, 1956

Wild Bill Davison, cornet; Cutty Cutshall, trombone; Pee Wee Russell, clarinet; Gene Schroeder, piano; Eddie Condon, guitar; Walter Page, bass; George Wettling, drums.

CO 54487 I'm Gonna Sit Right Down And Write Myself A Letter
    45: Columbia (J) EM 159
    33: CBS Coronet (Au) KLP-673, >Columbia CL 881, Columbia
           (Arg) 8058, Columbia (C) CL 881, Columbia (J) TD-1006,
           Philips (E) BBL 7131, Philips (E) BBL 7173, Philips (Eu)
           429233BE, Philips (H) B 07193 L

CO 54488 Don't Get Around Much Anymore
    33: CBS Cornet (Au) KLP-673, >Columbia CL 881, Columbia
           (Arg) 8058, Columbia (C) CL 881, Columbia (J) TD-1006,
           Philips (E) BBL 7131, Philips (Eu) 429233BE, Philips (H) B
           07193 L

CO 54489 Three-Two-One Blues
   33: >Columbia CL 881, Columbia (Arg) 8058, Columbia (J) TD-
          1006, Musica Jazz Presenta (I) 2MJP 1071, Philips (E) BBL
          7131, Philips (Eu) 429233BE, Philips (H) B 07193 L, Time-
          Life STL-J17 (P 15735), Time-Life (Au) STL-J17 (P 15735),
          Time-Life (C) STL-J17
   CT: Time-Life 4TL-J17
   8T: Time-Life 8TL-J17

CO 54490 I'm Confessin'
   45: Columbia (J) EM 159, Philips (E) bbe 12365
   33: CBS Coronet (Au) KLP-673, >Columbia CL 881, Columbia
          (Arg) 8058, Columbia (C) CL 881, Columbia (J) TD-1006,
          Philips (E) BBL 7131, Philips (Eu) 429886BE, Philips (H) B
          O7193 L

CO 54491 Sometimes I'm Happy
   33: CBS Coronet (Au) KLP-673, >Columbia CL 881, Columbia
          (Arg) 8058, Columbia (C) CL 881, Columbia (J) TD-1006,
          Philips (E) BBL 7131, Philips (H) B 07193 L

NOTE: Produced by George Avakian.

Eddie Condon And His All Stars
NYC, February 20, 1956

Wild Bill Davison, cornet; Billy Butterfield, trumpet; Cutty Cutshall,
trombone; Pee Wee Russell, clarinet; Peanuts Hucko, clarinet, tenor;
Gene Schroeder, piano; Eddie Condon, guitar; Walter Page, bass;
George Wettling, drums.

CO 54494 Since My Best Gal Turned Me Down
   33: CBS Coronet (Au) KLP-673, >Columbia CL 881, Columbia
          (Arg) 8058, Columbia (C) CL 881, Columbia (J) TD-1006,
          Columbia (J) PL 5064, Philips (E) BBL 7131, Philips (Eu) B
          07901 R, Philips (H) B O7193 L

CO 54495 Just Friends
   45: Philips bbe 12280
   33: CBS Coronet (Au) KLP-673, >Columbia CL 881, Columbia
          (Arg) 8058, Columbia (C) CL 881, Columbia (J) TD-1006,
          Philips (E) BBL 7131, Philips (Eu) 429586BE, Philips (Eu)
          BQ 7901 R, Philips (H) B 07193 L

CO 54496 Someday You'll Be Sorry
  33:    CBS Coronet (Au) KLP-673, >Columbia CL 881, Columbia
         (Arg) 8058, Columbia (C) CL 881, Columbia (J) TD-1006,
         Philips (E) BBL 7131, Philips (H) B 07193 L

NOTE: Produced by George Avakian.

Brother Matthew with Eddie Condon's Jazz Band
                                          NYC, April 2, 1956

Wild Bill Davison, cornet; Cutty Cutshall, trombone; Pee Wee Russell,
clarinet; Boyce "Brother Matthew" Brown, alto; Ernie Caceres,
baritone; Gene Schroeder, piano; Eddie Condon, guitar, leader; Bob
Casey, bass; George Wettling, drums.

5162 Out of Nowhere
  33:    >ABC Paramount ABC-121, ABC Paramount (J) PC 2,
         Sparton (C) ABC-121, W&G (Au) WG-PJN-208

5163 I Never Knew
  33:    >ABC Paramount ABC-121, ABC Paramount (J) PC 2,
         Sparton (C) ABC-121, W&G (Au) WG-PJN-208

5164 Someday Sweetheart
  33:    >ABC Paramount ABC-121, ABC Paramount (J) PC 2,
         Sparton (C) ABC-121, W&G (Au) WG-PJN-208

5165 The World Is Waiting For The Sunrise
  33:    >ABC Paramount ABC-121, ABC Paramount (J) PC 2,
         Sparton (C) ABC-121, W&G (Au) WG-PJN-208

5166 My Blue Heaven
  33:    >ABC Paramount ABC-121, ABC Paramount (J) PC 2,
         Sparton (C) ABC-121, W&G (Au) WG-PJN-208

5167 Linger Awhile
  33:    >ABC Paramount ABC-121, ABC Paramount (J) PC 2,
         Sparton (C) ABC-121, W&G (Au) WG-PJN-208

NOTE: This session was recorded at Columbia studios. Produced by
Creed Taylor. Brother Matthew was a monk in the Servite Order of the
Catholic Church.

248

Brother Matthew with Eddie Condon's Jazz Band

NYC, April 3, 1956

Same personnel

5168   Blues For Boyce
   33:   >ABC Paramount ABC-121, ABC Paramount (J) PC 2,
       Sparton (C) ABC-121, Musica Jazz (I) 2MJP 1042, W&G
       (Au) WG-PJN-208

5169   Sister Kate
   45:   HMV 7EG 8312
   33:   >ABC Paramount ABC-121, ABC Paramount (J) PC 2,
       Sparton (C) ABC-121, W&G (Au) WG-PJN-208

5170   Sweet Georgia Brown
   45:   HMV 7EG 8312
   33:   >ABC Paramount ABC-121, ABC Paramount (J) PC 2,
       Sparton (C) ABC-121, W&G (Au) WG-PJN-208

NOTE: This session was recorded at Columbia studios. Produced by Creed Taylor.

Music Inn Concert

Lenox, Mass., August 30, 1956

Pee Wee Russell, clarinet; Jimmy Giuffre, clarinet; George Wein, piano; Oscar Pettiford, bass; Connie Kay, drums.

Blues In E Flat
   33:   >Atlantic LP 1298, Atlantic (J) ATL 5025

NOTE: Recorded at a concert in the Music Barn at Music Inn.

In January, 1957, Pee Wee Russell and Ruby Braff recorded several sessions, produced by George Avakian, for Epic records. Other personnel is said to have included Coleman Hawkins and Vic Dickenson. According to Avakian, the master tapes were destroyed.

Bud Freeman's Summa Cum Laude Orchestra

Jimmy McPartland, cornet; Pee Wee Russell, clarinet; Bud Freeman, tenor; Dick Cary, piano; Al Casamenti, guitar; Milt Hinton, bass; George Wettling, drums.

H2J B 2160 Lisa [*sic*]
    45:   >Victor EPA 3-1508
    33:   Camden (J) RGP-1088, >Victor LPM 1508, Victor (J) LS 5056

H2J B 2161 China Boy
    45:   >Victor EPA 1-1508
    33:   Camden (J) RGP-1088, >Victor LPM 1508, Victor (J) LS 5056

H2J B 2162 Sugar
    45:   >Victor EPA 2-1508
    33:   Camden (J) RGP-1088, >Victor LPM 1508, Victor (J) LS 5056

H2J B 2163 Nobody's Sweetheart
    45:   >Victor EPA 2-1508
    33:   Camden (J) RGP-1088, >Victor LPM 1508, Victor (J) LS 5056

NOTE: Produced by Fred Reynolds. Recored in RCA studio 3. The correct title for H2J B 2160 is "Liza."

Ruby Braff And His Men

Ruby Braff, cornet; Benny Morton, trombone; Pee Wee Russell, clarinet; Dick Hafer, tenor; Nat Pierce, piano; Steve Jordan, guitar; Walter Page, bass; Buzzy Drootin, drums.

H2J B 2793 It's Been So Long
    45:   >Victor EPA 1-1510
    33:   Camden (J) RGP 1188, RCA (Au) L 10822, >Victor LPM 1510
    CD: Bluebird 6456-2-RB
    CT: Bluebird 6456-4-RB

H2J B 2794 I'm Comin' Virginia
   45: >Victor EPA 2-1510
   33: Camden (J) RGP 1188, RCA (Au) L 10822, >Victor LPM
         1510
   CD: Bluebird 6456-2-RB
   CT: Bluebird 6456-4-RB

H2J B 2795 Keep Smiling At Trouble
   45: >Victor EPA 3-1510
   33: Camden (J) RGP 1188, RCA (Au) L 10822, >Victor LPM
         1510

NOTE: Produced by Fred Reynolds. Recorded in RCA studio 3.

Bud Freeman's Summa Cum Laude Orchestra

NYC, April 3, 1957

Billy Butterfield, trumpet; Tyree Glenn, trombone; Pee Wee Russell,
clarinet; Bud Freeman, tenor; Dick Cary, piano; Al Casamenti, guitar;
Al Hall, bass; George Wettling, drums.

H2J B 3214 Chicago
   45: >Victor EPA 3-1508
   33: Camden (J) RGP-1088, RCA (F) PM 43267, >Victor LPM
         1508, Victor (J) LS 5056

H2J B 3215 At Sundown
   45: >Victor EPA 1-1508
   33: Camden (J) RGP-1088, >Victor LPM 1508, Victor (J) LS
         5056

H2J B 3216 Sunday
   33: Camden (J) RGP-1088, >Victor LPM 1644, Victor (J) RA
         5014

H2J B 3217 The Reverend's In Town
   33: Camden (J) RGP-1088, >Victor LPM 1644, Victor (J) RA
         5014

NOTE: Produced by Fred Reynolds. Recorded in RCA studio 3.

Ruby Braff And His Men

Ruby Braff, cornet; Benny Morton, trombone; Pee Wee Russell, clarinet; Dick Hafer, tenor; Nat Pierce, piano; Steve Jordan, guitar; Walter Page, bass; Buzzy Drootin, drums.

H2J B 3273 I Can't Get Started
    45:   >Victor EPA 1-1510
    33:   Camden (J) RGP-1188, RCA (Au) L 10822, >Victor LPM 1510
    CD: Bluebird 6456-2-RB
    CT: Bluebird 6456-4-RB

H2J B 3274 Marie
    45:   >Victor EPA 2-1510
    33:   Camden (J) RGP-1188, RCA (Au) L 10822, >Victor LPM 1510
    CD: Bluebird 6456-2-RB
    CT: Bluebird 6456-4-RB

H2J B 3275 I Got It Bad And That Ain't Good
    45:   >Victor EPA 3-1510
    33:   Camden (J) RGP-1188, RCA (Au) L 10822, >Victor LPM 1510
    CD: Bluebird 6456-2-RB
    CT: Bluebird 6456-4-RB

NOTE: Produced by Fred Reynolds. Recorded in RCA studio 3.

Ruby Braff And His Men

Same personnel

H2J B 3415 Somebody Else Is Taking My Place
    45:   >Victor EPA 3-1510
    33:   Camden (J) RGP-1188, RCA (Au) L 10822, >Victor LPM 1510

H2J B 3416 Downhearted Blues
    45: >Victor EPA 3-1510
    33: Camden (J) RGP-1188, RCA (Au) L 10822, >Victor LPM
         1510
    CD: Bluebird 6456-2-RB
    CT: Bluebird 6456-4-RB

H2L B 3417 Did I Remember?
    33: >Victor LPM 1644, Victor (J) RA 5014
    CD: Bluebird 6456-2-RB
    CT: Bluebird 6456-4-RB

NOTE: Produced by Fred Reynolds. Recorded in RCA studio 3.

Bud Freeman All Stars/George Wettling's All Stars

NYC, April 22, 1957

Max Kaminsky, trumpet; Cutty Cutshall, trombone; Pee Wee Russell,
clarinet; Bud Freeman, tenor; Dick Cary, piano, arranger; Eddie
Condon, guitar; Leonard Gaskin, bass; George Wettling, drums.

CO 57831 Ginger Brown
    33: >Harmony HL 7046

CO 57832 Runnin' Wild
    33: >Harmony HL 7080, Harmony (C) HL 7080

C0 57833 Dinah
    33: >Harmony HL 7046

CO 57834 Odd Aardvark
    33: >Harmony HL 7080, Harmony (C) HL 7080

NOTE: Harmony HL 7046 was issued as Bud Freeman; Harmony HL
7080 as George Wettling.

The Ruby Braff Octet with Pee Wee Russell

Newport, Rhode Island, July 5, 1957

Ruby Braff, cornet; Jimmy Welsh, valve trombone; Pee Wee Russell, clarinet; Sam Margolis, tenor; Nat Pierce, piano; Steve Jordan, guitar; Walter Page, bass; Buzzy Drootin, drums.

It Don't Mean A Thing
- 33: American Recording Society G 439, Columbia (E) 33CX 10104, Reader's Digest RD4-129, >Verve MGV 8241, Verve (G) 845 150-1, Verve (J) MV 2625
- CD: Verve (G) 845 150-2
- CT: Verve (G) 845 150-4

These Foolish Things
- 33: American Recording Society G 439, Columbia (E) 33CX 10104, >Verve MGV 8241, Verve (G) 845 151-1, Verve (J) MV 2625
- CD: Verve (G) 845 151-2
- CT: Verve (G) 845 151-4

Oh, Lady Be Good
- 33: American Recording Society G 439, Columbia (E) 33CX 10104, Reader's Digest RD4-129, Metro (E) 2356 017, >Verve MGV 8241, Verve (J) MV 2625

NOTE: Recorded at the Newport Jazz Festival. The band also played "No One Else But You," but this has not been issued.

Pee Wee Russell Quintet

NYC, 1957

Pee Wee Russell, clarinet; Nat Pierce, piano; Steve Jordan, guitar; Walter Page, bass; George Wettling, drums.

Muskogee Blues
- 45: Stere-o-craft EPS 303
- 33: Bell BLP 42, Hi-Life 42, Hi-Life 69, >Stere-o-craft RTN 105, World Record Club (E) T 308, Xanadu 192
- CD: Fresh Sound (Sp) FSR-CD 126, Rockin' Chair (Sw) (no number)
- RT: Hi-Life 42, Stere-o-Tone TN 105

254

Pee Wee's Song
   45: Stere-o-craft EPS 303
   33: Bell BLP 42, Hi-Life 42, >Stere-o-craft RTN 105, World
        Record Club (E) T 308, Xanadu 192
   CD: Fresh Sound (Sp) FSR-CD 126, Rockin' Chair (Sw) (no
        number)
   RT: Hi-Life 42, Stere-o-Tone TN 105

Exactly Like You
   33: Bell BLP 42, Hi-Life 42, Hi-Life 69, >Stere-o-craft RTN
        105, World Record Club (E) T 308, Xanadu 192
   CD: Fresh Sound (Sp) FSR-CD 126, Rockin' Chair (Sw) (no
        number)
   RT: Hi-Life 42, Stere-o-Tone TN 105

I'd Climb The Highest Mountain (take "1")
   33: Bell BLP 42, Hi-Life 42, >Stere-o-craft RTN 105, Time-Life
        STL-J17 (P 15735), Time-Life (Au) STL-J17 (P 15735),
        Time-Life (C) STL-J17, World Record Club (E) T 308,
        Xanadu 192
   CD: Fresh Sound (Sp) FSR-CD 126, Rockin' Chair (Sw) (no
        number)
   CT: Time-Life 4TL-J17
   8T: Time-Life 8TL-J17

I'd Climb The Highest Mountain (take "2")
   45: Stere-o-craft EPS 303
   33: Bell BLP 42, Hi-Life 42, >Stere-o-craft RTN 105, Xanadu
        192
   CD: Fresh Sound (Sp) FSR-CD 126, Rockin' Chair (Sw) (no
        number)
   RT: Hi-Life 42, Stere-o-Tone TN 105

Over The Rainbow
   33: Bell BLP 42, Hi-Life 42, >Stere-o-craft RTN 105, World
        Record Club (E) T 308, Xanadu 192
   CD: Fresh Sound (Sp) FSR-CD 126, Rockin' Chair (Sw) (no
        number)
   RT: Hi-Life 42, Stere-o-Tone TN 105

255

I Would Do Anything For You
 33: Bell BLP 42, Hi-Life 42, >Stere-o-craft RTN 105, World
   Record Club (E) T 308, Xanadu 192
 CD: Fresh Sound (Sp) FSR-CD 126, Rockin' Chair (Sw) (no
   number)
 RT: Hi-Life 42, Stere-o-Tone TN 105

I'm In The Market For You
 45: Stere-o-craft EPS 303
 33: Bell BLP 42, Hi-Life 42, >Stere-o-craft RTN 105, World
   Record Club (E) T 308, Xanadu 192
 CD: Fresh Sound (Sp) FSR-CD 126, Rockin' Chair (Sw) (no
   number)
 RT: Hi-Life 42, Stere-o-Tone TN 105

The Lady's In Love With You
 33: Bell BLP 42, Hi-Life 42, >Stere-o-craft RTN 105, World
   Record Club (E) T 308, Xanadu 192
 CD: Fresh Sound (Sp) FSR-CD 126, Rockin' Chair (Sw) (no
   number)
 RT: Hi-Life 42, Stere-o-Tone TN 105

Swingin' Down The Lane
 33: Hi-Life 69

Take numbers have been assigned to the two takes of "I'd Climb The
Highest Mountain" based on the sequence in which they appear on the
Stere-o-craft, Bell and Hi-Life LPs. The actual recording sequence is
not known. Despite liner notes for the reel tape issue on Hi-Life and
Stere-o-Tone, only one take of "I'd Climb the Highest Mountain" is
included. All liner notes suggest a 1958 date for this session, but Walter
Page died on December 20, 1957. "Muskogee Blues" (labeled
"Muskeegie Blues" on Bell, Hi-Life, Fresh Sound and Rockin' Chair)
and "Pee Wee's Song" are both Pee Wee Russell compositions. "Pee
Wee's Song" is the same composition as "Pee Wee's Tune" (see
February 23 and 24, 1959).

Ruby Braff - Pee Wee Russell Sextet

NYC, August 10, 1957

Ruby Braff, trumpet; Pee Wee Russell, clarinet; Nat Pierce, piano; Steve Jordan, guitar; Walter Page, bass; Bobby Donaldson, drums.

I'm Crazy 'Bout My Baby
    33: >Spook Jazz (D) SPJ 6607
    CT: Holmia (E) HM 06

Blue Turning Grey Over You (incomplete)
    Unissued

The above titles are from a "Bandstand U.S.A." broadcast from the Village Vanguard.

Pee Wee Russell with the Charlie Byrd Quartet

Washington, D.C., December 1, 1957

Pee Wee Russell, clarinet; Eddie Diamond, piano, trumpet; Charlie Byrd, guitar; Keter Betts, bass; Eddie Phyfe, drums.

"C" Jam Blues
    Unissued

Rose Room
    Unissued

'S Wonderful
    Unissued

Rosetta
    Unissued

Blues
    Unissued

Indiana
    Unissued

St. James Infirmary
    Unissued

Whispering
    Unissued

Blues
    Unissued

Ja Da
    Unissued

Blue Room
    Unissued

NOTE: From a benefit concert for the Washington, D.C., Jazz Club. Recorded at the Bayou Club.

The Sound Of Jazz

NYC, December 5, 1957

Rex Stewart, cornet; Henry "Red" Allen, trumpet, vocal; Vic Dickenson, trombone; Pee Wee Russell, clarinet; Coleman Hawkins, tenor; Nat Pierce, piano; Danny Barker, guitar; Milt Hinton, bass; Jo Jones, drums.

CO 59469 Wild Man Blues
    33:    CBS (H) CBS 57036, CBS Coronet (Au) KLP 657, CBS Sony (J) 15 AP 551, CBS Sony (J) SONP-50342, >Columbia CL 1098, Columbia JCL 1098, >Columbia CS 8040, Columbia CJ 45234, Columbia (Arg) 8159, Columbia (J) YL 101, Columbia (J) YS 109, Fontana (C) 682.015TL, Fontana (E) TFL 5025, Philips Realities (F) V 15
    CD: CBS (E) 465.683-2, CBS Sony (J) 25DP-5322, Columbia CK 45234
    CT: Columbia BT 8040, Columbia CJT 45234

CO 59470 Rosetta (HA vocal)
    33:   CBS (H) CBS 57036, CBS Coronet (Au) KLP 657, CBS
           Sony (J) 15 AP 551, CBS Sony (J) SONP-50342, >Columbia
           CL 1098, Columbia JCL 1098, >Columbia CS 8040,
           Columbia CJ 45234, Columbia (Arg) 8159, Columbia (J) YL
           101, Columbia (J) YS 109, Fontana (C) 682015TL, Fontana
           (E) TFL 5025, Philips Realities (F) V 15
    CD: CBS (E) 465.683-2, CBS Sony (J) 25DP-5322, Columbia CK
           45234
    CT: Columbia BT 8040, Columbia CJT 45234

Jimmy Giuffre, Pee Wee Russell, clarinet; Danny Barker, guitar; Milt
Hinton, bass; Jo Jones, drums.

CO 59472 Blues
    45:   Fontana (E) tfe 17081, Columbia (J) EM 227
    33:   CBS (H) CBS 57036, CBS Coronet (Au) KLP 657, CBS
           Sony (J) 15 AP 551, CBS Sony (J) SONP-50342, >Columbia
           CL 1098, Columbia JCL 1098, >Columbia CS 8040,
           Columbia CJ 45234, Columbia (Arg) 8159, Columbia (J) YL
           101, Columbia (J) YS 109, Fontana (C) 682015TL, Fontana
           (E) TFL 5025
    CD: CBS (E) 465.683-2, CBS Sony (J) 25DP-5322, Columbia CK
           45234
    CT: Columbia BT 8040, Columbia CJT 45234

NOTE: Recorded at Columbia's 30th Street studio. This session served
as a rehearsal for the live telecast of December 8, 1957.

The Sound Of Jazz
NYC, December 8, 1957

Rex Stewart, cornet; Henry "Red" Allen, trumpet, vocal; Vic
Dickenson, trombone; Pee Wee Russell, clarinet; Coleman Hawkins,
tenor; Nat Pierce, piano; Danny Barker, guitar; Milt Hinton, bass; Jo
Jones, drums.

Wild Man Blues
    33:   >Phoenix LP 24, Pumpkin 116
    CD: Bandstand (I) BDCD 1517
    VD: Kay Jazz (J) KJ-013, Toei Video Co. (J) TE-D 104
    VT: A Vision 50238-3, Vintage Jazz Classics Video VJC-2001-4,
           Warner Music Vision (E) 9031 74506 3

Rosetta (HA vocal)
- 33: >Phoenix LP 24, Pumpkin 116
- CD: Bandstand (I) BDCD 1517
- VD: Kay Jazz (J) KJ-013, Toei Video Co. (J) TE-D 104
- VT: A Vision 50238-3, Vintage Jazz Classics Video VJC-2001-4, Warner Music Vision (E) 9031 74506 3

Jimmy Giuffre, Pee Wee Russell, clarinet; Danny Barker, guitar; Milt Hinton, bass; Jo Jones, drums.

Blues (incomplete)
- 33: >Pumpkin 116
- CD: Bandstand (I) BDCD 1517
- VD: Kay Jazz (J) KJ-013, Toei Video Co. (J) TE-D 104
- VT: A Vision 50238-3, Vintage Jazz Classics Video VJC-2001-4, Warner Music Vision (E) 9031 74506 3

NOTE: Live telecast from CBS studio 58. This program was part of the series "The Seven Lively Arts," hosted by John Crosby. Executive producer was John Houseman. Robert Herridge was the producer and Jack Smight was the director. Musical advisors were Whitney Balliett and Nat Hentoff.

Jimmy McPartland's All Stars

NYC, January 3, 1958

Jimmy McPartland, Max Kaminsky, Johnny Glasel, trumpet; Dick Cary, "F" trumpet, alto horn, arranger; Al Gusikoff, Lou McGarity, Cutty Cutshall, trombone; Pee Wee Russell, Bob Wilber, clarinet; Bud Freeman, tenor; Marian McPartland, piano; Eddie Condon, guitar; Bill Crow, bass; William Stanley, tuba; George Wettling, drums.

CO 60300 Gary, Indiana
- 33: >Epic LN 3463, Epic BN 506, Fontana (E) Z4060, Philips (Au) 682139-BL

Dick Cary plays prepared piano.

CO 60301 The Wells Fargo Wagon
- 33: >Epic LN 3463, Epic BN 506, Fontana (E) Z4060, Philips (Au) 682139-BL

NOTE: Produced by James Foglesong.

Dixieland At Carnegie Hall

NYC, February 1 and 2, 1958

Jimmy McPartland, trumpet; Vic Dickenson, trombone; Pee Wee Russell, clarinet; Bud Freeman, tenor; Gene Schroeder, piano; Tommy Potter, bass; Mousey Alexander, drums.

Royal Garden Blues
33:   Columbia (E) 33SX 1122, Forum F 9011, Forum SF 9011, >Roulette R 25038, Roulette SR 25038, Roulette (J) RET 5006, Storyville (D) SLP 105

Basin Street Blues
33:   Columbia (E) 33SX 1122, Forum F 9011, Forum SF 9011, >Roulette R 25038, Roulette SR 25038, Roulette (J) RET 5006, Storyville (D) SLP 105

Add Wild Bill Davison, cornet; Joe Barufaldi and Tony Parenti, clarinet.

High Society
33:   Columbia (E) 33SX 1122, Forum F 9011, Forum SF 9011, >Roulette R 25038, Roulette SR 25038, Roulette (J) RET 5006, Storyville (D) SLP 105

Add Zutty Singleton and Cozy Cole, drums.

When The Saints Go Marching In
33:   Columbia (E) 33SX 1122, Forum F 9011, Forum SF 9011, >Roulette R 25038, Roulette SR 25038, Roulette (J) RET 5006, Storyville (D) SLP 105

Add Miff Mole and Tyree Glenn, trombone.

That's A Plenty
33:   Columbia (E) 33SX 1122, Forum F 9011, Forum SF 9011, >Roulette R 25038, Roulette SR 25038, Roulette (J) RET 5006, Storyville (D) SLP 105

Joe Barufaldi, Tony Parenti, Pee Wee Russell, clarinet; Gene Schroeder, piano; Tommy Potter, bass; Mousey Alexander, drums.

Tin Roof Blues (Clarinet Challenge)
    33: Columbia (E) 33SX 1122, Forum F 9011, Forum SF 9011, >Roulette R 25038, Roulette SR 25038, Roulette (J) RET 5006, Storyville (D) SLP 105

NOTE: From the Carnegie Hall concerts, "Dody in Dixieland," 8:30 p.m. and midnight. Produced by Rudy Taylor. Portions of the concerts were broadcast by CBS. Pee Wee Russell does not appear on other titles.

Pee Wee Russell

                                          NYC, February 18 and 19, 1958

Ruby Braff, cornet; Vic Dickenson, trombone; Pee Wee Russell, clarinet; Bud Freeman, tenor; Nat Pierce, piano, arranger; Tommy Potter, bass; Karl Kiffe, drums.

That Old Feeling
    33: America (F) 30 AM 6097, >Counterpoint CPST 562, >Counterpoint CPT 565, Ember (E) CJS 824, Everest FS 233, Fresh Sound (Sp) FSR-126, Globe (J) SMJ 7165, I Grande Del Jazz (I) GDJ 07, Opus (Arg) OJC 20011, Quadrifaglio (I) VDS 348, Society (E) SOC 1013, Vendette (I) VPA 8099
    CD: DCC DJZ-611, Fresh Sound (Sp) FSR-CD-126, Rockin' Chair (Sw) (no number)

I've Got The World On A String
    33: America (F) 30 AM 6097, >Counterpoint CPST 562, >Counterpoint CPT 565, Ember (E) CJS 824, Everest FS 233, Fresh Sound (Sp) FSR-126 Globe (J) SMJ 7165, I Grande Del Jazz (I) GDJ 07, Opus (Arg) OJC 20011, Quadrifaglio (I) VDS 348, Society (E) SOC 1013, Vendette (I) VPA 8099
    CD: DCC DJZ-611, Fresh Sound (Sp) FSR-CD-126, Rockin' Chair (Sw) (no number)

It All Depends On You
  33: America (F) 30 AM 6097, >Counterpoint CPST 562,
       >Counterpoint CPT 565, Ember (E) CJS 824, Everest FS 233,
       Fresh Sound (Sp) FSR-126, Globe (J) SMJ 7165, I Grande
       Del Jazz (I) GDJ 07, Opus (Arg) OJC 20011, Quadrifaglio (I)
       VDS 348, Society (E) SOC 1013, Vendette (I) VPA 8099
  CD: DCC DJZ-611, Fresh Sound (Sp) FSR-CD-126, Rockin'
       Chair (Sw) (no number)
  RT: Sentry 3S-106

Out Of Nowhere
  33: America (F) 30 AM 6097, >Counterpoint CPST 562,
       >Counterpoint CPT 565, Ember (E) CJS 824, Everest FS 233,
       Fresh Sound (Sp) FSR-126, Globe (J) SMJ 7165, I Grande
       Del Jazz (I) GDJ 07, Opus (Arg) OJC 20011, Quadrifaglio (I)
       VDS 348, Society (E) SOC 1013, Vendette (I) VPA 8099
  CD: DCC DJZ-611, Fresh Sound (Sp) FSR-CD-126, Rockin'
       Chair (Sw) (no number)

I Used To Love You
  33: America (F) 30 AM 6097, >Counterpoint CPST 562,
       >Counterpoint CPT 565, Ember (E) CJS 824, Everest FS 233,
       Fresh Sound (Sp) FSR-126, Globe (J) SMJ 7165, I Grande
       Del Jazz (I) GDJ 07, Opus (Arg) OJC 20011, Quadrifaglio (I)
       VDS 348, Society (E) SOC 1013, Vendette (I) VPA 8099
  CD: DCC DJZ-611, Fresh Sound (Sp) FSR-CD-126, Rockin'
       Chair (Sw) (no number)
  RT: Sentry 3S-106

Oh No
  33: America (F) 30 AM 6097, >Counterpoint CPST 562,
       >Counterpoint CPT 565, Ember (E) CJS 824, Everest FS 233,
       Fresh Sound (Sp) FSR-126, Globe (J) SMJ 7165, I Grande
       Del Jazz (I) GDJ 07, Opus (Arg) OJC 20011, Quadrifaglio (I)
       VDS 348, Society (E) SOC 1013, Vendette (I) VPA 8099
  CD: DCC DJZ-611, Fresh Sound (Sp) FSR-CD-126, Rockin'
       Chair (Sw) (no number)
  RT: Sentry 3S-106

Omit Braff, Dickenson and Freeeman.

Exactly Like You
33: America (F) 30 AM 6097, >Counterpoint CPST 562,
>Counterpoint CPT 565, Ember (E) CJS 824, Everest FS 233,
Fresh Sound (Sp) FSR-126, Globe (J) SMJ 7165, I Grande
Del Jazz (I) GDJ 07, Opus (Arg) OJC 20011, Quadrifaglio (I)
VDS 348, Society (E) SOC 1013, Vendette (I) VPA 8099,
Xanadu 192
CD: DCC DJZ-611, Fresh Sound (Sp) FS-RCD-126, Rockin'
Chair (Sw) (no number)
RT: Sentry 3S-106

If I Had You
33: America (F) 30 AM 6097, >Counterpoint CPST 562,
>Counterpoint CPT 565, DGR (H) DGR 2004, Ember (E)
CJS 824, Everest FS 233, Fresh Sound (Sp) FSRCD-126,
Globe (J) SMJ 7165, I Grande Del Jazz (I) GDJ 07, Opus
(Arg) OJC 20011, Quadrifaglio (I) VDS 348, Society (E)
SOC 1013, Vendette (I) VPA 8099, Xanadu 192
CD: DCC DJZ-611, Fresh Sound (Sp) FSR-CD-126, Rockin'
Chair (Sw) (no number)

Pee Wee's Blues
33: America (F) 30 AM 6097, >Counterpoint CPST 562,
>Counterpoint CPT 565, Ember (E) CJS 824, Everest FS 233,
Fresh Sound (Sp) FSR-126, Globe (J) SMJ 7165, I Grande
Del Jazz (I) GDJ 07, Mecca (E) OSL 63, Omega OSLF-63,
Opus (Arg) OJC 20011, Overseas (J) ULS 1598, Sutton SU
240, Tiara TST 518, Tiara TST 532, Tiara TMT 7518, Tiara
TMT 7532, Quadrifaglio (I) VDS 348, Society (E) SOC
1013, Sutton 240, Vendette (I) VPA 8099, Viking VK 001,
Viking VK 010, Viking VKS 1001, Viking VKS 1010,
Xanadu 192
CD: DCC DJZ-611, Fresh Sound (Sp) FSR-CD-126, Rockin'
Chair (Sw) (no number)
RT: Sentry 3S-106

NOTE: Recorded at Beltone Recording studios. "Pee Wee's Blues" is
entitled "Pee Wee Blues" on Counterpoint, Fresh Sound and Rockin'
Chair; "Buck's Blues" on Viking VK 101 and Viking VKS 1001; and
"Vic's Victory" on Viking VK 010 and Viking VK 1010. "Oh No" and
"Pee Wee's Blues" were composed by Pee Wee Russell.

Max Kaminsky Band

NYC, May 3, 1958

Max Kaminsky, trumpet, vocal; Pee Wee Russell, clarinet; Bob Wilber, tenor; Dick Cary, piano; Johnny Giuffreda, bass; Charlie Smith, drums.

Sugar
    Unissued

Indiana
    Unissued

Yellow Dog Blues
    Unissued

Sister Kate (MK vocal)
    Unissued

Sweet Georgia Brown
    Unissued

NOTE: From a WOR "Bandstand USA" broadcast from the Gothic Room of the Hotel Duane, 237 Madison Avenue. Russell does not perform on one other tune (Deep Purple) from this broadcast.

Art Ford's Jazz Party

Newark, New Jersey, May 8, 1958

Rex Stewart, cornet; Wilbur DeParis, trombone; Pee Wee Russell, clarinet; Dick Grifoldi, tenor; Harry Sheppard, vibes; Joe Baque, piano; Chuck Wayne, electric guitar; Aaron Bell, bass; Zutty Singleton, drums. Art Ford, announcer.

Basin Street Blues
    CT: Jazz Connoisseur Cassette (E) AF.10/DP

Royal Garden Blues
    CT: Jazz Connoisseur Cassette (E) AF.10/DP

Hindustan
    CT: Jazz Connoisseur Cassette (E) AF.10/DP

Sugar
    CT: Jazz Connoisseur Cassette (E) AF.10/DP

This Can't Be Love
    CT: Jazz Connoisseur Cassette (E) AF.10/DP

Rex's Blues
    CT: Jazz Connoisseur Cassette (E) AF.10/DP

The Sheik Of Araby
    CT: Jazz Connoisseur Cassette (E) AF.10/DP

Honeysuckle Rose
    CT: Jazz Connoisseur Cassette (E) AF.10/DP

Add Joe Mack, trombone.

Joe Mack Blues
    CT: Jazz Connoisseur Cassette (E) AF.10/DP

"C" Jam Blues
    CT: Jazz Connoisseur Cassette (E) AF.10/DP

NOTE: This telecast on WNTA-TV was announced on the program as being broadcast from Rex Stewart's apartment, 108th Street and Broadway, but it was telecast from a set in the station's Newark studios. This was the first telecast in the "Jazz Party" series. All programs were directed by Don Luftig and produced and hosted by Art Ford. Other titles from this broadcast do not include Russell.

Art Ford's Jazz Party
                                    Newark, New Jersey, May 22, 1958

Charlie Shavers, trumpet; Tyree Glenn, trombone; Pee Wee Russell, clarinet; Bud Freeman, tenor; Harry Sheppard, vibes; Marty Napoleon, piano; Mundell Lowe, electric guitar; Vinnie Burke, bass; Zutty Singleton, drums. Art Ford and Anita O'Day, voice.

Basin Street Blues
    Unissued

Rose Room
    Unissued

Blues Background (Ford, O'Day, voice)
    Unissued

That's A Plenty
    Unissued

Blues Background (Ford, voice)
    Unissued

Exactly Like You
    Unissued

Chinatown, My Chinatown
    Unissued

Add Joe Holiday, tenor.

Undecided
    Unissued

Two O'Clock Jump
    Unissued

Basin Street Blues
    Unissued

NOTE: This session and all following Art Ford Jazz Party programs were telecast with stereophonic sound; one channel broadcast on WNTA-AM and the other on WNTA-FM. The television transmission on WNTA-TV carried a combined signal. Jazz Parties were kinescoped for re-broadcast to U.S. armed forces in 22 nations, but only a few segments have been discovered. Pee Wee Russell does not appear on other selections from this telecast.

Pee Wee Russell And His Jazz Band

Toronto, Canada, May 24, 1958

Ruby Braff, cornet; Steve Richards, trombone; Pee Wee Russell, clarinet; Wally Gurd, piano; Jack Richardson, bass; Doug McLeod, drums; Phyllis Marshall, vocal.

Oh, Lady Be Good
    Unissued

Who's Sorry Now (PM vocal)
    Unissued

NOTE: From a Canadian Broadcasting Corporation telecast, "Cross-Canada Hit Parade." A kinescope exists.

Art Ford's Jazz Party

Newark, New Jersey, June 12, 1958

Charlie Shavers, trumpet; J.C. Higginbotham, trombone; Pee Wee Russell, clarinet; Hal Singer, tenor; Harry Sheppard, vibes; Marty Napoleon, piano; unknown electric guitar; Vinnie Burke, bass; Panama Francis, drums; Beulah Bryant, Ham Jackson, vocal.

Basin Street Blues
    Unissued

Indiana
    Unissued
Blues (BB vocal)
    Unissued

Limehouse Blues
    Unissued

Fascinatin' Rhythm
    Unissued

Nobody Knows You When You're Down And Out (HJ vocal)
    Unissued

Cottontail
    Unissued

Stompin' At The Savoy
    Unissued

I Would Do Anything For You
    Unissued

St. Louis Blues (BB vocal)
    Unissued

When You're Smiling
    Unissued

Add Bill Graham, alto.

What A Difference A Day Made
    Unissued

I've Found A New Baby
    Unissued

Basin Street Blues
    Unissued

NOTE: From a WNTA-TV telecast. See note for May 22, 1958, session. Pee Wee Russell does not appear on other selections from this telecast.

Newport All Stars

Newport, Rhode Island, July 5 and 6, 1958

Buck Clayton, trumpet; Jack Teagarden, trombone; Pee Wee Russell, clarinet; Lester Young, tenor; Don Ewell, piano; Tommy Bryant, bass; Jo Jones, drums.

Royal Garden Blues
    RT: >VOA Music USA R-1330-B

I Cover The Waterfront
    33: Pres Box (I) PB.22, Unique Jazz (I) UJ 14
    RT: >VOA Music USA R-1330-B

Muskrat Ramble
    RT: >VOA Music USA R-1330-B

Jump The Blues
    33: CBS (E) 88605, CBS Sony (J) 40AP-2771-2, Columbia C2
         38262, Pres Box (I) PB.22, Unique Jazz (I) UJ-14
    RT: >VOA Music USA R-1330-B

NOTE: Recorded at the Newport Jazz Festival.

269

Ruby Braff - Pee Wee Russell Sextet

NYC, July 11, 1958

Ruby Braff, trumpet;   Wayne Andre, trombone; Pee Wee Russell, clarinet; Jimmy Jones, piano; Bill Takas, bass; Nat Ray, drums.

Theme
   33:   Shoestring SS 109
   TX: >AFRS Bandstand USA 37

When You're Smiling
   33:   Shoestring SS 109
   TX: >AFRS Bandstand USA 37

What Is There To Say?
   33:   Shoestring SS 109
   TX: >AFRS Bandstand USA 37 (incomplete)

I Would Do Anything For You (incomplete)
   Unissued

NOTE: This is a broadcast from the Gothic Room, Hotel Duane, 237 Madison Avenue. "What Is There to Say," interrupted by a news report on the broadcast, is faded out after the trombone solo on the transcription.

Tony Scott And The All Stars

NYC, August 6, 1958

Joe Thomas, trumpet; Wilbur DeParis, J.C. Higginbotham, trombone; Pee Wee Russell, Tony Scott, clarinet; Sonny White, piano; Al Casey, guitar; Oscar Pettiford, bass; Denzil Best, drums.

105428   Blues For The Street
   33:   >Coral CRL 57239, >Coral CRL 757239, Coral (E) LVA 9109, Coral (J) LPCM 1062, Jasmine (E) JASM 1011, MCA (J) MCA 3036

Omit Casey.

105431   Love Is Just Around the Corner
   33:   >Coral CRL 57239, >Coral CRL 757239, Coral (E) LVA
         9l09, Coral (J) LPCM 1062, Jasmine (E) JASM 1011, MCA
         (J) MCA 3036

Art Ford's Jazz Party

Newark, New Jersey, September 25, 1958

Charlie Shavers, trumpet, vocal; J.C. Higginbotham, trombone; Pee
Wee Russell, clarinet; Coleman Hawkins, tenor; Harry Sheppard, vibes;
Willie "The Lion" Smith, piano; Dicky Thompson, electric guitar;
Vinnie Burke, bass; Sonny Greer, drums, Mae Barnes, vocal.

When I Grow Too Old To Dream
   Unissued

St. James Infirmary (CS vocal)
   33:   >Enigma 301, Jazz Anthology (F) 30JA 5217

Sweet Georgia Brown (MB vocal)
   Unissued

Runnin' Wild
   Unissued

Indian Summer
   33:   >Enigma 301, Jazz Anthology (F) 30JA-5217, Musidisc (E)
         5217, Queen Disc (I) Bean 11
   CT: Jazz Connoisseur Cassettes (E) AFJP 6, Jazz Connoisseur
         Cassettes (E) CC 31

I May Be Wrong
   Unissued

Avalon
   33:   >Phoenix LP 21, Queen Disc (I) Bean 11
   CT: Jazz Connoisseur Cassettes (E) AFJP 6

271

I Can't Get Started
>
33: >Enigma 301, Jazz Anthology (F) 30JA 5217
CT: Jazz Connoisseur Cassettes AFJP (E) 6, Jazz Connoisseur
Cassettes (E) JCC 31

St. Louis Blues
Unissued

Indiana (MB vocal)
Unissued

Add Lester Young, tenor.

Mean To Me
33: >Enigma 301, Jazz Anthology (F) 30JA-5217, Musidisc (E)
5217, Pres Box (I) PB.22
CT: Jazz Connoisseur Cassettes (E) AFJP 6, Jazz Connoisseur
Cassettes (E) JCC 31

Jumpin' With Symphony Sid
33: >Enigma 301, Jazz Anthology (F) 30JA-5217, Musidisc (E)
5217, Pres Box (I) PB.22, Queen Disc (I) Bean 11
CT: Jazz Connoisseur Cassettes (E) AFJP 6, Jazz Connoisseur
Cassettes (E) JCC 31

NOTE: From a WNTA-TV telecast, directed by Don Luftig, produced
and hosted by Art Ford. See note for May 22, 1958, session. A
kinescope of a portion of this program exists. It is not certain that the
last two titles are from this session.

Art Ford's Jazz Party

Newark, New Jersey, November 20, 1958

Rex Stewart, cornet; J. C. Higginbotham, Tyree Glenn, Bob Brookmeyer, trombone; Pee Wee Russell, clarinet; Paul Quinichette, tenor; Nat Pierce, piano; Vinnie Burke, bass; Elvin Jones, drums.

I've Found A New Baby
    Unissued

Swing That Music
    Unissued

NOTE: From a WNTA telecast, directed by Don Luftig, produced and hosted by Art Ford. See note for May 22, 1958, session. This entire telecast has not been available for audition; Russell might appear on other selections.

On February 16, 1959, the Eddie Condon band with Pee Wee Russell accompanied vocalist Mary Mulligan in a session for Dot records. Nothing has been issued from this session and details are unknown.

Pee Wee Russell And His Orchestra

NYC, February 23 and 24, 1959

Buck Clayton, trumpet; Vic Dickenson, trombone; Pee Wee Russell, clarinet; Bud Freeman, tenor; Dick Cary, piano; Eddie Condon, guitar; Bill Takas, bass; George Wettling, drums.

Pee Wee's Blues
    33:   ABC Impulse IA-9359/2, >Dot DLP 3253, >Dot DLPS 25253, Dot DLP 25878, MCA 2-4150, Musica Jazz Presenta (I) 2MJP 1071, Rediffusion (E) 0100 174

What's The Pitch
    33:   ABC Impulse IA-9359/2, >Dot DLP 3253, >Dot DLPS 25878, MCA 2-4150

Dreaming And Schemin'
    33:   ABC Impulse IA-9359/2, >Dot DLP 3253, >Dot DLPS 25878, MCA 2-4150

Cutie Pie
33:    ABC Impulse IA-9359/2, >Dot DLP 3253, >Dot DLPS
25878, MCA 2-4150

Oh No
33:    ABC Impulse IA-9359/2, >Dot DLP 3253, >Dot DLPS
25878, MCA 2-4150

Pee Wee's Tune
33:    ABC Impulse IA-9359/2, >Dot DLP 3253, >Dot DLPS
25878, MCA 2-4150

Oh Yes
33:    ABC Impulse IA-9359/2, >Dot DLP 3253, >Dot DLPS
25878, MCA 2-4150

Missy
33:    ABC Impulse IA-9359/2, >Dot DLP 3253, >Dot DLPS
25878, MCA 2-4150

Are You Here?
33:    ABC Impulse IA-9359/2, >Dot DLP 3253, >Dot DLPS
25878, MCA 2-4150

Write Me A Love Song Baby
33:    ABC Impulse IA-9359/2, >Dot DLP 3253, >Dot DLPS
25878, MCA 2-4150

This Is It
33:    ABC Impulse IA-9359/2, >Dot DLP 3253, >Dot DLPS
25878, MCA 2-4150

But Why?
33:    ABC Impulse IA-9359/2, >Dot DLP 3253, >Dot DLPS
25878, MCA 2-4150

NOTE: Supervised by Bob Thiele. This session was recorded in RCA
studios. All compositions are by Pee Wee Russell, arrangements by
Dick Cary. "Pee Wee's Tune" is another title for "Pee Wee's Song."

Eddie Condon and His Chicagoans

NYC, February 26, 1959

Max Kaminsky, trumpet; Cutty Cutshall, trombone; Pee Wee Russell, clarinet; Bud Freeman, tenor; Dick Cary, piano; Eddie Condon, guitar; Leonard Gaskin, bass; George Wettling, drums.

B 50230 There'll Be Some Changes Made
    33: Atlantic 90461-1-Y, >Warner W 1315, >Warner WS 1315,
         Warner (E) WM 4009, Warner (E) WS 8009, Warner (J) WB
         1029, Warner (J) SB 1037
    TX: AFRS APM 289
    CT: Atlantic 90461-4

B 50231 I've Found A New Baby
    33: Atlantic 90461-1-Y, >Warner W 1315, >Warner WS 1315,
         Warner (E) WM 4009, Warner (E) WS 8009, Warner (J) WB
         1029, Warner (J) SB 1037
    TX: AFRS APM 289
    CT: Atlantic 90461-4

B 50232 Oh Baby
    33: Atlantic 90461-1-Y, >Warner W 1315, >Warner WS 1315,
         Warner (E) WM 4009, Warner (E) WS 8009, Warner (J) WB
         1029, Warner (J) SB 1037
    TX: AFRS APM 478
    CT: Atlantic 90461-4

B 50233 Love Is Just Around the Corner
    33: Atlantic 90461-1-Y, >Warner W 1315, >Warner WS 1315,
         Warner (E) WM 4009, Warner (E) WS 8009, Warner (J) WB
         1029, Warner (J) SB 1037
    TX: AFRS APM 289
    CT: Atlantic 90461-4

B 50234 Nobody's Sweetheart
    33: Atlantic 90461-1-Y, >Warner W 1315, >Warner WS 1315,
         Warner (E) WM 4009, Warner (E) WS 8009, Warner (J) WB
         1029, Warner (J) SB 1037
    CT: Atlantic 90461-4

NOTE: Produced by George Avakian to celebrate the twentieth anniversary of his recording of the "Chicago Jazz" album for Decca.

Eddie Condon And His Chicagoans

NYC, February 27, 1959

Max Kaminsky, trumpet; Cutty Cutshall, trombone; Pee Wee Russell, clarinet; Bud Freeman, tenor; Dick Cary, piano; Eddie Condon, guitar; Al Hall, bass; George Wettling, drums.

B 50235 Chicago
- 33: Atlantic 90461-1-Y, >Warner W 1315, >Warner WS 1315, Warner (E) WM 4009, Warner (E) WS 8009, WB 1725, Warner (J) WB 1029, Warner (J) SB 1037
- TX: AFRS APM 1105
- CT: Atlantic 90461-4

B 50236 Shim-Me-Sha-Wabble
- 33: Atlantic 90461-1-Y, >Warner W 1315, >Warner WS 1315, Warner (E) WM 4009, Warner (E) WS 8009, Warner (J) WB 1029, Warner (J) SB 1037
- TX: AFRS APM 289, AFRS APM 478
- CT: Atlantic 90461-4

B 50237 Someday Sweetheart
- 33: Atlantic 90461-1-Y, >Warner W 1315, >Warner WS 1315, Warner (E) WM 4009, Warner (E) WS 8009, Warner (J) WB 1029, Warner (J) SB 1037
- TX: AFRS APM 289, AFRS APM 478
- CT: Atlantic 90461-4

B 50238 Friar's Point Shuffle
- 33: Atlantic 90461-1-Y, >Warner W 1315, >Warner WS 1315, Warner (E) WM 4009, Warner (E) WS 8009, Warner (J) WB 1029, Warner (J) SB 1037
- TX: AFRS APM 289
- CT: Atlantic 90461-4

B 50239 Liza
- 33: Atlantic 90461-1-Y, >Warner W 1315, >Warner WS 1315, Warner (E) WM 4009, Warner (E) WS 8009, Warner (J) WB 1029, Warner (J) SB 1037
- TX: AFRS APM 289
- CT: Atlantic 90461-4

NOTE: Produced by George Avakian.

On March 16, 1959, Mercury records recorded a charity concert for Friendship House at the Washington Jazz Jubilee Concert. The concert was entitled "A History of Jazz from Congo Square to Carnegie Hall." Included was Dick Cary's band, which included Buck Clayton, trumpet; Pee Wee Russell, clarinet; Bud Freeman, tenor; Dick Cary, piano, trumpet, alto horn, arranger, unknown bass, Jo Jones, drums. Nothing has been issued from this concert.

Pee Wee Russell

Toronto, Canada, April 6, 1959

Pee Wee Russell interviewed by Joyce Davison
    Unissued

NOTE: A kinescope of this program, "Tabloid," exists. Produced at the Canadian Broadcasting Corporation studios.

Art Hodes-Jimmy McPartland Orchestras

Chicago, May 7, 1959

Art Hodes band: Nap Trottier, trumpet; George Brunies, trombone, vocal; Pee Wee Russell, clarinet; Art Hodes, piano; Earl Murphy, bass; Buddy Smith, drums.
Jimmy McPartland band: Jimmy McPartland, trumpet, vocal; Vic Dickenson, trombone; John Maheu, clarinet; Bud Freeman, tenor; Floyd Bean, piano; John Frigo, bass; George Wettling, drums.

18566   Chicago
    33:   >Mercury MG 20460, >Mercury SR 60143, Mercury (J) SMC 11, Mercury (J) MC 45, Mercury (J) SM 7113, Philips (J) SM 9005, World Record Club (E) T297

18567   Logan Square (JMcP vocal)
    33:   >Mercury MG 20460, >Mercury SR 60l43, Mercury (J) SMC 11, Mercury (J) MC 45, World Record Club (E) T297

John Frigo switches to violin; Earl Murphy doubles on banjo.

18568   Bill Bailey, Won't You Please Come Home?
    33:   >Mercury MG 20460, >Mercury SR 60143, Mercury (J) SMC 11, Mercury (J) MC 45, World Record Club (E) T297

Frigo and Murphy return to bass.

18569   You Gotta See Mama Ev'ry Night
    33:   >Mercury MG 20460, >Mercury SR 60143, Mercury (J)
        SMC 11, Mercury (J) MC 45, World Record Club (E) T297

18570   Somebody Stole My Girl
    33:   >Mercury MG 20460, >Mercury SR 60l43, Mercury (J) SMC
        11, Mercury (J) MC 45, World Record Club (E) T297

18571   I Never Knew
    33:   >Mercury MG 20460, >Mercury SR 60143, Mercury (J)
        SMC 11, Mercury (J) MC 45, World Record Club (E) T297

18572   Deed I Do
    33:   >Mercury MG 20460, >Mercury SR 60l43, Mercury (J) SMC
        11, Mercury (J) MC 45, World Record Club (E) T297

18573   Sister Kate (GB vocal)
    33:   >Mercury MG 20460, >Mercury SR 60143, Mercury (J)
        SMC 11, Mercury (J) MC 45, Mercury (J) SM 7113, Philips
        (J) SM 9005, World Record Club (E) T297

18574   Meet Me In Chicago
    33:   >Mercury MG 20460, >Mercury SR 60143, Mercury (J)
        SMC 11, Mercury (J) MC 45, World Record Club (E) T297

18575   Runnin' Wild
    Unissued

NOTE: On Mercury SR 60143, each band is heard on a separate
channel. Philips (J) SM 9005 is in album SFL 9001-5. Recorded at
Universal Recording studios, the session was produced by Jack Tracy.

Eddie Condon
                                New York, c. May, 1959

Wild Bill Davison, cornet; Pee Wee Russell, clarinet; Willie "The
Lion" Smith, piano; Morey Feld, drums. Helen Ward, vocal.

I've Got A Crush On You (HW, vocal)
    Unissued

Love Is Just Around The Corner (partial)
  Unissued

Pee Wee Russell, clarinet; Willie "The Lion" Smith, piano

Pee Wee's Blues #1 (fragment)
  Unissued

Pee Wee's Blues #2 (fragment)
  Unissued

Pee Wee's Blues #3 (fragment)
  Unissued

Add Wild Bill Davison, cornet; Morey Feld, drums.

Blues
  Unissued

From a television program, "After Hours At Eddie Condon's," broadcast from the night club.   Most selections have voice-over by the narrator and by Eddie Condon.   Other selections from this program ("I'm Confessin'" and "Struttin' With Some Barbecue") do not include Pee Wee Russell.

Bud Freeman's All Stars

Boston, June 3, 1959

Buck Clayton, trumpet; Vic Dickenson, trombone; Pee Wee Russell, clarinet; Bud Freeman, tenor; Lou Carter, piano; Champ Jones, bass; Jo Jones, drums.

'Deed I Do
  Unissued

Dinah
  Unissued

Sunday
  Unissued

NOTE: From a "Dateline Boston" telecast, hosted by John McLellan.

279

Dixieland All Stars

Boston, c. June 6 and 18, 1959

Buck Clayton, trumpet; Vic Dickenson, trombone; Pee Wee Russell, clarinet; Bud Freeman, tenor; Lou Carter, piano; Champ Jones, bass; Jo Jones, drums.

Ballin' The Jack
33: Celebrity UTS 113, Coronet CX-14, Coronet CX 163, Coronet CSX 5163, Gala (E) GLP 359, Master MAL 3006, >Omega OSL 52, Omnibus OML-4006, Overseas (J) ULS 1598, Promenade LP 2134, Silver Seal UT 113
RT: >Omegatape STF-7

Billboard
33: Allegro (E) ALL 791, Celebrity UTS 113, Coronet CX-14, Coronet CX 163, Coronet CSX 5163, Crown CST 246, Crown CLP 5242, Design DLP 148, Design DLP 266; Everest FS 274, Everest 924730, Gala (E) GLP 359, Hollywood H 1026, Jazz Club (F) 1652.371, Master MAL 3006, Mecca (E) OSL 63, Murray Hill S53968/5, Music for Pleasure (F) 165.237, >Omega OSLF-63, Omnibus OML-4006, Overseas (J) JLS 1598, Palace M-644, Palace PST 751, Pickwick PR 111, Promenade LP 2134, Silver Seal UT 113, Sutton SU 240, Sutton SU 286, Sutton SU 287, Sutton SU 313, Tiara TST 532, Tiara TST 551, Tiara TMT 7532, Tiara TMT 7551, Viking VK 002, Viking VK 010, Viking VKS 1002, Viking VKS 1010
RT: Sentry 3S-106

Bugle Call Rag
33: Album Set Productions GT 1002 (excerpt), Celebrity UTS 113, Coronet CX-14, Coronet CX 163, Coronet CSX 5163, Gala (E) GLP 359, Guest Star G 1401, Guest Star GS 1401, Guest Star G 1451, Guest Star GS 1451, Guest Star G 1477, Guest Star GS 1477, Master MAL 3006, >Omega OSL 52, Omnibus OML-4006, Overseas (J) ULS 1598, Promenade LP 2134, Silver Seal UT 113
RT: >Omegatape STF-7

Embraceable You
33: >Omega OSL 52, Overseas (J) ULS 1598, Society (E) SOC 1019
CT: Star Line SLC-61083

280

Fascinating Rhythm
    33:   >Omega OSL 52, Overseas (J) ULS 1598, Society (E) SOC
           1019
    CT: Star Line SLC-61083

Muskrat Ramble
    33:   Celebrity UTS 113, Coronet CX-14, Coronet CX 163,
           Coronet CSX 5163, Gala (E) GLP 359, Guest Star G 1401,
           Guest Star GS 1401, Guest Star G 1451, Guest Star GS 1451,
           Guest Star G 1477, Guest Star GS 1477, Master MAL 3006,
           >Omega OSL 52, Omnibus OML-4006, Overseas (J) ULS
           1598, Promenade LP 2134, Silver Seal UT 113
    RT: >Omegatape STF-7

St. James Infirmary
    33:   Celebrity UTS 113, Coronet CX-14, Coronet CX 163,
           Coronet CSX 5163, Design DLP 182, Design SDLP 182,
           Everest FS 257, Gala (E) GLP 359, Halo 50223, Halo 50268,
           Master MAL 3006, >Omega OSL 52, Omnibus OML-4006,
           Opus (Arg) OJC 20004, Overseas (J) ULS 1598, Promenade
           LP 2134, Silver Seal UT 113, Ultraphonic 50268
    RT: >Omegatape STF-7

Somebody Loves Me
    33:   >Omega OSL 52, Overseas (J) ULS 1598, Society (E) SOC
           1019
    CT: Star Line SLC-61083

Someone To Watch Over Me
    33:   >Omega OSL 52, Overseas (J) ULS 1598, Society (E) SOC
           1019
    CT: Star Line SLC-61083

Strike Up The Band
    33:   Mecca (E) OSL 63, >Omega OSL 52, Omega OSLF-63,
           Overseas (J) ULS 1598, Society (E) SOC 1019
    CT: Star Line SLC-61083

Sweet Sue
    33:   Celebrity UTS 113, Coronet CX-14, Coronet CX 163,
           Coronet CSX 5163, Gala (E) GLP 359, Master MAL 3006,
           Omnibus OML-4006, Overseas (J) ULS 1598, >Promenade
           LP 2134, Silver Seal UT 113
    RT: >Omegatape STF-7

Synthetic Blues
33: Allegro (E) ALL 791, Brookville LCA 0003, Celebrity UTS 113, Coronet CX-14, Coronet CX 163, Coronet CSX 5163, Crown CST 246, Crown CLP 5242, Design DLP 148, Everest FS 274, Everest 924730, Gala (E) GLP 359, Hollywood H 1026, Jazz Club (F) 1652.371, Master MAL 3006, Mecca (E) OSL 63, Murray Hill S53968/5, Music for Pleasure (F) 165.237, >Omega OSLF-63, Omnibus OML-4006, Overseas (J) ULS 1598, Palace M-644, Pickwick PR 111, Promenade LP 2134, Silver Seal UT 113, Sutton SU 240, Sutton SU 286, Sutton SU 287, Tiara TST 532, Tiara TST 551, Tiara TMT 7532, Tiara TMT 7551, Universal (C) MS 171, Viking VK 001, Viking VK 010, Viking VKS 1001, Viking VKS 1010
RT: >Omegatape STF-7

When The Saints Go Marching In
33: Allegro (E) ALL 791, Celebrity UTS 113, Coronet CX-14, Coronet CX 163, Coronet CSX 5163, Crown CST 246, Crown CLP 5242, Design DLP 148, Design DLP-182, Design SDLP-182, Design DLP 266; Everest FS 257, Gala (E) GLP 359, Guest Star G 1401, Guest Star GS 1401, Guest Star G 1451, Guest Star GS 1451, Guest Star G 1477, Guest Star GS 1477, Hollywood H 1026, Master MAL 3006, Mecca (E) OSL 63, >Omega OSF-63, Omnibus OML-4006, Opus (Arg) OJC 20004, Overseas (J) ULS 1598, Palace M-644, Palace PST 751, Pickwick PR 111, Promenade LP 2134, Silver Seal UT 113, Sutton SU 240, Sutton SU 313, Tiara TMT 7532, Tiara TST 532, Tiara TMT 7551, Tiara TST 551, Viking VK 002, Viking VK 010, Viking VKS 1002, Viking VKS 1010, Way-Wolff (no number), Xtra 1120
RT: >Omegatape STF-7, Sentry 3S-106

NOTE: Recorded at Ace Recording studios. The recording sequence is unknown. Although the Omega issues have been designated as the original issues, it is likely many of the American issues appeared around the same time. The LPs were issued as follows:

Album Set Productions GT 1002 (3-LP set): A Century of American Music
Allegro ALL 791: Eddie Condon & Dixieland All Stars
Brookville LCA 0003 (5-LP set, LCA 5000): 50 Great Hits of the 30's and 40's
Celebrity UTS 113 Dixieland
Coronet CX-14: Mardi Gras in Dixieland

Coronet CX 163/CSX 5163: Dixieland
Crown CST 246/CLP 5242: Kings of Dixieland, Vol. 6
Design DLP/SDLP 148: Eddie Condon & Dixieland All Stars
Design DLP/SDLP 182: Pete Fountain & The New Orleans All Stars
Design DLP/SDLP 266: Thoroughly Modern Millie and the Dixie Hits
    of the Jazz Age
Everest FS 257: Pete Fountain - New Orleans All Stars
Everest FS 274 and 924730: Roots of Dixieland Jazz
Gala GLP 359: Dixieland USA
Guest Star G and GS 1401: The Original Dukes of Dixieland & the
    Dixieland Greats
Guest Star G and GS 1451: Pete Fountain: Broadway to Bourbon
    Street
Guest Star G and GS 1477: Dixieland Greats
Halo 50223: All Star Jazz
Halo 50268: Dixieland
Jazz Club 1652.371: Aux Sources du Jazz Dixieland
Master MAL 3006: New Orleans Dixieland
Mecca OSL 63: Dixieland A La Carte
Murray Hill S53968/5: Collector's History of Dixieland Jazz
Omega OSL 52: Dixieland A La Carte
Omega OSLF-63: Dixieland!
Omegatape STF-7: Dixieland Special Vol. 1
Omnibus OML-4006: Delightful Dixieland
Opus OJC 20004: Dixieland All Stars
Overseas ULS 1598 Play Back!
Palace M-644: Dixieland: The Dixie Rebels
Palace PST 751: Dixieland: Jimmy McPartland Vol. 2, Dixie Rebels
Pickwick PR 111: Spotlight on Eddie Condon
Promenade LP 2134: Dixieland USA
Sentry (RT) 3S-106 Three Hour Jazz Marathon
Silver Seal UT 113: Barons of Dixieland Visit the Bowery
Society SOC 1019: Buck Clayton Plays
Star Line SLC-61083: Buck Clayton
Sutton SU 240: Empire City Six in Dixie
Sutton SU 286: Fletcher Henderson with Slam Stewart and the Jazz
    Tones
Sutton SU 313: Rockin' Rhythm featuring Harry "The Hipster" Gibson
Tiara TST 518, TMT 7518: Dizzy Gillespie & Chuck Lewis
Tiara TST 532, TMT 7532: Spotlite on the Dixie Greats
Tiara TST 551, TMT 7551: Red Nichols and his Five Pennies
Ultraphonic 50268: Dixieland
Viking VK 001, VKS 1001: Duke Ellington Meets Buck Clayton
Viking VK 002, VKS 1002: Dizzy Gillespie Meets Pee Wee Russell

Viking VK 010, VKS 1010: Vic Dickenson--Young Man with a Horn
Xtra 1120: New Orleans All Stars

A quartet performance of "Pee Wee's Blues" is included on Mecca (E) OSL 63, Omega OSL 63, Overseas (J) ULS 1598, Sutton SU 240, Tiara TMT 7518, Tiara TMT 7532, Tiara TST 532, Viking VK 001, Viking VK 010, Viking VKS 1001 and Viking VKS 1010, but it is from Russell's Counterpoint session of February 18 and 19, 1958, q.v.

"Bugle Call Rag" is entitled "Diamonds and Pearls" on Guest Star GS 1401 and GS 1477. The opening bugle call has been edited out.

"Muskrat Ramble" is entitled "Billboard Blues" on Guest Star GS 1401 and "Duke's Blues" on Guest Star GS 1451 and GS 1477.

"Synthetic Blues" is entitled "Deep Royal Blues" on Allegro ALL 791, Brookville LCA 0002, Design DLP 148, Everest 924730, FS 274, Murray Hill S523968/5, MFP 165.237, and Jazz Club 1652.371; "School's Out" on Sutton SU 286 (end fades out after tenor solo); "Billboard March" on Omega OSL 63; "Dixieland Blues" on Palace M-644; "Mason-Dixon Line Blues" on Universal MS 171, and "Too Darn Much" on Viking VK 001.

"Strike Up the Band" is entitled "Chiribiribin" on Omega OSL 63 and Mecca OSL 63.

"Billboard" is entitled "Goodbye Big Town" on Sutton SU 286; "Billboard Blues" on Guest Star G and GS 1401, "Billboard Dixieland" on Allegro ALL 79l, Design DLP 148, Everest 924730, FS 274, Murray Hill S53968/5, MFP 165.237, and Jazz Club 1652.371; "Peace Pipe" on Viking VK 002; "Billboard March" on Crown CLP 5242, Palace M-644, Sutton SU 313, Tiara TST 532, Tiara TST 551, Tiara TMT 7532, Tiara TMT 7551, Everest 924730, Everest FS 274, Sentry (RT) 3S-106; "Georgia Blues" on Palace PST 751; and "Basic Blues" on Viking VK 010.

"When The Saints Go Marching In" Guest Star 1451 repeats, following the trombone solo, the trumpet, tenor, piano and trombone solos. Entitled "Those Saints" on Viking VK 010, "When the Saints Come Marching Home" on Omnibus OML-4006, "Saints Go Marching In" on Omegatape STF-7, Sentry 3S-106 and Silver Seal UT 113.

The ending of "Sweet Sue" is faded out on Omegatape STF-7

Newport Jazz Festival All Stars

Newport, Rhode Island, July 2, 1959

Buck Clayton, trumpet; Vic Dickenson, trombone; Pee Wee Russell, clarinet; Bud Freeman, tenor; Ray Bryant, piano; Champ Jones, bass; Buzzy Drootin, drums; Jimmy Rushing, vocal.

Sweet Sue, Just You
    33:   >Europa Jazz (I) EJ-1023, Curcio/I Giganti del Jazz (I) GJ
            29, Los Grandes del Jazz (Sp) GJ 29
    CT: Curcio/I Giganti del Jazz (I) GJ-29

Add Freddie Green, guitar.

Avalon
    33:   >Musica Jazz Presenta (I) 2MJP 1071

Wrap Your Troubles In Dreams
    33:   >Musica Jazz Presenta (I) 2MJP 1071

Add Ruby Braff, cornet.

I'm Gonna Sit Right Down And Write Myself A Letter (JR vocal)
    Unissued

Goin' To Chicago (JR vocal)
    Unissued

St. Louis Blues (JR vocal)
    Unissued

NOTE: "Sweet Sue, Just You" issued as Buck Clayton's All Stars. The rhythm section is shown as Hank Jones, piano; Aaron Bell, bass; Herbie Lovelle, drums; and the date as 1958, but this is incorrect.

The Big Three

Frank Hubbell, trumpet; Dick Rath, trombone; Pee Wee Russell, Paul Hubbell, clarinet, Marty Napoleon, piano; Chubby Jackson, bass; Mickey Sheen, drums.

(Pee Wee Russell introduces the band, voice over rhythm section)
    33:    >Everest LPBR 5041, >Everest SDBR 1041

Jazz Band Ball
    33:    >Everest LPBR 5041, >Everest SDBR 1041

Struttin' With Some Barbecue
    33:    >Everest LPBR 5041, >Everest SDBR 1041

NOTE: Aaron Nathanson was the recording director.

Jimmy McPartland

French Lick, Indiana, August 2, 1959

Jimmy McPartland, cornet; Buck Clayton, trumpet; Vic Dickenson, trombone; Pee Wee Russell, clarinet; Marian McPartland, piano; unknown bass and drums.

Crazy Rhythm
    CT: >Alphorn ALH-120

Royal Garden Blues
    CT: >Alphorn ALH-120

If I Had You
    CT: >Alphorn ALH-120

Add Jimmy Rushing, vocal.

Sunny Side Of The Street (JR vocal)
    CT: >Alphorn ALH-120

Add Jack Teagarden, trombone.

Harvard Blues; Goin' To Chicago (JR vocal)
    CT: >Alphorn ALH-120

Rock This Joint Tonight (JR vocal)
    CT: >Alphorn ALH-120

NOTE: Other selections issued from this concert do not include Pee Wee Russell. "Goin' to Chicago" is labeled "Chicago" on Alphorn ALH-120.

The Austin High Gang

Chicago, August 9, 1959

Jimmy McPartland, cornet, vocal; Pee Wee Russell, clarinet; Bud Freeman, tenor; Art Hodes, piano; George Wettling, drums.

China Boy
    Unissued

Sugar (JMcP vocal)
    TX: >AFRS TIJ-8

High Society
    TX: >AFRS TIJ-8

Nobody's Sweetheart
    TX: >AFRS TIJ-8

Add George Brunies, trombone

Blues For Austin
    TX: >AFRS TIJ-8

Royal Garden Blues
    Unissued

NOTE: From the Playboy Jazz Festival, Chicago Stadium.

Max Kaminsky And The Storyville All Stars

Boston, October 22, 1959

Max Kaminsky, trumpet; Vic Dickenson, trombone; Pee Wee Russell, clarinet; Bob Pillsbury, piano; Champ Jones, bass; Butch Atsmith, drums.

Royal Garden Blues
    Unissued

Ja Da
    Unissued

Muskrat Ramble
    Unissued

Mack The Knife
    Unissued

I've Found A New Baby
    Unissued

Blues (announcer voice-over)
    Unissued

Note: From a "Dateline Boston" telecast, hosted by John McLellan.

Stan Rubin

NYC, November 26, 1959

Wild Bill Davison, cornet; Irvin (Marky) Markowitz, Jack Honeywill, Joe Shepley, Ike Iacommetta, Max Kaminsky, Pee Wee Erwin, trumpet; J.C. Higginbotham, Ben Long, trombone; Pee Wee Russell, Tony Parenti, Stan Rubin, clarinet; Bob Wilber, clarinet, tenor; Bill Cooper, tenor; Danny Derasmo, Vinnie Riccitelli, alto; Kenny Arzberger, baritone; Harry Sheppard, vibes, Marty Napoleon, piano; Mel Rose, bass; Gary Chester, drums; Bob Friedlander, arranger.

Hindustan
    33:    >United Artists UAL 3085, >United Artists UAS 6085

Omit Pee Wee Erwin, trumpet

Limehouse Blues
    33:    >United Artists UAL 3085, >United Artists UAS 6085

NOTE: Recorded at a concert in the Grand Ballroom, Hotel Astor. Other titles do not include Pee Wee Russell. Produced by Jack Lewis.

Newport Jazz Festival All Stars

Boston, Mass., December, 1959

Buck Clayton, trumpet; Vic Dickenson, trombone; Pee Wee Russell, clarinet; Bud Freeman, tenor; George Wein, piano; Champ Jones, bass; Jake Hanna, drums.

4017   Royal Garden Blues
    33:    >Atlantic LP 1331, >Atlantic SD 1331, London (E) LTZ-K
           15202, London (E) SAH-K 6116

4018-1 Rose Room
    33:    >Atlantic LP 1331, >Atlantic SD 1331, London (E) LTZ-K
           15202, London (E) SAH-K 6116

4019-1 You Took Advantage Of Me
    33:    >Atlantic LP 1331, >Atlantic SD 1331, London (E) LTZ-K
           15202, London (E) SAH-K 6116

289

4020   Sunday
    33:    >Atlantic LP 1331, >Atlantic SD 1331, London (E) LTZ-K
           15202, London (E) SAH-K 6116

4021   Dinah
    33:    >Atlantic LP 1331, >Atlantic SD 1331, London (E) LTZ-K
           15202, London (E) SAH-K 6116

4022   'Deed I Do
    33:    >Atlantic LP 1331, >Atlantic SD 1331, London (E) LTZ-K
           15202, London (E) SAH-K 6116

4023-1 Pee Wee Russell's Unique Sound (breakdown)
        Unissued

4023-2 Pee Wee Russell's Unique Sound
    33:    >Atlantic LP 1331, >Atlantic SD 1331, London (E) LTZ-K
           15202, London (E) SAH-K 6116

NOTE: Five takes were recorded of 4021 and two takes were recorded
of 4022. The take numbers of the issued versions are not known. 4017
and 4019 were single takes. Supervised by George Wein and Paul
Nossiter.

Pee Wee Russell

                        Englewood Cliffs, New Jersey, March 29, 1960

Buck Clayton, trumpet; Pee Wee Russell, clarinet; Tommy Flanagan,
piano; Wendell Marshall, bass; Osie Johnson, drums.

2094   Wrap Your Troubles In Dreams
    33:    Fontana (H) 688 403SL, Prestige 7672, Prestige (J) SMJ
           7568, Prestige/Swingville (E) SVLP 2008, >Swingville
           SVLP 2008, Time-Life STL-J17 (P 15735), Time-Life (Au)
           STL-J17 (P 15735), Time-Life (C) STL-J17, Transatlantic
           (E) PR 2008
    CT: Time-Life 4TL-J17
    8T: Time-Life 8TL-J17

2095   What Can I Say, Dear (sic)
    33:    Fontana (H) 688 403SL, Prestige 7672, Prestige (J) SMJ
           7568, Prestige/Swingville (E) SVLP 2008, >Swingville
           SVLP 2008, Transatlantic (E) PR 2008

2096   Midnight Blue
    33:    Fontana (H) 688 403SL, Prestige 7672, Prestige (J) SMJ
           7568, Prestige/Swingville (E) SVLP 2008, >Swingville
           SVLP 2008, Transatlantic (E) PR 2008

2097   I Would Do Anything For You
    33:    Fontana (H) 688 403SL, Prestige 7672, Prestige (J) SMJ
           7568, Prestige/Swingville (E) SVLP 2008, >Swingville
           SVLP 2008, Transatlantic (E) PR 2008

2098   Englewood
    33:    Fontana (H) 688 403SL, Prestige 7672, Prestige (J) SMJ
           7568, Prestige/Swingville (E) SVLP 2008, >Swingville
           SVLP 2008, Time-Life STL-J17 (P 15735), Time-Life (Au)
           STL-J17, Time-Life (C) STL-J17, Transatlantic (E) PR 2008
    CT: Time-Life 4TL-J17
    8T: Time-Life 8TL-J17

2099   Lulu's Back In Town
    33:    Fontana (H) 688 403SL, Prestige 7672, Prestige (J) SMJ
           7568, Prestige/Swingville (E) SVLP 2008, >Swingville
           SVLP 2008, Transatlantic (E) PR 2008

2100   The Very Thought Of You
    33:    Fontana (H) 688 403SL, Franklin Mint 48, Prestige 7672,
           Prestige (J) SMJ 7568, Prestige/Swingville (E) SVLP 2008,
           >Swingville SVLP 2008, Transatlantic (E) PR 2008

NOTE: Produced by Esmond Edwards.   "Midnight Blue" and
"Englewood" were composed by Pee Wee Russell.

The Storyville Sextet

Boston, Mass., April 20, 1960

Shorty Baker, trumpet; Pee Wee Russell, clarinet; Bud Freeman, tenor; George Wein, piano; Bill Crow, bass; Marquis Foster, drums.

Please Don't Talk About Me When I'm Gone
    Unissued

Tin Roof Blues
    Unissued

Struttin' With Some Barbecue
    Unissued

NOTE: From "The Jazz Scene," telecast at 6 p.m. on WHDH-TV. Host John McLellan interviews Wein during the program.

George Wein and The Storyville Sextet

NYC, June 16, 1960

Shorty Baker, trumpet; Tyree Glenn, trombone; Pee Wee Russell, clarinet; George Wein, piano; Bill Crow, bass; Mickey Sheen, drums.

That's A Plenty
    33:    >Bethlehem BCP 6050, Parlophone (E) PMC 1156

I Ain't Got Nobody
    33:    >Bethlehem BCP 6050, Parlophone (E) PMC 1156

September In The Rain
    33:    >Bethlehem BCP 6050, Parlophone (E) PMC 1156

Undecided
    33:    >Bethlehem BCP 6050, Parlophone (E) PMC 1156

Rosetta
    33:    >Bethlehem BCP 6050, Parlophone (E) PMC 1156

Do Nothing Till You Hear From Me
    33:    >Bethlehem BCP 6050, Parlophone (E) PMC 1156

NOTE: Recorded at a concert in the sculpture garden of the Museum of Modern Art. Other titles were recorded at this concert, which was produced by Bill Coss and Metronome magazine. Recording produced by Teddy Charles.

Newport Jazz Festival All Stars
Newport, Rhode Island, July 2, 1960

Ruby Braff, cornet; Pee Wee Russell, clarinet; George Wein, piano; Don Kenney, bass; Buzzy Drootin, drums.

Just You, Just Me
Unissued

Rosetta (incomplete)
Unissued

NOTE: Part of a WJAR-TV telecast. These selections were released in the 26-film series, "Jazz USA," made at the festival for the United States Information Services. Russell may appear on other films in the series, but these are the only titles to surface so far.

Bobby Hackett
Unknown location, Cape Cod, Massachusetts, July 31, 1960

Bobby Hackett, cornet; Pee Wee Russell, clarinet; Peanuts Hucko, tenor sax; unknown piano, unknown bass, possibly Joe Testa, drums.

Struttin' With Some Barbecue
Unissued

Omit Hackett and Hucko

If I Had You
Unissued

Hackett, Hucko return and add unknown trombone

Caravan
Unissued

Oh, Baby (incomplete)
Unissued

St. James Infirmary
   Unissued

Muskrat Ramble (incomplete)
   Unissued

Omit Hackett and unknown trombone.

Ain't Misbehavin' (incomplete)
   Unissued

NOTE: Privately recorded by Bobby Hackett. One other title was recorded but it does not include Russell.

Gene Krupa Sextet
                          Philadelphia, Pennsylvania, August 28, 1960

Buck Clayton, trumpet; Pee Wee Russell, clarinet; Eddie Wasserman, tenor; probably Ronnie Ball, piano; possibly Kenny O'Brien, bass; Gene Krupa, drums.

I've Found A New Baby
   33: >Sunbeam SB 225

NOTE: From a CBS radio program, "World Series of Jazz: Quaker City Jazz Festival," broadcast from Connie Mack Stadium.

Eddie Condon Sextet
                                        Chicago, November, 1960

Johnny Windhurst, trumpet; Roswell Rudd, trombone; Pee Wee Russell, clarinet; Johnny Varro, piano; Eddie Condon, guitar; possibly Phil Failla, drums.

That's The Blues
   TX >AFRTS ONS 5263

Muskrat Ramble
   TX: >AFRTS ONS 5263

Black And Blue
    TX: >AFTRS ONS 5263

Clarinet Marmalade
    TX: >AFRTS ONS 5263

Medley: After Awhile, September In The Rain, Pennies From Heaven
    33:   IAJRC IAJRC-28
    TX: >AFRTS ONS 5263

That Da Da Strain
    TX: >AFRTS ONS 5263

As Long As I Live
    TX: >AFRTS ONS 5263

Royal Garden Blues
    TX: >AFRTS ONS 5270

Improvisation For The March Of Time
    TX: >AFRTS ONS 5263

NOTE: Recorded at the London House. "As Long As I Live" is
announced as "Down Basin Street Way." Russell does not play on two
titles from the medley, "After Awhile" and "Pennies from Heaven."
Only "September In The Rain" from the medley was issued on IAJRC
IAJRC-28.

Eddie Condon Sextet

Chicago, November 1960

Johnny Windhurst, trumpet; Roswell Rudd, trombone; Pee Wee
Russell, clarinet; Johnny Varro, piano; Eddie Condon, guitar; unknown
bass; possibly Phil Failla, drums.

That's A Plenty
    TX: >AFRTS ONS 5270

Ain't Misbehavin'
    TX: >AFRTS ONS 5270

Love Is Just Around The Corner
    TX: >AFRTS ONS 5270

Diane
    TX: >AFRTS ONS 5270

NOTE: From the London House. A few bars of an unidentified tune
are played before the first and after the last titles.

Pee Wee Russell - Coleman Hawkins All Stars

NYC, February 23, 1961

Emmett Berry, trumpet; Bob Brookmeyer, valve trombone; Pee Wee
Russell, clarinet; Coleman Hawkins, tenor; Nat Pierce, piano, arranger;
Milt Hinton, bass; Jo Jones, drums.

All Too Soon
    33:   Barnaby BR-5018, >Candid CM 8020, >Candid CS 9020,
          Candid (E) CS-9020, Candid (F) CANF 5018, Candid (J)
          SMJ 6214, Candid (J) SOPC 57017, Jazz Man JAZ 5042
    CD: Candid (G) CCD 79020, Candid (J) 32JDC-143

If I Could Be With You
    33:   Barnaby BR-5018, >Candid CM 8020, >Candid CS 9020,
          Candid (E) CS-9020, Candid (F) CANF 5018, Candid (J)
          SMJ 6214, Candid (J) SOPC 57107, Jazz Man JAZ 5042,
          Time-Life STL-J17 (P 15735), Time-Life (Au) STL-J17,
          Time-Life (C) STL-J17
    CD: Candid (G) CCD 79020, Candid (J) 32JDC-143
    CT: Time-Life 4TL-J17
    8T: Time-Life 8TL-J17

Tin Tin Deo
    33:   Barnaby BR-5018, >Candid CM 8020, >Candid CS 9020,
          Candid (E) CS 9020, Candid (F) CANF 5018, Candid (J)
          SMJ 6214, Candid (J) SOPC 57017, Jazz Man JAZ 5042
    TX: AFRS SH 1853, AFRS MMM 73, AFRS MOMM 17
    CD: Candid (G) CCD 79020, Candid (J) 32JDC-143

28th And 8th
    33:    Barnaby BR-5018, >Candid CM 8020, >Candid CS 9020,
           Candid (E) CS 9020, Candid (F) CANF 5018, Candid (J)
           SMJ 6214, Candid (J) SOPC 57017, Jazz Man JAZ 5042
    CD: Candid (G) CCD 79000, Candid (G) CCD 79020, Candid (J)
           32JDC-143, Candid (J) 32JDC-193

What Am I Here For?
    33:    Barnaby BR-5018, >Candid CM 8020, >Candid CS 9020,
           Candid (E) CS 9020, Candid (F) CANF 5018, Candid (J)
           SMJ 6214, Candid (J) SOPC 57017, Jazz Man JAZ 5042
    CD: Candid (G) CCD 79020, Candid (J) 32JDC-143

Omit Berry, Brookmeyer and Hawkins

Mariooch
    33:    Barnaby BR-5018, >Candid CM 8020, >Candid CS 9020,
           Candid (E) CS 9020, Candid (F) CANF 5018, Candid (J)
           SMJ 6214, Candid (J) SOPC 57017, Jazz Man JAZ 5042,
           Time-Life STL-J17 (P 15735), Time-Life (Au) STL-J17,
           Time-Life (C) STL-J17
    CD: Candid (G) CCD 79020, Candid (J) 32JDC-143
    CT: Time-Life 4TL-J17
    8T: Time-Life 8TL-J17

NOTE: Supervised by Nat Hentoff. Recorded at Nola Penthouse
Sound studios. "28th and 8th" refers to the location of the Russell's
apartment in New York. That tune and "Mariooch," his nickname for
his wife, Mary, were both composed by him. Jazz Man JAZ 5042 was
issued as by Coleman Hawkins. All arrangements by Nat Pierce.

Newport Jazz Festival All Stars

                                        Essen, West Germany, April 14, 1961.

Ruby Braff, cornet; Vic Dickenson, trombone; Pee Wee Russell,
clarinet; George Wein, piano; Jimmy Woode, bass; Buzzy Drootin,
drums.

Royal Garden Blues
    Unissued

297

Basin Street Blues
    Unissued

Just You, Just Me
    Unissued

Exactly Like You
    Unissued

Sugar
    Unissued

I've Found A New Baby
    Unissued

NOTE: From a broadcast of the Essen Jazz Festival. An additional title, "Blue and Sentimental," does not include Pee Wee Russell.

George Wein's Newport Jazz Festival All Stars

Paris, France, April 15, 1961.

Ruby Braff, cornet; Vic Dickenson, trombone; Pee Wee Russell, clarinet; George Wein, piano; Jimmy Woode, bass; Buzzy Drootin, drums.

Sweet Georgia Brown
    33: Mercury International (E) SMWL 21047, Philips (E) BL
         7665, Philips (J) SM 7104, >Smash 27023, >Smash S67023

When My Sugar Walks Down The Street
    33: Mercury International (E) SMWL 21047, Philips (E) BL
         7665, Philips (J) SM 7104, >Smash 27023, >Smash S67023

Blue And Sentimental
    33: Mercury International (E) SMWL 21047, Philips (E) BL
         7665, Philips (J) SM 7104, >Smash 27023, >Smash S67023
    CT: Philips 7552005

Blues Pour Commencer
    33: Mercury International (E) SMWL 21047, Philips (E) BL
         7665, Philips (J) SM 7104, >Smash 27023, >Smash S67023
    CT: Philips 7552005

Sugar
    33:    Mercury International (E) SMWL 21047, Philips (E) BL
           7665, Philips (J) SM 7104, >Smash 27023, >Smash S67023

I've Found A New Baby
    33:    Mercury International (E) SMWL 21047, Philips (E) BL
           7665, Philips (J) SM 7104, >Smash 27023, >Smash S67023

Lover, Come Back To Me
    33:    Mercury International (E) SMWL 21047, Philips (E) BL
           7665, Philips (J) SM 7104, >Smash 27023, >Smash S67023

NOTE: Recorded at a concert at the Olympia Theatre.

Newport Festival All Stars

                              Baden-Baden, West Germany, April-May, 1961

Ruby Braff, cornet; Vic Dickenson, trombone; Pee Wee Russell,
clarinet; George Wein, piano; Jimmy Woode, bass; Buzzy Drootin,
drums.

Jazz Train Blues
    Unissued

Sugar
    Unissued

NOTE: From a telecast. An additional title, "Lover, Come Back To
Me," does not include Pee Wee Russell.

"First Annual Prestige Swing Festival"

Englewood Cliffs, New Jersey, May 19, 1961

Joe Thomas, trumpet; Vic Dickenson, trombone; Pee Wee Russell, clarinet; Buddy Tate, clarinet, tenor; Al Sears, tenor, arranger; Cliff Jackson, piano; Danny Barker, guitar; Joe Benjamin, bass; J.C. Heard, drums.

3037   Things Ain't What They Used To Be
   33:   Prestige P 24051, >Swingville SVLP 2024, Top Rank (J) RANK 7042, Transatlantic (E) XTRA 5031

3038   So Glad
   33:   Prestige P 24051, >Swingville SVLP 2024

3039   Vic's Spot
   33:   Prestige P 24051, >Swingville SVLP 2024, Top Rank (J) RANK 7042, Transatlantic (E) XTRA 5031

3040   I May Be Wrong
   33:   Prestige P 24051, >Swingville SVLP 2024, Top Rank (J) RANK 7042, Transatlantic (E) XTRA 5031

3041   Phoenix
   33:   Prestige P 24051, >Swingville SVLP 2024, Top Rank (J) RANK 7042, Transatlantic (E) XTRA 5031

3042   Years Ago
   33:   Prestige P 24051, >Swingville SVLP 2024, Top Rank (J) RANK 7042, Transatlantic (E) XTRA 5031

NOTE: Session supervised by Esmond Edwards. This was a studio session, not a live performance as the title implies. Swingville SVLP 2024 and 2025 were first issued in a double album as SV 4001, although the records bore the numbers of the individual LPs as shown above. The Swingville issues also appeared as Prestige/Swingville and, on even later pressings, as Prestige, although still retaining the same issue numbers.

Eddie Condon And His Chicagoans

NYC, October 30, 1961

Jimmy McPartland, trumpet; Jack Teagarden, trombone, vocal; Pee Wee Russell, clarinet; Bud Freeman, tenor; Joe Sullivan, piano; Eddie Condon, guitar; Bob Haggart, bass; Gene Krupa, drums.

61VK514 Logan Square (JT vocal)
    33:    Metro (Arg) 4094, Metro (E) 2356 017, Metro (E) 2683.051, Metro (F) 2355015, >Verve V-8441, >Verve V6-8441, Verve (E) VLP 9003, Verve (G) 845 149-1, Verve (J) MV 2019, Verve (J) MV 2535, Verve (J) 20MJ 0092, Verve (J) VLS 1043, Verve (J) VL 1049
    CD: Verve (G) 845 149-2
    RT: Verve VSTC 266
    CT: Verve (G) 845 149-4

61VK515 Chicago
    33:    Metro (Arg) 4094, Metro (E) 2356 017, Metro (E) 2683.051, Metro (F) 2355015, >Verve V-8441, >Verve V6-8441, Verve (E) VLP 9003, Verve (J) MV 2019, Verve (J) MV 2535, Verve (J) 20MJ 0092, Verve (J) VLS 1043, Verve (J) VL 1049
    RT: Verve VSTC 266

61VK516 After You've Gone (JT vocal)
    33:    Metro (Arg) 4094, Metro (E) 2356 017, Metro (E) 2683.051, Metro (F) 2355015, >Verve V-8441, >Verve V6-8441, Verve (E) VLP 9003, Verve (G) 845 144-1, Verve (J) MV 2019, Verve (J) MV 2535, Verve (J) 20MJ 0092, Verve (J) VLS 1043, Verve (J) VL 1049
    CD: Verve (G) 845 144-2
    RT: Verve VSTC 266
    CT: Verve (G) 845 144-4

61VK517   China Boy
  33:   Metro (Arg) 4094, Metro (E) 2356 017, Metro (E) 2683.051,
         Metro (F) 2355015, >Verve V-8441, >Verve V6-8441, Verve
         845 149-1, Verve (E) VLP 9003, Verve (J) MV 2019, Verve
         (J) MV 2535, Verve (J) 20MJ 0092, Verve (J) VLS 1043,
         Verve (J) VL 1049
  CD: Verve 845 149-2
  RT: Verve VSTC 266
  CT: Verve 845 149-4

NOTE: Produced by Creed Taylor.   "Four or Five Times" has also
been reported as being recorded at this session, but Verve files do not
confirm this.

Eddie Condon And His Chicagoans

NYC, October 31, 1961.

Jimmy McPartland, trumpet, vocal; Jack Teagarden, trombone, vocal;
Pee Wee Russell, clarinet; Bud Freeman, tenor; Lil Armstrong, piano;
Eddie Condon, guitar; Bob Haggart, bass; Gene Krupa, drums.
Blossom Seeley, vocal.

61VK518 Take Me To The Land Of Jazz (JT, LA, BS, vocal)
  33:   Metro (Arg) 4094, Metro (E) 2356 017, Metro (E) 2683.051,
         Metro (F) 2355015, >Verve V-8441, >Verve V6-8441, Verve
         (E) VLP 9003, Verve (J) MV 2019, Verve (J) MV 2535,
         Verve (J) 20MJ 0092, Verve (J) VLS 1043, Verve (J) VL
         1049
  RT: Verve VSTC 266

Sullivan replaces Armstrong, piano.

61VK519 Sugar (JMcP, vocal)
  33:   Metro (Arg) 4094, Metro (E) 2356 017, Metro (E) 2683.051,
         Metro (F) 2355015, >Verve V-8441, >Verve V6-8441, Verve
         (E) VLP 9003, Verve (J) MV 2019, Verve (J) MV 2535,
         Verve (J) 20MJ 0092, Verve (J) VLS 1043, Verve (J) VL
         1049
  RT: Verve VSTC 266

61VK521   Nobody's Sweetheart
33:    Metro (Arg) 4094, Metro (E) 2356 017, Metro (E) 2683.051,
Metro (F) 2355015, >Verve V-8441, >Verve V6-8441, Verve
(E) VLP 9003, Verve (J) MV 2019, Verve (J) MV 2535,
Verve (J) 20MJ 0092, Verve (J) VLS 1043, Verve (J) VL
1049
RT: Verve VSTC 266

61VK523   Wolverine Blues
33:    Metro (Arg) 4094, Metro (E) 2356 017, Metro (E) 2683.051,
Metro (F) 2355015, >Verve V-8441, >Verve V6-8441, Verve
(E) VLP 9003, Verve (G) 2615044, Verve (J) MV 2019,
Verve (J) MV 2535, Verve (J) 20MJ 0092, Verve (J) VLS
1043, Verve (J) VL 1049
RT: Verve VSTC 266

61VK524   Chicago (JT, LA, BS, vocal)
33:    Metro (Arg) 4094, Metro (E) 2356 017, Metro (E) 2683.051,
Metro (F) 2355015, >Verve V-8441, >Verve V6-8441, Verve
(E) VLP 9003, Verve (J) MV 2019, Verve (J) MV 2535,
Verve (J) 20MJ 0092, Verve (J) VLS 1043, Verve (J) VL
1049
RT: Verve VSTC 266

NOTE: Produced by Creed Taylor. Missing matrix numbers 61VK520
and 61VK522 are piano solos by Lil Armstrong.

Chicago And All That Jazz

NYC, October 31, 1961

Jimmy McPartland, trumpet; Jack Teagarden, trombone, vocal; Pee
Wee Russell, clarinet; Bud Freeman, tenor; Joe Sullivan, piano; Eddie
Condon, guitar; Bob Haggart, bass; Gene Krupa, drums; Garry Moore,
announcer.

Garry Moore Introduces The Band
33:    >Pumpkin 115, Sounds Great SG 8007
VT: Vintage Jazz Classics Video VJC-2002

China Boy
33:    >Pumpkin 115, Sounds Great SG 8007
VT: Jazz Pioneer (C) JMV 101691, Vintage Jazz Classics Video
VJC-2002

303

After You've Gone (JT vocal)
  33: >Sounds Great SG 8007
  VT: Vintage Jazz Classics Video VJC-2002

Wolverine Blues
  33: >Sounds Great SG 8007
  VT: Jazz Pioneer (C) JMV 101691, Vintage Jazz Classics Video
       VJC-2002

Add Henry "Red" Allen, trumpet; Kid Ory, trombone; Buster Bailey,
clarinet; Lil Armstrong, piano; Johnny St. Cyr, banjo; Milt Hinton,
bass; Zutty Singleton, drums, and others.

Tiger Rag
  33: >Sounds Great SG 8007
  VT: Jazz Pioneer (C) JMV 101691, Vintage Jazz Classics Video
       VJC-2002

NOTE: From the NBC Special Projects television series, "Dupont
Show of the Week," directed by James Elson. Executive producer was
Donald Hyatt and the producer and writer was William Nichols. The
program was broadcast on November 26, 1961. The date above is the
video recording date. A kinescope exists of the telecast. "Garry Moore
Introduces The Band" entitled "Untitled Blues" on Sounds Great SG
8007, and "Blues For Gene" on Vintage Jazz Classics Video VJC-2002.

Today All Star Jazz Band

NYC, October 31, 1961

Jimmy McPartland, trumpet; Jack Teagarden, trombone; Pee Wee
Russell, clarinet; Bud Freeman, tenor; Joe Sullivan, piano; Eddie
Condon, guitar; Bob Haggart, bass; Gene Krupa, drums.

China Boy
  Unissued

Indiana
  33: >Pumpkin 115

Sugar (see note)
  Unissued

After You've Gone (JT vocal)
  33: >Pumpkin 115

Royal Garden Blues
    33:   >Pumpkin 115

Blues For Today
    33:   >Pumpkin 115

NOTE: Recorded 7 a.m. to 9 a.m. from the "Today" television
program. Frank Blair interviewed Condon. "Sugar" begins with the
McKenzie and Condon Chicagoans' recording (Okeh 41011, matrix
82030-A); the band joins in during the first chorus.

Newport All Stars
                                    Newport, Rhode Island, July 8, 1962

Ruby Braff, cornet; Marshall Brown, valve trombone; Pee Wee Russell,
clarinet; George Wein, piano; John Neves, bass; Jo Jones, drums,
Louise Tobin, vocal.

You Can Depend On Me
    Unissued

Blue And Sentimental
    Unissued

Add Bud Freeman, tenor

Crazy Rhythm
    Unissued

St. Louis Blues
    Unissued

Pee Wee's Blues
    Unissued

Should I (LT vocal)
    Unissued

I Got It Bad And That Ain't Good (LT vocal)
    Unissued

'Deed I Do (LT vocal)
    Unissued

305

Add Duke Ellington's Orchestra: Cat Anderson, Ray Nance, Bill Berry, Ray Burrowes, trumpet; Lawrence Brown, Buster Cooper, Chuck Connors, trombone; Jimmy Hamilton, clarinet; Johnny Hodges, Gene Hull, alto; Paul Gonsalves, tenor; Harry Carney, baritone; Duke Ellington, piano; Aaron Bell, bass; Sam Woodyard, drums.

Take The "A" Train
    Unissued

NOTE: Recorded at Freebody Park at the Newport Jazz Festival. A portion of "You Can Depend On Me" was released on the soundtrack of the film "Newport Jazz Festival - 1962."

The Pee Wee Russell Quartet with Marshall Brown
                                                    NYC, Summer, 1962.

Marshall Brown, valve trombone, bass trumpet; Pee Wee Russell, clarinet; Russell George, bass; Ron Lundberg, drums.

Moten Swing
    33:   >MB-91062

'Round Midnight
    33:   >MB-91062

My Mother's Eyes
    33:   >MB-91062

Lester Leaps In
    33:   >MB-91062

Scrapple From The Apple Bossa Nova (#1)
    33:   >MB-91062

Scrapple From The Apple Bossa Nova (#2)
    Unissued

Scrapple From The Apple Bossa Nova (#3)
    Unissued

Georgia On My Mind
    33:   MB-91062

You Took Advantage Of Me
    33:   MB-91062

Goose Pimples (#1)
    33:   MB-91062

Goose Pimples (#2)
    Unissued

I'd Climb The Highest Mountain
    Unissued

Holy Roller (#1)
    Unissued

Holy Roller (#2)
    Unissued

Holy Roller (#3)
    Unissued

Mathew (Ferris Wheel) (#1) (false start)
    Unissued

Mathew (Ferris Wheel) (#2)
    Unissued

Mathew (Ferris Wheel) (#3)
    Unissued

Humph (#1) (false start)
    Unissued

Humph (#2)
    Unissued

Humph (#3)
    Unissued

A Garden In The Rain
    Unissued

Sonny Boy
    Unissued

NOTE: Recorded in Marshall Brown's rehearsal studio, West 72nd Street, prior to September 10, 1962. The LP does not have a label name. One hundred copies were pressed, intended for use as a demonstration disc and not released commercially. The sequence of recording of these titles is not known. It is likely that some of the titles issued on the LP were edited composites of various takes. Take numbers have been assigned arbitrarily.

George Wein And The Newport All Stars

Englewood Cliffs, New Jersey, October 12, 1962.

Ruby Braff, cornet; Marshall Brown, valve trombone, bass trumpet; Pee Wee Russell, clarinet; Bud Freeman, tenor; George Wein, piano, celeste on 11131; Bill Takas, bass; Marquis Foster, drums.

11129 At the Jazz Band Ball
    33:    ABC Impulse 1A-9359/2, HMV (E) CLP 1651, >Impulse! A 31, >Impulse! AS 31, Impulse!/Sparton (C) A 31, Impulse!/Sparton (C) A 31S

11130 Crazy Rhythm
    33:    ABC Impulse 1A-9359/2, HMV (E) CLP 1651, >Impulse! A 31, >Impulse! AS 31, Impulse! (E) 8046, Impulse/Sparton (C) A 31, Impulse!/Sparton (C) A 31S

11131 Blue Turning Grey Over You
    33:    ABC Impulse 1A-9359/2, HMV (E) CLP 1651, >Impulse! A 31, >Impulse! AS 31, Impulse! (E) 8046, Impulse!/Sparton (C) A 31, Impulse!/Sparton (C) A 31S

11132 Lulu's Back in Town
    33:    ABC Impulse 1A-9359/2, HMV (E) CLP 1651, >Impulse! A 31, >Impulse! AS 31, Impulse! (E) 8046, Impulse!/Sparton (C) A 31, Impulse!/Sparton (C) A 31S

Omit Braff and Freeman.

11133 The Bends Blues
    33:    ABC Impulse 1A-9359/2, HMV (E) CLP 1651, >Impulse! A 31, >Impulse! AS 31, Impulse! (E) 8046, Impulse!/Sparton (C) A 31, Impulse!/Sparton (C) A 31S

Braff and Freeman return.

11134 Keepin' Out Of Mischief Now
  33:   ABC Impulse 1A-9359/2, HMV (E) CLP 1651, >Impulse! A
        31, >Impulse! AS 31, Impulse! (E) 8046, Impulse!/Sparton
        (C) A 31, Impulse!/Sparton (C) A 31S

11135 Ja Da
  33:   ABC Impulse 1A-9359/2, HMV (E) CLP 1651, >Impulse! A
        31, >Impulse! AS 31, Impulse! (E) 8046, Impulse!/Sparton
        (C) A 31, Impulse!/Sparton (C) A 31S

11136 Slowly
  33:   ABC Impulse 1A-9359/2, HMV (E) CLP 1651, >Impulse! A
        31, >Impulse! AS 31, Impulse! (E) 8046, Impulse!/Sparton
        (C) A 31, Impulse!/Sparton (C) A 31S

NOTE: Produced by Bob Thiele. "The Bends Blues" was composed
by Pee Wee Russell.

Pee Wee Russell Quartet

NYC, November 12, 1962

Marshall Brown, valve trombone, bass trumpet; Pee Wee Russell,
clarinet; Russell George, bass; Ron Lundberg, drums.

CO 76992 Taps Miller
  Unissued

CO 76993 'Round Midnight
  Unissued

CO 76994 My Mother's Eyes
  Unissued

CO 76995 Pee Wee's Blues
  33:   CBS (E) SBPG 62242, >Columbia CL 1985, >Columbia CS
        8785, I Grande Del Jazz (I) GDJ-07, Time-Life STL-J17 (P
        15735), Time-Life (Au) STL-J17, Time-Life (C) STL-J17
  CT: Time-Life 4TL-J17
  8T: Time-Life 8TL-J17

CO 76996 Moten Swing
  Unissued

309

NOTE: Produced by Frank Driggs.

Pee Wee Russell Quartet

NYC, November 13, 1962

Same personnel.

CO 76997   Good Bait
  Unissued

CO 76998   Chelsea Bridge
  33:   CBS (E) SBPG 62242, >Columbia CL 1985, >Columbia CS
    878
CO 76999   Red Planet
  Unissued

CO 77000   Lester Leaps In
  Unissued

CO 77001   Old Folks
  33:   CBS (E) SBPG 62242, >Columbia CL 1985, >Columbia CS
    8785

NOTE: Produced by Frank Driggs

Pee Wee Russell Quartet

NYC, November 19, 1962

Same personnel.

CO 76994   My Mother's Eyes
  33:   CBS (E) SBPG 62242, >Columbia CL 1985, >Columbia CS
    8785

CO 76997   Good Bait
  33:   CBS (E) SBPG 62242, >Columbia CL 1985, >Columbia CS
    8785

CO 76999   Red Planet
  Unissued

NOTE: Produced by Frank Driggs.

310

Pee Wee Russell Quartet

NYC, November 26, 1962

Same personnel.

CO 76992   Taps Miller
    33:   CBS (E) SBPG 62242, >Columbia CL 1985, >Columbia CS
         8785, I Grande Del Jazz (I) DJ-07

CO 76996   Moten Swing
    33:   CBS (E) SBPG 62242, >Columbia CL 1985, >Columbia CS
         8785

CO 77000   Lester Leaps In
    Unissued

NOTE: Produced by Frank Driggs.

Pee Wee Russell Quartet

NYC, December 4, 1962

Same personnel.

CO 76993   'Round Midnight
    33:   CBS (E) SBPG 62242, >Columbia CL 1985, >Columbia CS
         8785

CO 76999   Red Planet
    33:   CBS (E) SBPG 62242, >Columbia CL 1985, >Columbia CS
         8785

NOTE: Produced by Frank Driggs.

Pee Wee Russell Quartet

NYC, April 9 & 10, 1963.

Marshall Brown, valve trombone, bass trumpet; Pee Wee Russell,
clarinet; Russell George, bass; Ronnie Bedford, drums.

90391   Turnaround
    33:   HMV (E) CLP 3552, HMV (E) CSD 3552, >Impulse! A 96,
         >Impulse! AS 96, Impulse! (NZ) ABCS 96, Impulse!/Sparton
         (C) A 96, Impulse!/Sparton (C) A 96S

90392   How About Me?
  33:    HMV (E) CLP 3552, HMV (E) CSD 3552, >Impulse! A 96,
         >Impulse! AS 96, Impulse (NZ) ABCS 96, Impulse!/Sparton
         (C) A 96, Impulse!/Sparton (C) A 96S

90393   Ask Me Now
  33:    HMV (E) CLP 3552, HMV (E) CSD 3552, >Impulse! A 96,
         >Impulse! AS 96 (see note), Impulse (NZ) ABCS 96,
         Impulse!/Sparton (C) A 96, Impulse!/Sparton (C) A 96S

90394   I'd Climb The Highest Mountain
  33:    HMV (E) CLP 3552, HMV (E) CSD 3552, >Impulse! A 96,
         >Impulse! AS 96 (see note), Impulse (NZ) ABCS 96,
         Impulse!/Sparton (C) A 96, Impulse!/Sparton (C) A 96S

90395   Some Other Blues
  33:    HMV (E) CLP 3552, HMV (E) CSD 3552, >Impulse! A 96,
         >Impulse! AS 96 (see note), Impulse (NZ) ABCS 96,
         Impulse!/Sparton (C) A 96, Impulse!/Sparton (C) AS 96S

90396   Licorice Stick
  33:    HMV (E) CLP 3552, HMV (E) CSD 3552, >Impulse! A 96,
         >Impulse! AS 96, Impulse (NZ) ABCS 96, Impulse!/Sparton
         (C) A 96, Impulse!/Sparton (C) A 96S

90397   Prelude To A Kiss
  33:    HMV (E) CLP 3552, HMV (E) CSD 3552, >Impulse! A 96,
         >Impulse! AS 96 (see note), Impulse (NZ) ABCS 96,
         Impulse!/Sparton (C) A 96, Impulse!/Sparton (C) A 96S

90398   Baby, You Can Count On Me
  33:    HMV (E) CLP 3552, HMV (E) CSD 3552, >Impulse! A 96,
         >Impulse! AS 96 (see note), Impulse (NZ) ABCS 96,
         Impulse!/Sparton (C) A 96, Impulse!/Sparton (C) AS 96S

90399   Hackensack
  33:    HMV (E) CLP 3552, HMV (E) CSD 3552, >Impulse! A 96,
         >Impulse! AS 96, Impulse (NZ) ABCS 96, Impulse!/Sparton
         (C) A 96, Impulse!/Sparton (C) A 96S
  TX: AFRS JF 25

90400   Angel Eyes
　　33: HMV (E) CLP 3552, HMV (E) CSD 3552, >Impulse! A 96,
　　　　 >Impulse! AS 96 (see note), Impulse (NZ) ABCS 96,
　　　　 Impulse!/Sparton (C) A 96, Impulse!/Sparton (C) A 96S

90401   Calypso Walk
　　33: HMV (E) CLP 3552, HMV (E) CSD 3552, >Impulse! A 96,
　　　　 >Impulse! AS 96 (see note), Impulse (NZ) ABCS 96,
　　　　 Impulse!/Sparton (C) A 96, Impulse!/Sparton (C) A 96S

Goose Pimples
　　Unissued

NOTE: Produced by George Avakian. Recorded at Plaza Sound
studios. Impulse! AS 96 was issued as a 12-inch LP, but the same issue
number was also used for a 7-inch disc (as noted), recorded at 33 1/3
rpm, designed for juke box use only.

Thelonious Monk Quartet with Pee Wee Russell

Newport, Rhode Island, July 4, 1963

Pee Wee Russell, clarinet; Charlie Rouse, tenor; Thelonious Monk,
piano; Butch Warren, bass; Frankie Dunlop, drums.

Co 81448   Nutty
　　33: CBS (Arg) 8.484, CBS (Arg) 9.059, CBS (E) BPG 62389,
　　　　 CBS (J) YS 392C, CBS (J) YS 957C, CBS Sony (J) SOPZ
　　　　 10, CBS Sony (J) 15AP541, CBS Sony (J) 20AP1404,
　　　　 >Columbia CL 2178, >Columbia CS 8978, Columbia PC
　　　　 8978, Columbia (C) CL 2178, Columbia (C) CS 8978
　　CD: CBS Sony (J) 30DP-522
　　RT: Columbia CQ 647

CO 81948   Blue Monk
     33:   CBS (Arg) 8.484, CBS (Arg) 9.059, CBS (E) BPG 62389,
            CBS (J) YS 392, CBS (J) YS 957C, CBS Sony (J) SOPZ 10,
            CBS Sony (J) SONE 70081, CBS Sony (J) 15AP541, CBS
            Sony (J) 20AP1404, CBS Sony (J) SONX 60048, >Columbia
            CL 2178, >Columbia CS 8978, Columbia CS 9775,
            Columbia PC 8978, Columbia (C) CL 2178, Columbia (C)
            CS 8978
     TX: AFRS JU 29
     CD: CBS Sony (J) 30DP-522, CBS Sony (J) 30DP-5029
     RT: Columbia CQ 647

NOTE: From the Newport Jazz Festival. Recording produced by Teo
Macero. CBS Sony (J) SONE 70081 is a 7-inch disc. Matrix numbers
were assigned later.

Jack Teagarden All Stars

Monterey, California, September 20, 1963

Charlie Teagarden, trumpet; Jack Teagarden, trombone, vocal; Pee Wee
Russell, clarinet; Gerry Mulligan, baritone; Joe Sullivan, piano; Jimmy
Bond, bass; Nick Ceroli, drums.

Struttin' With Some Barbecue
     33:   >Musica Jazz Presenta (I) 2MJP 1071
     CD: Grudge 4523-2-F

St. James Infirmary (JT vocal)
     CD: >Grudge 4523-2-F

I've Found A New Baby
     CD: >Grudge 4523-2-F

Omit Charlie Teagarden, Jack Teagarden and Joe Sullivan.

New Blues
     33:   >IAJRC IAJRC 28, Musica Jazz Presenta (I) 2MJP 1071
     CD: Grudge 4523-2-F

Full band personnel.

Basin Street Blues (JT vocal)
     33:   >Musica Jazz Presenta (I) 2MJP 1071
     CD: Grudge 4523-2-F

Add Sleepy Matsumoto, tenor

Sweet Georgia Brown
    CD: >Grudge 4523-2-F

Monterey Blues
    CD: >Grudge 4523-2-F

NOTE: Recorded at the sixth annual Monterey Jazz Festival, Monterey
Fairgrounds, 9 p.m. "New Blues" as "Pee Wee's and Gerry's Blues" on
Grudge 4523-2-F.

Jack Teagarden All Stars
                        Monterey, California, September 21, 1963.

Charlie Teagarden, trumpet; Jack Teagarden, trombone, vocal; Pee Wee
Russell, clarinet; Joe Sullivan, piano; George Tucker, bass; Nick
Ceroli, drums.

Indiana
    CD: >Grudge 4523-2-F

Casanova's Lament (JT vocal)
    33: >Giants of Jazz GOJ-1026
    CD: Grudge 4523-2-F

Norma Teagarden, piano, replaces Sullivan.

Body And Soul
    CD: >Grudge 4523-2-F

A Hundred Years From Today (JT vocal)
    33: >Giants of Jazz GOJ-1026
    CD: Grudge 4523-2-F

Basin Street Blues (JT vocal)
    33: >Giants of Jazz GOJ-1026
    CD: Grudge 4523-2-F

Sugar
    CD: >Grudge 4523-2-F

NOTE: From the sixth annual Monterey Jazz Festival, Monterey Fairgrounds, 1:30 p.m. A symposium entitled "What Happened to Dixieland?" was held at the festival during the afternoon of September 21. The symposium was moderated by Downbeat editor Don DeMicheal and included Jack Teagarden, Charlie Teagarden, Pee Wee Russell, Joe Sullivan and Darnell Howard.

Pee Wee Russell

East Providence, Rhode Island, February, 1964.

Tommy Tomasso, trumpet; Zolman "Porky" Cohen, trombone; Pee Wee Russell, clarinet; Ed Soares, piano; John Pell, bass, tuba; Ray Cerce, drums.

Sunday
    33:    >blank label 4, Honeydew HD 6614

I'd Do Anything For You
    33:    >blank label 4, Honeydew HD 6614

Black And Blue
    33:    >blank label 4, Honeydew HD 6614

I Found A New Baby
    33:    >blank label 4, Honeydew HD 6614

Sugar
    33:    >blank label 4, Honeydew HD 6614

Love Is Just Around the Corner
    33:    >blank label 4, Honeydew HD 6614

Washington and Lee Swing
    33:    >blank label 4, Honeydew HD 6614

When It's Sleepy Time Down South
    33:    >blank label 4, Honeydew HD 6614

Oh Baby
    33:    >blank label 3, Honeydew HD 6616

Keepin' Out Of Mischief Now
    33:    >blank label 3, Honeydew HD 6616

316

Omit Tomasso and Cohen.

Sugar
    33:    >blank label 3, Honeydew HD 6616

Tomasso and Cohen return.

Blues
    33:    >blank label 3, Honeydew HD 6616

Struttin' With Some Barbecue
    33:    >blank label 3, Honeydew HD 6616

Ain't Misbehavin'
    33:    >blank label 3, Honeydew HD 6616

There Will Be Some Changes Made (sic)
    33:    >blank label 3, Honeydew HD 6616

That's A Plenty
    33:    >blank label 3, Honeydew HD 6616

Closing Announcements and Chaser
    33:    >blank label 3, Honeydew HD 6616

NOTE: Recorded at Bovi's Town Tavern. The accompanying group performed as "The Jewels of Dixieland" in the Providence area for many years. "That's A Plenty" is labeled "Varsity Drag" on blank label 3.

The Eddie Condon tour of the Far East started in Australia. The intinerary there was:

March 5 Arrived Sydney, flew on to Adelaide. Possibly that night, the band was interviewed on television.
March 6 Interview with Kym Bonython for radio show, "Tempo of the Times." First of the four shows for the Adelaide Festival of Arts in Regent Theatre.
March 11 8:15 p.m. concert, Melbourne Festival Hall.
March 12 8:15 p.m. concert, Melbourne Festival Hall.
March 13 8:15 p.m. concert, Melbourne Festival Hall.
March 14 2:15 p.m. concert, Sydney Stadium
      8:15 p.m. concert, Sydney Stadium
March 15 2:00, 3:30 and 7 p.m. shows at the Playboy Club, Melbourne, but Russell, Condon and Rushing were not present as they stayed in Sydney. The band flew to Auckland, New Zealand, that night.

Eddie Condon All Stars
                        Melbourne, Australia, March 11, 1964

Buck Clayton, trumpet; Vic Dickenson, trombone; Pee Wee Russell, clarinet; Bud Freeman, tenor: Dick Cary, piano; Eddie Condon, guitar; Jack Lesberg, bass; Cliff Leeman, drums; Jimmy Rushing, vocal.

I Can't Believe That You're In Love With Me
    Unissued

Am I Blue? (JR vocal)
    Unissued

St. Louis Blues
    Unissued

Dick Cary switches to alto horn.

Caravan
    Unissued

Pee Wee Russell, clarinet; Dick Cary, piano; Eddie Condon, guitar; Jack Lesberg, bass; Cliff Leeman, drums.

Pee Wee's Blues
    Unissued

Full band personnel.

Blues medley: Goin' To Chicago; Outskirts Of Town; Harvard Blues;
St. Louis Blues (JR vocal)
    Unissued

There'll Be Some Changes Made (JR vocal)
    Unissued

Love Is Just Around The Corner (incomplete)
    Unissued

NOTE: From radio station 3AW broadcast of portions of the concert at
Festival Hall. Pee Wee Russell does not appear on other titles from this
broadcast.

Eddie Condon All Stars
                                        Sydney, Australia, March 14, 1964
Same personnel.

Caravan
    Unissued

Dick Cary switches to piano.

St. Louis Blues
    Unissued

Buck Clayton, trumpet; Pee Wee Russell, clarinet; Eddie Condon,
guitar; Dick Cary, piano, alto horn; Jack Lesberg, bass; Cliff Leeman,
drums.

Sugar
    33: >IAJRC IAJRC-28

Full band personnel; Cary plays piano only.

Am I Blue? (JR vocal)
    Unissued

When You're Smiling (JR vocal)
    Unissued

Blues medley: Going To Chicago, See See Rider, Outskirts Of Town,
St. Louis Blues (JR vocal)
 Unissued

Sent For You Yesterday (JR vocal)
 Unissued

That's A Plenty (incomplete)
 Unissued

NOTE: From an Australian Broadcast Corporation radio broadcast of
the concert at Sydney Stadium. Pee Wee Russell does not appear on
other titles from this concert.

The Eddie Condon All Stars appeared in ten concerts in New Zealand,
one at 6 p.m. and the second at 8:30 p.m. on each of the following
dates: Monday, March 16th at Auckland Town Hall, March 17 at
Hamilton Embassy Theatre, March 18th at Wellington Town Hall,
March 19 at Dunedin Town Hall and March 20 at Christchurch Civic
Theatre. The New Zealand Broadcasting Corporation, which arranged
for the tour in New Zealand, included rights to record the concerts for
four thirty-minute programs. The following listing is probably a
composite of several of these concerts as broadcast by NZBC. Pee
Wee Russell does not appear on other titles from these broadcasts.

Eddie Condon All Stars
New Zealand, March 16 - 20, 1964
Same personnel.

First Program:

Muskrat Ramble
 Unissued

Do You Know What It Means To Miss New Orleans
 Unissued

Full band, but Dick Cary, alto horn, piano.

Rose Room
 Unissued

Second Program:

Full band, Dick Cary, piano

I Would Do Anything For You
    Unissued

St. Louis Blues
    Unissued

Third Program:

Full band:

Basin Street Blues
    Unissued

Dick Cary plays both alto horn and piano.

I Can't Believe That You're In Love With Me
    Unissued

Pee Wee Russell, clarinet; Dick Cary, piano; Jack Lesberg, bass; Cliff
Leeman, drums.

Pee Wee's Blues
    Unissued

Dick Cary plays both alto horn and piano.

Sugar
    Unissued

Fourth Program.

Full band, Dick Cary, alto horn.

Caravan
    Unissued

Full band, Dick Cary, piano.

All Of Me (JR vocal)
  Unissued

When You're Smiling (JR vocal)
  Unissued

Blues medley (JR vocal)
  Unissued

Sent For You Yesterday (JR vocal)
  Unissued

On March 23, the band arrived in Japan. They appeared in concert in Tokyo on March 24 and 25. From March 26 through April 1, they toured Osaka, Nagoya, Sapporo and Kyoto. They returned to Tokyo on April 2 and performed at Sankei Hall. On April 3, they left Japan to return to the United States.

Eddie Condon All Stars

                                              Tokyo, Japan, March 24, 1964
Same personnel

Muskrat Ramble
  33: Chiaroscuro (J) ULS 1684-CH, >Chiaroscuro (J) UPS2069-
       CH

Do You Know What It Means To Miss New Orleans?
  Unissued

Dick Cary plays alto horn and piano.

Rose Room
  33: >Chiaroscuro CR 154, Chiaroscuro (C) CR 154, Chiaroscuro
       (J) ULS 1684-CH, Chiraroscuro (J) UPS2069-CH
  CD: Chiaroscuro CR(D) 154
  CT: Jazz Connoisseur Cassette (E) JCC 117

Dick Cary plays alto horn only.

Caravan
    CD: >Chiaroscuro CR(D) 154

Dick Cary plays piano.

I Would Do Anything For You
    33: >Chiaroscuro CR 154, Chiaroscuro (C) CR 154, Chiaroscuro
        (J) ULS 1684-CH, Chiaroscuro (J) UPS2069-CH
    CD: Chiaroscuro CR(D) 154
    CT: Jazz Connoisseur Cassette (E) JCC 117

St. Louis Blues
    33: Chiaroscuro (J) ULS 1684-CH, >Chiaroscuro UPS2069-CH

Basin Street Blues
    33: Chiaroscuro (J) ULS 1685-CH, >Chiaroscuro UPS2070-CH
    CD: Chiaroscuro CR(D) 154

Dick Cary plays alto horn and piano.

I Can't Believe That You're In Love With Me
    33: >Chiaroscuro CR 154, Chiaroscuro (C) CR 154, Chiaroscuro
        (J) ULS 1685-CH, Chiaroscuro (J) UPS2070-CH
    CD: Chiaroscuro CR(D) 154
    CT: Jazz Connoisseur Cassette (E) JCC 117

Pee Wee Russell, clarinet; Dick Cary, piano; Eddie Condon, guitar; Jack Lesberg, bass; Cliff Leeman, drums.

Pee Wee's Blues
    33: >Chiaroscuro CR 154, Chiaroscuro (C) CR 154, Chiaroscuro
        (J) ULS 1685-CH, Chiaroscuro (J) UPS2070-CH
    CD: Chiaroscuro CR(D) 154
    CT: Jazz Connoisseur Cassette (E) JCC 117

Full band personnel; Dick Cary plays piano.

All Of Me (JR vocal)
33: >Chiaroscuro CR 154, Chiaroscuro (C) CR 154, Chiaroscuro (J) ULS 1685-CH, Chiaroscuro (J) UPS2070-CH
CD: Chiarosocuro CR(D) 154
CT: Jazz Connoisseur Cassette (E) JCC 117

Am I Blue (JR, vocal)
33: Chiaroscuro (J) ULS 1685-CH, >Chiaroscuro (J) UPS2070-CH
CD: Chiaroscuro CR(D) 154
CT: Jazz Connoisseur Cassette (E) JCC 117

When You're Smiling (JR, vocal)
33: >Chiaroscuro CR 154, Chiaroscuro (C) CR 154, Chiaroscuro (J) ULS 1685-CH, Chiaroscuro (J) UPS2070-CH
CD: Chiaroscuro CR(D) 154
CT: Jazz Connoisseur Cassette (E) JCC 117

Blues Medley: Goin' To Chicago; Every Day, C. C. Rider; St. Louis Blues (JR, vocal)
CD: >Chiaroscuro CR(D) 154

Royal Garden Blues
33: >Chiaroscuro CR 154, Chiaroscuro (C) CR 154, Chiaroscuro (J) ULS 1684-5CH, Chiaroscuro (J) UPS2069-70CH
CD: Chiaroscuro CR(D) 154
CT: Jazz Connoisseur Cassette (E) JCC 117

NOTE: From a concert at Hibiya Civic Auditorium. Pee Wee Russell does not appear on other titles from this concert. Recording produced by Hank O'Neal. Original recording by Tokyo Broadcasting Service. Chiaroscuro CR(D) 154 is an American issue.

Eddie Condon All Stars
Osaka, Japan, March 27, 1964

Buck Clayton, trumpet; Vic Dickenson, trombone; Pee Wee Russell, clarinet; Bud Freeman, tenor; Dick Cary, piano; Eddie Condon, guitar; Jack Lesberg, bass; Cliff Leeman, drums, Jimmy Rushing, vocals.

Muskrat Ramble
33: >blank label (E) no number

St. Louis Blues
    33:   >blank label (E) no number

Basin Street Blues
    33:   >blank label (E) no number

Dick Cary switches from piano to alto horn.

Caravan
    33:   >blank label (E) no number

Pee Wee Russell, clarinet, Dick Cary, piano; Eddie Condon, guitar;
Jack Lesberg, bass; Cliff Leeman, drums.

Pee Wee's Blues
    33:   >blank label (E) no number

Full band personnel.

All Of Me (JR vocal)
    33:   >blank label (E) no number

Am I Blue? (JR vocal)
    33:   >blank label (E) no number

When You're Smiling (JR vocal)
    33:   >blank label (E) no number

Blues Medley: Goin' To Chicago; Outskirts Of Town; See See Rider;
St. Louis Blues (JR vocal)
    33:   >blank label (E) no number

Blues Medley (encore): Sent For You Yesterday; Rock And Roll; Sent
For You Yesterday (JR vocal)
    33:   >blank label (E) no number

NOTE: Fifty copies of the LP of this concert were pressed on a blank
label issue with no serial number. Other selections from this concert do
not include Pee Wee Russell.

Tribute to Eddie Condon

NYC, July 20, 1964

Jimmy McPartland, trumpet; Cutty Cutshall, trombone; Pee Wee Russell, clarinet; Bud Freeman, tenor; unknown piano, bass and drums.

At The Jazz Band Ball (partial)
Unissued

Add Henry "Red" Allen, vocal.

I Ain't Got Nobody (HA vocal)
Unissued

Yank Lawson, trumpet; Cutty Cutshall, trombone; Pee Wee Russell, clarinet; possibly Dick Hyman, piano; unknown bass and drums.

The Jazz Me Blues
Unissued

Bobby Hackett, cornet; Yank Lawson, trumpet; J.C. Higginbotham, trombone; Pee Wee Russell, clarinet; Bob Wilber, clarinet; Willie "The Lion" Smith, piano; unknown bass; Zutty Singleton, drums.

Royal Garden Blues (partial)
Unissued

NOTE: Recorded from the audience in Carnegie Hall.

Newport All Stars

Possibly NYC, August 31, 1964

Ruby Braff, cornet; Pee Wee Russell, clarinet; Bud Freeman, tenor; George Wein, piano; unknown bass; unknown drums.

Three Little Words
Unissued

St. Louis Blues (incomplete)
Unissued

326

Newport All Stars
                    Berlin, West Germany, September 26, 1964

Ruby Braff, cornet; Pee Wee Russell, clarinet; Bud Freeman, tenor;
George Wein, piano; Jimmy Woode, bass; Joe Nay, drums.

Royal Garden Blues
  Unissued

Ain't Misbehavin'
  Unissued

Indiana
  Unissued

Omit Braff and Freeman.

Pee Wee's Blues
  Unissued

Newport All Stars

                    Basel, Switzerland, September 28, 1964

Same personnel.

Indiana
  Unissued

Birth Of The Blues
  Unissued

I've Found A New Baby
  Unissued

St. Louis Blues
  Unissued

Omit Braff and Freeman.

Pee Wee's Blues
  Unissued

NOTE: Russell does not play on other titles from this broadcast.

327

Newport All Stars

Copenhagen, Denmark, early October, 1964.

Same personnel.

I've Found A New Baby
    Unissued

Ain't Misbehavin'
    Unissued

Omit Braff and Freeman.

Pee Wee's Blues
    Unissued

Newport All Stars

London, England, October 11, 1964

Ruby Braff, cornet; Pee Wee Russell, clarinet; Bud Freeman, tenor; George Wein, piano; Brian Brocklehurst, bass; Lennie Hastings, drums.

Royal Garden Blues
    Unissued

Ain't Misbehavin'
    Unissued

Omit Braff and Freeman.

Pee Wee's Blues
    Unissued

Full band personnel.

St. Louis Blues
    Unissued

NOTE: From a "Jazz 625" telecast recorded at the Marque Club. Program also includes two other titles which do not include Pee Wee Russell. ".i.Sugar;" may also have been recorded, but was edited out of the finished program.

Pee Wee Russell

Interview, broadcast by Humphrey Lyttleton, BBC.
      Unissued

*Following the tour with the Newport All Stars, Pee Wee stayed in
England for the rest of October and appeared with the Alex Welsh band
(except where noted). The intinerary was:*

October 15: Press reception at Manchester
October 16: Manchester Sports Guild and Social Center
October 17: Same, with Johnny Armatage Jump Band
October 18: Same, with Freddie Randall Band
October 20: George and Dragon, Bedford
October 22: Manchester Sports Guild, with Gary Cox Quartet
October 23: Palace Hotel, Southport
October 24   The Dancing Slipper, Nottingham
October 25: Coatham Hotel, Redcar
October 26: Condon's Club, Red Lion Hotel, Hatfield
October 27: Crown Hotel, Morden, Surrey
October 28: Dolphin Hotel, Botley
October 30: Conway Hall, London
October 31: Midland Jazz Club, Birmingham
November 1: Manchester Sports Guild

Pee Wee Russell with the Johnny Armatage Jump Band

Manchester, England, October 17, 1964.

Ray Crane, trumpet; Pete Strange, trombone; Archie Semple, Pee Wee
Russell, clarinet; Cyril Keefer, tenor; Keith Ingham, piano; Dave
Green, bass; Johnny Armatage, drums.

Rose Room
      Unissued

If I Had You
      Unissued

Indiana
      Unissued

329

'Deed I Do
    Unissued

Rosetta
    Unissued

There'll Be Some Changes Made
    Unissued

Sugar
    Unissued

Pee Wee Russell, clarinet; Keith Ingham, piano; Dave Green, bass; Johnny Armatage, drums.

Pee Wee's Blues
    Unissued

Add Sandy Brown, Archie Semple, clarinet.

Midnight Blue
    Unissued

NOTE: From a concert at the Manchester Sports Guild and Social Center.

Pee Wee Russell with the Alex Welsh Band

Nottingham, England, October 24, 1964.

Alex Welsh, trumpet; Roy Crimmins, trombone; Pee Wee Russell, clarinet; Johnny Barnes, clarinet, alto, baritone; Fred Hunt, piano; Jim Douglas, guitar; Ron Mathewson, bass; Lennie Hastings, drums.

If I Had You
    Unissued

Rose Room
    Unissued

Sugar
    Unissued

Someday Sweetheart
    Unissued

Indiana
    Unissued

Omit Welsh, Crimmins and Barnes.

Pee Wee's Blues
    Unissued

Add Welsh, Crimmins and Barnes.

It's Right Here For You
    Unissued

'S Wonderful
    Unissued

Ain't Misbehavin'
    Unissued

I'm Confessin'
    Unissued

Recorded at the Dancing Slipper. The tape of this performance includes closing comments by Russell.

Pee Wee Russell with the Alex Welsh Band

Manchester, England, November 1, 1964.

Alex Welsh, trumpet; Roy Crimmins, trombone; Pee Wee Russell, clarinet; Johnny Barnes, baritone; Fred Hunt, piano; Jim Douglas, guitar; Ron Mathewson, bass; Lennie Hastings, drums.

If I Had You
    Unissued

Rose Room
    Unissued

It's Right Here For You
    Unissued

331

Sugar
    Unissued

I Can't Believe That You're In Love With Me
    Unissued

Omit Welsh, Crimmins and Barnes.

Pee Wee's Blues
    Unissued

Clancy Hayes with the Lawson-Haggart Jazz Band

NYC, April 1, 1965

Yank Lawson, trumpet; Cutty Cutshall, trombone; Pee Wee Russell, clarinet; Dave McKenna, piano; Clancy Hayes, banjo, vocal; Bob Haggart, bass; Osie Johnson, drums.

12565 Copenhagen
    33: >ABC Paramount ABC-519, >ABC Paramount ABCS-519

12566 After You've Gone
    33: >ABC Paramount ABC-519, >ABC Paramount ABCS-519

12567 Tin Roof Blues
    33: >ABC Paramount ABC-519, >ABC Paramount ABCS-519

12568 Basin Street Blues (CH vocal)
    33: >ABC Paramount ABC-519, >ABC Paramount ABCS-519

12569 Don't Forget 127th Street (CH vocal)
    33: >ABC Paramount ABC-519, >ABC Paramount ABCS-519

12570 A Good Man Is Hard To Find (CH vocal)
    33: >ABC Paramount ABC-519, >ABC Paramount ABCS-519

12571 Fidgety Feet
    33: >ABC Paramount ABC-519, >ABC Paramount ABCS-519

12574 I Ain't Got Nobody (CH vocal)
    33: >ABC Paramount ABC-519, >ABC Paramount ABCS-519

12575 Nobody's Sweetheart (CH vocal)
    33:    >ABC Paramount ABC-519, >ABC Paramount ABCS-519

12576 .Dinah
    33:    >ABC Paramount ABC-519, >ABC Paramount ABCS-519

NOTE: Two additional titles from this LP, ".i.She's Just Perfect for Me;" (matrix 12572) and ".i.Fickle Finger of Fate;" (matrix 12573), do not include Pee Wee Russell.

Pee Wee Russell Quintet

NYC, July 22, 1965

Bobby Hackett, cornet; Pee Wee Russell, clarinet; Dave Frishberg, piano; George Tucker, bass; Oliver Jackson, drums.

'Deed I Do
    Unissued

I'm In The Market For You
    33:    >IAJRC IAJRC-28, Xanadu 192

Swing That Music
    Unissued

St. Louis Blues
    Unissued

Pennies From Heaven
    Unissued

In A Mellotone
    Unissued

'S Wonderful
    Unissued

Summertime
    Unissued

Midnight Blue
    Unissued

Pee Wee's Blues
    Unissued

NOTE: This concert, produced by Dan Morgenstern and Down Beat
magazine, was held in the sculpture garden of the Museum of Modern
Art. It was filmed by NBC television and shown in part on its
"Kaleidoscope 4" program on September 4, 1965. (The film is not
known to have survived.) The announcer speaks over a portion of
".i.Swing That Music.;" Only the first three titles, plus "The.i. Man
With The Horn,;" which did not include Pee Wee Russell, were
broadcast. The order of performance is not known.

Austin High School Reunion Band
                                    Chicago, August 14, 1965

Jimmy McPartland, cornet, vocals; Floyd O'Brien, trombone; Pee Wee
Russell, clarinet; Bud Freeman, tenor; Art Hodes, piano; Jim Lanigan,
bass; George Wettling, drums.

China Boy
    Unissued

Tin Roof Blues
    Unissued

Nobody's Sweetheart (incomplete)
    Unissued

St. James Infirmary (JMcP, vocal)
    Unissued

You Took Advantage Of Me
    Unissued

Sugar (JMcP, vocal)
    Unissued

Royal Garden Blues
    Unissued.

NOTE: Recorded at the Down Beat Jazz Festival, Soldier Field.

Earl Hines

NYC, January 11, 1966

Cat Anderson, Ray Nance, trumpet; Lawrence Brown, trombone; Pee Wee Russell, clarinet; Jimmy Hamilton, clarinet, tenor; Paul Gonsalves, tenor; Earl Hines, piano; Aaron Bell, bass; Elvin Jones, drums.

90461 Blues In My Flat (RN vocal)
- 33: HMV (E) CLP 3560, >Impulse! A 9108, >Impulse! AS 9108, Impulse! (E) IMPL-8011, Impulse! (J) YP 8597AI, Impulse!/Sparton (C) A 9108, Impulse!/Sparton (C) AS 9108, Jasmine (E) JAS 42, MCA MCA-29070
- CT: Jasmine (E) JASC 42

90462 You Can Depend On Me
- 33: HMV (E) CLP 3560, >Impulse! A 9108, >Impulse! AS 9108, Impulse! (E) IMPL-8011, Impulse! (J) YP 8597AI, Impulse!/Sparton (C) A 9108, Impulse!/Sparton (C) AS 9108, Jasmine (E) JAS 42, MCA MCA-29070
- CT: Jasmine (E) JASC 42

Add Johnny Hodges, Russell Procope, alto; Harold Ashby, tenor. Sonny Greer, drums, replaces Jones.

90464 Black And Tan Fantasy
- 33: HMV (E) CLP 3560, >Impulse! A 9108, >Impulse! AS 9108, Impulse! (E) IMPL-8011, Impulse! ASH-9 285-2, Impulse! (J) YP 8597AI, Impulse!/Sparton (C) A 9108, Impulse!/Sparton (C) AS 9108

Omit Ray Nance, trumpet.

90465 Hash Brown
- 33: HMV (E) CLP 3560, >Impulse! A 9108, >Impulse! AS 9108, Impulse! (E) IMPL-8011, Impulse! (J) YP 8597AI, Impulse!/Sparton (C) A 9108, Impulse!/Sparton (C) AS 9108, Jasmine (E) JAS 42, MCA MCA-29070
- CT: Jasmine (E) JASC 42

NOTE: Produced by Bob Thiele.

Pee Wee Russell with Tommy Gwaltney's Band

Washington, D.C., March, 1966.

Pee Wee Russell, clarinet; Tommy Gwaltney, clarinet, vibes; Steve Jordan, guitar; John Phillips, piano; William "Keter" Betts, bass; Bertell Knox, drums.

Ain't Misbehavin' (TG vibes)
  Unissued

I Want A Little Girl (TG clarinet)
  Unissued

Oh, Baby (TG clarinet and vibes) (incomplete)
  Unissued

Pee Wee's Blues (TG vibes)
  Unissued

St. Louis Blues (incomplete) (TG vibes)
  Unissued

NOTE: From a live performance at Blues Alley.

Pee Wee Russell

Washington, D.C., March, 1966

Felix Grant interviews Pee Wee Russell and Tommy Gwaltney.
  Unissued

Yank Lawson and His Orchestra

NYC, May 2, 1966

Yank Lawson, trumpet; Cutty Cutshall, trombone; Pee Wee Russell, clarinet; Dave McKenna, piano; Bucky Pizzarelli, guitar; Bob Haggart, bass; Chico Hamilton, drums; Willie Bobo, Victor Pantora, percussion.

13318 Wolverine Blues
  33: >ABC Paramount ABC-567, >ABC Paramount ABCS-567,
       ABC Paramount (J) YW 8530-AB

13319   Muscrat Ramble (sic)
    33:   >ABC Paramount ABC-567, >ABC Paramount ABCS-567,
        ABC Paramount (J) YW 8530-AB

13320   Bossa Nova Noche
    33:   >ABC Paramount ABC-567, >ABC Paramount ABCS-567,
        ABC Paramount (J) YW 8530-AB

13321   Fidgety Feet
    33:   >ABC Paramount ABC-567, >ABC Paramount ABCS-567,
        ABC Paramount (J) YW 8530-AB

NOTE: Produced by Bob Thiele

Yank Lawson and His Orchestra

NYC, May 18, 1966

Yank Lawson, trumpet; Cutty Cutshall, trombone; Pee Wee Russell, clarinet; Dave McKenna, piano; Tony Mottola, guitar, Bob Haggart, bass, whistling; Ed Shaughnessy, drums; Bob Rosengarden, percussion.

13322   Daydream (BH whistling)
    33:   >ABC Paramount ABC-567, >ABC Paramount ABCS-567,
        ABC Paramount (J) YW 8530-AB

13324   Tijuana
    33:   >ABC Paramount ABC-567, >ABC Paramount ABCS-567,
        ABC Paramount (J) YW 8530AB

13325   Bang Bang (My Baby Shot Me Down)
    33:   >ABC Paramount ABC-567, >ABC Paramount ABCS-567,
        ABC Paramount (J) YW 8530-AB

NOTE: Pee Wee Russell does not appear on mx. 13323, "What's New." Produced by Bob Thiele.

Yank Lawson and His Orchestra

NYC, May 19, 1966

Yank Lawson, trumpet; Cutty Cutshall, trombone; Pee Wee Russell, clarinet; Dave McKenna, piano; Bucky Pizzarelli, guitar; Bob Haggart, bass; Chico Hamilton, drums; Bob Rosengarden, percussion.

13326   Where Did I Find You?
    33:     >ABC Paramount ABC-567, >ABC Paramount ABCS-567,
           ABC Paramount (J) YW 8530-AB

13327   Ka Boom Boom
    33:     >ABC Paramount ABC-567, >ABC Paramount ABCS-567,
           ABC Paramount (J) YW 8530-AB

13328   South Rampart Street Parade
    Unissued

13329   I Cried In The Night
    33:     >ABC Paramount ABC-567, >ABC Paramount ABCS-567,
           ABC Paramount (J) YW 8530-AB

NOTE: Produced by Bob Thiele.

Newport All Stars

Atlanta, Georgia, May 27, 1966

Ruby Braff, cornet; Lou McGarity, trombone; Pee Wee Russell, clarinet; George Wein, piano; Eddie Condon, guitar; Jack Lesberg, bass; Dick Berk, drums.

Indiana
    Unissued

At The Jazz Band Ball
    Unissued

Blues For The Delta
    Unissued

Oh, Baby
    Unissued

NOTE: Recorded at the Atlanta Jazz Festival, Atlanta Stadium.

338

Henry "Red" Allen and Pee Wee Russell

Cambridge, Mass., October 29, 1966

Henry "Red" Allen, trumpet, vocal; Pee Wee Russell, clarinet; Steve Kuhn, piano; Charlie Haden, bass; Marty Morell, drums.

90708 Blue Monk
    33:   >Impulse! A-9137, >Impulse! AS-9137, Impulse! (E) MILP
          509, Impulse! (E) SILP 509, Impulse!/Sparton (C) A 9137,
          Impulse!/Sparton (C) AS 9137, Jasmine (E) JAS 78
    CT: Jasmine (E) JASC 78

90709 I Want A Little Girl
    33:   >Impulse! A-9137, >Impulse! AS-9137, Impulse! (E) MILP
          509, Impulse! (E) SILP 509, Impulse!/Sparton (C) A 9137,
          Impulse!/Sparton (C) AS 9137, Jasmine (E) JAS 78
    CT: Jasmine (E) JASC 78

90710 Body And Soul (HA vocal)
    33:   >Impulse! A-9137, >Impulse! AS-9137, Impulse! (E) MILP
          509, Impulse! (E) SILP 509, Impulse!/Sparton (C) A 9137,
          Impulse!/Sparton (C) AS 9137, Jasmine (E) JAS 78
    CT: Jasmine (E) JASC 78

Omit Allen.

90711 Pee Wee's Blues
    33:   >Impulse! A-9137, >Impulse! AS-9137, Impulse! (E) MILP
          509, Impulse! (E) SILP 509, Impulse!/Sparton (C) A 9137,
          Impulse!/Sparton (C) AS 9137, Jasmine (E) JAS 78
    CT: Jasmine (E) JASC 78

Allen returns.

90712 Two Degrees East, Three Degrees West
    33:   >Impulse! A-9137, >Impulse! AS-9137, Impulse! (E) MILP
          509, Impulse! (E) SILP 509, Impulse!/Sparton (C) A 9137,
          Impulse!/Sparton (C) AS 9137, Jasmine (E) JAS 78
    CT: Jasmine (E) JASC 78

90713 Graduation Blues (HA vocal)
>   33:   >Impulse! A-9137, >Impulse! AS-9137, Impulse! (E) MILP
509, Impulse! (E) SILP 509, Impulse!/Sparton (C) A 9173,
Impulse!/Sparton (C) AS 1937, Jasmine (E) JAS 78
>   CT: Jasmine (E) JASC 78

NOTE: These performances were recorded at the Massachusetts
Institute of Technology where they were used to illustrate a lecture by
Whitney Balliett.

Pee Wee Russell

NYC, December 20, 1966

Pee Wee Russell interviewed by Henry Whiston
Unissued

NOTE: Recorded by the Canadian Broadcasting Corporation which
broadcast the interview on the radio program "Jazz At Its Best" in
March, 1967. The taping took place in the Russells' apartment.

Bob Thiele And His New Happy Times Orchestra

NYC, February 13, 1967

Max Kaminsky, Jimmy McPartland, trumpet; Urbie Green, Lou
McGarity, trombone; Pee Wee Russell, clarinet; Milt Hinton or George
Duvivier, bass; Don Butterfield, tuba; others unknown. Teresa Brewer,
vocal. Tommy Goodman, Glenn Osser, arranger.

13862 Thoroughly Modern Millie (TB, vocal)
>   33:   >ABC Paramount ABC-605, >ABC Paramount ABCS-605,
HMV (E) CLP 3624

13863 Jimmy (TB, vocal)
>   33:   >ABC Paramount ABC-605, >ABC Paramount ABCS-605,
HMV (E) CLP 3624

13864 San
>   33:   >ABC Paramount ABC-605, >ABC Paramount ABCS-605,
HMV (E) CLP 3624

13865 Charleston
   33:   >ABC Paramount ABC-605, >ABC Paramount ABCS-605,
         HMV (E) CLP 3624

NOTE: Produced by Bob Thiele. Russell can be heard only on 13864
and 13865.

Pee Wee Russell and Oliver Nelson and his Orchestra

NYC, February 14, 1967

Joe Wilder, Ed Williams, Snooky Young, Clark Terry, trumpet; Jimmy
Cleveland, Richard Hixson, Urbie Green, Tony Studd, trombone; Pee
Wee Russell, clarinet; Phil Woods, alto; Jerry Dodgion, alto, flute;
Frank Wess, tenor; Seldon Powell, tenor, flute; Danny Bank, baritone,
bass clarinet; Hank Jones, piano; Howard Collins, guitar; George
Duvivier, bass; Grady Tate, drums; Oliver Nelson, leader, arranger.

90738 Ja Da
   33:   >Impulse! A 9147, >Impulse! AS 9147, Impulse!/Sparton (C)
         A 9147, Impulse!/Sparton (E) AS 9147

90739 This Is It
   33:   >Impulse! A 9147, >Impulse! AS 9147, Impulse!/Sparton (C)
         A 9147, Impulse!/Sparton (C) AS 9147

90740 Memories Of You
   33:   >Impulse! A 9147, >Impulse! AS 9147, Impulse!/Sparton (C)
         A 9147, Impulse!/Sparton (C) AS 9147

90741 Pee Wee's Blues
   33:   >Impulse! A 9147, >Impulse! AS 9147, Impulse!/Sparton (C)
         A 9147, Impulse!/Sparton AS 9147

90742 The Shadow Of Your Smile
   33:   >Impulse! A 9147, >Impulse! AS 9147, Impulse!/Sparton (C)
         A 9147, Impulse!/Sparton (C) AS 9147

NOTE: Produced by Bob Thiele. "This Is It" and "Pee Wee's Blues" were composed by Pee Wee Russell.

Pee Wee Russell and Oliver Nelson and his Orchestra

NYC, February 15, 1967

Marvin Stamm, Thad Jones, Jimmy Nottingham, John Frosk, trumpet; Thomas Mitchell, Tom McIntosh, Paul Faulise, trombone; Pee Wee Russell, clarinet; Phil Woods, alto; Jerry Dodgion, alto, flute; Bob Ashton, tenor; Seldon Powell, tenor, flute; Gene Allen, baritone; Patti Bown, piano; Howard Collins, guitar; George Duvivier, bass; Grady Tate, drums; Oliver Nelson, leader, arranger.

90743 Love Is Just Around The Corner
    33: >Impulse! A 9147, >Impulse! AS 9147, Impulse!/Sparton (C)
          A 9147, Impulse!/Sparton (C) AS 9147
    TX: AFRS JU 9l

90744 I'm Coming Virginia
    33: >Impulse! A 9147, >Impulse! AS 9147, Impulse!/Sparton (C)
          A 9147, Impulse!/Sparton AS 9147

90745 A Good Man Is Hard To Find
    33: >Impulse! A 9147, >Impulse! AS 9147, Impulse!/Sparton (C)
          A 9147, Impulse!/Sparton (C) AS 9147

90746 Bopol
    33: >Impulse! A 9l47, >Impulse! AS 9147, Impulse!/Sparton (C)
          A 9147, Impulse!/Sparton (C) AS 9147

90747 Six And Four
    33: >Impulse! A 9147, >Impulse! AS 9147, Impulse!/Sparton (C)
          A 9147, Impulse!/Sparton (C) AS 9147

NOTE: Produced by Bob Thiele.

Bob Thiele and His New Happy Times Orchestra

NYC, March 1, 1967.

Max Kaminsky, Jimmy McPartland, trumpet; Urbie Green, Lou McGarity, trombone; Pee Wee Russell, clarinet; Milt Hinton or George Duvivier, bass; Don Butterfield, tuba; others unknown.

13881 Changes
    33:   >ABC Paramount ABC-605, >ABC Paramount ABCS-605, HMV (E) CLP 3624

13882 Betty Co-ed
    33:   >ABC Paramount ABC-605, >ABC Paramount ABCS-605, HMV (E) CLP 3624

13883 Give Me Your Kisses
    33:   >ABC Paramount ABC-605, >ABC Paramount ABCS-605, HMV (E) CLP 3624

13884 Sugar Blues
    33:   >ABC Paramount ABC-605, >ABC Paramount ABCS-605, HMV (E) CLP 3624

NOTE: Produced by Bob Thiele. Russell is audible only on 13881 and 13882. The arrangement of "Changes" is based on the Bill Challis chart as recorded by Paul Whiteman.

Bob Thiele and His New Happy Times Orchestra

NYC, March 2, 1967

Max Kaminsky, Jimmy McPartland, trumpet; Urbie Green, Lou McGarity, trombone; Pee Wee Russell, clarinet; Milt Hinton or George Duvivier, bass; Don Butterfield, tuba; others unknown. Teresa Brewer, Steve Allen, "The Happy Girls" (Toni Wein, Valerie Simpson, Leslie Miller) vocal. Tommy Goodman, Glenn Osser, arranger.

13885 Barnacle Bill The Sailor (SA vocal)
    33:   >ABC Paramount ABC-605, >ABC Paramount ABCS-605, HMV (E) CLP 3624

13886 Japanese Sandman (THG, vocal)
   33: >ABC Paramount ABC-605, >ABC Paramount ABCS-605,
       HMV (E) CLP 3624

13887 Whispering (THG, vocal)
   33: >ABC Paramount ABC-605, >ABC Paramount ABCS-605,
       HMV (E) CLP 3624

13888 I'm Just A Vagabond Lover (SA, vocal)
   33: >ABC Paramount ABC-605, >ABC Paramount ABCS-605,
       HMV (E) CLP 3624

NOTE: Produced by Bob Thiele. Russell is audible only on 13885. It is possible that the jazz segments on these sessions were all recorded at a different time, perhaps in one session, from the rest of the music and spliced into the arrangements. This is Pee Wee Russell's last known studio recording.

George Wein

                Mexico City and Puebla, Mexico, May 12, 13, 14, 1967

Ruby Braff, cornet; Pee Wee Russell, clarinet; Bud Freeman, tenor; George Wein, piano; Jack Lesberg, bass; Don Lamond, drums.

I Never Knew
   33: >Columbia CS 9631, Columbia (C) CS 9631

Take The "A" Train
   33: >Columbia CS 9631, Columbia (C) CS 9631

All Of Me
   33: >Columbia CS 9631, Columbia (C) CS 9631

Blue And Sentimental
   33: >Columbia CS 9631, Columbia (C) CS 9631

If I Had You
   33: >Columbia CS 9631, Columbia (C) CS 9631

The World Is Waiting For The Sunrise
   33: >Columbia CS 9631, Columbia (C) CS 9631

These Foolish Things
    Unissued

'Deed I Do
    Unissued

Blue
    Unissued

Rose Room
    Unissued

Blues For Puebla
    Unissued

Rosetta
    Unissued

Undecided
    Unissued

'S Wonderful
    Unissued

Sugar
    Unissued

Lullaby Of The Leaves
    Unissued

Just One Of Those Things
    Unissued

Don Lamond Solo
    Unissued

NOTE: From concerts at the Belle Artes Opera House, Mexico City
(April 12); City of Puebla (April 13), and National Auditorium, Mexico
City (April 14). "Disc Jockey" monaural copies with the same issue
number (Columbia CS 9631) were made available to radio stations that
had not switched over to stereo equipment.

345

Newport All Stars

Montreal, Canada, May 25, 1967.

Ruby Braff, cornet; Pee Wee Russell, clarinet; Bud Freeman, tenor; George Wein, piano; Jack Lesberg, bass; Don Lamond, drums.

Royal Garden Blues
    Unissued

Les Blues Fait Froid Aujourd'hui
    Unissued

Just You, Just Me
    Unissued

The World Is Waiting For The Sunrise
    Unissued

NOTE: From Jazz Festival, U.S.A., Place de Nations, Expo 67. Produced by George Wein.

Newport Jazz Festival All Stars

NYC, June 29, 1967

Ruby Braff, cornet; Pee Wee Russell, clarinet; Bud Freeman, tenor; George Wein, piano; Jack Lesberg, bass; Don Lamond, drums.

St. Louis Blues
    Unissued

Honeysuckle Rose
    Unissued

Just One Of Those Things
    Unissued

Omit Braff and Freeman

Sugar
    Unissued

Braff and Freeman return.

I Can't Give You Anything But Love
 Unissued

NOTE: From an NBC "Today" show telecast.

Art Hodes

Chicago, October 12, 1967

Jimmy McPartland, cornet, vocal; Pee Wee Russell, clarinet; Art Hodes, piano; Robert "Rail" Wilson, bass; Harry Hawthorne, drums.

China Boy
 VT: Jazz Pioneer (C) JMV 101691

St. James Infirmary (JMcP vocal)
 VT: Jazz Pioneer (C) JMV 101691

Oh, Baby
 VT: Jazz Pioneer (C) JMV 101691

Meet Me In Chicago
 VT: Jazz Pioneer (C) JMV 101691

Sugar (JMcP vocal) (incomplete)
 VT: Jazz Pioneer (C) JMV 101691

NOTE: This WTTW-TV telecast was part of the National Educational Television series "Jazz Alley," hosted by Art Hodes and directed by Robert Kaiser. A kinescope exists that bears the serial number 1, and is dated August 27, 1968. That date, however, may be date the kinescope print was processed and not the date it was originally recorded since the program was mentioned in Down Beat as early as April 4, 1968.

Pee Wee Russell with Tommy Gwaltney's Quintet

Washington, D.C., December 11, 1967

Pee Wee Russell, clarinet; Tommy Gwaltney, clarinet, vibes; John Phillips, piano; Steve Jordan, guitar; Keter Betts, bass; Bertell Knox, drums.

Sunday (TG vibes)
    Unissued

Omit Gwaltney.

Pee Wee's Blues
    Unissued

Gwaltney returns.

Royal Garden Blues (TG clarinet)
    Unissued

Love Is Just Around The Corner (TG vibes)
    Unissued

Prelude To A Kiss (TG vibes)
    Unissued

NOTE: From a live performance at Blues Alley.

Pee Wee Russell with Tommy Gwaltney's Quintet

Washington, D.C., December 13, 1967

Pee Wee Russell, clarinet; Tommy Gwaltney, clarinet, vibes; John Phillips, piano; Steve Jordan, guitar; Keter Betts, bass; Bertell Knox, drums.

Sunday (TG vibes)
    Unissued

Old Folks (TG vibes)
    Unissued

Royal Garden Blues (TG clarinet)
    Unissued

Love Is Just Around The Corner (TG vibes)
    Unissued

Pee Wee's Blues (TG vibes)
    Unissued

Nobody's Sweetheart (TG clarinet)
    Unissued

Prelude To A Kiss (TG vibes)
    Unissued

I've Found A New Baby (TG clarinet)
    Unissued

NOTE: From a live performance at Blues Alley.

Pee Wee Russell

                              Alexandria, Va., January 23, 1968

Pee Wee Russell, clarinet; Bob Greene, piano.

Singin' The Blues (fast tempo)
    Unissued

Singin' The Blues (slow tempo)
    Unissued

Nobody Knows You When You're Down And Out
    Unissued

I've Found A New Baby
    Unissued

I'll Be A Friend With Pleasure (incomplete)
    Unissued

Add Johnson "Fat Cat" McRee, Jr., whistling, kazoo and vocal.

I'll Be A Friend With Pleasure (JMcR whistling, vocal)
  Unissued

Blues (JMcR, vocal, kazoo)
  Unissued.

NOTE: Privately recorded in Helen Decker's apartment.

Max Kaminsky's New York Jazz Band

New Orleans, May 15, 1968

Max Kaminsky, trumpet; Herb Gardner, trombone; Pee Wee Russell, clarinet; Dick Hyman, piano; Bob Haggart, bass; Bob Haggart, Jr., drums.

Dippermouth Blues
  Unissued

Squeeze Me
  Unissued

Muskrat Ramble
  Unissued

NOTE: Privately recorded by Bill Bacin at "Jazzfest '68," aboard the S.S. President on the Mississippi River. This is the last performance by Pee Wee Russell known to have been preserved. He died in Alexandria, Virginia, on February 15, 1969.

PERSONNEL INDEX

352

354

Gabler, Milt 53, 57, 60, 78, 80, 96, 98, 101, 106, 108, 109, 111, 113, 118, 123, 124, 126, 128, 130, 161, 163, 165, 180, 182, 184, 186, 194, 219
Garcia, Louis 42
Gardner, Herb 350
Gardner, Jack 223
Gaskin, Leonard 253, 275
Gauvin, Aime 229
George, Russell 306, 309, 311
Gibson, Harry "The Hipster" 283
Gillespie, Dizzy 283
Giuffre, Jimmy 249, 259, 260
Giuffreda, Johnny 265
Glasel, Johnny 260
Glenn, Tyree 251, 261, 266, 273, 292
Goffin, Maurice 17, 19, 20, 21
Gold, Al 61
Gonsalves, Paul 306, 335
Gooding, Sally 50
Goodman, Benny 13, 23, 24
Goodman, Harry 13, 29
Goodman, Tommy 340, 343
Goodson, Ernie 244
Gorman, Jerry 244
Gott, Tommy 13
Gowans, Brad 58, 60, 63, 64, 67, 68, 69, 70, 72, 74, 75, 76, 78, 79, 80, 81, 83, 84, 92, 99, 101, 102, 111, 116, 205, 219
Grace, Teddy 92
Granato, Jimmy 42
Grant, Felix 336
Grauso, Joe 116, 119, 124, 127, 128, 131, 132, 134, 135, 137, 138, 139, 141, 142, 145, 146, 148, 149, 150, 151, 152, 153, 155, cont.

Grauso, Joe cont. 157, 168, 169, 172, 175, 178, 180, 197, 199, 213
Green, Dave 329, 330
Green, Freddie 61, 285
Green, Urbie 340, 341, 343
Greene, Bob 349
Greer, Sonny 132, 133, 229, 271, 335
Grifoldi, Dick 265
Gross, Walter 58
Gurd, Wally 267
Gusikoff, Al 260
Gussak, Bobby 58
Gwaltney, Tommy 336, 348

Hackett, Bobby 51, 53, 54, 55, 57, 58, 59, 60, 63, 64, 65, 66, 67, 68, 69, 70, 101, 120, 128, 130, 132, 133, 134, 135, 136, 137, 138, 140, 141, 142, 143, 144, 145, 146, 147, 149, 150, 151, 152, 153, 154, 155, 158, 159, 160, 178, 183, 184, 187, 188, 189, 191, 196, 203, 204, 221, 222, 293, 294, 326, 333
Haden, Charlie 339
Hafer, Dick 250, 252
Hagan, Cass 10
Haggart, Bob 102, 135, 137, 138, 139, 141, 142, 146, 147, 148, 149, 151, 153, 154, 156, 157, 161, 167, 170, 171, 178, 183, 184, 198, 200, 214, 301, 302, 303, 304, 332, 336, 337, 338, 350
Haggart, Jr., Bob 350
Hale, Teddy 220
Hall, Al 54, 251, 276

355

Hall, Ed 102, 120, 121, 135, 146, 149, 153, 166, 170
Hamilton, Chico 336, 338
Hamilton, Jimmy 306, 335
Hammond, John 51, 55, 82
Hampton, Lionel 66
Hanlon, Allen 198
Hanna, Jake 289
Hansen, Jack 7, 8, 10, 12, 17, 18, 19
Harris, Bill 139, 141, 153, 154
Hart, Clyde 139, 141
Hastings, Lennie 328, 330, 331
Hawkins, Coleman 22, 249, 258, 259, 271, 296, 297
Hawthorne, Harry 347
Hayes, Clancy 332
Hayton, Lennie 2, 7, 8, 10
Heard, J. C. 300
Henderson, Fletcher 283
Hentoff, Nat 260, 297
Herridge, Robert 260
Higginbotham, J. C. 101, 102, 268, 270, 271, 273, 289, 326
Hill, Alex 39, 40
Hines, Earl 102, 192, 194, 222, 335
Hinton, Milt 243, 250, 258, 259, 260, 296, 304, 340, 343
Hirsch, Godfrey 49
Hixson, Richard 341
Hodes, Art 115, 215, 220, 277, 287, 334, 347
Hodges, Johnny 306, 335
Hohengarten, Carl 1, 2
Honeywill, Jack 289
Houseman, John 260
Howard, Darnell 316
Hubbell, Frank 286
Hubbell, Paul 286
Hucko, Peanuts 217, 220, 247, 293
Hull, Gene 306

Hunt, Fred 330, 331
Hyatt, Donald 304
Hyman, Arnold 232
Hyman, Dick 326, 350

Iacommetta, Ike 289
Ingham, Keith 329, 330
Isaacs, Hank 98

Jackson, Chubby 286
Jackson, Cliff 118, 120, 177, 178, 213, 300
Jackson, Ham 268
Jackson, Oliver 333
Jacobs, Sid 68, 69
Jacobson, Bud 223
James, Jimmy 223
James, Lewis 10
John, Kenny 224
Johnson, James P. 61, 62, 102, 121, 132, 141, 216
Johnson, Joe 1, 2
Johnson, Osie 290, 332
Johnson, Robert 58
Jones, Champ 279, 280, 285, 288, 289
Jones, Elvin 273, 335
Jones, Hank 285, 341
Jones, Jimmy 270
Jones, Jo 258, 259, 260, 269, 277, 279, 280, 296, 305
Jones, Jonah 144, 145, 146, 147, 155
Jones, Thad 342
Jordan, Steve 250, 252, 254, 257, 336, 348
Justice, Tommy 244

Kaiser, Robert 347
Kaminsky, Max 39, 41, 61, 70, 72, 74, 75, 76, 79, 80, 81, 83, 84, 90, 92, 99, 101, 102, 108, 111, 113, 115,

356

360

TITLE INDEX

I've Got A Crush On You, 75, 150, 278
I've Got My Fingers Crossed 46
I've Got The World On A String, 181, 262
I've Gotta Get Up And Go To Work, 37
Ida, Sweet As Apple Cider, 3, 4, 5, 16, 180, 218
If Dreams Come True, 53
If I Could Be With You, 119, 296 See also: One Hour
If I Had Somebody To Love, 37
If I Had You, 117, 118, 228, 240, 242, 243, 264, 286, 293, 329, 330, 331, 344
If It Ain't Love, 142
If You Believed In Me, 21
Imagination, 5, 8, 86
Impromptu Ensemble No. 1, 183
Impromptu Ensemble, 120, 132, 133, 134, 135, 141, 145, 146, 147, 149, 151, 153, 154, 155, 157, 159, 166, 169, 172, 174, 175, 176, 178, 187, 189, 190, 191, 192, 195, 196, 201, 202, 203, 204, 205
Improvisation ('Cheri'), 115
Improvisation For The March Of Time, 295
In A Little Gypsy Tea Room, 44
In A Mellotone, 333
In Blinky, Winky, Chinky Chinatown, 42
In The Dim, Dim Dawnin, 37
Indian Summer, 271
Indiana, 199, 238, 240, 257, 265, 268, 272, 304, 315, 327, 329, 331, 338

Information, My Ahss, 84
Interview, 235, 277, 329, 336, 340
Isle Of Capri, 47
It All Depends On You, 263
It Don't Mean A Thing, 254
It Had To Be You, 211, 240
It's A Wonderful World, 86
It's All Right Here For You, 77 See also: It's Right Here For You
It's Been So Long, 46, 250
It's Gonna Be You, 36
It's Right Here For You, 77, 78, 331
It's So Good, 14
It's The Talk Of The Town, 245

Ja Da, 52, 53, 88, 120, 138, 140, 155, 188, 206, 208, 223, 232, 258, 288, 309, 341
Jack Hits The Road, 89
Jam On Jazz, 115, 116
Jam Session Blues, 184
Jam Session Jump, 184
Jam Session, 222
Jammin' At The Three Deuces, 221
Japanese Sandman, 344
Jazz Band Ball, 67, 286 See also: At The Jazz Band Ball
Jazz Me Blues, The 67, 98, 143, 148, 167, 193, 194, 203, 210, 237, 326
Jazz Train Blues, 299
Jelly Roll, 200 See also: I Ain't Gonna Give Nobody None Of My Jelly Roll, etc.
Jig Walk, 96
Jimmy, 340
Jingle Bells, 187
Joe Mack Blues, 266
Joint Is Jumpin', The, 141

369

375

ABOUT THE AUTHOR

Robert Hilbert began collecting and studying jazz recordings in 1953, when he was 14 years old. While in high school he struggled to learn how to play the clarinet which, although the lessons were subsequently forgotten, resulted in a deeper appreciation of the accomplishments of the instrument's jazz greats. His biography of Pee Wee Russell, *Jazzman: The Jazz Life of Pee Wee Russell*, has been published by Oxford University Press. Hilbert has written extensively about various jazz subjects through the years; Scarecrow Press has published his discography of James P. Johnson (*A Case of Mistaken Identity*, coauthored with Scott Brown, 1986), and his "Discographical Forum" column appears regularly in Joslin's Jazz Journal. He is also active in record production work, having released a series of jazz LPs on his Pumpkin label. He is currently president of the International Association of Jazz Record Collectors.